BEST
CUSTOMERS
DEMOGRAPHICS OF CONSUMER DEMAND

BEST
CUSTOMERS

DEMOGRAPHICS OF CONSUMER DEMAND

9th EDITION

New Strategist Press, LLC
Amityville, New York

New Strategist Press, LLC
P.O. Box 635, 26 Austin Avenue, Amityville, NY 11701
800/848-0842; 631/608-8795
www.newstrategist.com

ISBN 978-1-937737-11-5 (paper)
ISBN 978-1-937737-10-8 (hardcover)

Printed in the United States of America

Table of Contents

Chapter 10. Health Care 489

Chapter 11. Household Services 529

Introduction

Welcome to the ninth edition of *Best Customers: Demographics of Consumer Demand,* a unique examination of how changing demographics are reshaping the consumer marketplace. *Best Customers* reveals who the best and biggest customers are for hundreds of individual products and services, alerting marketers to potential booms and busts in the years ahead.

Based on data from the Bureau of Labor Statistics' 2010 Consumer Expenditure Survey, *Best Customers* examines spending patterns by the demographic characteristics of households. For most consumer products and services, demographics drive demand. *Best Customers* analyzes household spending on more than 300 products and services by age of householder, household income, household type, race and Hispanic origin of householder, region of residence, and educational attainment of householder. It identifies which households spend the most on a product or service (the best customers) and which control the largest share of spending (the biggest customers).

Household demographics are not static, but ever changing, influencing the consumer market during good times and bad. Today, the aging of the population is one of the most-important factors in determining consumer demand. The rapid growth of the Asian, black, and Hispanic populations makes their spending ever more important to business success. Education, living arrangements, and geography also determine who spends what—critical information as the consumer marketplace becomes increasingly competitive. *Best Customers* reveals the demographic trends behind spending, allowing marketers to prepare for what lies ahead.

Demographic Trends

Two demographic trends are key to today's consumer markets: the aging of the baby-boom generation and the rise of Asian, black, and Hispanic consumers.

Born between 1946 and 1964, the baby-boom generation spanned the ages of 46 through 64 in 2010. As boomers filled the 55-to-64 age group during the past decade, the percentage of households headed by empty-nesters grew each year. Having children leave home is one of life's major transitions, and spending patterns change accordingly. Empty-nesters spend less on groceries, for example, and more on meals in full-service restaurants. Spending on alcoholic beverages increases after the teetotaler years of child rearing. Empty-nesters are the biggest spenders on travel. And instead of buying children's clothes, they devote more to men's and women's apparel. Although boomers have been severely affected by the economic downturn, their financial problems are going to make them even more important consumers in the years ahead. Millions of two-earner baby-boom couples in their peak earning years will remain in the labor force much longer than they or the experts had expected. This will boost the incomes and spending power of older Americans, delaying the shift to a reduced standard of living after retirement. An understanding of the spending patterns of these older Americans is vital to staying afloat during the coming years.

Asians, blacks, Hispanics, and other minorities account for a growing share of the nation's population. In 2010, the 5 million Asian, 15 million black, and 15 million Hispanic consumer units accounted for 29 percent of the national total and for 25 percent of American consumer spending. The average Asian household has a higher income and spends more money than the average non-Hispanic white household. Although the incomes and spending of blacks and Hispanics are below average, both groups spend much more than average on many individual products and services. The distinct spending patterns of Asians, blacks, and Hispanics make them a major force in many consumer markets. As competition for customers becomes ever more heated, effective wooing of Asians, blacks, and Hispanics has never been more important.

How to Use This Book

Best Customers is divided into 21 chapters, arranged alphabetically, each focusing on a major spending category as defined by the Bureau of Labor Statistics—such as entertainment, groceries (or what the bureau calls "food at home"), transportation, and so on. Within each chapter, individual products and services are arranged alphabetically. Three chapters of *Best Customers*—computers, telephone, and travel—are unique groupings produced by New Strategist to highlight important spending patterns. The Bureau of Labor Statistics includes computer and telephone spending in its housing category, and it groups the various travel items into the entertainment, food, housing, and transportation categories.

Most individual products and services included in the Consumer Expenditure Survey are analyzed in *Best Customers*. Two types of items are excluded from the book: "other" categories, such as "other food at home," for which an analysis of spending patterns cannot provide meaningful conclusions; and products and services with spending data considered unreliable by New Strategist because of small sample sizes.

Each table in *Best Customers* analyzes household spending on a particular product or service, showing average spending, indexed spending, and market share of spending by age of householder, household income, household type, race and Hispanic origin of householder, region of residence, and educational attainment of householder. New Strategist has calculated the indexes and market shares to reveal the trends. Text accompanies each table that identifies the best and biggest customers, analyzes spending patterns, describes spending trends for the product over the past few years, and predicts future trends based on the nation's changing demographics.

Spending Data

Best Customers is based on unpublished, detailed data collected by the Bureau of Labor Statistics' Consumer Expenditure Survey, an ongoing, nationwide survey of household spending. A complete accounting of household expenditures, the Consumer Expenditure Survey includes everything from big-ticket items such as homes and cars, to small purchases like laundry detergent and video games. The survey does not include expenditures by government, business, or nonprofit institutions.

The Consumer Expenditure Survey uses "consumer unit" rather than "household" as its sampling unit. In this book, the terms consumer unit and household are used interchangeably. The Bureau of Labor Statistics defines consumer unit as "a single person or group of persons in a sample household related by blood, marriage, adoption or other legal arrangement or who share responsibility for at least two out of three major types of expenses—food, housing, and other expenses." For more information about the Consumer Expenditure Survey and consumer units, see Appendix A.

Spending Data

Average Spending. The average spending figures in *Best Customers* are unpublished data from the Bureau of Labor Statistics' 2010 Consumer Expenditure Survey. The Bureau of Labor Statistics calculates average spending for all households in a segment, not just for those who bought an item. When examining the averages, it is important to remember that by including both purchasers and nonpurchasers in the calculation of the average, the average spending amount is often greatly reduced—especially for infrequently purchased items. For example, the average household spent $239 on day care centers, nursery schools, and preschools in 2010. Since only a small percentage of households spends money on day care, this figure greatly underestimates the amount spent on day care centers by those who use them. To get a more-realistic picture of how much buyers spend on an item, Appendix B shows the percentage of households that purchased individual products and services during the average quarter of 2010, and the amount purchasers spent per quarter. According to Appendix B, only 4.7 percent of households spent on day care centers during the average quarter of 2010. The purchasers spent an average of $1,258 per quarter, for an estimated annual cost of $5,032—a much more realistic figure than the average of $239 for all households. For frequently purchased items—such as bread—the average spending figures give a fairly accurate account of actual spending. But for most of the products and services examined in *Best Customers*, average spending figures are less revealing than indexes and market shares.

Average spending figures are useful for determining the market potential of a product or service in a local area. By multiplying the average amount married couples spend on children's clothing by the number of married couple households in the San Diego metropolitan area, for example, marketers can estimate the size of the market for children's clothing in San Diego. The San Diego media could show those figures to potential advertisers to prove the demand for children's clothing in the area.

(Note: Because of sampling errors, average values can vary—especially for infrequently purchased items. To examine the standard errors for detailed average spending data, contact the Bureau of Labor Statistics Consumer Expenditure Survey statisticians by phone at 202-691-6900 or by email at cexinfo@bls.gov.)

• **Indexed Spending (Best Customers).** Indexed spending figures compare the spending of demographic segments with that of the average household. To compute the indexes, New Strategist's statisticians divide the average amount a household segment spends on a particular item by how much the average household spends on the item, then multiply the resulting figure by 100. An index of 100 is the average for all households. An index of 125 means average spending by households in a segment is 25 percent above average (100 plus 25). An index of 80 means average spending by households in a segment is 20 percent below average (100 minus 20).

Spending indexes can reveal hidden markets—household segments with a high propensity to buy a particular product or service but which are overshadowed by larger household segments that account for a bigger share of the total market. Householders aged 65 to 74, for example, account for 13 percent of the market for full-service breakfasts, less than the 16 percent share accounted for by householders aged 25 to 34. But a look at the indexed spending figures reveals that, in fact, the older householders are the better customers. Householders aged 65 to 74 spend 18 percent *more* than the average household on full-service breakfasts, while householders aged 25 to 34 spend 6 percent *less* than the average household on this item. Using the index column in the spending tables, marketers can see that older householders are in fact their better customers and adjust their business strategy accordingly. (Note: Because of sampling errors, small differences in index values are usually insignificant. But the broader patterns revealed by indexes can guide marketers to the best customers.)

• **Market Share (Biggest Customers).** To calculate market share figures, New Strategist first determines the total amount all households spend on an item by multiplying average household spending on that item by the total number of consumer units (121,107,000). New Strategist then calculates total household spending for each demographic segment by multiplying the segment's average spending on an item by the number of households in the segment. To calculate the percentage of total spending on the item controlled by a demographic segment—i.e., its market share—New Strategist divides each segment's spending on the item by total household spending on the item.

In 2010, for example, college graduates accounted for 62 percent of total household spending on ship fares. The cruise industry could reach most of its customers if it targeted only this demographic segment. Of course, by single-mindedly targeting the biggest customers, businesses cannot nurture potential growth markets. An additional danger of focusing only on the biggest customers is that businesses may end up ignoring their best customers. This is especially problematic because market shares are unstable, thanks to baby booms and busts over the past half-century. Right now, for example, householders aged 45 to 54 are one of the biggest customers of housekeeping services and control 23 percent of the market—but only because the age group is filled with the large baby-boom generation. In fact, the best customers of housekeeping services are the oldest householders. Those aged 75 or older spend 89 percent more than the average household on housekeeping services, whereas the 45-to-54 age group spends only 13 percent more than average on this item. Although the older age group controls only 18 percent of the housekeeping services market today, the share will expand greatly as boomers age into their seventies. The best customers of housekeeping services will become the biggest customers as well. Marketers who ignore their best customers in favor of the biggest customers may end up with no customers.

• **Age of Householder.** Age is one of the best predictors of spending because lifestage determines most consumer wants and needs. Ongoing changes in the age structure of the population will have a profound effect on consumer spending. This is why *Best Customers* explores spending by age in so much detail, using it as the primary guide to consumer trends in the years ahead.

Changes in the size of age groups will dramatically affect spending in many categories over the next few years. The number of adults under age 35 is expanding as the age group fills with the millennial generation. This will boost average household spending on products and services for infants and young children. The small generation X is filling the 35-to-44 age group, reducing the share of the consumer market controlled by that age group. Now that the large baby-boom generation has completely filled the 55-to-64 age group and is entering the empty-nest lifestage, look for more spending on full-service restaurants, alcoholic beverages, women's clothing, and travel. Not only will the sizes of age groups change but, as younger generations replace older ones, attitudes and behavior will also change. Younger generations, for example, devote a larger share of their household budget to computers, cell phones and other high-tech gadgets. In making predictions of future spending trends, New Strategist takes into account not only the changing numbers, but also changing attitudes and lifestyles.

• **Household Income.** It is no surprise that the most-affluent households spend the most. For most of the products and services examined in *Best Customers,* households with the highest incomes appear to be the best and biggest customers. Yet the story behind spending is more complex than income alone. Most spending is driven by lifestage (age) or lifestyle (household type), and secondarily by income. For that reason *Best Customers* identifies high-income households as the best and biggest customers only when income has an extraordinary effect on spending or when an item is a purely discretionary expense—such as spending on wine at restaurants and bars. While most businesses would do well to target the affluent, they will find it difficult to design a product or craft a message if they ignore the lifestage and lifestyle reasons for spending.

• **Household Type.** Household type is one of the most important determinants of spending for several reasons. The presence of children, for example, means the household spends on products and services children want and need. Not only that, but households with children tend to include more people than those without children, and household size is an important determinant of spending. Because married couples head most of the nation's households, they account for the majority of spending in most categories. But single parents are important in some markets, and single-person households account for a large share of spending on many items. The most-important household change to occur in the next few years is the rapid expansion of the number of married couples without children at home as more boomers become empty-nesters. (Note: Market shares by household type do not sum to 100 percent because not all household types are shown.)

• **Race and Hispanic Origin of Householder.** The Bureau of Labor Statistics classifies households by the self-identified race and Hispanic origin of the householder. The bureau classifies households into three racial groups: Asian, black, and "white and other" where "other" includes Alaska Natives, American Indians, Native Hawaiians and other Pacific Islanders, as well as those who report more than one race. Because Hispanics may be of any race, the bureau separately classifies all households into one of two Hispanic origin categories: Hispanic or non-Hispanic. Within the non-Hispanic origin group there are blacks and "whites and all other races," which in this classification include non-Hispanic Alaska Natives, American Indians, Asians, Native Hawaiians and other Pacific Islanders, as well as non-Hispanics reporting more than one race.

To simplify things for *Best Customers*, we narrowed the race and Hispanic origin categories to four: Asians (including Hispanic Asians), blacks (including Hispanic blacks), Hispanics (a group that also includes Hispanic Asians and blacks), and non-Hispanic whites and others (a group that also includes non-Hispanic Asians). Because there is overlap among the four race and Hispanic origin groups, numbers by race and Hispanic origin do not sum to the total.

On average, Asian households spend more than non-Hispanic white households, whereas black and Hispanic households spend less. But there is great variation by individual product and service category. Asians do not spend much on pets, for example. Blacks and Hispanics spend disproportionately on children's clothes.

The spending of Asians, blacks, and Hispanics differs from that of non-Hispanic whites for a variety of reasons. Asians are, on average, younger and better educated than non-Hispanic whites. Blacks and Hispanics are more likely to have children at home. Food preferences differ by race and Hispanic origin as well. Geographic location can influence purchasing patterns, and Asians and Hispanics are concentrated in the West, while most blacks live in the South. As the numbers of Asians, blacks, and Hispanics grow, their spending is becoming increasingly important to the nation's economy. Consequently it is important to understand spending patterns by race and Hispanic origin.

• **Region of Residence.** For many products and services, regional differences in spending are small. But for some items, spending differences by region are pronounced. There are several reasons for this, including differences in regional economies, climate, physical infrastructure, racial and ethnic composition, and access to resources. Differences in regional population growth rates also affect household spending patterns.

• **Educational Attainment of Householder.** The population is becoming increasingly educated, and the spending of educated consumers differs from that of those with less education. College graduates headed 30 percent of the nation's households in 2010. Because income rises directly with education, households headed by college graduates tend to spend more on most discretionary items than those headed by people who went no further than high school. Because older generations are less educated than younger ones, older Americans are overrepresented among householders with a high school diploma or less education. Consequently, the spending of less-educated householders reflects their older age. As well-educated boomers enter the older age groups in the years ahead, the spending of older Americans is going to change. This is one of the most-important spending trends of the coming decade.

Appendices

Best Customers includes four appendices and a glossary of terms.

• **Appendix A** describes the Consumer Expenditure Survey in more detail and tells readers how to contact the Bureau of Labor Statistics.

• **Appendix B** shows the percentage of households that purchased the products and services examined in the Consumer Expenditure Survey during the average quarter of 2010. It also shows how much purchasers spent on items during the average quarter. In some cases, the quarterly spending figure alone is a good estimate of how much a typical purchaser spends. Take new cars, for example, which is a one-time rather than an ongoing expense. In the average quarter of 2010, 0.7 percent of households bought a new car, spending on average $21,959. (The Consumer Expenditure Survey counts the net cost of an item at the time of purchase, whether households pay for it at once or over time.) For ongoing expenses, however, the quarterly spending figure must be multiplied by four to get an estimate of how much households spend annually on the product or service. Forty-one percent of households bought women's clothes during the average quarter of 2010, for example, and spent $202 during the quarter. The annual spending of households that buy women's clothes can reasonably be estimated at four times $202, or $808. Appendix B not only supplies readers with invaluable insight into the propensity of households to buy individual products and services, but also provides a more realistic view of how much purchasers spend.

• **Appendix C** ranks products and services by the amount the average household spends on them, from highest to lowest. It shows which categories are most important to the household budget. The relative standing of products and services is often surprising. To know that gasoline is the fifth-biggest expense of the average household puts the media's focus on gasoline prices into perspective. The fact that out-of-pocket health insurance cost is the seventh-biggest household expense, ahead of property taxes and electricity, for example, explains why many households feel strapped by health care costs.

• **Appendix D** shows trends in household spending by major category between 2000 and 2010. During those years, spending by the average household was essentially unchanged, after adjusting for inflation. But this overall constancy masks the spending decline that has taken place over the past few years. Average household spending increased 9 percent between 2000 and 2006 (the year overall household spending peaked), then fell 8 percent between 2006 and 2010 as the Great Recession took hold. Households have cut their spending deeply on many items during the past few years, revealing the typical American householder to be a cautious spender. This caution can be seen in the spending trends for many of the individual products and services analyzed in *Best Customers*.

For More Information

The ninth edition of *Best Customers* examines the demographics of spending on individual products and services and describes how changing demographics will boost or reduce average household spending in the future. To compare and contrast spending patterns on the entire range of goods and services included in the Consumer Expenditure Survey, see the companion volume, the 17th edition of *Household Spending: Who Spends How Much on What*. For analysis of household spending trends by single product category, see New Strategist's Who's Buying reports.

To find out more about these books and reports and to view tables of contents and sample pages, visit New Strategist's web site at http://www.newstrategist.com. All New Strategist books and reports are available in print or as downloads with links to the Excel version of each table.

Chapter 1.

Alcoholic Beverages

Household Spending on Alcoholic Beverages, 2010

The average household spent $412 on alcoholic beverages in 2010, 12 percent less than in 2000 after adjusting for inflation. Spending on alcoholic beverages climbed by a substantial 14 percent between 2000 and 2006 (the year when household spending peaked), then fell 23 percent between 2006 and 2010 as the recession took hold (see Appendix D for overall household spending trends). Behind the earlier increase was the aging of the baby-boom generation into the empty-nest lifestage, when spending on alcoholic beverages rises.

Alcoholic beverage spending is changing. While the largest share of the alcoholic beverage dollar is still devoted to beer (40 percent), the percentage is lower than the 47 percent of 2000. Wine accounted for 29 percent of the alcoholic beverage budget in 2010, up from 26 percent in 2000. Whiskey and other alcoholic beverages accounted for 20 percent of the budget in 2010; the share had been just under 18 percent in 2000.

Spending on alcoholic beverages

(average annual spending of households on alcoholic beverages, 2000, 2006, and 2010; in 2010 dollars)

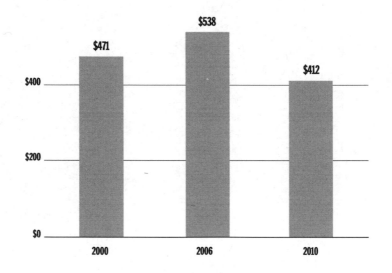

Table 1.1 Alcoholic beverage spending, 2000 to 2010

(average annual and percent distribution of household spending on alcoholic beverages by category, 2000 to 2010; percent change and percentage point change in spending, 2000–06, 2006–10, and 2000–10; in 2010 dollars; ranked by amount spent)

	2010 average household spending	2006 average household spending (in 2010$)	2000 average household spending (in 2010$)	percent change		
				2006–10	2000–06	2000–10
AVERAGE ANNUAL SPENDING						
Average household spending on alcoholic beverages	**$411.97**	**$537.63**	**$470.82**	**–23.4%**	**14.2%**	**–12.5%**
Beer and ale	165.79	225.68	220.93	–26.5	2.2	–25.0
Beer and ale at home	102.83	133.95	141.84	–23.2	–5.6	–27.5
Beer and ale at restaurants, bars	62.96	91.73	79.09	–31.4	16.0	–20.4
Wine	120.99	156.18	123.88	–22.5	26.1	–2.3
Wine at home	87.69	111.16	101.35	–21.1	9.7	–13.5
Wine at restaurants, bars	33.30	45.02	22.53	–26.0	99.8	47.8
Whiskey and other alcohol	82.48	108.87	82.65	–24.2	31.7	–0.2
Whiskey and other alcohol at restaurants, bars	51.31	70.20	38.85	–26.9	80.7	32.1
Whiskey and other alcohol at home	31.17	38.67	43.80	–19.4	–11.7	–28.8
Alcoholic beverages on trips	42.71	46.90	43.36	–8.9	8.2	–1.5

				percentage point change		
	2006–10	2000–06	2000–10	2006–10	2000–06	2000–10
PERCENT DISTRIBUTION OF SPENDING						
Average household spending on alcoholic beverages	**100.0%**	**100.0%**	**100.0%**	**–**	**–**	**–**
Beer and ale	40.2	42.0	46.9	–1.7	–4.9	–6.7
Beer and ale at home	25.0	24.9	30.1	0.1	–5.2	–5.2
Beer and ale at restaurants, bars	15.3	17.1	16.8	–1.8	0.3	–1.5
Wine	29.4	29.1	26.3	0.3	2.7	3.1
Wine at home	21.3	20.7	21.5	0.6	–0.9	–0.2
Wine at restaurants, bars	8.1	8.4	4.8	–0.3	3.6	3.3
Whiskey and other alcohol	20.0	20.2	17.6	–0.2	2.7	2.5
Whiskey and other alcohol at restaurants, bars	12.5	13.1	8.3	–0.6	4.8	4.2
Whiskey and other alcohol at home	7.6	7.2	9.3	0.4	–2.1	–1.7
Alcoholic beverages on trips	10.4	8.7	9.2	1.6	–0.5	1.2

Note: "–" means not applicable.

Source: Bureau of Labor Statistics, 2000, 2006, and 2010 Consumer Expenditure Surveys; calculations by New Strategist

Alcoholic Beverages Purchased on Trips

Best customers: **Householders aged 45 to 54**
Married couples without children at home
Asians and non-Hispanic whites
Households in the Northeast and West

Customer trends: **Average household spending on alcoholic beverages while traveling should begin to grow again as more boomers become empty-nesters, but only if discretionary income grows.**

The biggest spenders on alcoholic beverages purchased on trips can be found in a variety of demographic categories. Householders aged 45 to 54, the most affluent, spend 16 percent more than average on this item. Married couples without children at home (most of them older) spend 64 percent more than average on alcoholic beverages while on trips. These empty-nesters spend more than other household types on alcoholic beverages while traveling because they no longer need to devote their time and money to children's wants and needs. Asians and Non-Hispanic whites spend, respectively, 16 and 19 percent more than average on alcoholic beverages while traveling, while blacks and Hispanics spend considerably less than average. Households in the Northeast and West spend 16 to 22 percent more than average on alcohol while traveling.

Average household spending on alcoholic beverages purchased on trips grew by an inflation-adjusted 8 percent between 2000 and 2006, then fell 9 percent between 2006 and 2010. Behind the decline was the Great Recession, which reduced spending on travel. In the years ahead, spending on this item should rise again as more boomers become empty-nesters, but only if discretionary income grows.

Table 1.2 Alcoholic beverages purchased on trips

Total household spending $5,172,479,970.00
Average household spends   42.71

	AVERAGE HOUSEHOLD SPENDING	BEST CUSTOMERS (index)	BIGGEST CUSTOMERS (market share)
AGE OF HOUSEHOLDER			
Average household	**$42.71**	**100**	**100.0%**
Under age 25	29.73	70	4.6
Aged 25 to 34	45.24	106	17.6
Aged 35 to 44	46.40	109	19.7
Aged 45 to 54	49.52	116	24.0
Aged 55 to 64	46.14	108	19.1
Aged 65 to 74	42.48	99	10.7
Aged 75 or older	19.50	46	4.4

	AVERAGE HOUSEHOLD SPENDING	BEST CUSTOMERS (index)	BIGGEST CUSTOMERS (market share)
HOUSEHOLD INCOME			
Average household	**$42.71**	**100**	**100.0%**
Under $20,000	7.88	18	4.0
$20,000 to $39,999	16.85	39	9.0
$40,000 to $49,999	30.53	71	6.8
$50,000 to $69,999	44.39	104	14.9
$70,000 to $79,999	51.66	121	7.2
$80,000 to $99,999	50.20	118	9.8
$100,000 or more	120.15	281	48.2
HOUSEHOLD TYPE			
Average household	**42.71**	**100**	**100.0**
Married couples	56.35	132	65.1
Married couples, no children	69.94	164	34.8
Married couples, with children	49.69	116	27.1
Oldest child under age 6	43.35	101	4.3
Oldest child aged 6 to 17	52.26	122	14.4
Oldest child aged 18 or older	49.27	115	8.3
Single parent with child under age 18	22.89	54	3.2
Single person	30.35	71	20.8
RACE AND HISPANIC ORIGIN			
Average household	**42.71**	**100**	**100.0**
Asian	49.68	116	4.9
Black	16.42	38	4.7
Hispanic	20.80	49	5.9
Non-Hispanic white and other	50.74	119	90.1
REGION			
Average household	**42.71**	**100**	**100.0**
Northeast	49.70	116	21.4
Midwest	44.63	104	23.3
South	32.35	76	27.8
West	51.97	122	27.6
EDUCATION			
Average household	**42.71**	**100**	**100.0**
Less than high school graduate	7.90	18	2.6
High school graduate	20.82	49	12.4
Some college	35.96	84	17.7
Associate's degree	38.45	90	8.5
Bachelor's degree or more	84.41	198	58.7
Bachelor's degree	81.72	191	36.1
Master's, professional, doctoral degree	89.11	209	22.6

Note: Market shares may not sum to 100.0 because of rounding and missing categories by household type. "Asian" and "black" include Hispanics and non-Hispanics who identify themselves as being of the respective race alone. "Hispanic" includes people of any race who identify themselves as Hispanic. "Other" includes people who identify themselves as non-Hispanic and as Alaska Native, American Indian, Asian (who are also included in the "Asian" row), or Native Hawaiian or other Pacific Islander as well as non-Hispanics reporting more than one race.

Source: Calculations by New Strategist based on the Bureau of Labor Statistics' 2010 Consumer Expenditure Survey

Beer and Ale at Home

Best customers:
  Householders aged 35 to 54
  Hispanics
  Households in the West

Customer trends:
  Average household spending on beer and ale consumed at home should stabilize
  or even grow in the years ahead as the millennial generation marries, has children,
  and spends more time at home.

Because beer and ale consumed at home is such a common purchase, average household spending on this item does not vary all that much by demographic segment. Householders aged 35 to 54 spend 15 to 31 percent more than the average household on beer and ale for home consumption. Hispanics spend 5 percent more than average despite their lower incomes. Households in the West outspend the average by 19 percent.

Average household spending on beer and ale consumed at home has been falling since 2000, but the Great Recession accelerated the decline. Spending on beer and ale consumed at home should stabilize or even grow in the years ahead as the millennial generation marries, has children, and spends more time at home

Table 1.3 Beer and ale at home

Total household spending $12,453,432,810.00
Average household spends   102.83

	AVERAGE HOUSEHOLD SPENDING	BEST CUSTOMERS (index)	BIGGEST CUSTOMERS (market share)
AGE OF HOUSEHOLDER			
Average household	**$102.83**	**100**	**100.0%**
Under age 25	99.97	97	6.4
Aged 25 to 34	111.74	109	18.1
Aged 35 to 44	134.93	131	23.7
Aged 45 to 54	117.85	115	23.7
Aged 55 to 64	100.76	98	17.3
Aged 65 to 74	66.34	65	6.9
Aged 75 or older	40.53	39	3.8

	AVERAGE HOUSEHOLD SPENDING	BEST CUSTOMERS (index)	BIGGEST CUSTOMERS (market share)
HOUSEHOLD INCOME			
Average household	**$102.83**	**100**	**100.0%**
Under $20,000	59.39	58	12.6
$20,000 to $39,999	62.71	61	14.0
$40,000 to $49,999	88.88	86	8.2
$50,000 to $69,999	131.18	128	18.3
$70,000 to $79,999	142.43	139	8.3
$80,000 to $99,999	154.16	150	12.5
$100,000 or more	159.88	155	26.7
HOUSEHOLD TYPE			
Average household	**102.83**	**100**	**100.0**
Married couples	121.11	118	58.1
Married couples, no children	128.23	125	26.5
Married couples, with children	114.86	112	26.0
Oldest child under age 6	120.16	117	5.0
Oldest child aged 6 to 17	113.90	111	13.0
Oldest child aged 18 or older	113.59	110	8.0
Single parent with child under age 18	47.78	46	2.7
Single person	63.19	61	18.0
RACE AND HISPANIC ORIGIN			
Average household	**102.83**	**100**	**100.0**
Asian	61.74	60	2.6
Black	66.31	64	7.9
Hispanic	107.79	105	12.8
Non-Hispanic white and other	108.31	105	79.9
REGION			
Average household	**102.83**	**100**	**100.0**
Northeast	94.61	92	16.9
Midwest	100.47	98	21.8
South	96.62	94	34.5
West	122.19	119	26.9
EDUCATION			
Average household	**102.83**	**100**	**100.0**
Less than high school graduate	66.71	65	9.3
High school graduate	100.86	98	25.0
Some college	110.46	107	22.6
Associate's degree	107.25	104	9.9
Bachelor's degree or more	113.52	110	32.8
Bachelor's degree	127.78	124	23.5
Master's, professional, doctoral degree	85.44	83	9.0

Note: Market shares may not sum to 100.0 because of rounding and missing categories by household type. "Asian" and "black" include Hispanics and non-Hispanics who identify themselves as being of the respective race alone. "Hispanic" includes people of any race who identify themselves as Hispanic. "Other" includes people who identify themselves as non-Hispanic and as Alaska Native, American Indian, Asian (who are also included in the "Asian" row), or Native Hawaiian or other Pacific Islander as well as non-Hispanics reporting more than one race.

Source: Calculations by New Strategist based on the Bureau of Labor Statistics' 2010 Consumer Expenditure Survey

Beer and Ale at Restaurants and Bars

Best customers: **Householders under age 35**
Non-Hispanic whites
Households in the Northeast, Midwest, and West

Customer trends: **Average household spending on beer and ale at restaurants and bars may rise in the years ahead as the recession loosens its grip—but only if discretionary income grows.**

Householders under age 35 are the best customers of beer and ale at restaurants and bars, spending 57 to 65 percent more than the average household on this item. Non-Hispanic whites spend 17 percent more than average on this item and account for 89 percent of the market. Households in the Northeast, Midwest, and West spend 17 to 26 percent more than the average on beer and ale at restaurants and bars.

Average household spending on beer and ale consumed at restaurants and bars grew 16 percent between 2000 and 2006, then fell 31 percent through 2010, after adjusting for inflation. Behind the spending decline was the Great Recession and consequent belt-tightening, as well as a shift in the preferences of young adults for whiskey and other alcohol when out at restaurants and bars. Spending on beer and ale at restaurants and bars may rise in the years ahead as the recession loosens its grip—but only if discretionary income grows.

Table 1.4 Beer and ale at restaurants and bars

Total household spending $7,624,896,720.00
Average household spends   62.96

	AVERAGE HOUSEHOLD SPENDING	BEST CUSTOMERS (index)	BIGGEST CUSTOMERS (market share)
AGE OF HOUSEHOLDER			
Average household	**$62.96**	**100**	**100.0%**
Under age 25	98.75	157	10.4
Aged 25 to 34	103.89	165	27.5
Aged 35 to 44	79.15	126	22.7
Aged 45 to 54	57.02	91	18.7
Aged 55 to 64	44.98	71	12.6
Aged 65 to 74	39.60	63	6.8
Aged 75 or older	8.72	14	1.3

	AVERAGE HOUSEHOLD SPENDING	BEST CUSTOMERS (index)	BIGGEST CUSTOMERS (market share)
HOUSEHOLD INCOME			
Average household	**$62.96**	**100**	**100.0%**
Under $20,000	27.39	44	9.5
$20,000 to $39,999	42.18	67	15.4
$40,000 to $49,999	61.98	98	9.3
$50,000 to $69,999	78.48	125	17.9
$70,000 to $79,999	59.21	94	5.6
$80,000 to $99,999	79.40	126	10.5
$100,000 or more	118.80	189	32.4
HOUSEHOLD TYPE			
Average household	**62.96**	**100**	**100.0**
Married couples	59.16	94	46.4
Married couples, no children	69.21	110	23.3
Married couples, with children	53.64	85	19.8
Oldest child under age 6	57.41	91	3.9
Oldest child aged 6 to 17	52.59	84	9.8
Oldest child aged 18 or older	53.28	85	6.1
Single parent with child under age 18	14.74	23	1.4
Single person	64.33	102	29.9
RACE AND HISPANIC ORIGIN			
Average household	**62.96**	**100**	**100.0**
Asian	36.94	59	2.5
Black	16.47	26	3.2
Hispanic	40.20	64	7.8
Non-Hispanic white and other	73.87	117	89.0
REGION			
Average household	**62.96**	**100**	**100.0**
Northeast	79.45	126	23.2
Midwest	73.53	117	26.0
South	38.82	62	22.6
West	78.53	125	28.3
EDUCATION			
Average household	**62.96**	**100**	**100.0**
Less than high school graduate	17.21	27	3.9
High school graduate	39.83	63	16.2
Some college	56.98	91	19.0
Associate's degree	71.02	113	10.7
Bachelor's degree or more	105.18	167	49.6
Bachelor's degree	122.82	195	36.8
Master's, professional, doctoral degree	70.44	112	12.1

Note: Market shares may not sum to 100.0 because of rounding and missing categories by household type. "Asian" and "black" include Hispanics and non-Hispanics who identify themselves as being of the respective race alone. "Hispanic" includes people of any race who identify themselves as Hispanic. "Other" includes people who identify themselves as non-Hispanic and as Alaska Native, American Indian, Asian (who are also included in the "Asian" row), or Native Hawaiian or other Pacific Islander as well as non-Hispanics reporting more than one race.

Source: Calculations by New Strategist based on the Bureau of Labor Statistics' 2010 Consumer Expenditure Survey

Whiskey and Other Alcohol (except Beer and Wine) at Home

Best customers: Householders aged 25 to 44 and 65 to 74
Married couples without children at home
Married couples with school-aged children
Households in the Northeast

Customer trends: Average household spending on whiskey and other alcohol consumed at home
could stabilize in the years ahead if the millennial generation emerges as a new
best customer of this category.

Traditionally, older couples are the best customers of whiskey and other alcohol (except beer and wine) consumed at home. Householders aged 65 to 74 spend 48 percent more than average on whiskey and other alcohol at home, while married couples without children at home (most of them empty-nesters) spend 70 percent more than average on this item. The millennial generation may be an emerging best customer of this category: Married couples with school-aged children spend 68 percent more than average on this item. Householders aged 25 to 44 spend 10 to 33 percent more than average on whiskey and other alcohol consumed at home. Households in the Northeast outspend the average by 34 percent.

Average household spending trends on whiskey and other alcohol consumed at home shows a different pattern from other types of alcoholic beverages. Spending on this item fell 12 percent between 2000 and 2006, while spending on other alcohol categories grew. Spending fell by another 19 percent between 2006 and 2010, in part because of the aging of the category's traditional best customers. Average household spending on whiskey and other alcohol consumed at home may stabilize in the years ahead as the millennial generation marries, has children, and spends more time at home.

Table 1.5 Whiskey and other alcohol (except beer and wine) at home

Total household spending $3,774,905,190.00
Average household spends 31.17

	AVERAGE HOUSEHOLD SPENDING	BEST CUSTOMERS (index)	BIGGEST CUSTOMERS (market share)
AGE OF HOUSEHOLDER			
Average household	**$31.17**	**100**	**100.0%**
Under age 25	20.10	64	4.3
Aged 25 to 34	34.23	110	18.3
Aged 35 to 44	41.59	133	24.1
Aged 45 to 54	22.93	74	15.2
Aged 55 to 64	29.53	95	16.7
Aged 65 to 74	46.24	148	16.0
Aged 75 or older	17.99	58	5.5

	AVERAGE HOUSEHOLD SPENDING	BEST CUSTOMERS (index)	BIGGEST CUSTOMERS (market share)
HOUSEHOLD INCOME			
Average household	**$31.17**	**100**	**100.0%**
Under $20,000	11.41	37	8.0
$20,000 to $39,999	21.97	70	16.2
$40,000 to $49,999	23.56	76	7.1
$50,000 to $69,999	46.80	150	21.5
$70,000 to $79,999	38.25	123	7.3
$80,000 to $99,999	34.51	111	9.2
$100,000 or more	56.00	180	30.8
HOUSEHOLD TYPE			
Average household	**31.17**	**100**	**100.0**
Married couples	42.40	136	67.1
Married couples, no children	52.98	170	36.1
Married couples, with children	37.11	119	27.7
Oldest child under age 6	17.82	57	2.4
Oldest child aged 6 to 17	52.50	168	19.8
Oldest child aged 18 or older	24.05	77	5.6
Single parent with child under age 18	12.29	39	2.3
Single person	17.92	57	16.8
RACE AND HISPANIC ORIGIN			
Average household	**31.17**	**100**	**100.0**
Asian	11.61	37	1.6
Black	28.87	93	11.3
Hispanic	21.40	69	8.4
Non-Hispanic white and other	33.41	107	81.3
REGION			
Average household	**31.17**	**100**	**100.0**
Northeast	41.83	134	24.6
Midwest	32.11	103	23.0
South	25.77	83	30.3
West	30.36	97	22.1
EDUCATION			
Average household	**31.17**	**100**	**100.0**
Less than high school graduate	21.05	68	9.6
High school graduate	19.22	62	15.7
Some college	28.05	90	18.9
Associate's degree	29.81	96	9.0
Bachelor's degree or more	48.85	157	46.6
Bachelor's degree	50.91	163	30.9
Master's, professional, doctoral degree	44.79	144	15.5

Note: Market shares may not sum to 100.0 because of rounding and missing categories by household type. "Asian" and "black" include Hispanics and non-Hispanics who identify themselves as being of the respective race alone. "Hispanic" includes people of any race who identify themselves as Hispanic. "Other" includes people who identify themselves as non-Hispanic and as Alaska Native, American Indian, Asian (who are also included in the "Asian" row), or Native Hawaiian or other Pacific Islander as well as non-Hispanics reporting more than one race.

Source: Calculations by New Strategist based on the Bureau of Labor Statistics' 2010 Consumer Expenditure Survey

Whiskey and Other Alcohol (except Beer and Wine) at Restaurants and Bars

Best customers:

Householders under age 35
People who live alone
Asians
Households in the Northeast

Customer trends:

Average household spending on whiskey and other alcohol at restaurants and bars may stabilize because the millennial generation appears to be an emerging best customer—but only if discretionary income grows.

Householders under age 35 spend one-and-one-half to two times the average on whiskey and other alcohol at restaurants and bars. People who live alone, whose spending is generally below average on most items, spend 6 percent more than average on cocktails and shots at bars. Asians outspend the average by 37 percent. Households in the Northeast spend 52 percent more than average on whiskey and other alcohol at restaurants and bars.

Average household spending on whiskey and other alcohol at restaurants and bars grew 81 percent between 2000 and 2006, then declined 27 percent over the remainder of the decade. Spending on whiskey and other alcohol at restaurants and bars may stabilize in the years ahead because the large millennial generation appears to be an emerging best customer—but only if discretionary income grows.

Table 1.6 Whiskey and other alcohol (except beer and wine) at restaurants and bars

Total household spending $6,214,000,170.00
Average household spends   51.31

	AVERAGE HOUSEHOLD SPENDING	BEST CUSTOMERS (index)	BIGGEST CUSTOMERS (market share)
AGE OF HOUSEHOLDER			
Average household	**$51.31**	**100**	**100.0%**
Under age 25	104.11	203	13.5
Aged 25 to 34	75.64	147	24.5
Aged 35 to 44	53.03	103	18.7
Aged 45 to 54	43.90	86	17.7
Aged 55 to 64	40.33	79	13.9
Aged 65 to 74	38.34	75	8.0
Aged 75 or older	19.66	38	3.7

	AVERAGE HOUSEHOLD SPENDING	BEST CUSTOMERS (index)	BIGGEST CUSTOMERS (market share)
HOUSEHOLD INCOME			
Average household	**$51.31**	**100**	**100.0%**
Under $20,000	15.58	30	6.6
$20,000 to $39,999	35.82	70	16.0
$40,000 to $49,999	42.79	83	7.9
$50,000 to $69,999	53.99	105	15.1
$70,000 to $79,999	40.62	79	4.7
$80,000 to $99,999	70.90	138	11.5
$100,000 or more	116.24	227	38.8
HOUSEHOLD TYPE			
Average household	**51.31**	**100**	**100.0**
Married couples	43.43	85	41.8
Married couples, no children	48.50	95	20.1
Married couples, with children	42.19	82	19.1
Oldest child under age 6	33.59	65	2.8
Oldest child aged 6 to 17	38.93	76	8.9
Oldest child aged 18 or older	51.45	100	7.2
Single parent with child under age 18	15.27	30	1.8
Single person	54.36	106	31.0
RACE AND HISPANIC ORIGIN			
Average household	**51.31**	**100**	**100.0**
Asian	70.55	137	5.8
Black	31.19	61	7.4
Hispanic	25.03	49	5.9
Non-Hispanic white and other	58.56	114	86.5
REGION			
Average household	**51.31**	**100**	**100.0**
Northeast	77.91	152	27.9
Midwest	50.87	99	22.1
South	32.98	64	23.6
West	60.13	117	26.5
EDUCATION			
Average household	**51.31**	**100**	**100.0**
Less than high school graduate	12.57	24	3.5
High school graduate	28.71	56	14.3
Some college	38.12	74	15.6
Associate's degree	50.49	98	9.3
Bachelor's degree or more	98.15	191	56.8
Bachelor's degree	109.26	213	40.2
Master's, professional, doctoral degree	76.28	149	16.1

Note: Market shares may not sum to 100.0 because of rounding and missing categories by household type. "Asian" and "black" include Hispanics and non-Hispanics who identify themselves as being of the respective race alone. "Hispanic" includes people of any race who identify themselves as Hispanic. "Other" includes people who identify themselves as non-Hispanic and as Alaska Native, American Indian, Asian (who are also included in the "Asian" row), or Native Hawaiian or other Pacific Islander as well as non-Hispanics reporting more than one race.

Source: Calculations by New Strategist based on the Bureau of Labor Statistics' 2010 Consumer Expenditure Survey

Wine at Home

Best customers: **Householders aged 65 to 74**
Married couples without children at home
Non-Hispanic whites
Households in the Northeast
College graduates

Customer trends: **Average household spending on wine consumed at home should begin to increase again as more boomers become empty-nesters—but only if discretionary income grows.**

The best customers of wine consumed at home are older, educated, non-Hispanic white married couples without children at home (empty-nesters). Couples without children at home spend 73 percent more than average on this item. Householders aged 65 to 74 spend 50 percent more than average on wine consumed at home. Non-Hispanic whites spend 20 percent more than average on wine at home and control 91 percent of the market. College graduates spend twice the average on this item. Households in the Northeast outspend the average for wine consumed at home by 53 percent.

Average household spending on wine consumed at home increased 10 percent between 2000 and 2006, after adjusting for inflation, then fell 21 percent from 2006 to 2010 because of the Great Recession. Spending on wine consumed at home should begin to increase again as more boomers become empty-nesters—but only if discretionary income grows.

Table 1.7 Wine at home

Total household spending	$10,619,872,830.00		
Average household spends	87.69		

	AVERAGE HOUSEHOLD SPENDING	BEST CUSTOMERS (index)	BIGGEST CUSTOMERS (market share)
AGE OF HOUSEHOLDER			
Average household	**$87.69**	**100**	**100.0%**
Under age 25	32.99	38	2.5
Aged 25 to 34	69.33	79	13.2
Aged 35 to 44	101.26	115	20.9
Aged 45 to 54	87.76	100	20.7
Aged 55 to 64	100.73	115	20.3
Aged 65 to 74	131.91	150	16.2
Aged 75 or older	57.09	65	6.2

	AVERAGE HOUSEHOLD SPENDING	BEST CUSTOMERS (index)	BIGGEST CUSTOMERS (market share)
HOUSEHOLD INCOME			
Average household	**$87.69**	**100**	**100.0%**
Under $20,000	28.31	32	7.0
$20,000 to $39,999	38.70	44	10.1
$40,000 to $49,999	64.64	74	7.0
$50,000 to $69,999	69.74	80	11.4
$70,000 to $79,999	89.40	102	6.1
$80,000 to $99,999	98.47	112	9.4
$100,000 or more	258.15	294	50.5
HOUSEHOLD TYPE			
Average household	**87.69**	**100**	**100.0**
Married couples	113.79	130	64.0
Married couples, no children	151.97	173	36.8
Married couples, with children	91.17	104	24.2
Oldest child under age 6	120.82	138	5.9
Oldest child aged 6 to 17	77.65	89	10.4
Oldest child aged 18 or older	96.15	110	7.9
Single parent with child under age 18	46.82	53	3.1
Single person	61.41	70	20.5
RACE AND HISPANIC ORIGIN			
Average household	**87.69**	**100**	**100.0**
Asian	41.09	47	2.0
Black	31.08	35	4.3
Hispanic	33.81	39	4.7
Non-Hispanic white and other	105.46	120	91.2
REGION			
Average household	**87.69**	**100**	**100.0**
Northeast	133.94	153	28.0
Midwest	59.61	68	15.2
South	75.81	86	31.7
West	97.74	111	25.2
EDUCATION			
Average household	**87.69**	**100**	**100.0**
Less than high school graduate	10.75	12	1.8
High school graduate	44.27	50	12.9
Some college	64.84	74	15.5
Associate's degree	90.85	104	9.8
Bachelor's degree or more	175.43	200	59.4
Bachelor's degree	160.83	183	34.6
Master's, professional, doctoral degree	204.19	233	25.2

Note: Market shares may not sum to 100.0 because of rounding and missing categories by household type. "Asian" and "black" include Hispanics and non-Hispanics who identify themselves as being of the respective race alone. "Hispanic" includes people of any race who identify themselves as Hispanic. "Other" includes people who identify themselves as non-Hispanic and as Alaska Native, American Indian, Asian (who are also included in the "Asian" row), or Native Hawaiian or other Pacific Islander as well as non-Hispanics reporting more than one race.

Source: Calculations by New Strategist based on the Bureau of Labor Statistics' 2010 Consumer Expenditure Survey

Wine at Restaurants and Bars

Best customers: **Householders aged 35 to 64**
                             High-income households
                             Married couples without children at home
                             Married couples with preschoolers
                             Asians and non-Hispanic whites
                             Households in the Northeast and West
                             College graduates

Customer trends: **Average household spending on wine at restaurants and bars should begin to increase again as more boomers enter the empty-nest lifestage—but only if discretionary income grows.**

The best customers of wine at restaurants and bars are householders with the time and money to relax with a glass of wine, perhaps over a meal. Married couples without children at home (most of them empty-nesters) spend 20 percent more than average on this item. Householders ranging in age from 35 to 64 spend 5 to 23 percent more than average on wine at restaurants and bars. Married couples with preschoolers outspend the average on this item by 41 percent. Households with incomes of $100,000 or more spend three times the average on wine consumed in restaurants and bars. Asians spend 50 percent more than average on wine at restaurants and bars. The same is true for households in the Northeast, while households in the West spend 53 percent more than average on this item. Households headed by college graduates spend more than twice the average and control 61 percent of the market.

Average household spending on wine at restaurants and bars doubled between 2000 and 2006, after adjusting for inflation, but spending fell 26 percent between 2006 and 2010. Behind the increase in the first part of the decade was the entry of the baby-boom generation into the best-customer lifestage. The Great Recession is largely responsible for the drop in the past few years. Spending on this item should begin to increase again as more boomers become empty-nesters—but only if discretionary income grows.

Table 1.8 Wine at restaurants and bars

Total household spending $4,032,863,100.00
Average household spends   33.30

	AVERAGE HOUSEHOLD SPENDING	BEST CUSTOMERS (index)	BIGGEST CUSTOMERS (market share)
AGE OF HOUSEHOLDER			
Average household	**$33.30**	**100**	**100.0%**
Under age 25	20.44	61	4.1
Aged 25 to 34	32.98	99	16.5
Aged 35 to 44	41.05	123	22.3
Aged 45 to 54	35.06	105	21.8
Aged 55 to 64	39.64	119	21.0
Aged 65 to 74	26.59	80	8.6
Aged 75 or older	20.18	61	5.8

	AVERAGE HOUSEHOLD SPENDING	BEST CUSTOMERS (index)	BIGGEST CUSTOMERS (market share)
HOUSEHOLD INCOME			
Average household	**$33.30**	**100**	**100.0%**
Under $20,000	8.39	25	5.5
$20,000 to $39,999	16.86	51	11.6
$40,000 to $49,999	18.07	54	5.1
$50,000 to $69,999	30.50	92	13.1
$70,000 to $79,999	22.45	67	4.0
$80,000 to $99,999	42.68	128	10.7
$100,000 or more	99.69	299	51.3
HOUSEHOLD TYPE			
Average household	**33.30**	**100**	**100.0**
Married couples	35.33	106	52.3
Married couples, no children	39.84	120	25.4
Married couples, with children	35.08	105	24.5
Oldest child under age 6	46.85	141	6.0
Oldest child aged 6 to 17	32.78	98	11.6
Oldest child aged 18 or older	32.50	98	7.0
Single parent with child under age 18	6.98	21	1.2
Single person	30.53	92	26.9
RACE AND HISPANIC ORIGIN			
Average household	**33.30**	**100**	**100.0**
Asian	49.96	150	6.4
Black	12.96	39	4.8
Hispanic	10.85	33	4.0
Non-Hispanic white and other	40.02	120	91.1
REGION			
Average household	**33.30**	**100**	**100.0**
Northeast	50.07	150	27.6
Midwest	19.03	57	12.7
South	22.95	69	25.3
West	51.03	153	34.7
EDUCATION			
Average household	**33.30**	**100**	**100.0**
Less than high school graduate	4.96	15	2.1
High school graduate	16.87	51	12.9
Some college	26.66	80	16.8
Associate's degree	22.77	68	6.5
Bachelor's degree or more	68.63	206	61.2
Bachelor's degree	69.03	207	39.2
Master's, professional, doctoral degree	67.84	204	22.0

Note: Market shares may not sum to 100.0 because of rounding and missing categories by household type. "Asian" and "black" include Hispanics and non-Hispanics who identify themselves as being of the respective race alone. "Hispanic" includes people of any race who identify themselves as Hispanic. "Other" includes people who identify themselves as non-Hispanic and as Alaska Native, American Indian, Asian (who are also included in the "Asian" row), or Native Hawaiian or other Pacific Islander as well as non-Hispanics reporting more than one race.

Source: Calculations by New Strategist based on the Bureau of Labor Statistics' 2010 Consumer Expenditure Survey

Chapter 2.

Apparel

Household Spending on Apparel, 2010

Average household spending on apparel has been falling for years, dropping from $2,350 in 2000, after adjusting for inflation, to just $1,700 in 2010—a 28 percent decline. The apparel category includes men's, women's, and children's clothes as well as shoes, jewelry, watches, dry cleaning, and coin-operated laundry. Falling prices are one factor behind the decline in spending on this category as cheaper imports allow people to buy more for less. Another factor is the shift toward casual dress in the workplace and at social functions.

Average household spending on women's clothes—which account for the largest share of apparel spending (33 percent in 2010)—fell by 27 percent between 2000 and 2010, after adjusting for inflation. Spending on men's clothes fell by an even larger 30 percent. Spending on women's shoes declined by 26 percent, and men's shoe spending was 32 percent lower. Spending on children's clothing has fared poorly as well, with 32 and 36 percent declines in average household spending on girls' and boys' clothes, respectively. Spending on infants' clothes fell by a smaller amount (down 13 percent). Jewelry spending declined 29 percent as households slashed discretionary spending in these financially turbulent times. Spending on professional laundry and dry cleaning declined by a large 46 percent.

Average household spending on apparel may continue to slip as boomers approach retirement and no longer need even business casual attire. At some point, however, apparel spending will bottom out and then stabilize.

Spending on apparel

(average annual spending of households on apparel, 2000, 2006, and 2010; in 2010 dollars)

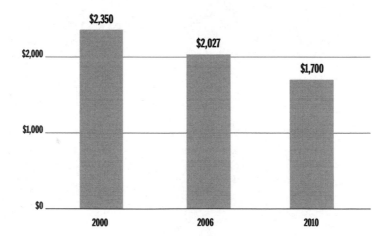

Table 2.1 Apparel spending, 2000 to 2010

(average annual and percent distribution of household spending on apparel by category, 2000 to 2010; percent change in spending and percentage point change in distribution, 2000–06, 2006–10, and 2000–10; in 2010 dollars; ranked by amount spent)

	2010 average household spending	2006 average household spending (in 2010$)	2000 average household spending (in 2010$)	percent change		
				2006–10	2000–06	2000–10
AVERAGE ANNUAL SPENDING						
Average household spending on apparel	**$1,699.80**	**$2,026.85**	**$2,350.45**	**–16.1%**	**–13.8%**	**–27.7%**
Women's apparel	561.50	679.90	768.78	–17.4	–11.6	–27.0
Men's apparel	304.05	381.36	435.97	–20.3	–12.5	–30.3
Women's shoes	146.30	155.36	197.48	–5.8	–21.3	–25.9
Men's shoes	101.14	106.88	148.85	–5.4	–28.2	–32.1
Girls' apparel	101.10	132.43	149.54	–23.7	–11.4	–32.4
Jewelry	96.48	135.63	135.90	–28.9	–0.2	–29.0
Infants' apparel	90.58	103.54	103.73	–12.5	–0.2	–12.7
Boys' apparel	77.77	98.36	121.26	–20.9	–18.9	–35.9
Children's shoes	55.94	66.48	88.12	–15.9	–24.6	–36.5
Professional apparel laundry and dry cleaning	49.53	67.01	91.68	–26.1	–26.9	–46.0
Coin-operated apparel laundry and dry cleaning	39.07	42.02	48.03	–7.0	–12.5	–18.7
Sewing material, patterns, and notions	10.15	20.01	11.95	–49.3	67.4	–15.1
Shoe and apparel repair and alteration	7.74	7.90	9.54	–2.0	–17.2	–18.8

				percentage point change		
	2006–10	2000–06	2000–10	2006–10	2000–06	2000–10
PERCENT DISTRIBUTION OF SPENDING						
Average household spending on apparel	**100.0%**	**100.0%**	**100.0%**	**–**	**–**	**–**
Women's apparel	33.0	33.5	32.7	–0.5	0.8	0.3
Men's apparel	17.9	18.8	18.5	–0.9	0.3	–0.7
Women's shoes	8.6	7.7	8.4	0.9	–0.7	0.2
Men's shoes	6.0	5.3	6.3	0.7	–1.1	–0.4
Girls' apparel	5.9	6.5	6.4	–0.6	0.2	–0.4
Jewelry	5.7	6.7	5.8	–1.0	0.9	–0.1
Infants' apparel	5.3	5.1	4.4	0.2	0.7	0.9
Boys' apparel	4.6	4.9	5.2	–0.3	–0.3	–0.6
Children's shoes	3.3	3.3	3.7	0.0	–0.5	–0.5
Professional apparel laundry and dry cleaning	2.9	3.3	3.9	–0.4	–0.6	–1.0
Coin-operated apparel laundry and dry cleaning	2.3	2.1	2.0	0.2	0.0	0.3
Sewing material, patterns, and notions	0.6	1.0	0.5	–0.4	0.5	0.1
Shoe and apparel repair and alteration	0.5	0.4	0.4	0.1	–0.0	0.1

Note: Numbers do not add to total because not all categories are shown. "–" means not applicable.
Source: Bureau of Labor Statistics, 2000, 2006, and 2010 Consumer Expenditure Surveys; calculations by New Strategist

Boys' Apparel

Best customers: **Married couples with children under age 18**
Single parents
Householders aged 25 to 44
Hispanics

Customer trends: **Average household spending on boys' apparel may increase as the large millennial generation has children.**

Not surprisingly, the best customers of boys' apparel are households with children, driven especially by those with school-aged children. Married couples with children at home spend more than twice the average on this category, while the subgroup with school-aged children spends over three times the average. Single parents spend two-and-one-half times the average on boys' clothes. Householders aged 35 to 44 spend over double the average on boys' clothes because most are parents, and those aged 25 to 34 spend one-third more than average on this item. Hispanic householders spend 51 percent more than the average household on this category. Behind the higher spending of Hispanics are their larger families.

Apparel spending fell 28 percent between 2000 and 2010 as less-expensive imports drove clothing prices down. Average household spending on boys' clothes fell by an even greater 36 percent during those years. As the large millennial generation has children, average household spending on boys' clothes may increase—especially if the downward spiral in clothing prices comes to an end.

Table 2.2 Boys' apparel

Total household spending $9,418,491,390.00
Average household spends   77.77

	AVERAGE HOUSEHOLD SPENDING	BEST CUSTOMERS (index)	BIGGEST CUSTOMERS (market share)
AGE OF HOUSEHOLDER			
Average household	**$77.77**	**100**	**100.0%**
Under age 25	41.24	53	3.5
Aged 25 to 34	103.90	134	22.2
Aged 35 to 44	166.27	214	38.7
Aged 45 to 54	79.29	102	21.1
Aged 55 to 64	38.80	50	8.8
Aged 65 to 74	26.80	34	3.7
Aged 75 or older	18.31	24	2.2

	AVERAGE HOUSEHOLD SPENDING	BEST CUSTOMERS (index)	BIGGEST CUSTOMERS (market share)
HOUSEHOLD INCOME			
Average household	**$77.77**	**100**	**100.0%**
Under $20,000	43.94	56	12.3
$20,000 to $39,999	57.76	74	17.0
$40,000 to $49,999	66.40	85	8.1
$50,000 to $69,999	77.27	99	14.2
$70,000 to $79,999	99.66	128	7.7
$80,000 to $99,999	87.69	113	9.4
$100,000 or more	143.09	184	31.5
HOUSEHOLD TYPE			
Average household	**77.77**	**100**	**100.0**
Married couples	109.31	141	69.3
Married couples, no children	24.80	32	6.8
Married couples, with children	176.99	228	52.9
Oldest child under age 6	105.93	136	5.8
Oldest child aged 6 to 17	258.10	332	39.0
Oldest child aged 18 or older	89.41	115	8.3
Single parent with child under age 18	195.00	251	14.8
Single person	11.25	14	4.2
RACE AND HISPANIC ORIGIN			
Average household	**77.77**	**100**	**100.0**
Asian	52.26	67	2.9
Black	86.42	111	13.6
Hispanic	117.25	151	18.4
Non-Hispanic white and other	70.07	90	68.3
REGION			
Average household	**77.77**	**100**	**100.0**
Northeast	92.18	119	21.8
Midwest	69.79	90	20.0
South	66.43	85	31.4
West	92.59	119	27.0
EDUCATION			
Average household	**77.77**	**100**	**100.0**
Less than high school graduate	77.16	99	14.2
High school graduate	68.50	88	22.5
Some college	71.34	92	19.3
Associate's degree	83.30	107	10.1
Bachelor's degree or more	89.18	115	34.1
Bachelor's degree	83.03	107	20.2
Master's, professional, doctoral degree	100.73	130	14.0

Note: Market shares may not sum to 100.0 because of rounding and missing categories by household type. "Asian" and "black" include Hispanics and non-Hispanics who identify themselves as being of the respective race alone. "Hispanic" includes people of any race who identify themselves as Hispanic. "Other" includes people who identify themselves as non-Hispanic and as Alaska Native, American Indian, Asian (who are also included in the "Asian" row), or Native Hawaiian or other Pacific Islander as well as non-Hispanics reporting more than one race.

Source: Calculations by New Strategist based on the Bureau of Labor Statistics' 2010 Consumer Expenditure Survey

Children's Shoes

Best customers: Married couples with school-aged children
Single parents
Householders aged 25 to 44
Blacks and Hispanics
Least-educated householders

Customer trends: Average household spending on shoes for children may increase as the large millennial generation enters parenthood.

Married couples with school-aged children spend more than three times the average on children's shoes and account for 38 percent of the market. Single parents spend more than twice the average on this item and account for another 13 percent of the market. Black and especially Hispanic householders are also big spenders on children's shoes. Blacks spend one-third more than average, while Hispanics spend well over twice the average on shoes for the kids. Because householders aged 25 to 44 are likely to have children at home, their spending on children's shoes is well above average. Householders without a high school diploma outspend the average by 79 percent and are the only educational group to exceed average spending on this item.

Average household spending on children's shoes fell 37 percent between 2000 and 2010, after adjusting for inflation, as less expensive imports allowed consumers to buy more for less. Spending on children's shoes may begin to rise in the years ahead as the large millennial generation has children and the black and Hispanic populations grow.

Table 2.3 Children's shoes

Total household spending $6,774,725,580.00
Average household spends   55.94

	AVERAGE HOUSEHOLD SPENDING	BEST CUSTOMERS (index)	BIGGEST CUSTOMERS (market share)
AGE OF HOUSEHOLDER			
Average household	**$55.94**	**100**	**100.0%**
Under age 25	42.39	76	5.0
Aged 25 to 34	92.88	166	27.6
Aged 35 to 44	124.51	223	40.3
Aged 45 to 54	49.81	89	18.4
Aged 55 to 64	19.02	34	6.0
Aged 65 to 74	9.64	17	1.9
Aged 75 or older	7.71	14	1.3

	AVERAGE HOUSEHOLD SPENDING	BEST CUSTOMERS (index)	BIGGEST CUSTOMERS (market share)
HOUSEHOLD INCOME			
Average household	**$55.94**	**100**	**100.0%**
Under $20,000	40.23	72	15.7
$20,000 to $39,999	52.43	94	21.5
$40,000 to $49,999	79.86	143	13.5
$50,000 to $69,999	49.27	88	12.6
$70,000 to $79,999	49.93	89	5.3
$80,000 to $99,999	47.96	86	7.1
$100,000 or more	77.64	139	23.8
HOUSEHOLD TYPE			
Average household	**55.94**	**100**	**100.0**
Married couples	74.57	133	65.8
Married couples, no children	7.88	14	3.0
Married couples, with children	117.41	210	48.8
Oldest child under age 6	58.93	105	4.5
Oldest child aged 6 to 17	178.54	319	37.5
Oldest child aged 18 or older	56.20	100	7.3
Single parent with child under age 18	124.99	223	13.2
Single person	3.81	7	2.0
RACE AND HISPANIC ORIGIN			
Average household	**55.94**	**100**	**100.0**
Asian	51.31	92	3.9
Black	75.48	135	16.5
Hispanic	132.50	237	28.9
Non-Hispanic white and other	40.98	73	55.5
REGION			
Average household	**55.94**	**100**	**100.0**
Northeast	48.04	86	15.8
Midwest	52.76	94	21.0
South	59.48	106	39.0
West	59.84	107	24.2
EDUCATION			
Average household	**55.94**	**100**	**100.0**
Less than high school graduate	100.38	179	25.6
High school graduate	49.54	89	22.6
Some college	52.47	94	19.7
Associate's degree	54.76	98	9.2
Bachelor's degree or more	44.80	80	23.8
Bachelor's degree	44.32	79	15.0
Master's, professional, doctoral degree	45.77	82	8.9

Note: Market shares may not sum to 100.0 because of rounding and missing categories by household type. "Asian" and "black" include Hispanics and non-Hispanics who identify themselves as being of the respective race alone. "Hispanic" includes people of any race who identify themselves as Hispanic. "Other" includes people who identify themselves as non-Hispanic and as Alaska Native, American Indian, Asian (who are also included in the "Asian" row), or Native Hawaiian or other Pacific Islander as well as non-Hispanics reporting more than one race.

Source: Calculations by New Strategist based on the Bureau of Labor Statistics' 2010 Consumer Expenditure Survey

Coin-Operated Apparel Laundry and Dry Cleaning

Best customers:

Householders under age 35
Low-income households
Single parents
Blacks and Hispanics
Households in the Northeast
Least-educated householders

Customer trends:

Average household spending on coin-operated apparel laundry and dry cleaning will climb as the large millennial generation fills the young-adult age group and the Hispanic population grows.

The biggest spenders at coin-operated laundries are householders under age 35, who spend 71 to 93 percent more than average. Not surprisingly, low-income households also spend more than average on this category. Many low-income householders are single parents, and the latter spend three-quarters more than average at laundromats. Black householders spend 70 percent more than average at coin-operated laundries, while Hispanic households spend nearly three times the average. Many black and Hispanic householders are renters and do not have a washer or dryer at home. Spending at laundromats by households in the Northeast is 72 percent above average. Householders without a high school diploma spend almost twice the average on this item.

Average household spending on coin-operated laundry and dry cleaning fell 19 percent between 2000 and 2010, after adjusting for inflation. This decline occurred despite the increase in the young-adult population. As millennials (the oldest of whom turned 33 in 2010) continue to fill the young-adult age group, average household spending on coin-operated laundries should rise. Also boosting spending in this category will be the rapidly growing Hispanic population.

Table 2.4 Coin-operated apparel laundry and dry cleaning

Total household spending $4,731,650,490.00
Average household spends   39.07

	AVERAGE HOUSEHOLD SPENDING	BEST CUSTOMERS (index)	BIGGEST CUSTOMERS (market share)
AGE OF HOUSEHOLDER			
Average household	**$39.07**	**100**	**100.0%**
Under age 25	75.38	193	12.8
Aged 25 to 34	66.63	171	28.4
Aged 35 to 44	43.69	112	20.2
Aged 45 to 54	34.02	87	18.0
Aged 55 to 64	24.00	61	10.8
Aged 65 to 74	21.74	56	6.0
Aged 75 or older	15.28	39	3.7

	AVERAGE HOUSEHOLD SPENDING	BEST CUSTOMERS (index)	BIGGEST CUSTOMERS (market share)
HOUSEHOLD INCOME			
Average household	**$39.07**	**100**	**100.0%**
Under $20,000	51.72	132	28.9
$20,000 to $39,999	56.11	144	32.9
$40,000 to $49,999	40.73	104	9.9
$50,000 to $69,999	32.59	83	12.0
$70,000 to $79,999	29.05	74	4.5
$80,000 to $99,999	23.42	60	5.0
$100,000 or more	15.78	40	6.9
HOUSEHOLD TYPE			
Average household	**39.07**	**100**	**100.0**
Married couples	26.38	68	33.3
Married couples, no children	17.12	44	9.3
Married couples, with children	29.95	77	17.8
Oldest child under age 6	44.46	114	4.9
Oldest child aged 6 to 17	26.39	68	7.9
Oldest child aged 18 or older	27.14	69	5.0
Single parent with child under age 18	68.77	176	10.4
Single person	40.66	104	30.5
RACE AND HISPANIC ORIGIN			
Average household	**39.07**	**100**	**100.0**
Asian	50.28	129	5.5
Black	66.60	170	20.9
Hispanic	109.01	279	34.0
Non-Hispanic white and other	23.67	61	45.9
REGION			
Average household	**39.07**	**100**	**100.0**
Northeast	67.10	172	31.5
Midwest	27.34	70	15.6
South	26.39	68	24.8
West	48.43	124	28.1
EDUCATION			
Average household	**39.07**	**100**	**100.0**
Less than high school graduate	76.10	195	27.8
High school graduate	39.09	100	25.5
Some college	35.21	90	18.9
Associate's degree	33.83	87	8.2
Bachelor's degree or more	25.63	66	19.5
Bachelor's degree	27.97	72	13.5
Master's, professional, doctoral degree	21.54	55	6.0

Note: Market shares may not sum to 100.0 because of rounding and missing categories by household type. "Asian" and "black" include Hispanics and non-Hispanics who identify themselves as being of the respective race alone. "Hispanic" includes people of any race who identify themselves as Hispanic. "Other" includes people who identify themselves as non-Hispanic and as Alaska Native, American Indian, Asian (who are also included in the "Asian" row), or Native Hawaiian or other Pacific Islander as well as non-Hispanics reporting more than one race.

Source: Calculations by New Strategist based on the Bureau of Labor Statistics' 2010 Consumer Expenditure Survey

Girls' Apparel

Best customers:

Married couples with children under age 18
Single parents
Householders aged 35 to 44
Hispanics

Customer trends:

Average household spending on children's apparel may increase as the large millennial generation has children.

The average household spends more on clothes for girls than for boys—an average of $101 for girls' clothes versus $78 for boys' clothes in 2010. The big spenders on girls' clothes are, not surprisingly, the same households that spend the most on boys' clothes. Married couples with school-aged children at home spend more than three-and-one-half times the average on girls' clothes, and single parents spend more than twice the average. Couples with preschoolers spend 73 percent more than average on girls' clothes. Householders aged 35 to 44 spend over twice the average because most are parents. Hispanic householders spend 44 percent more than average on girls' clothes.

Average household spending on girls' clothes fell 32 percent between 2000 and 2010, after adjusting for inflation, as less expensive imports drove clothing prices down. As the large millennial generation has children, spending on girls' clothes may increase—especially if the downward spiral in clothing prices comes to a halt.

Table 2.5 **Girls' apparel**

Total household spending $12,243,917,700.00
Average household spends   101.10

	AVERAGE HOUSEHOLD SPENDING	BEST CUSTOMERS (index)	BIGGEST CUSTOMERS (market share)
AGE OF HOUSEHOLDER			
Average household	**$101.10**	**100**	**100.0%**
Under age 25	42.15	42	2.8
Aged 25 to 34	124.63	123	20.5
Aged 35 to 44	210.18	208	37.6
Aged 45 to 54	115.60	114	23.7
Aged 55 to 64	49.93	49	8.7
Aged 65 to 74	43.32	43	4.6
Aged 75 or older	24.91	25	2.4

	AVERAGE HOUSEHOLD SPENDING	BEST CUSTOMERS (index)	BIGGEST CUSTOMERS (market share)
HOUSEHOLD INCOME			
Average household	$101.10	100	100.0%
Under $20,000	59.89	59	12.9
$20,000 to $39,999	75.51	75	17.1
$40,000 to $49,999	74.56	74	7.0
$50,000 to $69,999	87.25	86	12.4
$70,000 to $79,999	104.10	103	6.2
$80,000 to $99,999	153.91	152	12.7
$100,000 or more	191.42	189	32.5
HOUSEHOLD TYPE			
Average household	101.10	100	100.0
Married couples	148.93	147	72.7
Married couples, no children	40.91	40	8.6
Married couples, with children	245.09	242	56.4
Oldest child under age 6	174.45	173	7.4
Oldest child aged 6 to 17	367.15	363	42.7
Oldest child aged 18 or older	96.51	95	6.9
Single parent with child under age 18	212.50	210	12.4
Single person	14.50	14	4.2
RACE AND HISPANIC ORIGIN			
Average household	101.10	100	100.0
Asian	112.75	112	4.7
Black	91.09	90	11.0
Hispanic	145.91	144	17.6
Non-Hispanic white and other	95.54	95	71.6
REGION			
Average household	101.10	100	100.0
Northeast	97.92	97	17.8
Midwest	91.57	91	20.2
South	103.14	102	37.4
West	110.05	109	24.7
EDUCATION			
Average household	101.10	100	100.0
Less than high school graduate	101.28	100	14.3
High school graduate	89.60	89	22.6
Some college	92.41	91	19.2
Associate's degree	102.00	101	9.5
Bachelor's degree or more	117.19	116	34.4
Bachelor's degree	120.42	119	22.5
Master's, professional, doctoral degree	110.74	110	11.9

Note: Market shares may not sum to 100.0 because of rounding and missing categories by household type. "Asian" and "black" include Hispanics and non-Hispanics who identify themselves as being of the respective race alone. "Hispanic" includes people of any race who identify themselves as Hispanic. "Other" includes people who identify themselves as non-Hispanic and as Alaska Native, American Indian, Asian (who are also included in the "Asian" row), or Native Hawaiian or other Pacific Islander as well as non-Hispanics reporting more than one race.

Source: Calculations by New Strategist based on the Bureau of Labor Statistics' 2010 Consumer Expenditure Survey

Infants' Apparel

Best customers: **Married couples with preschoolers**
                                          Single parents
                                          Householders under age 35
                                          Hispanics and Asians

Customer trends: **Average household spending on infants' apparel may increase as the large**
                                          millennial generation has children.

The average household spent $91 on clothes for infants in 2010. By far the biggest spenders on infants' clothes are married couples with preschoolers. This household type spends nearly seven times the average on baby clothes. The spending on infants' apparel by single parents is 23 percent above average. Householders aged 25 to 34 spend over twice the average because many have newborns and toddlers. Those under age 25 spend 62 percent more. Hispanic householders spend 65 percent more than average on infants' clothes because of their larger families, and Asians outspend the average by 46 percent.

Spending on infants' apparel fell 13 percent between 2000 and 2010, a much smaller decline in spending than most other apparel categories. In fact, infants' apparel spending held steady in the first half of the decade, and began to decline only in 2006. One factor behind the relative stability is the growing Hispanic population. As the large millennial generation has children during the next few years, average household spending on infants' clothes may increase—especially if the downward spiral in clothing prices comes to a halt.

Table 2.6 Infants' apparel

Total household spending $10,969,872,060.00
Average household spends   90.58

	AVERAGE HOUSEHOLD SPENDING	BEST CUSTOMERS (index)	BIGGEST CUSTOMERS (market share)
AGE OF HOUSEHOLDER			
Average household	**$90.58**	**100**	**100.0%**
Under age 25	146.46	162	10.7
Aged 25 to 34	195.40	216	35.9
Aged 35 to 44	116.98	129	23.4
Aged 45 to 54	58.73	65	13.4
Aged 55 to 64	54.11	60	10.5
Aged 65 to 74	33.81	37	4.0
Aged 75 or older	21.91	24	2.3

	AVERAGE HOUSEHOLD SPENDING	BEST CUSTOMERS (index)	BIGGEST CUSTOMERS (market share)
HOUSEHOLD INCOME			
Average household	**$90.58**	**100**	**100.0%**
Under $20,000	55.36	61	13.3
$20,000 to $39,999	78.17	86	19.8
$40,000 to $49,999	88.19	97	9.2
$50,000 to $69,999	85.93	95	13.6
$70,000 to $79,999	105.22	116	7.0
$80,000 to $99,999	107.40	119	9.9
$100,000 or more	144.02	159	27.3
HOUSEHOLD TYPE			
Average household	**90.58**	**100**	**100.0**
Married couples	131.50	145	71.6
Married couples, no children	54.41	60	12.8
Married couples, with children	185.58	205	47.7
Oldest child under age 6	612.60	676	29.0
Oldest child aged 6 to 17	115.43	127	15.0
Oldest child aged 18 or older	68.00	75	5.4
Single parent with child under age 18	111.26	123	7.2
Single person	16.93	19	5.5
RACE AND HISPANIC ORIGIN			
Average household	**90.58**	**100**	**100.0**
Asian	132.68	146	6.2
Black	80.43	89	10.9
Hispanic	149.80	165	20.1
Non-Hispanic white and other	83.25	92	69.7
REGION			
Average household	**90.58**	**100**	**100.0**
Northeast	91.37	101	18.5
Midwest	83.33	92	20.5
South	89.07	98	36.1
West	99.67	110	24.9
EDUCATION			
Average household	**90.58**	**100**	**100.0**
Less than high school graduate	83.34	92	13.1
High school graduate	81.46	90	23.0
Some college	78.91	87	18.3
Associate's degree	106.89	118	11.2
Bachelor's degree or more	105.17	116	34.5
Bachelor's degree	96.09	106	20.0
Master's, professional, doctoral degree	122.03	135	14.6

Note: Market shares may not sum to 100.0 because of rounding and missing categories by household type. "Asian" and "black" include Hispanics and non-Hispanics who identify themselves as being of the respective race alone. "Hispanic" includes people of any race who identify themselves as Hispanic. "Other" includes people who identify themselves as non-Hispanic and as Alaska Native, American Indian, Asian (who are also included in the "Asian" row), or Native Hawaiian or other Pacific Islander as well as non-Hispanics reporting more than one race.

Source: Calculations by New Strategist based on the Bureau of Labor Statistics' 2010 Consumer Expenditure Survey

Jewelry

Best customers: Householders aged 25 to 34 and 55 to 64
Married couples without children at home
Married couples with preschoolers
Asians

Customer trends: Average household spending on jewelry may continue to fall in the years ahead as tighter budgets limit discretionary spending.

Householders aged 25 to 34 spend 19 percent more than average on jewelry, as do those aged 55 to 64. Married couples without children at home (most of them empty-nesters) spend 41 percent more than average on jewelry. Those with preschoolers spend 65 percent more than average on this item. Asian householders outspend the average by 68 percent.

Average household spending on jewelry fell 29 percent between 2000 and 2010, after adjusting for inflation. Behind the decline was belt tightening due to the Great Recession, as spending on jewelry had held steady from 2000 to 2006 (the year average household spending peaked), and all the decline occurred between 2006 and 2010. Spending on jewelry may continue to fall in the years ahead as tighter budgets limit discretionary spending.

Table 2.7 Jewelry

Total household spending $11,684,403,360.00
Average household spends 96.48

	AVERAGE HOUSEHOLD SPENDING	BEST CUSTOMERS (index)	BIGGEST CUSTOMERS (market share)
AGE OF HOUSEHOLDER			
Average household	**$96.48**	**100**	**100.0%**
Under age 25	65.65	68	4.5
Aged 25 to 34	115.25	119	19.9
Aged 35 to 44	101.22	105	19.0
Aged 45 to 54	102.59	106	22.0
Aged 55 to 64	114.52	119	20.9
Aged 65 to 74	95.94	99	10.7
Aged 75 or older	30.17	31	3.0

	AVERAGE HOUSEHOLD SPENDING	BEST CUSTOMERS (index)	BIGGEST CUSTOMERS (market share)
HOUSEHOLD INCOME			
Average household	**$96.48**	**100**	**100.0%**
Under $20,000	21.31	22	4.8
$20,000 to $39,999	39.98	41	9.5
$40,000 to $49,999	62.99	65	6.2
$50,000 to $69,999	69.31	72	10.3
$70,000 to $79,999	128.77	133	8.0
$80,000 to $99,999	125.64	130	10.9
$100,000 or more	283.38	294	50.4
HOUSEHOLD TYPE			
Average household	**96.48**	**100**	**100.0**
Married couples	121.61	126	62.2
Married couples, no children	135.68	141	29.9
Married couples, with children	118.39	123	28.5
Oldest child under age 6	159.34	165	7.1
Oldest child aged 6 to 17	115.27	119	14.1
Oldest child aged 18 or older	99.20	103	7.4
Single parent with child under age 18	27.68	29	1.7
Single person	52.55	54	16.0
RACE AND HISPANIC ORIGIN			
Average household	**96.48**	**100**	**100.0**
Asian	162.24	168	7.2
Black	39.40	41	5.0
Hispanic	49.47	51	6.2
Non-Hispanic white and other	113.08	117	88.9
REGION			
Average household	**96.48**	**100**	**100.0**
Northeast	91.18	95	17.3
Midwest	97.62	101	22.6
South	90.99	94	34.6
West	108.54	113	25.5
EDUCATION			
Average household	**96.48**	**100**	**100.0**
Less than high school graduate	20.11	21	3.0
High school graduate	73.11	76	19.3
Some college	75.46	78	16.4
Associate's degree	86.78	90	8.5
Bachelor's degree or more	171.25	177	52.7
Bachelor's degree	159.39	165	31.2
Master's, professional, doctoral degree	191.95	199	21.5

Note: Market shares may not sum to 100.0 because of rounding and missing categories by household type. "Asian" and "black" include Hispanics and non-Hispanics who identify themselves as being of the respective race alone. "Hispanic" includes people of any race who identify themselves as Hispanic. "Other" includes people who identify themselves as non-Hispanic and as Alaska Native, American Indian, Asian (who are also included in the "Asian" row), or Native Hawaiian or other Pacific Islander as well as non-Hispanics reporting more than one race.

Source: Calculations by New Strategist based on the Bureau of Labor Statistics' 2010 Consumer Expenditure Survey

Men's Apparel

Best customers: **Householders aged 45 to 54**
                             Married couples with school-aged or older children at home
                             Asians
                             Households in the Northeast and West

Customer trends: **Average household spending on men's clothes will continue to decline as the large baby-boom generation approaches retirement.**

In 2010, the average household spent $304.05 on men's clothes versus a larger $561.50 on women's clothes. Both figures are more than one-quarter lower than in 2000, after adjusting for inflation. Falling prices are one reason for the decline in spending, as cheaper imports allow consumers to buy more for less. Also behind the decline is the trend toward more casual attire in the workplace and at social functions. A third factor is the Great Recession, which worsened the decline in spending on men's clothes.

The biggest spenders on men's clothes are households with working men. This explains why married couples with adult children at home spend 73 percent more than average on this item, since many of these households include more than one working man. Couples with school-aged children outspend the average by 36 percent. Householders aged 45 to 54 spend 28 percent more than average on men's clothes. Asians outspend the average by 84 percent. Households in the Northeast spend 31 percent more than average on men's apparel, and those in the West spend 23 percent more.

Average household spending on men's clothes fell 30 percent between 2000 and 2010 as clothing prices fell and more casual attire became the norm in the workplace. Spending on men's clothes will continue to decline as the large baby-boom generation approaches retirement and no longer requires business attire.

Table 2.8 Men's apparel

Total household spending $36,822,583,350.00
Average household spends 304.05

	AVERAGE HOUSEHOLD SPENDING	BEST CUSTOMERS (index)	BIGGEST CUSTOMERS (market share)
AGE OF HOUSEHOLDER			
Average household	**$304.05**	**100**	**100.0%**
Under age 25	218.67	72	4.8
Aged 25 to 34	324.76	107	17.8
Aged 35 to 44	320.29	105	19.1
Aged 45 to 54	390.11	128	26.5
Aged 55 to 64	331.11	109	19.2
Aged 65 to 74	246.44	81	8.7
Aged 75 or older	119.46	39	3.7

	AVERAGE HOUSEHOLD SPENDING	BEST CUSTOMERS (index)	BIGGEST CUSTOMERS (market share)
HOUSEHOLD INCOME			
Average household	**$304.05**	**100**	**100.0%**
Under $20,000	102.04	34	7.3
$20,000 to $39,999	189.66	62	14.3
$40,000 to $49,999	215.26	71	6.7
$50,000 to $69,999	245.62	81	11.6
$70,000 to $79,999	357.20	117	7.0
$80,000 to $99,999	421.17	139	11.5
$100,000 or more	752.28	247	42.4
HOUSEHOLD TYPE			
Average household	**304.05**	**100**	**100.0**
Married couples	380.53	125	61.7
Married couples, no children	347.40	114	24.3
Married couples, with children	423.02	139	32.4
Oldest child under age 6	251.08	83	3.5
Oldest child aged 6 to 17	413.70	136	16.0
Oldest child aged 18 or older	525.08	173	12.5
Single parent with child under age 18	214.96	71	4.2
Single person	173.94	57	16.8
RACE AND HISPANIC ORIGIN			
Average household	**304.05**	**100**	**100.0**
Asian	560.34	184	7.8
Black	202.36	67	8.1
Hispanic	297.96	98	11.9
Non-Hispanic white and other	321.11	106	80.1
REGION			
Average household	**304.05**	**100**	**100.0**
Northeast	399.31	131	24.1
Midwest	259.07	85	19.0
South	242.06	80	29.2
West	373.30	123	27.8
EDUCATION			
Average household	**304.05**	**100**	**100.0**
Less than high school graduate	192.21	63	9.0
High school graduate	195.40	64	16.4
Some college	300.70	99	20.8
Associate's degree	327.21	108	10.2
Bachelor's degree or more	443.83	146	43.4
Bachelor's degree	430.46	142	26.7
Master's, professional, doctoral degree	467.72	154	16.6

Note: Market shares may not sum to 100.0 because of rounding and missing categories by household type. "Asian" and "black" include Hispanics and non-Hispanics who identify themselves as being of the respective race alone. "Hispanic" includes people of any race who identify themselves as Hispanic. "Other" includes people who identify themselves as non-Hispanic and as Alaska Native, American Indian, Asian (who are also included in the "Asian" row), or Native Hawaiian or other Pacific Islander as well as non-Hispanics reporting more than one race.

Source: Calculations by New Strategist based on the Bureau of Labor Statistics' 2010 Consumer Expenditure Survey

Men's Shoes

Best customers:
Householders aged 35 to 44
Married couples with school-aged or older children at home
Asians and Hispanics
Least-educated householders

Customer trends:
Average household spending on men's shoes will decline as the large baby-boom generation approaches retirement.

The best customers of men's shoes are married couples with adult children at home. These households spend 74 percent more than the average on men's shoes because there are more men in the household. Couples with school-aged children outspend the average by 44 percent. Householders aged 35 to 44 spend 42 percent more than average on men's shoes. Asians and Hispanics spend, respectively, 91 and 52 percent more than average on this item. Householders without a high school diploma outspend the average by 31 percent.

In 2010, the average household spent $101 on men's shoes, 32 percent less than in 2000 after adjusting for inflation. Low-cost imports are behind the steep decline. Although the growing Asian and Hispanic populations should boost spending on men's shoes, the bigger trend is the aging of the baby-boom generation, which is likely to continue to dampen spending on this item.

Table 2.9 Men's shoes

Total household spending $12,248,761,980.00
Average household spends   101.14

	AVERAGE HOUSEHOLD SPENDING	BEST CUSTOMERS (index)	BIGGEST CUSTOMERS (market share)
AGE OF HOUSEHOLDER			
Average household	**$101.14**	**100**	**100.0%**
Under age 25	117.98	117	7.7
Aged 25 to 34	97.79	97	16.1
Aged 35 to 44	143.83	142	25.7
Aged 45 to 54	111.51	110	22.8
Aged 55 to 64	95.03	94	16.6
Aged 65 to 74	80.40	79	8.6
Aged 75 or older	26.15	26	2.5

	AVERAGE HOUSEHOLD SPENDING	BEST CUSTOMERS (index)	BIGGEST CUSTOMERS (market share)
HOUSEHOLD INCOME			
Average household	$101.14	100	100.0%
Under $20,000	56.44	56	12.2
$20,000 to $39,999	82.55	82	18.7
$40,000 to $49,999	108.66	107	10.2
$50,000 to $69,999	98.95	98	14.0
$70,000 to $79,999	99.97	99	5.9
$80,000 to $99,999	108.31	107	8.9
$100,000 or more	180.71	179	30.6
HOUSEHOLD TYPE			
Average household	101.14	100	100.0
Married couples	118.17	117	57.6
Married couples, no children	85.07	84	17.9
Married couples, with children	144.86	143	33.3
Oldest child under age 6	79.56	79	3.4
Oldest child aged 6 to 17	146.14	144	17.0
Oldest child aged 18 or older	176.36	174	12.6
Single parent with child under age 18	83.16	82	4.8
Single person	59.51	59	17.2
RACE AND HISPANIC ORIGIN			
Average household	101.14	100	100.0
Asian	193.08	191	8.1
Black	107.08	106	13.0
Hispanic	153.65	152	18.5
Non-Hispanic white and other	91.78	91	68.8
REGION			
Average household	101.14	100	100.0
Northeast	116.59	115	21.2
Midwest	79.13	78	17.4
South	95.42	94	34.6
West	120.19	119	26.9
EDUCATION			
Average household	101.14	100	100.0
Less than high school graduate	132.02	131	18.6
High school graduate	78.72	78	19.9
Some college	80.57	80	16.7
Associate's degree	96.56	95	9.0
Bachelor's degree or more	123.63	122	36.3
Bachelor's degree	136.53	135	25.5
Master's, professional, doctoral degree	98.23	97	10.5

Note: Market shares may not sum to 100.0 because of rounding and missing categories by household type. "Asian" and "black" include Hispanics and non-Hispanics who identify themselves as being of the respective race alone. "Hispanic" includes people of any race who identify themselves as Hispanic. "Other" includes people who identify themselves as non-Hispanic and as Alaska Native, American Indian, Asian (who are also included in the "Asian" row), or Native Hawaiian or other Pacific Islander as well as non-Hispanics reporting more than one race.

Source: Calculations by New Strategist based on the Bureau of Labor Statistics' 2010 Consumer Expenditure Survey

Professional Apparel Laundry and Dry Cleaning

Best customers: Householders aged 35 to 64
                           High-income households
                           Married couples
                           Asians
                           Households in the Northeast
                           College graduates

Customer trends: Average household spending on professional apparel laundry and dry cleaning
                           is likely to fall as boomers approach retirement and their need for this service
                           declines.

The biggest spenders on professional laundry and dry cleaning are affluent, educated, middle-aged and older householders. Households with incomes of $100,000 or more spend three-and-one-half times the average on professional laundry and dry cleaning. College graduates spend more than double the average. Married couples spend 35 percent more than average on this item, the figure peaking at 71 percent among those with school-aged children. Householders ranging in age from 35 to 64 spend 17 to 35 percent more than average. Spending on professional laundry and dry cleaning by households in the Northeast is 40 percent higher than average.

Average household spending on professional apparel laundry and dry cleaning declined by a substantial 46 percent between 2000 and 2010, after adjusting for inflation, as casual attire became more common in the workplace. Spending on professional laundry and dry cleaning should continue to decline as boomers retire and fewer dress in business clothes.

Table 2.10 Professional apparel laundry and dry cleaning

Total household spending	$5,998,429,710.00
Average household spends	49.53

	AVERAGE HOUSEHOLD SPENDING	BEST CUSTOMERS (index)	BIGGEST CUSTOMERS (market share)
AGE OF HOUSEHOLDER			
Average household	**$49.53**	**100**	**100.0%**
Under age 25	10.35	21	1.4
Aged 25 to 34	41.31	83	13.9
Aged 35 to 44	62.68	127	22.9
Aged 45 to 54	66.76	135	27.9
Aged 55 to 64	57.76	117	20.6
Aged 65 to 74	43.16	87	9.4
Aged 75 or older	20.79	42	4.0

	AVERAGE HOUSEHOLD SPENDING	BEST CUSTOMERS (index)	BIGGEST CUSTOMERS (market share)
HOUSEHOLD INCOME			
Average household	**$49.53**	**100**	**100.0%**
Under $20,000	9.08	18	4.0
$20,000 to $39,999	13.76	28	6.4
$40,000 to $49,999	23.63	48	4.5
$50,000 to $69,999	33.28	67	9.6
$70,000 to $79,999	53.46	108	6.5
$80,000 to $99,999	55.60	112	9.4
$100,000 or more	172.37	348	59.7
HOUSEHOLD TYPE			
Average household	**49.53**	**100**	**100.0**
Married couples	67.11	135	66.8
Married couples, no children	60.67	122	26.0
Married couples, with children	77.09	156	36.2
Oldest child under age 6	64.81	131	5.6
Oldest child aged 6 to 17	84.78	171	20.1
Oldest child aged 18 or older	71.84	145	10.5
Single parent with child under age 18	25.60	52	3.0
Single person	31.99	65	18.9
RACE AND HISPANIC ORIGIN			
Average household	**49.53**	**100**	**100.0**
Asian	59.04	119	5.1
Black	52.93	107	13.1
Hispanic	40.88	83	10.1
Non-Hispanic white and other	50.60	102	77.5
REGION			
Average household	**49.53**	**100**	**100.0**
Northeast	69.43	140	25.7
Midwest	32.83	66	14.8
South	47.13	95	34.9
West	53.74	108	24.6
EDUCATION			
Average household	**49.53**	**100**	**100.0**
Less than high school graduate	11.12	22	3.2
High school graduate	21.75	44	11.2
Some college	35.22	71	14.9
Associate's degree	40.53	82	7.7
Bachelor's degree or more	104.87	212	62.9
Bachelor's degree	82.81	167	31.6
Master's, professional, doctoral degree	143.39	290	31.3

Note: Market shares may not sum to 100.0 because of rounding and missing categories by household type. "Asian" and "black" include Hispanics and non-Hispanics who identify themselves as being of the respective race alone. "Hispanic" includes people of any race who identify themselves as Hispanic. "Other" includes people who identify themselves as non-Hispanic and as Alaska Native, American Indian, Asian (who are also included in the "Asian" row), or Native Hawaiian or other Pacific Islander as well as non-Hispanics reporting more than one race.

Source: Calculations by New Strategist based on the Bureau of Labor Statistics' 2010 Consumer Expenditure Survey

Sewing Materials, Patterns, and Notions

Best customers:

Householders aged 55 to 74
Married couples without children at home
Married couples with school-aged or older children at home
Households in the Midwest

Customer trends:

Average household spending on sewing materials, patterns, and notions is likely to fall in the years ahead as younger generations with little sewing experience fill the best-customer age groups.

The biggest spenders on sewing materials for clothing are older householders. Householders aged 55 to 74 spend 31 to 34 percent more than average on sewing materials. Married couples without children at home—most of them empty-nesters—spend 65 percent more than average on this item, and those with school-aged or older children at home spend 44 to 54 percent more than average on sewing materials, patterns, and notions. Households in the Midwest spend 40 percent more than average on sewing materials, patterns, and notions

Average household spending on sewing materials, patterns, and notions fell by 15 percent between 2000 and 2010, after adjusting for inflation. The Great Recession changed spending patterns on this item. Spending on sewing materials, patterns, and notions had grown by 67 percent between 2000 and 2006, but then declined by 49 percent during the remainder of the decade. Unless sewing experiences a revival among younger generations, household spending on this item is destined to decline.

Table 2.11 Sewing materials, patterns, and notions

Total household spending	$1,229,236,050.00		
Average household spends	10.15		

	AVERAGE HOUSEHOLD SPENDING	BEST CUSTOMERS (index)	BIGGEST CUSTOMERS (market share)
AGE OF HOUSEHOLDER			
Average household	**$10.15**	**100**	**100.0%**
Under age 25	3.45	34	2.3
Aged 25 to 34	7.90	78	13.0
Aged 35 to 44	12.00	118	21.4
Aged 45 to 54	8.76	86	17.9
Aged 55 to 64	13.57	134	23.6
Aged 65 to 74	13.28	131	14.1
Aged 75 or older	8.47	83	8.0

	AVERAGE HOUSEHOLD SPENDING	BEST CUSTOMERS (index)	BIGGEST CUSTOMERS (market share)
HOUSEHOLD INCOME			
Average household	**$10.15**	**100**	**100.0%**
Under $20,000	5.55	55	11.9
$20,000 to $39,999	8.01	79	18.1
$40,000 to $49,999	9.44	93	8.8
$50,000 to $69,999	6.78	67	9.6
$70,000 to $79,999	19.06	188	11.2
$80,000 to $99,999	11.05	109	9.1
$100,000 or more	18.96	187	32.0
HOUSEHOLD TYPE			
Average household	**10.15**	**100**	**100.0**
Married couples	14.94	147	72.6
Married couples, no children	16.77	165	35.1
Married couples, with children	14.61	144	33.5
Oldest child under age 6	11.54	114	4.9
Oldest child aged 6 to 17	15.67	154	18.2
Oldest child aged 18 or older	14.61	144	10.4
Single parent with child under age 18	1.59	16	0.9
Single person	3.97	39	11.5
RACE AND HISPANIC ORIGIN			
Average household	**10.15**	**100**	**100.0**
Asian	5.08	50	2.1
Black	7.44	73	9.0
Hispanic	6.66	66	8.0
Non-Hispanic white and other	11.12	110	83.1
REGION			
Average household	**10.15**	**100**	**100.0**
Northeast	8.84	87	16.0
Midwest	14.16	140	31.1
South	8.65	85	31.3
West	9.64	95	21.5
EDUCATION			
Average household	**10.15**	**100**	**100.0**
Less than high school graduate	12.75	126	17.9
High school graduate	9.16	90	23.0
Some college	8.65	85	17.9
Associate's degree	12.78	126	11.9
Bachelor's degree or more	10.09	99	29.5
Bachelor's degree	7.68	76	14.3
Master's, professional, doctoral degree	14.82	146	15.8

Note: Market shares may not sum to 100.0 because of rounding and missing categories by household type. "Asian" and "black" include Hispanics and non-Hispanics who identify themselves as being of the respective race alone. "Hispanic" includes people of any race who identify themselves as Hispanic. "Other" includes people who identify themselves as non-Hispanic and as Alaska Native, American Indian, Asian (who are also included in the "Asian" row), or Native Hawaiian or other Pacific Islander as well as non-Hispanics reporting more than one race.

Source: Calculations by New Strategist based on the Bureau of Labor Statistics' 2010 Consumer Expenditure Survey

Shoe and Apparel Repair and Alteration

Best customers: Householders aged 55 to 64
High-income households
Married couples without children at home
Married couples with school-aged or older children at home
Asians
Households in the West
College graduates

Customer trends: Average household spending on shoe and apparel repair and alteration should continue to decline as boomers retire and have less need for maintaining professional clothes.

The biggest spenders on shoe and apparel repair and alteration are high-income households, which spend three times the average on this item. College graduates, a well-to-do demographic, spend more than twice the average on shoe and apparel repair and alteration. Married couples without children at home spend 47 percent more than average on shoe and apparel repair and alteration, and those with school-aged or older children at home spend 29 to 37 percent more than average on this item. Spending on this item by Asians is 90 percent above average. Households in the West outspend the average by 24 percent.

Average household spending on shoe and apparel repair and alteration fell 19 percent between 2000 and 2010, after adjusting for inflation. Spending on this item is likely to continue to decline as boomers retire and have less need for maintaining professional clothes.

Table 2.12 Shoe and apparel repair and alteration

| Total household spending | $937,368,180.00 |
| Average household spends | 7.74 |

	AVERAGE HOUSEHOLD SPENDING	BEST CUSTOMERS (index)	BIGGEST CUSTOMERS (market share)
AGE OF HOUSEHOLDER			
Average household	**$7.74**	**100**	**100.0%**
Under age 25	3.65	47	3.1
Aged 25 to 34	7.82	101	16.8
Aged 35 to 44	7.96	103	18.6
Aged 45 to 54	8.22	106	22.0
Aged 55 to 64	10.56	136	24.1
Aged 65 to 74	7.05	91	9.8
Aged 75 or older	4.55	59	5.6

	AVERAGE HOUSEHOLD SPENDING	BEST CUSTOMERS (index)	BIGGEST CUSTOMERS (market share)
HOUSEHOLD INCOME			
Average household	**$7.74**	**100**	**100.0%**
Under $20,000	2.30	30	6.5
$20,000 to $39,999	3.79	49	11.2
$40,000 to $49,999	3.92	51	4.8
$50,000 to $69,999	6.49	84	12.0
$70,000 to $79,999	5.62	73	4.3
$80,000 to $99,999	8.62	111	9.3
$100,000 or more	23.41	302	51.9
HOUSEHOLD TYPE			
Average household	**7.74**	**100**	**100.0**
Married couples	10.15	131	64.7
Married couples, no children	11.39	147	31.3
Married couples, with children	9.48	122	28.5
Oldest child under age 6	6.26	81	3.5
Oldest child aged 6 to 17	9.95	129	15.1
Oldest child aged 18 or older	10.61	137	9.9
Single parent with child under age 18	5.32	69	4.1
Single person	4.42	57	16.7
RACE AND HISPANIC ORIGIN			
Average household	**7.74**	**100**	**100.0**
Asian	14.72	190	8.1
Black	4.19	54	6.6
Hispanic	6.13	79	9.6
Non-Hispanic white and other	8.59	111	84.1
REGION			
Average household	**7.74**	**100**	**100.0**
Northeast	8.13	105	19.3
Midwest	6.77	87	19.5
South	6.99	90	33.1
West	9.59	124	28.1
EDUCATION			
Average household	**7.74**	**100**	**100.0**
Less than high school graduate	1.97	25	3.6
High school graduate	3.06	40	10.1
Some college	4.93	64	13.4
Associate's degree	6.52	84	8.0
Bachelor's degree or more	16.91	218	64.9
Bachelor's degree	14.48	187	35.3
Master's, professional, doctoral degree	21.16	273	29.6

Note: Market shares may not sum to 100.0 because of rounding and missing categories by household type. "Asian" and "black" include Hispanics and non-Hispanics who identify themselves as being of the respective race alone. "Hispanic" includes people of any race who identify themselves as Hispanic. "Other" includes people who identify themselves as non-Hispanic and as Alaska Native, American Indian, Asian (who are also included in the "Asian" row), or Native Hawaiian or other Pacific Islander as well as non-Hispanics reporting more than one race.

Source: Calculations by New Strategist based on the Bureau of Labor Statistics' 2010 Consumer Expenditure Survey

Women's Apparel

Best customers: **Householders aged 45 to 54**
                           Married couples with school-aged or older children at home
                           Single parents
                           Asians

Customer trends: **Average household spending on women's clothes is likely to continue to decline as**
                           aging boomer women retire from the workforce and have fewer reasons to shop
                           for clothes.

The average household spends more on women's clothes than on any other apparel category—$561.50 in 2010, or one-third of the apparel dollar. The biggest spenders on women's clothes are householders aged 45 to 54, who spend 29 percent more than the average household on this item. Married couples with school-aged children spend 32 percent more than average on women's clothes, and those with adult children at home outspend the average by 36 percent because there are more women in the household. Single parents, who are predominantly women, spend 26 percent more than average on women's clothes. Asians spend 37 percent more than average on women's clothes.

Average household spending on women's clothes declined by 27 percent between 2000 and 2010, after adjusting for inflation. Falling prices are one reason for the decline in spending, as cheaper imports allow consumers to buy more for less. Spending on women's clothes is likely to continue to decline as aging boomer women retire from the workforce and have fewer reasons to shop for clothes.

Table 2.13 Women's apparel

Total household spending   **$68,001,580,500.00**
Average household spends   **561.50**

	AVERAGE HOUSEHOLD SPENDING	BEST CUSTOMERS (index)	BIGGEST CUSTOMERS (market share)
AGE OF HOUSEHOLDER			
Average household	**$561.50**	**100**	**100.0%**
Under age 25	628.27	112	7.4
Aged 25 to 34	550.23	98	16.3
Aged 35 to 44	554.98	99	17.9
Aged 45 to 54	722.38	129	26.6
Aged 55 to 64	563.98	100	17.7
Aged 65 to 74	449.75	80	8.6
Aged 75 or older	307.87	55	5.2

	AVERAGE HOUSEHOLD SPENDING	BEST CUSTOMERS (index)	BIGGEST CUSTOMERS (market share)
HOUSEHOLD INCOME			
Average household	**$561.50**	**100**	**100.0%**
Under $20,000	236.03	42	9.2
$20,000 to $39,999	394.66	70	16.1
$40,000 to $49,999	457.85	82	7.7
$50,000 to $69,999	612.23	109	15.6
$70,000 to $79,999	602.43	107	6.4
$80,000 to $99,999	574.41	102	8.5
$100,000 or more	1,208.37	215	36.9
HOUSEHOLD TYPE			
Average household	**561.50**	**100**	**100.0**
Married couples	674.86	120	59.3
Married couples, no children	646.29	115	24.4
Married couples, with children	707.52	126	29.3
Oldest child under age 6	503.81	90	3.8
Oldest child aged 6 to 17	741.62	132	15.5
Oldest child aged 18 or older	761.18	136	9.8
Single parent with child under age 18	706.07	126	7.4
Single person	287.96	51	15.0
RACE AND HISPANIC ORIGIN			
Average household	**561.50**	**100**	**100.0**
Asian	768.47	137	5.8
Black	466.49	83	10.2
Hispanic	549.94	98	11.9
Non-Hispanic white and other	577.94	103	78.0
REGION			
Average household	**561.50**	**100**	**100.0**
Northeast	601.59	107	19.7
Midwest	512.25	91	20.3
South	516.54	92	33.8
West	652.45	116	26.3
EDUCATION			
Average household	**561.50**	**100**	**100.0**
Less than high school graduate	369.41	66	9.4
High school graduate	434.72	77	19.8
Some college	407.53	73	15.3
Associate's degree	741.12	132	12.5
Bachelor's degree or more	810.09	144	42.9
Bachelor's degree	827.89	147	27.9
Master's, professional, doctoral degree	774.94	138	14.9

Note: Market shares may not sum to 100.0 because of rounding and missing categories by household type. "Asian" and "black" include Hispanics and non-Hispanics who identify themselves as being of the respective race alone. "Hispanic" includes people of any race who identify themselves as Hispanic. "Other" includes people who identify themselves as non-Hispanic and as Alaska Native, American Indian, Asian (who are also included in the "Asian" row), or Native Hawaiian or other Pacific Islander as well as non-Hispanics reporting more than one race.

Source: Calculations by New Strategist based on the Bureau of Labor Statistics' 2010 Consumer Expenditure Survey

Women's Shoes

Best customers:	Householders aged 45 to 64
	Married couples without children at home
	Married couples with school-aged or older children at home
	Single parents
	Asians and Hispanics
Customer trends:	Average household spending on women's shoes may continue to decline as boomer women retire from the workforce and need fewer shoes.

The best customers of women's shoes are married couples with adult children at home. They spend 25 percent more than average on women's shoes. Behind the higher spending are their larger households, many of which include more than one adult female. Married couples without children at home, most of them empty-nesters, spend 22 percent more than average on this item. Couples with school-aged children and single parents spend, respectively, 21 and 23 percent more than average on women's shoes. Householders aged 45 to 54 outspend the average on women's shoes by 36 percent. Those aged 55 to 64 spend 22 percent more than average on this item. Asian and Hispanic households spend, respectively, 70 and 30 percent more than average on women's shoes.

Average household spending on women's shoes fell 26 percent between 2000 and 2010, after adjusting for inflation. Falling prices are one factor behind the decline in spending on women's shoes as cheaper imports allow consumers to buy more for less. Spending on women's shoes may continue to decline as boomer women retire from the workforce and need fewer shoes.

Table 2.14 Women's shoes

Total household spending $17,717,954,100.00
Average household spends 146.30

	AVERAGE HOUSEHOLD SPENDING	BEST CUSTOMERS (index)	BIGGEST CUSTOMERS (market share)
AGE OF HOUSEHOLDER			
Average household	**$146.30**	**100**	**100.0%**
Under age 25	144.96	99	6.6
Aged 25 to 34	122.14	83	13.9
Aged 35 to 44	145.73	100	18.0
Aged 45 to 54	198.32	136	28.0
Aged 55 to 64	178.03	122	21.5
Aged 65 to 74	85.92	59	6.3
Aged 75 or older	83.87	57	5.5

	AVERAGE HOUSEHOLD SPENDING	BEST CUSTOMERS (index)	BIGGEST CUSTOMERS (market share)
HOUSEHOLD INCOME			
Average household	**$146.30**	**100**	**100.0%**
Under $20,000	74.24	51	11.1
$20,000 to $39,999	129.43	88	20.3
$40,000 to $49,999	121.82	83	7.9
$50,000 to $69,999	130.28	89	12.8
$70,000 to $79,999	143.69	98	5.9
$80,000 to $99,999	163.86	112	9.3
$100,000 or more	283.00	193	33.2
HOUSEHOLD TYPE			
Average household	**146.30**	**100**	**100.0**
Married couples	173.83	119	58.6
Married couples, no children	177.83	122	25.8
Married couples, with children	164.63	113	26.2
Oldest child under age 6	92.11	63	2.7
Oldest child aged 6 to 17	177.14	121	14.2
Oldest child aged 18 or older	183.09	125	9.0
Single parent with child under age 18	179.43	123	7.2
Single person	87.84	60	17.6
RACE AND HISPANIC ORIGIN			
Average household	**146.30**	**100**	**100.0**
Asian	249.02	170	7.2
Black	140.10	96	11.7
Hispanic	189.63	130	15.8
Non-Hispanic white and other	140.30	96	72.7
REGION			
Average household	**146.30**	**100**	**100.0**
Northeast	168.64	115	21.2
Midwest	127.17	87	19.4
South	140.06	96	35.1
West	157.63	108	24.4
EDUCATION			
Average household	**146.30**	**100**	**100.0**
Less than high school graduate	133.30	91	13.0
High school graduate	109.90	75	19.2
Some college	120.43	82	17.3
Associate's degree	177.73	121	11.5
Bachelor's degree or more	192.28	131	39.0
Bachelor's degree	195.90	134	25.3
Master's, professional, doctoral degree	185.16	127	13.7

Note: Market shares may not sum to 100.0 because of rounding and missing categories by household type. "Asian" and "black" include Hispanics and non-Hispanics who identify themselves as being of the respective race alone. "Hispanic" includes people of any race who identify themselves as Hispanic. "Other" includes people who identify themselves as non-Hispanic and as Alaska Native, American Indian, Asian (who are also included in the "Asian" row), or Native Hawaiian or other Pacific Islander as well as non-Hispanics reporting more than one race.

Source: Calculations by New Strategist based on the Bureau of Labor Statistics' 2010 Consumer Expenditure Survey

Chapter 3.

Computers

Household Spending on Computers, 2010

Thirty years ago the average household spent nothing on computers. By now computers have become a central appliance in most homes and an important expenditure category. Average household spending on computer information services (Internet service) more than tripled since 2000, after adjusting for inflation. The average household spends twice as much on computer information services as on computers themselves. In 2000, computer hardware accounted for 70 percent of the average household's computer budget, while computer information services accounted for just 23 percent. By 2010, computer hardware accounted for a much smaller 31 percent of the computer budget, while Internet service accounted for a much larger 62 percent.

The average household spent $463 on computer hardware, software, and information services in 2010—36 percent more than in 2000, after adjusting for inflation. Falling prices for computer equipment is one factor behind the relatively small increase in overall spending on computers during the past 10 years. In fact, spending on computer hardware fell 39 percent between 2000 and 2010, after adjusting for inflation. Spending on computer software and accessories fell 24 percent, while spending on computer information services surged by 267 percent as online access became a necessity for a growing share of households. Average annual household spending on repair of computer systems more than doubled between 2000 and 2010, after adjusting for inflation.

Spending on computers

(average annual spending of households on computer hardware, software, and information services, 2000 and 2010; in 2010 dollars)

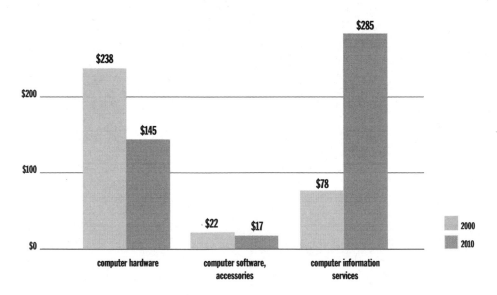

Table 3.1 Computer spending, 2000 to 2010

(average annual household spending on computer equipment and services, 2000, 2006, and 2010; percent change in spending, 2000–06, 2000–10, and 2006–10; in 2010 dollars; ranked by amount spent)

	2010 average household spending	2006 average household spending (in 2010$)	2000 average household spending (in 2010$)	percent change		
				2006–10	2000–06	2000–10
AVERAGE ANNUAL SPENDING						
Average household spending on computer equipment and services for nonbusiness use	**$462.82**	**$377.29**	**$341.18**	**22.7%**	**10.6%**	**35.7%**
Computer information services	285.14	190.84	77.70	49.4	145.6	267.0
Computers and computer hardware	144.58	154.23	237.85	–6.3	–35.2	–39.2
Computer software and accessories	16.89	23.47	22.15	–28.0	6.0	–23.7
Repair of computer systems for nonbusiness use	7.29	6.98	3.48	4.5	100.3	109.3
Portable memory	7.06	–	–	–	–	–
Internet services away from home	1.86	1.77	–	4.9	–	–

	2010	2006	2000	percentage point change		
				2006–10	2000–06	2000–10
PERCENT DISTRIBUTION OF SPENDING						
Average household spending on computer equipment and services for nonbusiness use	**100.0%**	**100.0%**	**100.0%**	**–**	**–**	**–**
Computer information services	61.6	50.6	22.8	11.0	27.8	38.8
Computers and computer hardware	31.2	40.9	69.7	–9.6	–28.8	–38.5
Computer software and accessories	3.6	6.2	6.5	–2.6	–0.3	–2.8
Repair of computer systems for nonbusiness use	1.6	1.8	1.0	–0.3	0.8	0.6
Portable memory	1.5	–	–	–	–	–
Internet services away from home	0.4	0.5	–	–0.1	–	–

Note: "–" means not applicable or data are unavailable.

Source: Bureau of Labor Statistics, 2000, 2006, and 2010 Consumer Expenditure Surveys; calculations by New Strategist

Computer Information Services

Best customers: **Householders aged 25 to 54**
                       Married couples with children at home

Customer trends: **Average household spending on computer information services will grow more slowly now that the majority of households are online, although some growth remains as younger householders replace older generations without Internet access.**

Average household spending on computer information services shows relatively little variation by demographic variables because the item is so universally bought. The best customers of Internet access are households with children. Householders aged 25 to 54 spend 10 to 18 percent more than the average household on Internet service and control 63 percent of household spending on this item. Married couples with children at home spend 29 percent more than average on Internet service.

Average household spending on computer information services more than tripled between 2000 and 2010, after adjusting for inflation, and Internet access became the fourth-largest information and consumer electronics category in terms of average household spending. The average household spends about seven times as much on computer information services as it does on newspaper and magazine subscriptions. The growth in spending for online services is likely to slow now that the majority of households are online, although some growth remains as younger householders replace older generations without Internet access.

Table 3.2 Computer information services

Total household spending $34,532,449,980.00
Average household spends   285.14

	AVERAGE HOUSEHOLD SPENDING	BEST CUSTOMERS (index)	BIGGEST CUSTOMERS (market share)
AGE OF HOUSEHOLDER			
Average household	**$285.14**	**100**	**100.0%**
Under age 25	203.60	71	4.7
Aged 25 to 34	314.01	110	18.3
Aged 35 to 44	337.54	118	21.4
Aged 45 to 54	320.23	112	23.2
Aged 55 to 64	302.00	106	18.7
Aged 65 to 74	246.74	87	9.3
Aged 75 or older	128.12	45	4.3

	AVERAGE HOUSEHOLD SPENDING	BEST CUSTOMERS (index)	BIGGEST CUSTOMERS (market share)
HOUSEHOLD INCOME			
Average household	**$285.14**	**100**	**100.0%**
Under $20,000	127.20	45	9.7
$20,000 to $39,999	219.05	77	17.6
$40,000 to $49,999	287.98	101	9.5
$50,000 to $69,999	324.54	114	16.3
$70,000 to $79,999	379.80	133	8.0
$80,000 to $99,999	416.92	146	12.2
$100,000 or more	442.85	155	26.6
HOUSEHOLD TYPE			
Average household	**285.14**	**100**	**100.0**
Married couples	342.89	120	59.3
Married couples, no children	317.87	111	23.7
Married couples, with children	366.82	129	29.9
Oldest child under age 6	370.24	130	5.6
Oldest child aged 6 to 17	373.89	131	15.4
Oldest child aged 18 or older	353.27	124	8.9
Single parent with child under age 18	264.72	93	5.5
Single person	188.84	66	19.4
RACE AND HISPANIC ORIGIN			
Average household	**285.14**	**100**	**100.0**
Asian	330.42	116	4.9
Black	238.27	84	10.2
Hispanic	222.66	78	9.5
Non-Hispanic white and other	302.69	106	80.5
REGION			
Average household	**285.14**	**100**	**100.0**
Northeast	295.51	104	19.0
Midwest	270.70	95	21.2
South	274.61	96	35.3
West	308.01	108	24.5
EDUCATION			
Average household	**285.14**	**100**	**100.0**
Less than high school graduate	136.20	48	6.8
High school graduate	238.75	84	21.4
Some college	288.66	101	21.3
Associate's degree	335.48	118	11.1
Bachelor's degree or more	378.14	133	39.4
Bachelor's degree	371.90	130	24.6
Master's, professional, doctoral degree	389.02	136	14.8

Note: Market shares may not sum to 100.0 because of rounding and missing categories by household type. "Asian" and "black" include Hispanics and non-Hispanics who identify themselves as being of the respective race alone. "Hispanic" includes people of any race who identify themselves as Hispanic. "Other" includes people who identify themselves as non-Hispanic and as Alaska Native, American Indian, Asian (who are also included in the "Asian" row), or Native Hawaiian or other Pacific Islander as well as non-Hispanics reporting more than one race.

Source: Calculations by New Strategist based on the Bureau of Labor Statistics' 2010 Consumer Expenditure Survey

Computer Software and Accessories for Nonbusiness Use

Best customers: **Householders aged 45 to 54 and 65 to 74**
     Married couples without children at home
     Married couples with school-aged children
     Asians

Customer trends: **Average household spending on computer software and accessories may begin to grow again as more people download apps for their smartphones.**

The best customers of computer software and accessories for nonbusiness use are middle-aged householders with children at home. Householders aged 45 to 54 spend 29 percent more than the average household on computer software. Married couples with school-aged children spend 80 percent more than average on software. Householders aged 65 to 74 spend 27 percent more than average on software. The spending on this item by Asian householders is 31 percent higher than average.

Average household spending on computer software and accessories grew by a modest 6 percent between 2000 and 2006 then fell 28 percent from 2006 to 2010. One factor that explains the lackluster spending is software bundling, whereby computer manufacturers include software with their hardware in an attempt to entice buyers. Spending on computer software may begin to grow again as more people download apps for their smartphones.

Table 3.3   Computer software and accessories for nonbusiness use

Total household spending $2,045,497,230.00
Average household spends   16.89

	AVERAGE HOUSEHOLD SPENDING	BEST CUSTOMERS (index)	BIGGEST CUSTOMERS (market share)
AGE OF HOUSEHOLDER			
Average household	**$16.89**	**100**	**100.0%**
Under age 25	11.61	69	4.6
Aged 25 to 34	15.76	93	15.5
Aged 35 to 44	17.32	103	18.6
Aged 45 to 54	21.85	129	26.8
Aged 55 to 64	17.57	104	18.3
Aged 65 to 74	21.42	127	13.6
Aged 75 or older	4.65	28	2.6

	AVERAGE HOUSEHOLD SPENDING	BEST CUSTOMERS (index)	BIGGEST CUSTOMERS (market share)
HOUSEHOLD INCOME			
Average household	**$16.89**	**100**	**100.0%**
Under $20,000	6.54	39	8.4
$20,000 to $39,999	11.09	66	15.0
$40,000 to $49,999	14.63	87	8.2
$50,000 to $69,999	13.99	83	11.9
$70,000 to $79,999	31.52	187	11.2
$80,000 to $99,999	21.97	130	10.8
$100,000 or more	33.93	201	34.4
HOUSEHOLD TYPE			
Average household	**16.89**	**100**	**100.0**
Married couples	21.36	126	62.4
Married couples, no children	20.25	120	25.5
Married couples, with children	24.19	143	33.3
Oldest child under age 6	18.51	110	4.7
Oldest child aged 6 to 17	30.45	180	21.2
Oldest child aged 18 or older	17.36	103	7.4
Single parent with child under age 18	13.10	78	4.6
Single person	11.14	66	19.3
RACE AND HISPANIC ORIGIN			
Average household	**16.89**	**100**	**100.0**
Asian	22.14	131	5.6
Black	10.97	65	7.9
Hispanic	15.52	92	11.2
Non-Hispanic white and other	18.04	107	81.0
REGION			
Average household	**16.89**	**100**	**100.0**
Northeast	19.97	118	21.7
Midwest	17.46	103	23.0
South	14.89	88	32.4
West	17.10	101	22.9
EDUCATION			
Average household	**16.89**	**100**	**100.0**
Less than high school graduate	6.50	38	5.5
High school graduate	8.77	52	13.3
Some college	15.94	94	19.8
Associate's degree	17.31	102	9.7
Bachelor's degree or more	29.41	174	51.7
Bachelor's degree	24.51	145	27.4
Master's, professional, doctoral degree	37.98	225	24.3

Note: Market shares may not sum to 100.0 because of rounding and missing categories by household type. "Asian" and "black" include Hispanics and non-Hispanics who identify themselves as being of the respective race alone. "Hispanic" includes people of any race who identify themselves as Hispanic. "Other" includes people who identify themselves as non-Hispanic and as Alaska Native, American Indian, Asian (who are also included in the "Asian" row), or Native Hawaiian or other Pacific Islander as well as non-Hispanics reporting more than one race.

Source: Calculations by New Strategist based on the Bureau of Labor Statistics' 2010 Consumer Expenditure Survey

Computers and Computer Hardware for Nonbusiness Use

Best customers: **Householders aged 45 to 54**
Married couples with school-aged or older children at home
Asians
Households in the Northeast and West

Customer trends: **Average household spending on computers and computer hardware for nonbusiness use may rise over the next few years as a growing share of households purchase tablet computers.**

The best customers of computers and computer hardware for nonbusiness use are households with children, especially children of college age. Householders aged 45 to 54—many with college-aged kids—spend 22 percent more than the average household on computers. Married couples with school-aged children spend 54 percent more than the average household on this item, and those with adult children at home spend 56 percent more. Asians spend 70 percent more than average on computers. Households in the Northeast and West spend one-fifth more than average on computers.

Average household spending on computers and computer hardware for nonbusiness use fell by 39 percent between 2000 and 2010, after adjusting for inflation. Most of the drop occurred between 2000 and 2006. Average household spending on computers declined just 6 percent between 2006 and 2010. Behind the decline were falling prices and market saturation as a growing majority of households has become computer owners. Spending on computer hardware may rise in the next few years as an increasing share of households purchase tablet computers.

Table 3.4 Computers and computer hardware for nonbusiness use

Total household spending $17,509,650,060.00
Average household spends   144.58

	AVERAGE HOUSEHOLD SPENDING	BEST CUSTOMERS (index)	BIGGEST CUSTOMERS (market share)
AGE OF HOUSEHOLDER			
Average household	**$144.58**	**100**	**100.0%**
Under age 25	142.86	99	6.6
Aged 25 to 34	148.32	103	17.1
Aged 35 to 44	161.05	111	20.2
Aged 45 to 54	176.87	122	25.3
Aged 55 to 64	154.10	107	18.8
Aged 65 to 74	119.90	83	8.9
Aged 75 or older	48.23	33	3.2

	AVERAGE HOUSEHOLD SPENDING	BEST CUSTOMERS (index)	BIGGEST CUSTOMERS (market share)
HOUSEHOLD INCOME			
Average household	**$144.58**	**100**	**100.0%**
Under $20,000	61.90	43	9.3
$20,000 to $39,999	84.62	59	13.4
$40,000 to $49,999	108.91	75	7.1
$50,000 to $69,999	142.01	98	14.1
$70,000 to $79,999	162.92	113	6.7
$80,000 to $99,999	180.01	125	10.4
$100,000 or more	328.13	227	38.9
HOUSEHOLD TYPE			
Average household	**144.58**	**100**	**100.0**
Married couples	189.54	131	64.7
Married couples, no children	168.53	117	24.8
Married couples, with children	214.53	148	34.5
Oldest child under age 6	173.20	120	5.1
Oldest child aged 6 to 17	222.87	154	18.1
Oldest child aged 18 or older	225.45	156	11.3
Single parent with child under age 18	100.26	69	4.1
Single person	92.91	64	18.8
RACE AND HISPANIC ORIGIN			
Average household	**144.58**	**100**	**100.0**
Asian	245.75	170	7.2
Black	78.74	54	6.7
Hispanic	114.60	79	9.7
Non-Hispanic white and other	159.77	111	83.8
REGION			
Average household	**144.58**	**100**	**100.0**
Northeast	172.81	120	21.9
Midwest	133.81	93	20.6
South	118.08	82	30.0
West	175.25	121	27.5
EDUCATION			
Average household	**144.58**	**100**	**100.0**
Less than high school graduate	58.51	40	5.8
High school graduate	92.81	64	16.4
Some college	146.55	101	21.3
Associate's degree	162.43	112	10.6
Bachelor's degree or more	223.40	155	45.9
Bachelor's degree	192.18	133	25.1
Master's, professional, doctoral degree	277.91	192	20.8

Note: Market shares may not sum to 100.0 because of rounding and missing categories by household type. "Asian" and "black" include Hispanics and non-Hispanics who identify themselves as being of the respective race alone. "Hispanic" includes people of any race who identify themselves as Hispanic. "Other" includes people who identify themselves as non-Hispanic and as Alaska Native, American Indian, Asian (who are also included in the "Asian" row), or Native Hawaiian or other Pacific Islander as well as non-Hispanics reporting more than one race.

Source: Calculations by New Strategist based on the Bureau of Labor Statistics' 2010 Consumer Expenditure Survey

Internet Services Away from Home

Best customers: Householders aged 25 to 44
                        Married couples with children under age 18
                        Hispanics and blacks
                        Households in the Northeast

Customer trends: Average household spending on Internet services away from home is likely to be
                        constrained by free wifi connections offered by hotels and coffee shops.

The best customers for Internet services away from home are younger householders with children. Married couples with preschoolers spend 53 percent more than average on Internet services away from home, and those with school-aged children, 22 percent more. Householders aged 25 to 44, most with children, spend 28 to 32 percent more and control a sizeable 45 percent of the market. Spending on Internet services away from home is 34 percent above average among Hispanic householders and 12 percent above average among blacks. Households in the Northeast spend 54 percent more than average on Internet services away from home.

Average household spending on Internet services away from home (a category added to the Consumer Expenditure Survey in 2005) grew by a slow 5 percent between 2006 and 2010. Average household spending on Internet services away from home may not rise much in the years ahead as free wifi reduces the need to buy this item.

Table 3.5 Internet services away from home

Total household spending	$225,259,020.00
Average household spends	1.86

	AVERAGE HOUSEHOLD SPENDING	BEST CUSTOMERS (index)	BIGGEST CUSTOMERS (market share)
AGE OF HOUSEHOLDER			
Average household	**$1.86**	**100**	**100.0%**
Under age 25	1.31	70	4.7
Aged 25 to 34	2.46	132	22.0
Aged 35 to 44	2.39	128	23.2
Aged 45 to 54	2.03	109	22.6
Aged 55 to 64	1.68	90	15.9
Aged 65 to 74	1.42	76	8.2
Aged 75 or older	0.63	34	3.2

	AVERAGE HOUSEHOLD SPENDING	BEST CUSTOMERS (index)	BIGGEST CUSTOMERS (market share)
HOUSEHOLD INCOME			
Average household	**$1.86**	**100**	**100.0%**
Under $20,000	1.28	69	15.0
$20,000 to $39,999	0.87	47	10.7
$40,000 to $49,999	1.76	95	8.9
$50,000 to $69,999	2.68	144	20.7
$70,000 to $79,999	2.88	155	9.3
$80,000 to $99,999	1.56	84	7.0
$100,000 or more	3.06	165	28.2
HOUSEHOLD TYPE			
Average household	**1.86**	**100**	**100.0**
Married couples	2.04	110	54.1
Married couples, no children	2.07	111	23.6
Married couples, with children	1.92	103	24.0
Oldest child under age 6	2.85	153	6.6
Oldest child aged 6 to 17	2.26	122	14.3
Oldest child aged 18 or older	0.80	43	3.1
Single parent with child under age 18	1.52	82	4.8
Single person	1.50	81	23.6
RACE AND HISPANIC ORIGIN			
Average household	**1.86**	**100**	**100.0**
Asian	1.63	88	3.7
Black	2.08	112	13.7
Hispanic	2.50	134	16.4
Non-Hispanic white and other	1.74	94	70.9
REGION			
Average household	**1.86**	**100**	**100.0**
Northeast	2.87	154	28.3
Midwest	1.08	58	12.9
South	1.87	101	36.9
West	1.77	95	21.6
EDUCATION			
Average household	**1.86**	**100**	**100.0**
Less than high school graduate	1.56	84	12.0
High school graduate	1.59	85	21.8
Some college	1.78	96	20.1
Associate's degree	1.32	71	6.7
Bachelor's degree or more	2.45	132	39.1
Bachelor's degree	2.61	140	26.5
Master's, professional, doctoral degree	2.19	118	12.7

Note: Market shares may not sum to 100.0 because of rounding and missing categories by household type. "Asian" and "black" include Hispanics and non-Hispanics who identify themselves as being of the respective race alone. "Hispanic" includes people of any race who identify themselves as Hispanic. "Other" includes people who identify themselves as non-Hispanic and as Alaska Native, American Indian, Asian (who are also included in the "Asian" row), or Native Hawaiian or other Pacific Islander as well as non-Hispanics reporting more than one race.

Source: Calculations by New Strategist based on the Bureau of Labor Statistics' 2010 Consumer Expenditure Survey

Portable Memory

Best customers: Householders aged 25 to 64
Married couples with school-aged children
Asians

Customer trends: Average household spending on portable memory may not increase much as the
growing use of cloud computing allows people to secure their documents and
access them from multiple devices.

The biggest spenders on portable memory are householders of working age and those with school-aged children at home. Householders ranging in age from 25 to 64 spend 14 to 28 percent more than the average household on USB sticks and other memory devices. Married couples with adult children at home spend 86 percent more than average on portable memory. Asian householders spend 52 percent more than average on this item.

Portable memory was not included in the Consumer Expenditure Survey until recently, which limits the analysis of spending trends. Average household spending on portable memory may not increase much as the growing use of cloud computing allows people to secure their documents and access them from multiple devices.

Table 3.6 Portable memory

Total household spending	$855,015,420.00
Average household spends	7.06

	AVERAGE HOUSEHOLD SPENDING	BEST CUSTOMERS (index)	BIGGEST CUSTOMERS (market share)
AGE OF HOUSEHOLDER			
Average household	**$7.06**	**100**	**100.0%**
Under age 25	5.69	81	5.3
Aged 25 to 34	8.02	114	18.9
Aged 35 to 44	9.01	128	23.1
Aged 45 to 54	8.56	121	25.1
Aged 55 to 64	8.23	117	20.6
Aged 65 to 74	3.15	45	4.8
Aged 75 or older	1.61	23	2.2

	AVERAGE HOUSEHOLD SPENDING	BEST CUSTOMERS (index)	BIGGEST CUSTOMERS (market share)
HOUSEHOLD INCOME			
Average household	**$7.06**	**100**	**100.0%**
Under $20,000	3.02	43	9.3
$20,000 to $39,999	4.34	61	14.1
$40,000 to $49,999	6.16	87	8.2
$50,000 to $69,999	7.19	102	14.6
$70,000 to $79,999	7.80	110	6.6
$80,000 to $99,999	9.06	128	10.7
$100,000 or more	15.00	212	36.4
HOUSEHOLD TYPE			
Average household	**7.06**	**100**	**100.0**
Married couples	8.73	124	61.0
Married couples, no children	7.22	102	21.7
Married couples, with children	10.40	147	34.3
Oldest child under age 6	8.09	115	4.9
Oldest child aged 6 to 17	13.14	186	21.9
Oldest child aged 18 or older	7.33	104	7.5
Single parent with child under age 18	5.57	79	4.7
Single person	5.04	71	20.9
RACE AND HISPANIC ORIGIN			
Average household	**7.06**	**100**	**100.0**
Asian	10.72	152	6.5
Black	6.68	95	11.6
Hispanic	5.15	73	8.9
Non-Hispanic white and other	7.63	108	81.9
REGION			
Average household	**7.06**	**100**	**100.0**
Northeast	6.25	89	16.2
Midwest	6.69	95	21.1
South	7.47	106	38.8
West	7.41	105	23.8
EDUCATION			
Average household	**7.06**	**100**	**100.0**
Less than high school graduate	2.04	29	4.1
High school graduate	3.77	53	13.6
Some college	6.98	99	20.8
Associate's degree	7.83	111	10.5
Bachelor's degree or more	12.11	172	51.0
Bachelor's degree	11.97	170	32.0
Master's, professional, doctoral degree	12.37	175	19.0

Note: Market shares may not sum to 100.0 because of rounding and missing categories by household type. "Asian" and "black" include Hispanics and non-Hispanics who identify themselves as being of the respective race alone. "Hispanic" includes people of any race who identify themselves as Hispanic. "Other" includes people who identify themselves as non-Hispanic and as Alaska Native, American Indian, Asian (who are also included in the "Asian" row), or Native Hawaiian or other Pacific Islander as well as non-Hispanics reporting more than one race.

Source: Calculations by New Strategist based on the Bureau of Labor Statistics' 2010 Consumer Expenditure Survey

Repair of Computer Systems for Nonbusiness Use

Best customers:	**Householders aged 55 to 74** **Married couples without children at home** **Married couples with adult children at home** **Households in the West and Northeast**
Customer trends:	**Average household spending on repair of computer systems for nonbusiness use is likely to continue to grow as boomers age and the economic downturn encourages repair rather than replacement.**

The best customers of repair of computer systems for nonbusiness use are older householders and households that include adult children. Householders aged 55 to 74 spend 38 to 57 percent more than the average household on computer repairs. Married couples without children at home, most older, spend 37 percent more than average on computer repair. Couples with adult children at home spend 84 percent above average on this item. Spending on computer repair by households in the West and Northeast is, respectively, 47 and 23 percent above average.

Average household spending on repair of computer systems for nonbusiness use doubled between 2000 and 2006, after adjusting for inflation, and grew by another 4 percent since then. With computers becoming the norm in most households, many people—particularly older adults—need help maintaining their systems. Average household spending on computer repair is likely to continue to grow as boomers age and the economic downturn encourages repair rather than replacement.

Table 3.7 Repair of computer systems for nonbusiness use

Total household spending	$882,870,030.00
Average household spends	7.29

	AVERAGE HOUSEHOLD SPENDING	BEST CUSTOMERS (index)	BIGGEST CUSTOMERS (market share)
AGE OF HOUSEHOLDER			
Average household	**$7.29**	**100**	**100.0%**
Under age 25	4.10	56	3.7
Aged 25 to 34	5.31	73	12.1
Aged 35 to 44	5.95	82	14.8
Aged 45 to 54	6.82	94	19.4
Aged 55 to 64	10.04	138	24.3
Aged 65 to 74	11.42	157	16.9
Aged 75 or older	6.84	94	8.9

	AVERAGE HOUSEHOLD SPENDING	BEST CUSTOMERS (index)	BIGGEST CUSTOMERS (market share)
HOUSEHOLD INCOME			
Average household	**$7.29**	**100**	**100.0%**
Under $20,000	3.30	45	9.9
$20,000 to $39,999	4.28	59	13.4
$40,000 to $49,999	12.88	177	16.7
$50,000 to $69,999	4.75	65	9.3
$70,000 to $79,999	17.97	247	14.8
$80,000 to $99,999	8.07	111	9.2
$100,000 or more	11.37	156	26.7
HOUSEHOLD TYPE			
Average household	**7.29**	**100**	**100.0**
Married couples	9.21	126	62.3
Married couples, no children	10.01	137	29.2
Married couples, with children	9.34	128	29.8
Oldest child under age 6	5.05	69	3.0
Oldest child aged 6 to 17	8.42	116	13.6
Oldest child aged 18 or older	13.38	184	13.3
Single parent with child under age 18	1.79	25	1.4
Single person	4.30	59	17.3
RACE AND HISPANIC ORIGIN			
Average household	**7.29**	**100**	**100.0**
Asian	6.96	95	4.1
Black	3.34	46	5.6
Hispanic	3.95	54	6.6
Non-Hispanic white and other	8.52	117	88.6
REGION			
Average household	**7.29**	**100**	**100.0**
Northeast	8.99	123	22.6
Midwest	6.99	96	21.4
South	4.52	62	22.8
West	10.73	147	33.3
EDUCATION			
Average household	**7.29**	**100**	**100.0**
Less than high school graduate	1.94	27	3.8
High school graduate	3.58	49	12.5
Some college	8.67	119	25.0
Associate's degree	8.69	119	11.3
Bachelor's degree or more	11.64	160	47.4
Bachelor's degree	10.63	146	27.5
Master's, professional, doctoral degree	13.42	184	19.9

Note: Market shares may not sum to 100.0 because of rounding and missing categories by household type. "Asian" and "black" include Hispanics and non-Hispanics who identify themselves as being of the respective race alone. "Hispanic" includes people of any race who identify themselves as Hispanic. "Other" includes people who identify themselves as non-Hispanic and as Alaska Native, American Indian, Asian (who are also included in the "Asian" row), or Native Hawaiian or other Pacific Islander as well as non-Hispanics reporting more than one race.

Source: Calculations by New Strategist based on the Bureau of Labor Statistics' 2010 Consumer Expenditure Survey

Chapter 4.

Education

Household Spending on Education, 2010

Because few households have educational expenses in a given year, average spending on education is relatively low. In 2010, the average household spent $1,074 on education, including $702 for college tuition. As public colleges cost thousands of dollars a year, and private colleges tens of thousands, this figure is so low because few households have education expenses. A more-realistic spending figure for college tuition can be found in Appendix B, which shows the spending of purchasers only. During the average quarter of 2010, just 5.2 percent of households spent on college tuition, but those who did spent $3,354 per quarter. Between 2000 and 2010, average household spending on college tuition increased 53 percent, after adjusting for inflation.

More important than average spending figures are the patterns of spending by demographic characteristic. Householders under age 25 and those aged 45 to 54 are the biggest spenders on college tuition. The younger householders are paying for their own college education, while the older ones are paying for their children's education. Because of volatility in the financial markets and tighter lending standards, average household spending on education may stabilize or even decline in the years ahead.

Spending on college tuition

(average annual household spending on college tuition, 2000, 2006, and 2010; in 2010 dollars)

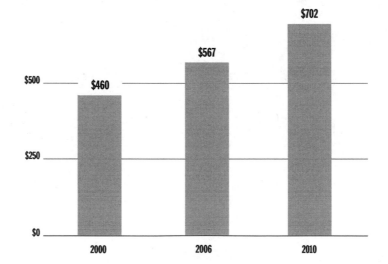

Table 4.1 Education spending, 2000 to 2010

(average annual household spending on education by category, 2000 to 2010; percent change and percentage point change in spending, 2000–06, 2006–10, and 2000–10; in 2010 dollars; ranked by amount spent)

	2010 average household spending	2006 average household spending (in 2010$)	2000 average household spending (in 2010$)	percent change		
				2006–10	2000–06	2000–10
AVERAGE ANNUAL SPENDING						
Average annual household spending on education	**$1,074.46**	**$960.25**	**$800.21**	**11.9%**	**20.0%**	**34.3%**
Tuition, college	701.62	566.63	460.03	23.8	23.2	52.5
Tuition, elementary and high school	156.02	169.23	128.43	–7.8	31.8	21.5
Books and supplies, college	63.79	65.19	66.68	–2.1	–2.2	–4.3
Miscellaneous school supplies	63.54	59.18	62.21	7.4	–4.9	2.1
Other school expenses including rentals	34.76	51.56	30.39	–32.6	69.7	14.4
Tuition, other schools	19.55	26.59	30.92	–26.5	–14.0	–36.8
Books and supplies, elementary and high school	13.14	18.04	17.63	–27.2	2.4	–25.5
Test preparation, tutoring services	10.20	–	–	–	–	–
Tuition, vocational and technical schools	9.19	–	–	–	–	–
Books and supplies, other schools	1.19	–	–	–	–	–
Books and supplies, vocational and technical schools	0.98	–	–	–	–	–
Books and supplies, day care and nursery	0.49	3.82	3.91	–87.2	–2.4	–87.5

				percentage point change		
	2006–10	2000–06	2000–10	2006–10	2000–06	2000–10
PERCENT DISTRIBUTION OF SPENDING						
Average annual household spending on education	**100.0%**	**100.0%**	**100.0%**	–	–	–
Tuition, college	65.3	59.0	57.5	6.3	1.5	7.8
Tuition, elementary and high school	14.5	17.6	16.1	–3.1	1.6	–1.5
Books and supplies, college	5.9	6.8	8.3	–0.9	–1.5	–2.4
Miscellaneous school supplies	5.9	6.2	7.8	–0.2	–1.6	–1.9
Other school expenses including rentals	3.2	5.4	3.8	–2.1	1.6	–0.6
Tuition, other schools	1.8	2.8	3.9	–0.9	–1.1	–2.0
Books and supplies, elementary and high school	1.2	1.9	2.2	–0.7	–0.3	–1.0
Test preparation, tutoring services	0.9	–	–	–	–	–
Tuition, vocational and technical schools	0.9	–	–	–	–	–
Books and supplies, other schools	0.1	–	–	–	–	–
Books and supplies, vocational and technical schools	0.1	–	–	–	–	–
Books and supplies, day care and nursery	0.1	0.4	0.5	–0.4	–0.1	–0.4

Note: "–" means data are unavailable.

Source: Bureau of Labor Statistics, 2000, 2006, and 2010 Consumer Expenditure Surveys; calculations by New Strategist

Books and Supplies, College

Best customers: Householders under age 25 and aged 45 to 54
Married couples with adult children at home
Asians

Customer trends: Average household spending on books and supplies for college will decline as college students search for less-expensive alternatives such as renting or downloading texts.

Not surprisingly, college students are the best customers of college books and supplies. Householders under age 25 spend over three-and-one-half times the average on this item and account for 24 percent of the market. Married couples with children aged 18 or older at home spend three-and-one-third times the average on college books and supplies. Asian households spend 77 percent more than average on this item.

Average household spending on college books and supplies fell 4 percent between 2000 and 2010, after adjusting for inflation. Behind the modest decline is the valiant attempt by students and parents to cut costs as tuition soars. Spending on books and supplies for college is likely to decline further in the future as students search for less-expensive books via the Internet.

Table 4.2 Books and supplies, college

Total household spending $7,725,415,530.00
Average household spends   63.79

	AVERAGE HOUSEHOLD SPENDING	BEST CUSTOMERS (index)	BIGGEST CUSTOMERS (market share)
AGE OF HOUSEHOLDER			
Average household	**$63.79**	**100**	**100.0%**
Under age 25	230.39	361	24.0
Aged 25 to 34	54.39	85	14.2
Aged 35 to 44	50.29	79	14.3
Aged 45 to 54	99.54	156	32.3
Aged 55 to 64	44.95	70	12.4
Aged 65 to 74	11.41	18	1.9
Aged 75 or older	6.27	10	0.9

	AVERAGE HOUSEHOLD SPENDING	BEST CUSTOMERS (index)	BIGGEST CUSTOMERS (market share)
HOUSEHOLD INCOME			
Average household	**$63.79**	**100**	**100.0%**
Under $20,000	67.53	106	23.1
$20,000 to $39,999	33.88	53	12.2
$40,000 to $49,999	45.61	72	6.8
$50,000 to $69,999	50.53	79	11.4
$70,000 to $79,999	39.63	62	3.7
$80,000 to $99,999	70.45	110	9.2
$100,000 or more	125.28	196	33.7
HOUSEHOLD TYPE			
Average household	**63.79**	**100**	**100.0**
Married couples	70.90	111	54.8
Married couples, no children	35.17	55	11.7
Married couples, with children	101.61	159	37.1
Oldest child under age 6	55.33	87	3.7
Oldest child aged 6 to 17	51.39	81	9.5
Oldest child aged 18 or older	210.84	331	23.9
Single parent with child under age 18	23.86	37	2.2
Single person	53.41	84	24.5
RACE AND HISPANIC ORIGIN			
Average household	**63.79**	**100**	**100.0**
Asian	112.63	177	7.5
Black	54.64	86	10.5
Hispanic	40.79	64	7.8
Non-Hispanic white and other	68.92	108	81.9
REGION			
Average household	**63.79**	**100**	**100.0**
Northeast	73.05	115	21.0
Midwest	72.38	113	25.3
South	51.51	81	29.6
West	67.72	106	24.0
EDUCATION			
Average household	**63.79**	**100**	**100.0**
Less than high school graduate	16.06	25	3.6
High school graduate	23.35	37	9.3
Some college	100.56	158	33.1
Associate's degree	66.70	105	9.9
Bachelor's degree or more	94.55	148	44.0
Bachelor's degree	92.39	145	27.4
Master's, professional, doctoral degree	98.32	154	16.7

Note: Market shares may not sum to 100.0 because of rounding and missing categories by household type. "Asian" and "black" include Hispanics and non-Hispanics who identify themselves as being of the respective race alone. "Hispanic" includes people of any race who identify themselves as Hispanic. "Other" includes people who identify themselves as non-Hispanic and as Alaska Native, American Indian, Asian (who are also included in the "Asian" row), or Native Hawaiian or other Pacific Islander as well as non-Hispanics reporting more than one race.

Source: Calculations by New Strategist based on the Bureau of Labor Statistics' 2010 Consumer Expenditure Survey

Books and Supplies, Elementary and High School

Best customers:	**Householders aged 35 to 54**
	Married couples with school-aged or older children at home
	Single parents
	Asians and Hispanics
Customer trends:	**Average household spending on books and supplies for elementary and high school may grow again in the years ahead as schools become increasingly dependent on parents to provide books and supplies.**

The best customers of books and supplies for elementary and high school are parents with school-aged children. Married couples with children aged 6 to 17 spend almost four times the average on this item. Single parents spend almost two-and-one-half times the average on books and supplies for elementary and high school. Together these groups control 60 percent of the market. Householders aged 35 to 54 spend nearly twice the average on this item because many have school-aged children. Asian householders spend 35 percent more than average on elementary and high school books and supplies, and Hispanics, 34 percent more.

Average household spending on books and supplies for elementary and high school grew 2 percent between 2000 and 2006 (the year overall household spending peaked), then fell by a sharp 27 percent as the Great Recession set in and parents cut back on their spending. With schools cutting budgets and increasingly dependent on parents to provide books and supplies, this category may grow again in the years ahead.

Table 4.3 Books and supplies, elementary and high school

Total household spending	$1,591,345,980.00
Average household spends	13.14

	AVERAGE HOUSEHOLD SPENDING	BEST CUSTOMERS (index)	BIGGEST CUSTOMERS (market share)
AGE OF HOUSEHOLDER			
Average household	**$13.14**	**100**	**100.0%**
Under age 25	3.04	23	1.5
Aged 25 to 34	13.57	103	17.2
Aged 35 to 44	26.08	198	35.9
Aged 45 to 54	23.78	181	37.4
Aged 55 to 64	3.55	27	4.8
Aged 65 to 74	3.05	23	2.5
Aged 75 or older	0.88	7	0.6

	AVERAGE HOUSEHOLD SPENDING	BEST CUSTOMERS (index)	BIGGEST CUSTOMERS (market share)
HOUSEHOLD INCOME			
Average household	**$13.14**	**100**	**100.0%**
Under $20,000	4.44	34	7.4
$20,000 to $39,999	7.28	55	12.7
$40,000 to $49,999	12.63	96	9.1
$50,000 to $69,999	17.31	132	18.9
$70,000 to $79,999	11.48	87	5.2
$80,000 to $99,999	18.85	143	12.0
$100,000 or more	26.62	203	34.7
HOUSEHOLD TYPE			
Average household	**13.14**	**100**	**100.0**
Married couples	18.94	144	71.1
Married couples, no children	0.89	7	1.4
Married couples, with children	33.92	258	60.0
Oldest child under age 6	7.22	55	2.4
Oldest child aged 6 to 17	51.80	394	46.4
Oldest child aged 18 or older	20.65	157	11.3
Single parent with child under age 18	31.37	239	14.1
Single person	2.06	16	4.6
RACE AND HISPANIC ORIGIN			
Average household	**13.14**	**100**	**100.0**
Asian	17.72	135	5.7
Black	13.90	106	12.9
Hispanic	17.62	134	16.3
Non-Hispanic white and other	12.33	94	71.1
REGION			
Average household	**13.14**	**100**	**100.0**
Northeast	9.02	69	12.6
Midwest	14.52	111	24.6
South	14.58	111	40.7
West	12.79	97	22.0
EDUCATION			
Average household	**13.14**	**100**	**100.0**
Less than high school graduate	9.32	71	10.1
High school graduate	12.13	92	23.6
Some college	10.62	81	17.0
Associate's degree	10.17	77	7.3
Bachelor's degree or more	18.56	141	42.0
Bachelor's degree	18.30	139	26.3
Master's, professional, doctoral degree	19.01	145	15.7

Note: Market shares may not sum to 100.0 because of rounding and missing categories by household type. "Asian" and "black" include Hispanics and non-Hispanics who identify themselves as being of the respective race alone. "Hispanic" includes people of any race who identify themselves as Hispanic. "Other" includes people who identify themselves as non-Hispanic and as Alaska Native, American Indian, Asian (who are also included in the "Asian" row), or Native Hawaiian or other Pacific Islander as well as non-Hispanics reporting more than one race.

Source: Calculations by New Strategist based on the Bureau of Labor Statistics' 2010 Consumer Expenditure Survey

Tuition, College

Best customers: **Householders under age 25 and aged 45 to 54**
High-income households
Married couples with adult children at home
Asians
Households in the Northeast
College graduates

Customer trends: **Average household spending on college tuition may stabilize or even decline in the**
years ahead as the nation's economic problems crimp the college market.

The biggest spenders on college tuition are, not surprisingly, young adults who attend college and the parents who pay for those expenses. This explains why householders under age 25 and householders aged 45 to 54 spend over twice the average amount on college tuition. Married couples with adult children at home spend more than three times the average on college tuition since many have children in school. Asian households spend more than two-and-one-half times the average, and households in the Northeast spend 71 percent more than average on this item. Households with incomes of $100,000 or more spend more than three times the average on college tuition. College graduates, a well-off demographic, spend more than twice the average on college tuition.

Average household spending on college tuition soared 53 percent between 2000 and 2010, after adjusting for inflation. Behind the increase was the growing proportion of households with children in college as boomers sent their children to school. Also behind the increase is the rapid rise in the cost of college. Average household spending on college tuition may stabilize or even decline in the years ahead as the nation's economic problems make college unaffordable for a growing share of families.

Table 4.4 Tuition, college

Total household spending   **$84,971,093,340.00**
Average household spends   **701.62**

	AVERAGE HOUSEHOLD SPENDING	BEST CUSTOMERS (index)	BIGGEST CUSTOMERS (market share)
AGE OF HOUSEHOLDER			
Average household	**$701.62**	**100**	**100.0%**
Under age 25	1,617.55	231	15.3
Aged 25 to 34	586.28	84	13.9
Aged 35 to 44	382.27	54	9.9
Aged 45 to 54	1,414.99	202	41.7
Aged 55 to 64	640.16	91	16.1
Aged 65 to 74	133.38	19	2.0
Aged 75 or older	79.13	11	1.1

	AVERAGE HOUSEHOLD SPENDING	BEST CUSTOMERS (index)	BIGGEST CUSTOMERS (market share)
HOUSEHOLD INCOME			
Average household	$701.62	100	100.0%
Under $20,000	466.82	67	14.5
$20,000 to $39,999	270.68	39	8.8
$40,000 to $49,999	251.77	36	3.4
$50,000 to $69,999	433.75	62	8.9
$70,000 to $79,999	445.90	64	3.8
$80,000 to $99,999	627.12	89	7.5
$100,000 or more	2,173.85	310	53.1
HOUSEHOLD TYPE			
Average household	701.62	100	100.0
Married couples	902.00	129	63.4
Married couples, no children	619.89	88	18.8
Married couples, with children	1,191.36	170	39.5
Oldest child under age 6	432.56	62	2.6
Oldest child aged 6 to 17	776.34	111	13.0
Oldest child aged 18 or older	2,317.22	330	23.8
Single parent with child under age 18	112.77	16	0.9
Single person	464.30	66	19.4
RACE AND HISPANIC ORIGIN			
Average household	701.62	100	100.0
Asian	1,868.85	266	11.3
Black	248.40	35	4.3
Hispanic	532.40	76	9.2
Non-Hispanic white and other	802.90	114	86.8
REGION			
Average household	701.62	100	100.0
Northeast	1,197.55	171	31.3
Midwest	737.12	105	23.4
South	418.42	60	21.9
West	723.72	103	23.4
EDUCATION			
Average household	701.62	100	100.0
Less than high school graduate	88.18	13	1.8
High school graduate	184.72	26	6.7
Some college	616.87	88	18.5
Associate's degree	637.31	91	8.6
Bachelor's degree or more	1,521.29	217	64.4
Bachelor's degree	1,444.55	206	38.9
Master's, professional, doctoral degree	1,655.27	236	25.5

Note: Market shares may not sum to 100.0 because of rounding and missing categories by household type. "Asian" and "black" include Hispanics and non-Hispanics who identify themselves as being of the respective race alone. "Hispanic" includes people of any race who identify themselves as Hispanic. "Other" includes people who identify themselves as non-Hispanic and as Alaska Native, American Indian, Asian (who are also included in the "Asian" row), or Native Hawaiian or other Pacific Islander as well as non-Hispanics reporting more than one race.

Source: Calculations by New Strategist based on the Bureau of Labor Statistics' 2010 Consumer Expenditure Survey

Tuition, Elementary and High School

Best customers: **Householders aged 35 to 54**
High-income households
Married couples with school-aged or older children at home
Asians
College graduates

Customer trends: **Average household spending on elementary and high school tuition may continue**
to decline as the nation's economic problems make private school unaffordable for
a growing share of families.

The biggest spenders on elementary and high school tuition are affluent parents with school-aged children. Householders aged 35 to 54 spend over twice the average on private school tuition because many are parents. Married couples with school-aged children spend five-and-one-half times the average on this item. Households with incomes of $100,000 or more spend four-and-one-half times the average on elementary and high school tuition. Asians spend more than four times the average amount on elementary and high school tuition and account for a 17 percent share of the market. College graduates, who rank among the most-affluent households, spend two-and-one-half the average on this item.

Average household spending on private school tuition rose 21 percent between 2000 and 2010, after adjusting for inflation. All the growth occurred before the overall peak-spending year of 2006, and spending on this item has declined 8 percent since then. Behind the increase was the burgeoning number of parents searching for alternatives to public school. Also behind the increase was the rapid rise in private school tuition. The Great Recession curtailed spending on private school education. Average household spending on elementary and high school tuition may continue to decline as the nation's economic problems make private school unaffordable for a growing share of families.

Table 4.5 Tuition, elementary and high school

Total household spending $18,895,114,140.00
Average household spends   156.02

	AVERAGE HOUSEHOLD SPENDING	BEST CUSTOMERS (index)	BIGGEST CUSTOMERS (market share)
AGE OF HOUSEHOLDER			
Average household	**$156.02**	**100**	**100.0%**
Under age 25	8.66	6	0.4
Aged 25 to 34	60.11	39	6.4
Aged 35 to 44	318.84	204	37.0
Aged 45 to 54	343.66	220	45.6
Aged 55 to 64	70.28	45	7.9
Aged 65 to 74	29.26	19	2.0
Aged 75 or older	11.61	7	0.7

	AVERAGE HOUSEHOLD SPENDING	BEST CUSTOMERS (index)	BIGGEST CUSTOMERS (market share)
HOUSEHOLD INCOME			
Average household	**$156.02**	**100**	**100.0%**
Under $20,000	22.71	15	3.2
$20,000 to $39,999	27.82	18	4.1
$40,000 to $49,999	54.74	35	3.3
$50,000 to $69,999	36.21	23	3.3
$70,000 to $79,999	80.50	52	3.1
$80,000 to $99,999	135.36	87	7.2
$100,000 or more	698.30	448	76.7
HOUSEHOLD TYPE			
Average household	**156.02**	**100**	**100.0**
Married couples	287.41	184	90.9
Married couples, no children	41.73	27	5.7
Married couples, with children	511.92	328	76.3
Oldest child under age 6	46.08	30	1.3
Oldest child aged 6 to 17	857.69	550	64.6
Oldest child aged 18 or older	225.03	144	10.4
Single parent with child under age 18	83.65	54	3.2
Single person	11.12	7	2.1
RACE AND HISPANIC ORIGIN			
Average household	**156.02**	**100**	**100.0**
Asian	641.12	411	17.5
Black	56.32	36	4.4
Hispanic	113.41	73	8.9
Non-Hispanic white and other	178.47	114	86.7
REGION			
Average household	**156.02**	**100**	**100.0**
Northeast	183.55	118	21.6
Midwest	185.76	119	26.5
South	96.58	62	22.7
West	200.74	129	29.1
EDUCATION			
Average household	**156.02**	**100**	**100.0**
Less than high school graduate	44.26	28	4.1
High school graduate	58.24	37	9.5
Some college	62.77	40	8.5
Associate's degree	72.02	46	4.4
Bachelor's degree or more	386.49	248	73.6
Bachelor's degree	236.14	151	28.6
Master's, professional, doctoral degree	648.99	416	45.0

Note: Market shares may not sum to 100.0 because of rounding and missing categories by household type. "Asian" and "black" include Hispanics and non-Hispanics who identify themselves as being of the respective race alone. "Hispanic" includes people of any race who identify themselves as Hispanic. "Other" includes people who identify themselves as non-Hispanic and as Alaska Native, American Indian, Asian (who are also included in the "Asian" row), or Native Hawaiian or other Pacific Islander as well as non-Hispanics reporting more than one race.

Source: Calculations by New Strategist based on the Bureau of Labor Statistics' 2010 Consumer Expenditure Survey

Tuition, Vocational and Technical Schools

Best customers: Householders aged 25 to 34 and 45 to 54
Married couples without children at home
Married couples with adult children at home
Hispanics
Households in the West

Customer trends: Average household spending on vocational and technical school tuition may rise in the years ahead as parents search for lower-cost alternatives to college.

The biggest spenders on vocational and technical school tuition are adults aged 25 to 34 who are attending these schools or parents who are paying for their children's tuition. Householders aged 45 to 54 spend 49 percent more than average on vocational and technical school tuition, and householders aged 25 to 34 spend 76 percent more. Married couples without children at home—most of them empty-nesters—spend 63 percent more than average on vocational and technical school tuition. Couples with adult children at home spend two-and-one-half times the average. Hispanics spend 73 percent above average on this item and represent 21 percent of the market. Households in the West, where many Hispanics reside, spend 54 percent more than average on vocational and technical school tuition.

Spending on vocational and technical schools tuition became part of the Consumer Expenditure Survey only in 2007, and data from earlier years are nonexistent. Average household spending on vocational and technical school tuition may rise in the years ahead as a burgeoning number of parents search for lower-cost alternatives to college.

Table 4.6 Tuition, vocational and technical schools

Total household spending $1,112,973,330.00
Average household spends 9.19

	AVERAGE HOUSEHOLD SPENDING	BEST CUSTOMERS (index)	BIGGEST CUSTOMERS (market share)
AGE OF HOUSEHOLDER			
Average household	**$9.19**	**100**	**100.0%**
Under age 25	0.42	5	0.3
Aged 25 to 34	16.21	176	29.4
Aged 35 to 44	7.63	83	15.0
Aged 45 to 54	13.70	149	30.8
Aged 55 to 64	9.20	100	17.7
Aged 65 to 74	2.62	29	3.1
Aged 75 or older	3.60	39	3.7

	AVERAGE HOUSEHOLD SPENDING	BEST CUSTOMERS (index)	BIGGEST CUSTOMERS (market share)
HOUSEHOLD INCOME			
Average household	**$9.19**	**100**	**100.0%**
Under $20,000	2.29	25	5.4
$20,000 to $39,999	7.29	79	18.2
$40,000 to $49,999	6.01	65	6.2
$50,000 to $69,999	5.09	55	7.9
$70,000 to $79,999	3.95	43	2.6
$80,000 to $99,999	11.36	124	10.3
$100,000 or more	27.01	294	50.4
HOUSEHOLD TYPE			
Average household	**9.19**	**100**	**100.0**
Married couples	13.17	143	70.7
Married couples, no children	14.98	163	34.6
Married couples, with children	13.49	147	34.1
Oldest child under age 6	2.27	25	1.1
Oldest child aged 6 to 17	11.83	129	15.1
Oldest child aged 18 or older	22.84	249	17.9
Single parent with child under age 18	1.77	19	1.1
Single person	4.45	48	14.2
RACE AND HISPANIC ORIGIN			
Average household	**9.19**	**100**	**100.0**
Asian	7.60	83	3.5
Black	3.52	38	4.7
Hispanic	15.88	173	21.1
Non-Hispanic white and other	9.19	100	75.8
REGION			
Average household	**9.19**	**100**	**100.0**
Northeast	5.14	56	10.3
Midwest	8.19	89	19.9
South	8.77	95	35.0
West	14.14	154	34.9
EDUCATION			
Average household	**9.19**	**100**	**100.0**
Less than high school graduate	3.02	33	4.7
High school graduate	5.28	57	14.7
Some college	7.45	81	17.0
Associate's degree	12.88	140	13.2
Bachelor's degree or more	15.57	169	50.3
Bachelor's degree	19.39	211	39.9
Master's, professional, doctoral degree	8.90	97	10.5

Note: Market shares may not sum to 100.0 because of rounding and missing categories by household type. "Asian" and "black" include Hispanics and non-Hispanics who identify themselves as being of the respective race alone. "Hispanic" includes people of any race who identify themselves as Hispanic. "Other" includes people who identify themselves as non-Hispanic and as Alaska Native, American Indian, Asian (who are also included in the "Asian" row), or Native Hawaiian or other Pacific Islander as well as non-Hispanics reporting more than one race.

Source: Calculations by New Strategist based on the Bureau of Labor Statistics' 2010 Consumer Expenditure Survey

Chapter 5.

Entertainment

Household Spending on Entertainment, 2010

Average household spending on entertainment climbed 6 percent between 2000 and 2010, rising from $2,360 to $2,504 after adjusting for inflation. The 114 percent rise in spending on video game hardware and software, the 53 percent increase in spending on cable television, the 44 percent increase in spending on (high-definition) television sets, and the explosion of spending on pet purchases, supplies, and medicines (up 237 percent) and veterinary services (up 36 percent) account for most of the increase in entertainment spending.

While overall entertainment spending rose slightly during the past 10 years, many entertainment categories saw declines in spending, some precipitous. Categories with the largest percentage losses in spending were film (down 95 percent); compact discs, records, and audio tapes (down 72 percent); photo processing (down 71 percent); video cassette recorders and video disc players (down 66 percent); musical instruments and accessories (down 60 percent); and rental of video cassettes, tapes, discs, films (down 59 percent). Household penny pinching is behind some of these declines, but changing technologies are an obvious factor. While, for example, digital cameras have slashed spending on film and photo processing, average household spending on photographic equipment declined a mere 5 percent between 2000 and 2010.

Average household spending on entertainment has been rising for more than a decade, but behind the increase are big gains in just a few categories. This is a troubling trend for the entertainment industry, which has become such an important part of the U.S. economy.

Spending on entertainment

(average annual spending of households on entertainment, 2000, 2006, and 2010; in 2010 dollars)

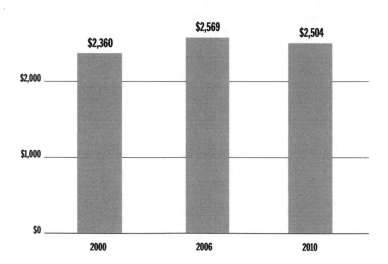

Table 5.1 Entertainment spending, 2000 to 2010

(average annual and percent distribution of household spending on entertainment by category, 2000 to 2010; percent change in spending and percentage point change in distribution, 2000–06, 2006–10, and 2000–10; in 2010 dollars; ranked by amount spent)

	2010 average household spending	2006 average household spending (in 2010$)	2000 average household spending (in 2010$)	percent change		
				2006–10	2000–06	2000–10
AVERAGE ANNUAL SPENDING						
Average household spending on entertainment	**$2,504.44**	**$2,569.44**	**$2,359.74**	**–2.5%**	**8.9%**	**6.1%**
Cable and satellite television services	621.49	583.04	406.71	6.6	43.4	52.8
Pet food	165.20	143.87	108.86	14.8	32.2	51.7
Pet purchase, supplies, and medicines	162.51	59.72	48.25	172.1	23.8	236.8
Movie, theater, amusement park, and other admissions (including on trips)	155.00	173.73	169.81	–10.8	2.3	–8.7
Recreational vehicles (boats, campers, trailers), purchase and rental	139.32	234.91	168.18	–40.7	39.7	–17.2
Club memberships (social, recreational, and health)	120.72	133.56	124.32	–9.6	7.4	–2.9
Television sets	118.73	141.03	82.70	–15.8	70.5	43.6
Toys, games, hobbies, and tricycles	117.78	93.37	153.17	26.1	–39.0	–23.1
Veterinarian services	113.52	101.42	83.58	11.9	21.4	35.8
Fees for participant sports (including on trips)	108.25	117.68	134.91	–8.0	–12.8	–19.8
Fees for recreational lessons	94.41	109.86	94.64	–14.1	16.1	–0.2
Admission to sports events (including on trips)	59.62	59.62	63.71	0.0	–6.4	–6.4
Video game hardware and software	50.80	36.88	23.71	37.7	55.6	114.3
Athletic gear, game tables, exercise equipment	47.28	62.85	74.26	–24.8	–15.4	–36.3
Recreational expenses on trips	43.16	61.11	64.56	–29.4	–5.3	–33.1
Pet services	38.87	36.79	24.52	5.7	50.1	58.6
Sound components, equipment, and accessories	27.67	36.68	53.75	–24.6	–31.8	–48.5
Video cassettes, tapes, and discs	27.38	44.56	26.34	–38.6	69.2	4.0
Hunting and fishing equipment	26.17	31.02	32.73	–15.6	–5.2	–20.1
Photographic equipment	24.25	35.22	25.59	–31.1	37.6	–5.2
Rental of video cassettes, tapes, discs, films	21.51	34.01	52.63	–36.7	–35.4	–59.1
Musical instruments and accessories, purchase, rental, and repair	16.68	18.20	41.84	–8.4	–56.5	–60.1
Photographer's fees	16.62	24.27	25.54	–31.5	–5.0	–34.9
Bicycles	15.43	14.12	14.85	9.3	–5.0	3.9
Satellite radio service	14.57	–	–	–	–	–
Compact discs, records, and audio tapes	13.79	36.81	49.97	–62.5	–26.3	–72.4
Camping equipment	13.41	11.25	21.55	19.2	–47.8	–37.8
Rental of party supplies for catered affairs	12.73	–	–	–	–	–
Personal digital audio players	11.42	18.83	–	–39.4	–	–
Photo processing	11.42	19.34	39.80	–40.9	–51.4	–71.3
Live entertainment for catered affairs	10.34	–	–	–	–	–
Video cassette recorders and video disc players	10.10	17.44	30.14	–42.1	–42.1	–66.5
Streamed and downloaded audio	6.70	3.92	–	71.1	–	–
Global positioning system devices	5.20	–	–	–	–	–
Stamp and coin collecting	2.77	6.08	–	–54.4	–	–
Repair of TV, radio, and sound equipment	2.69	5.98	4.09	–55.0	46.2	–34.2
Online gaming services	2.55	–	–	–	–	–
Streamed and downloaded video	1.94	1.11	–	74.1	–	–
Film	1.23	6.91	27.01	–82.2	–74.5	–95.5

	2006–10	2000–06	2000–10	percentage point change		
				2006–10	2000–06	2000–10
PERCENT DISTRIBUTION OF SPENDING						
Average household spending on entertainment	**100.0%**	**100.0%**	**100.0%**	–	–	–
Cable and satellite television services	24.8	22.7	17.2	2.1	5.5	7.6
Pet food	6.6	5.6	4.6	1.0	1.0	2.0
Pet purchase, supplies, and medicines	6.5	2.3	2.0	4.2	0.3	4.4
Movie, theater, amusement park, and other admissions (including on trips)	6.2	6.8	7.2	–0.6	–0.4	–1.0
Recreational vehicles (boats, campers, trailers), purchase and rental	5.6	9.1	7.1	–3.6	2.0	–1.6
Club memberships (civic, recreational, and health)	4.8	5.2	5.3	–0.4	–0.1	–0.4
Television sets	4.7	5.5	3.5	–0.7	2.0	1.2
Toys, games, hobbies, and tricycles	4.7	3.6	6.5	1.1	–2.9	–1.8
Veterinarian services	4.5	3.9	3.5	0.6	0.4	1.0
Fees for participant sports (including on trips)	4.3	4.6	5.7	–0.3	–1.1	–1.4
Fees for recreational lessons	3.8	4.3	4.0	–0.5	0.3	–0.2
Admission to sports events (including on trips)	2.4	2.3	2.7	0.1	–0.4	–0.3
Video game hardware and software	2.0	1.4	1.0	0.6	0.4	1.0
Athletic gear, game tables, exercise equipment	1.9	2.4	3.1	–0.6	–0.7	–1.3
Recreational expenses on trips	1.7	2.4	2.7	–0.7	–0.4	–1.0
Pet services	1.6	1.4	1.0	0.1	0.4	0.5
Sound components, equipment, and accessories	1.1	1.4	2.3	–0.3	–0.9	–1.2
Video cassettes, tapes, and discs	1.1	1.7	1.1	–0.6	0.6	–0.0
Hunting and fishing equipment	1.0	1.2	1.4	–0.2	–0.2	–0.3
Photographic equipment	1.0	1.4	1.1	–0.4	0.3	–0.1
Rental of video cassettes, tapes, discs, films	0.9	1.3	2.2	–0.5	–0.9	–1.4
Musical instruments and accessories, purchase, rental, and repair	0.7	0.7	1.8	–0.0	–1.1	–1.1
Photographer's fees	0.7	0.9	1.1	–0.3	–0.1	–0.4
Bicycles	0.6	0.5	0.6	0.1	–0.1	–0.0
Satellite radio service	0.6	–	–	–	–	–
Compact discs, records, and audio tapes	0.6	1.4	2.1	–0.9	–0.7	–1.6
Camping equipment	0.5	0.4	0.9	0.1	–0.5	–0.4
Rental of party supplies for catered affairs	0.5	–	–	–	–	–
Personal digital audio players	0.5	0.7	–	–0.3	–	–
Photo processing	0.5	0.8	1.7	–0.3	–0.9	–1.2
Live entertainment for catered affairs	0.4	–	–	–	–	–
Video cassette recorders and video disc players	0.4	0.7	1.3	–0.3	–0.6	–0.9
Streamed and downloaded audio	0.3	0.2	–	0.1	–	–
Global positioning system devices	0.2	–	–	–	–	–
Stamp and coin collecting	0.1	0.2	–	–0.1	–	–
Repair of TV, radio, and sound equipment	0.1	0.2	0.2	–0.1	0.1	–0.1
Online gaming services	0.1	–	–	–	–	–
Streamed and downloaded video	0.1	0.0	–	0.0	–	–
Film	0.1	0.3	1.1	–0.2	–0.9	–1.1

Note: Numbers do not add to total because not all categories are shown. "–" means not applicable or data are unavailable.

Source: Bureau of Labor Statistics, 2000, 2006, and 2010 Consumer Expenditure Surveys; calculations by New Strategist

Admission to Sports Events (Including on Trips)

Best customers:	**Householders aged 35 to 54** **High-income households** **Married couples with children at home** **Non-Hispanic whites** **College graduates**
Customer trends:	**Average household spending on admissions to sports events may resume its decline in the years ahead as high-definition television and online streaming of sports events substitute for the real thing.**

The best customers of sports events are married couples with children at home. Households with school-aged children spend more than twice the average on this item, while those with adult children at home spend 39 percent more than average. Householders aged 35 to 54, many of them parents, spend 25 to 38 percent more than average on admissions to sports events and control just over half the market. Non-Hispanic whites control 91 percent of the market for admission to sporting events, and they spend 19 percent more than average on this item. Households with incomes of $100,000 or more spend over three times the average on sports events and control 53 percent of the market. College graduates spend twice the average and control 60 percent of the market.

Average household spending on admissions to sports events declined 6 percent between 2000 and 2006, after adjusting for inflation, then remained flat between 2006 and 2010. One factor behind the decline was the aging of the baby-boom generation out of the best customer age groups. Spending on sports events may resume its decline in the years ahead as high-definition television and online streaming of sports events substitute for the real thing.

Table 5.2 Admission to sports events (including on trips)

Total household spending $7,220,399,340.00
Average household spends   59.62

	AVERAGE HOUSEHOLD SPENDING	BEST CUSTOMERS (index)	BIGGEST CUSTOMERS (market share)
AGE OF HOUSEHOLDER			
Average household	**$59.62**	**100**	**100.0%**
Under age 25	28.06	47	3.1
Aged 25 to 34	54.29	91	15.2
Aged 35 to 44	74.43	125	22.6
Aged 45 to 54	82.55	138	28.6
Aged 55 to 64	61.51	103	18.2
Aged 65 to 74	50.30	84	9.1
Aged 75 or older	20.01	34	3.2

	AVERAGE HOUSEHOLD SPENDING	BEST CUSTOMERS (index)	BIGGEST CUSTOMERS (market share)
HOUSEHOLD INCOME			
Average household	**$59.62**	**100**	**100.0%**
Under $20,000	16.44	28	6.0
$20,000 to $39,999	22.69	38	8.7
$40,000 to $49,999	29.66	50	4.7
$50,000 to $69,999	53.29	89	12.8
$70,000 to $79,999	52.28	88	5.2
$80,000 to $99,999	66.42	111	9.3
$100,000 or more	184.96	310	53.2
HOUSEHOLD TYPE			
Average household	**59.62**	**100**	**100.0**
Married couples	82.88	139	68.6
Married couples, no children	59.62	100	21.2
Married couples, with children	108.65	182	42.4
Oldest child under age 6	73.26	123	5.3
Oldest child aged 6 to 17	137.27	230	27.1
Oldest child aged 18 or older	83.01	139	10.1
Single parent with child under age 18	35.34	59	3.5
Single person	32.27	54	15.9
RACE AND HISPANIC ORIGIN			
Average household	**59.62**	**100**	**100.0**
Asian	58.83	99	4.2
Black	16.83	28	3.5
Hispanic	29.67	50	6.1
Non-Hispanic white and other	71.18	119	90.5
REGION			
Average household	**59.62**	**100**	**100.0**
Northeast	61.80	104	19.0
Midwest	70.31	118	26.3
South	46.64	78	28.7
West	68.36	115	26.0
EDUCATION			
Average household	**59.62**	**100**	**100.0**
Less than high school graduate	7.30	12	1.7
High school graduate	33.52	56	14.4
Some college	46.37	78	16.4
Associate's degree	46.92	79	7.4
Bachelor's degree or more	120.60	202	60.1
Bachelor's degree	108.42	182	34.4
Master's, professional, doctoral degree	141.87	238	25.7

Note: Market shares may not sum to 100.0 because of rounding and missing categories by household type. "Asian" and "black" include Hispanics and non-Hispanics who identify themselves as being of the respective race alone. "Hispanic" includes people of any race who identify themselves as Hispanic. "Other" includes people who identify themselves as non-Hispanic and as Alaska Native, American Indian, Asian (who are also included in the "Asian" row), or Native Hawaiian or other Pacific Islander as well as non-Hispanics reporting more than one race.

Source: Calculations by New Strategist based on the Bureau of Labor Statistics' 2010 Consumer Expenditure Survey

Athletic Gear, Game Tables, and Exercise Equipment

Best customers: **Householders aged 35 to 44**
Married couples with school-aged children

Customer trends: **Average household spending on athletic gear is likely to continue to decline as households tighten their belts and the small generation X fills the best-customer lifestage.**

The best customers of athletic gear, game tables, and exercise equipment are married couples with school-aged children. Householders aged 35 to 44, most with children, spend almost twice the average on athletic equipment, and married couples with school-aged children, almost three times the average. Householders aged 65 to 74 spent 53 percent more than average on this category in 2010.

Average household spending on athletic gear, game tables, and exercise equipment fell 36 percent between 2000 and 2010, after adjusting for inflation. The decline began long before the peak-spending year of 2006 and continued intensified with the Great Recession. As households tighten their belts and the small generation X fills the best-customer lifestage, average household spending on athletic gear is likely to decline further.

Table 5.3 Athletic gear, game tables, and exercise equipment

Total household spending $5,725,938,960.00
Average household spends 47.28

	AVERAGE HOUSEHOLD SPENDING	BEST CUSTOMERS (index)	BIGGEST CUSTOMERS (market share)
AGE OF HOUSEHOLDER			
Average household	**$47.28**	**100**	**100.0%**
Under age 25	25.59	54	3.6
Aged 25 to 34	32.62	69	11.5
Aged 35 to 44	86.54	183	33.1
Aged 45 to 54	42.53	90	18.6
Aged 55 to 64	43.44	92	16.2
Aged 65 to 74	72.17	153	16.4
Aged 75 or older	3.11	7	0.6

	AVERAGE HOUSEHOLD SPENDING	BEST CUSTOMERS (index)	BIGGEST CUSTOMERS (market share)
HOUSEHOLD INCOME			
Average household	**$47.28**	**100**	**100.0%**
Under $20,000	11.12	24	5.1
$20,000 to $39,999	49.15	104	23.8
$40,000 to $49,999	29.04	61	5.8
$50,000 to $69,999	39.20	83	11.9
$70,000 to $79,999	89.73	190	11.4
$80,000 to $99,999	41.45	88	7.3
$100,000 or more	96.69	205	35.1
HOUSEHOLD TYPE			
Average household	**47.28**	**100**	**100.0**
Married couples	69.55	147	72.6
Married couples, no children	56.62	120	25.4
Married couples, with children	89.10	188	43.8
Oldest child under age 6	24.84	53	2.2
Oldest child aged 6 to 17	136.59	289	34.0
Oldest child aged 18 or older	51.18	108	7.8
Single parent with child under age 18	40.60	86	5.1
Single person	21.39	45	13.3
RACE AND HISPANIC ORIGIN			
Average household	**47.28**	**100**	**100.0**
Asian	41.19	87	3.7
Black	35.60	75	9.2
Hispanic	26.05	55	6.7
Non-Hispanic white and other	52.49	111	84.2
REGION			
Average household	**47.28**	**100**	**100.0**
Northeast	52.99	112	20.6
Midwest	36.15	76	17.0
South	48.91	103	38.0
West	51.18	108	24.5
EDUCATION			
Average household	**47.28**	**100**	**100.0**
Less than high school graduate	44.86	95	13.6
High school graduate	35.13	74	19.0
Some college	36.48	77	16.2
Associate's degree	50.41	107	10.1
Bachelor's degree or more	65.83	139	41.4
Bachelor's degree	52.67	111	21.0
Master's, professional, doctoral degree	91.74	194	21.0

Note: Market shares may not sum to 100.0 because of rounding and missing categories by household type. "Asian" and "black" include Hispanics and non-Hispanics who identify themselves as being of the respective race alone. "Hispanic" includes people of any race who identify themselves as Hispanic. "Other" includes people who identify themselves as non-Hispanic and as Alaska Native, American Indian, Asian (who are also included in the "Asian" row), or Native Hawaiian or other Pacific Islander as well as non-Hispanics reporting more than one race.

Source: Calculations by New Strategist based on the Bureau of Labor Statistics' 2010 Consumer Expenditure Survey

Bicycles

Best customers: **Householders aged 25 to 54**
Married couples with children at home
Households in the Midwest and West
College graduates

Customer trends: **Average household spending on bicycles is likely to decline because the small**
generation X is in the best-customer lifestage—unless communities aggressively
promote the use of bicycles as an alternative to automobiles.

Parents are the best customers of bicycles, buying them for their children. Married couples with school-aged children spend two-and-one-half times the average on bicycles and control 30 percent of the market. Householders aged 25 to 54—most of them parents—spend 29 to 77 percent more than average on bicycles. Those aged 35 to 44 alone account for nearly one-third of the market as they spend 77 percent more than average on bicycles. Households in the Midwest and West outspend the average by 23 and 31 percent, respectively. College graduates spend a bit more than twice the average on this item.

Average household spending on bicycles fell 5 percent between 2000 and 2006, after adjusting for inflation, then increased 9 percent between 2006 and 2010. Spending on bicycles may decline in the years ahead because the small generation X is in the best-customer lifestage—unless communities aggressively promote the use of bicycles as an alternative to automobiles.

Table 5.4 Bicycles

Total household spending	$1,868,681,010.00
Average household spends	15.43

	AVERAGE HOUSEHOLD SPENDING	BEST CUSTOMERS (index)	BIGGEST CUSTOMERS (market share)
AGE OF HOUSEHOLDER			
Average household	**$15.43**	**100**	**100.0%**
Under age 25	10.28	67	4.4
Aged 25 to 34	19.92	129	21.5
Aged 35 to 44	27.29	177	32.0
Aged 45 to 54	20.15	131	27.0
Aged 55 to 64	10.54	68	12.0
Aged 65 to 74	3.35	22	2.3
Aged 75 or older	1.07	7	0.7

	AVERAGE HOUSEHOLD SPENDING	BEST CUSTOMERS (index)	BIGGEST CUSTOMERS (market share)
HOUSEHOLD INCOME			
Average household	**$15.43**	**100**	**100.0%**
Under $20,000	8.28	54	11.7
$20,000 to $39,999	5.95	39	8.8
$40,000 to $49,999	11.90	77	7.3
$50,000 to $69,999	12.67	82	11.8
$70,000 to $79,999	21.10	137	8.2
$80,000 to $99,999	20.45	133	11.1
$100,000 or more	37.00	240	41.1
HOUSEHOLD TYPE			
Average household	**15.43**	**100**	**100.0**
Married couples	20.00	130	63.9
Married couples, no children	10.30	67	14.2
Married couples, with children	30.62	198	46.2
Oldest child under age 6	28.06	182	7.8
Oldest child aged 6 to 17	38.71	251	29.5
Oldest child aged 18 or older	18.98	123	8.9
Single parent with child under age 18	11.11	72	4.2
Single person	7.07	46	13.4
RACE AND HISPANIC ORIGIN			
Average household	**15.43**	**100**	**100.0**
Asian	12.78	83	3.5
Black	7.37	48	5.8
Hispanic	10.27	67	8.1
Non-Hispanic white and other	17.54	114	86.2
REGION			
Average household	**15.43**	**100**	**100.0**
Northeast	8.55	55	10.2
Midwest	19.03	123	27.5
South	13.68	89	32.5
West	20.28	131	29.8
EDUCATION			
Average household	**15.43**	**100**	**100.0**
Less than high school graduate	6.36	41	5.9
High school graduate	5.81	38	9.6
Some college	13.02	84	17.7
Associate's degree	8.41	55	5.1
Bachelor's degree or more	31.99	207	61.6
Bachelor's degree	25.97	168	31.8
Master's, professional, doctoral degree	42.50	275	29.8

Note: Market shares may not sum to 100.0 because of rounding and missing categories by household type. "Asian" and "black" include Hispanics and non-Hispanics who identify themselves as being of the respective race alone. "Hispanic" includes people of any race who identify themselves as Hispanic. "Other" includes people who identify themselves as non-Hispanic and as Alaska Native, American Indian, Asian (who are also included in the "Asian" row), or Native Hawaiian or other Pacific Islander as well as non-Hispanics reporting more than one race.

Source: Calculations by New Strategist based on the Bureau of Labor Statistics' 2010 Consumer Expenditure Survey

Cable and Satellite Television Services

Best customers: **Householders aged 35 to 74**
                               Married couples

Customer trends: **Average household spending on cable and satellite television services will continue to rise if cable and satellite television can continue to innovate.**

Cable and satellite television service is the number-one entertainment expenditure of the average household. Because cable service is nearly universal, average household spending on the service does not vary much by demographic characteristic. By age, the best customers are householders ranging in age from 35 to 74, who spend 6 to 12 percent more than average on this item. Married couples without children at home (most of them empty-nesters) spend 18 percent more than average on cable television, while couples with children at home spend 12 percent more.

Spending on cable and satellite television service grew by a substantial 53 percent between 2000 and 2010, after adjusting for inflation. Behind the increase were more cable channels and services. If cable and satellite television can continue to innovate, households will continue to spend—at the expense of other entertainment categories, however.

Table 5.5 Cable and satellite television services

Total household spending $75,266,789,430.00
Average household spends   621.49

	AVERAGE HOUSEHOLD SPENDING	BEST CUSTOMERS (index)	BIGGEST CUSTOMERS (market share)
AGE OF HOUSEHOLDER			
Average household	**$621.49**	**100**	**100.0%**
Under age 25	329.23	53	3.5
Aged 25 to 34	551.25	89	14.8
Aged 35 to 44	656.52	106	19.1
Aged 45 to 54	672.62	108	22.4
Aged 55 to 64	693.65	112	19.7
Aged 65 to 74	679.94	109	11.8
Aged 75 or older	570.64	92	8.8

	AVERAGE HOUSEHOLD SPENDING	BEST CUSTOMERS (index)	BIGGEST CUSTOMERS (market share)
HOUSEHOLD INCOME			
Average household	**$621.49**	**100**	**100.0%**
Under $20,000	402.92	65	14.1
$20,000 to $39,999	539.35	87	19.9
$40,000 to $49,999	624.88	101	9.5
$50,000 to $69,999	678.92	109	15.7
$70,000 to $79,999	720.15	116	6.9
$80,000 to $99,999	763.70	123	10.2
$100,000 or more	855.93	138	23.6
HOUSEHOLD TYPE			
Average household	**621.49**	**100**	**100.0**
Married couples	716.92	115	56.9
Married couples, no children	733.12	118	25.1
Married couples, with children	697.41	112	26.1
Oldest child under age 6	646.55	104	4.5
Oldest child aged 6 to 17	699.24	113	13.2
Oldest child aged 18 or older	724.59	117	8.4
Single parent with child under age 18	554.39	89	5.3
Single person	471.21	76	22.2
RACE AND HISPANIC ORIGIN			
Average household	**621.49**	**100**	**100.0**
Asian	480.15	77	3.3
Black	621.57	100	12.2
Hispanic	499.85	80	9.8
Non-Hispanic white and other	641.16	103	78.2
REGION			
Average household	**621.49**	**100**	**100.0**
Northeast	678.72	109	20.0
Midwest	573.33	92	20.6
South	649.80	105	38.4
West	576.63	93	21.0
EDUCATION			
Average household	**621.49**	**100**	**100.0**
Less than high school graduate	472.07	76	10.9
High school graduate	614.70	99	25.3
Some college	591.35	95	20.0
Associate's degree	683.78	110	10.4
Bachelor's degree or more	700.69	113	33.5
Bachelor's degree	693.72	112	21.1
Master's, professional, doctoral degree	712.86	115	12.4

Note: Market shares may not sum to 100.0 because of rounding and missing categories by household type. "Asian" and "black" include Hispanics and non-Hispanics who identify themselves as being of the respective race alone. "Hispanic" includes people of any race who identify themselves as Hispanic. "Other" includes people who identify themselves as non-Hispanic and as Alaska Native, American Indian, Asian (who are also included in the "Asian" row), or Native Hawaiian or other Pacific Islander as well as non-Hispanics reporting more than one race.

Source: Calculations by New Strategist based on the Bureau of Labor Statistics' 2010 Consumer Expenditure Survey

Camping Equipment

The best customers of camping equipment are parents with children. Couples with children at home spend nearly two-and-one-half times the average on camping equipment. Householders aged 35 to 44, most with children, spend well over twice the average on this item and control 41 percent of the camping equipment market. Single parents spend 35 percent more than average. Households in the Midwest and West spend, respectively, 20 and 45 percent more than average on this item.

Average household spending on camping equipment dropped by half between 2000 and 2006, after adjusting for inflation, then rebounded by 19 percent between 2006 and 2010. One factor behind the decline was the exit of the baby-boom generation from the best-customer lifestage, and the increase could be due to belt-tightening as more families with children choose to camp rather than spend money on hotel rooms. Spending on camping equipment is likely may stabilize or even rise in the years ahead as the large millennial generation enters the best-customer lifestage

---

Table 5.6 **Camping equipment**

Total household spending $1,624,044,870.00
Average household spends   13.41

	AVERAGE HOUSEHOLD SPENDING	BEST CUSTOMERS (index)	BIGGEST CUSTOMERS (market share)
AGE OF HOUSEHOLDER			
Average household	**$13.41**	**100**	**100.0%**
Under age 25	0.43	3	0.2
Aged 25 to 34	16.73	125	20.8
Aged 35 to 44	30.37	226	41.0
Aged 45 to 54	15.13	113	23.3
Aged 55 to 64	6.58	49	8.7
Aged 65 to 74	5.59	42	4.5
Aged 75 or older	2.75	21	2.0

	AVERAGE HOUSEHOLD SPENDING	BEST CUSTOMERS (index)	BIGGEST CUSTOMERS (market share)
HOUSEHOLD INCOME			
Average household	**$13.41**	**100**	**100.0%**
Under $20,000	3.94	29	6.4
$20,000 to $39,999	8.01	60	13.7
$40,000 to $49,999	4.76	35	3.4
$50,000 to $69,999	12.38	92	13.2
$70,000 to $79,999	41.13	307	18.4
$80,000 to $99,999	15.08	112	9.4
$100,000 or more	29.00	216	37.1
HOUSEHOLD TYPE			
Average household	**13.41**	**100**	**100.0**
Married couples	19.10	142	70.3
Married couples, no children	7.23	54	11.5
Married couples, with children	32.31	241	56.0
Oldest child under age 6	19.31	144	6.2
Oldest child aged 6 to 17	38.16	285	33.5
Oldest child aged 18 or older	30.24	226	16.3
Single parent with child under age 18	18.15	135	8.0
Single person	5.11	38	11.2
RACE AND HISPANIC ORIGIN			
Average household	**13.41**	**100**	**100.0**
Asian	9.93	74	3.1
Black	5.96	44	5.4
Hispanic	11.04	82	10.0
Non-Hispanic white and other	14.95	111	84.5
REGION			
Average household	**13.41**	**100**	**100.0**
Northeast	7.36	55	10.1
Midwest	16.05	120	26.7
South	11.15	83	30.5
West	19.42	145	32.8
EDUCATION			
Average household	**13.41**	**100**	**100.0**
Less than high school graduate	8.35	62	8.9
High school graduate	3.80	28	7.2
Some college	14.01	104	22.0
Associate's degree	8.13	61	5.7
Bachelor's degree or more	25.41	189	56.3
Bachelor's degree	28.74	214	40.5
Master's, professional, doctoral degree	18.86	141	15.2

Note: Market shares may not sum to 100.0 because of rounding and missing categories by household type. "Asian" and "black" include Hispanics and non-Hispanics who identify themselves as being of the respective race alone. "Hispanic" includes people of any race who identify themselves as Hispanic. "Other" includes people who identify themselves as non-Hispanic and as Alaska Native, American Indian, Asian (who are also included in the "Asian" row), or Native Hawaiian or other Pacific Islander as well as non-Hispanics reporting more than one race.

Source: Calculations by New Strategist based on the Bureau of Labor Statistics' 2010 Consumer Expenditure Survey

Club Memberships (Social, Recreational, Health)

Best customers:

Householders aged 35 to 54
High-income households
Married couples without children at home
Married couples with school-aged or older children at home
Non-Hispanic whites
College graduates

Customer trends:

Average household spending on club memberships should begin to grow again in the years ahead as aging boomers gain more free time and look for ways to plug into their community—but only if discretionary income grows.

Club memberships are the sixth most important entertainment expenditure. Affluent, educated, middle-aged married couples are the best customers of clubs. These households are the glue of every community, funding and supporting a variety of organizations ranging from civic groups to the YMCA to country clubs. Householders aged 35 to 54 spend 20 to 43 percent more than the average household on memberships. Married couples without children at home (most of them empty-nesters) spend 47 percent more than average on this item. Couples with school-aged children spend well over twice the average, and those with adult children at home spend 56 percent more than average on club memberships. Non-Hispanic whites outspend minorities by a wide margin on this item and constitute 93 percent of the market. Households with incomes of $100,000 or more spend over three times the average on club memberships, and college graduates spend more than twice the average.

Average household spending on club memberships dropped 3 percent between 2000 and 2010, after adjusting for inflation. Between 2000 and 2006 (the year household spending peaked), households devoted more money to clubs. Then the Great Recession hit, and average household spending on club memberships dropped 10 percent between 2006 and 2010. Spending on club memberships should grow again in the years ahead as aging boomers gain more free time and look for ways to plug into their community—but only if discretionary income grows.

Table 5.7 Club memberships (social, recreational, health)

Total household spending $14,620,037,040.00
Average household spends   120.72

	AVERAGE HOUSEHOLD SPENDING	BEST CUSTOMERS (index)	BIGGEST CUSTOMERS (market share)
AGE OF HOUSEHOLDER			
Average household	**$120.72**	**100**	**100.0%**
Under age 25	34.62	29	1.9
Aged 25 to 34	97.43	81	13.4
Aged 35 to 44	172.47	143	25.8
Aged 45 to 54	144.86	120	24.8
Aged 55 to 64	126.69	105	18.5
Aged 65 to 74	101.47	84	9.0
Aged 75 or older	81.47	67	6.4

	AVERAGE HOUSEHOLD SPENDING	BEST CUSTOMERS (index)	BIGGEST CUSTOMERS (market share)
HOUSEHOLD INCOME			
Average household	$120.72	100	100.0%
Under $20,000	21.65	18	3.9
$20,000 to $39,999	37.23	31	7.1
$40,000 to $49,999	57.82	48	4.5
$50,000 to $69,999	90.12	75	10.7
$70,000 to $79,999	102.62	85	5.1
$80,000 to $99,999	132.26	110	9.1
$100,000 or more	419.37	347	59.6
HOUSEHOLD TYPE			
Average household	120.72	100	100.0
Married couples	185.29	153	75.7
Married couples, no children	177.70	147	31.3
Married couples, with children	215.55	179	41.5
Oldest child under age 6	109.25	90	3.9
Oldest child aged 6 to 17	271.08	225	26.4
Oldest child aged 18 or older	188.15	156	11.3
Single parent with child under age 18	56.68	47	2.8
Single person	52.77	44	12.8
RACE AND HISPANIC ORIGIN			
Average household	120.72	100	100.0
Asian	114.89	95	4.0
Black	29.36	24	3.0
Hispanic	40.34	33	4.1
Non-Hispanic white and other	148.14	123	93.0
REGION			
Average household	120.72	100	100.0
Northeast	128.39	106	19.5
Midwest	108.17	90	20.0
South	122.07	101	37.1
West	124.67	103	23.4
EDUCATION			
Average household	120.72	100	100.0
Less than high school graduate	13.31	11	1.6
High school graduate	43.62	36	9.2
Some college	79.08	66	13.8
Associate's degree	85.84	71	6.7
Bachelor's degree or more	279.21	231	68.7
Bachelor's degree	207.46	172	32.5
Master's, professional, doctoral degree	404.48	335	36.3

Note: Market shares may not sum to 100.0 because of rounding and missing categories by household type. "Asian" and "black" include Hispanics and non-Hispanics who identify themselves as being of the respective race alone. "Hispanic" includes people of any race who identify themselves as Hispanic. "Other" includes people who identify themselves as non-Hispanic and as Alaska Native, American Indian, Asian (who are also included in the "Asian" row), or Native Hawaiian or other Pacific Islander as well as non-Hispanics reporting more than one race.

Source: Calculations by New Strategist based on the Bureau of Labor Statistics' 2010 Consumer Expenditure Survey

Compact Disks, Audio Tapes, and Records

Best customers:
Householders aged 35 to 54
Married couples with school-aged or older children at home
Households in the West

Customer trends:
Average household spending on compact disks, audio tapes, and records will continue to decline as online downloads dominate music purchases.

Households with school-aged or older children at home dominate spending on compact disks, audio tapes, and records. Married couples with adult children at home spend 37 percent more than average on CDs, audio tapes, and records whereas those with school-aged children outspend the average by 29 percent. Householders aged 35 to 54 spend 15 to 22 percent more than average on this item. Households in the West spend 25 percent more than average on recordings.

Average household spending on CDs, audio tapes, and records fell by an enormous 72 percent between 2000 and 2010, after adjusting for inflation. The decline in spending will continue as downloads replace compact disks as the preferred way to purchase music.

Table 5.8 Compact disks, audio tapes, and records

Total household spending $1,670,065,530.00
Average household spends   13.79

	AVERAGE HOUSEHOLD SPENDING	BEST CUSTOMERS (index)	BIGGEST CUSTOMERS (market share)
AGE OF HOUSEHOLDER			
Average household	**$13.79**	**100**	**100.0%**
Under age 25	10.23	74	4.9
Aged 25 to 34	14.60	106	17.6
Aged 35 to 44	15.92	115	20.9
Aged 45 to 54	16.86	122	25.3
Aged 55 to 64	14.85	108	19.0
Aged 65 to 74	10.61	77	8.3
Aged 75 or older	5.76	42	4.0

	AVERAGE HOUSEHOLD SPENDING	BEST CUSTOMERS (index)	BIGGEST CUSTOMERS (market share)
HOUSEHOLD INCOME			
Average household	**$13.79**	**100**	**100.0%**
Under $20,000	6.30	46	10.0
$20,000 to $39,999	10.72	78	17.8
$40,000 to $49,999	12.67	92	8.7
$50,000 to $69,999	13.85	100	14.4
$70,000 to $79,999	16.29	118	7.1
$80,000 to $99,999	20.59	149	12.4
$100,000 or more	23.80	173	29.6
HOUSEHOLD TYPE			
Average household	**13.79**	**100**	**100.0**
Married couples	15.54	113	55.6
Married couples, no children	14.02	102	21.6
Married couples, with children	17.11	124	28.9
Oldest child under age 6	12.30	89	3.8
Oldest child aged 6 to 17	17.77	129	15.2
Oldest child aged 18 or older	18.89	137	9.9
Single parent with child under age 18	13.36	97	5.7
Single person	9.85	71	20.9
RACE AND HISPANIC ORIGIN			
Average household	**13.79**	**100**	**100.0**
Asian	12.75	92	3.9
Black	14.13	102	12.5
Hispanic	13.57	98	12.0
Non-Hispanic white and other	13.73	100	75.5
REGION			
Average household	**13.79**	**100**	**100.0**
Northeast	13.90	101	18.5
Midwest	12.41	90	20.1
South	12.41	90	33.0
West	17.27	125	28.4
EDUCATION			
Average household	**13.79**	**100**	**100.0**
Less than high school graduate	7.67	56	7.9
High school graduate	11.08	80	20.5
Some college	13.25	96	20.2
Associate's degree	15.58	113	10.7
Bachelor's degree or more	18.86	137	40.6
Bachelor's degree	18.74	136	25.7
Master's, professional, doctoral degree	19.07	138	15.0

Note: Market shares may not sum to 100.0 because of rounding and missing categories by household type. "Asian" and "black" include Hispanics and non-Hispanics who identify themselves as being of the respective race alone. "Hispanic" includes people of any race who identify themselves as Hispanic. "Other" includes people who identify themselves as non-Hispanic and as Alaska Native, American Indian, Asian (who are also included in the "Asian" row), or Native Hawaiian or other Pacific Islander as well as non-Hispanics reporting more than one race.

Source: Calculations by New Strategist based on the Bureau of Labor Statistics' 2010 Consumer Expenditure Survey

Fees for Participant Sports
(Including on Trips)

Best customers:	**Householders aged 35 to 54**
	Married couples without children at home
	Married couples with school-aged or older children at home
	Non-Hispanic whites
Customer trends:	**Average household spending on fees for participant sports is likely to continue to decline because the small generation X is in the best-customer lifestage.**

Fees for participant sports include a broad range of recreational charges from greens fees for golfers to fees for children's sports leagues. Those who spend the most on fees for participant sports are middle-aged married couples with children at home. Householders aged 35 to 54 spend 33 to 44 percent more than average on fees for participant sports and account for 54 percent of the market. Married couples without children at home (most of them empty-nesters) spend 22 percent more than average on this item. Couples with school-aged children spend more than twice the average on fees for participant sports, and those with adult children at home spend 68 percent more than average. Non-Hispanic whites outspend the minorities by a wide margin on this item and control 92 percent of the market for participant sports fees.

Average household spending on fees for participant sports declined 20 percent between 2000 and 2010, after adjusting for inflation. Spending on this category is likely to continue to decline because the small generation X is in the best-customer lifestage.

Table 5.9 Fees for participant sports (including on trips)

Total household spending $13,109,832,750.00
Average household spends   108.25

	AVERAGE HOUSEHOLD SPENDING	BEST CUSTOMERS (index)	BIGGEST CUSTOMERS (market share)
AGE OF HOUSEHOLDER			
Average household	**$108.25**	**100**	**100.0%**
Under age 25	34.83	32	2.1
Aged 25 to 34	78.52	73	12.1
Aged 35 to 44	155.91	144	26.1
Aged 45 to 54	143.84	133	27.5
Aged 55 to 64	93.35	86	15.2
Aged 65 to 74	101.82	94	10.1
Aged 75 or older	78.93	73	7.0

	AVERAGE HOUSEHOLD SPENDING	BEST CUSTOMERS (index)	BIGGEST CUSTOMERS (market share)
HOUSEHOLD INCOME			
Average household	**$108.25**	**100**	**100.0%**
Under $20,000	26.15	24	5.3
$20,000 to $39,999	40.98	38	8.7
$40,000 to $49,999	90.67	84	7.9
$50,000 to $69,999	107.44	99	14.2
$70,000 to $79,999	160.50	148	8.9
$80,000 to $99,999	138.74	128	10.7
$100,000 or more	284.15	262	45.0
HOUSEHOLD TYPE			
Average household	**108.25**	**100**	**100.0**
Married couples	160.18	148	73.0
Married couples, no children	131.61	122	25.8
Married couples, with children	196.58	182	42.2
Oldest child under age 6	47.62	44	1.9
Oldest child aged 6 to 17	257.85	238	28.0
Oldest child aged 18 or older	182.24	168	12.2
Single parent with child under age 18	79.64	74	4.3
Single person	48.28	45	13.1
RACE AND HISPANIC ORIGIN			
Average household	**108.25**	**100**	**100.0**
Asian	95.33	88	3.7
Black	25.78	24	2.9
Hispanic	45.67	42	5.1
Non-Hispanic white and other	131.20	121	91.9
REGION			
Average household	**108.25**	**100**	**100.0**
Northeast	110.24	102	18.7
Midwest	113.60	105	23.4
South	94.43	87	32.0
West	124.00	115	25.9
EDUCATION			
Average household	**108.25**	**100**	**100.0**
Less than high school graduate	36.56	34	4.8
High school graduate	74.54	69	17.6
Some college	75.49	70	14.7
Associate's degree	80.02	74	7.0
Bachelor's degree or more	203.16	188	55.8
Bachelor's degree	182.93	169	31.9
Master's, professional, doctoral degree	241.67	223	24.2

Note: Market shares may not sum to 100.0 because of rounding and missing categories by household type. "Asian" and "black" include Hispanics and non-Hispanics who identify themselves as being of the respective race alone. "Hispanic" includes people of any race who identify themselves as Hispanic. "Other" includes people who identify themselves as non-Hispanic and as Alaska Native, American Indian, Asian (who are also included in the "Asian" row), or Native Hawaiian or other Pacific Islander as well as non-Hispanics reporting more than one race.

Source: Calculations by New Strategist based on the Bureau of Labor Statistics' 2010 Consumer Expenditure Survey

Fees for Recreational Lessons

Best customers:	**Householders aged 35 to 54** **High-income households** **Married couples with school-aged children at home** **Asians** **Households in the Northeast and West** **College graduates**
Customer trends:	**Average household spending on fees for recreational lessons may continue to decline in the years ahead as households tighten their belts and because the small generation X is in the best-customer lifestage.**

Married couples with school-aged children spend four-and-one-half times the average on fees for recreational lessons and control 53 percent of the market. Householders aged 35 to 54, who are likely to be parents, spend from 70 percent more to over twice the average on this category. Households with incomes of $100,000 or more spend three-and-one-half times the average on recreational lessons and control 60 percent of the market. Asians spend three times the average on fees for recreational lessons, and college graduates well over twice the average. Households in the Northeast spend 58 percent more than average on fees for recreational lessons, and those in the West spend 30 percent more.

Average household spending on fees for recreational lessons climbed 16 percent between 2000 and 2006, after adjusting for inflation. Behind the rise was the parental frenzy to ensure that children are well rounded. The Great Recession disrupted those dreams, however, and in the 2006-to-2010 time period spending on this item fell by 14 percent. Spending on fees for recreational lessons may continue to decline in the years ahead as households tighten their belts and because the small generation X is in the best-customer lifestage.

Table 5.10 Fees for recreational lessons

Total household spending $11,433,711,870.00
Average household spends   94.41

	AVERAGE HOUSEHOLD SPENDING	BEST CUSTOMERS (index)	BIGGEST CUSTOMERS (market share)
AGE OF HOUSEHOLDER			
Average household	**$94.41**	**100**	**100.0%**
Under age 25	32.62	35	2.3
Aged 25 to 34	62.44	66	11.0
Aged 35 to 44	205.28	217	39.3
Aged 45 to 54	160.76	170	35.2
Aged 55 to 64	42.53	45	7.9
Aged 65 to 74	27.59	29	3.1
Aged 75 or older	10.29	11	1.0

	AVERAGE HOUSEHOLD SPENDING	BEST CUSTOMERS (index)	BIGGEST CUSTOMERS (market share)
HOUSEHOLD INCOME			
Average household	**$94.41**	**100**	**100.0%**
Under $20,000	15.20	16	3.5
$20,000 to $39,999	22.96	24	5.6
$40,000 to $49,999	41.99	44	4.2
$50,000 to $69,999	61.39	65	9.3
$70,000 to $79,999	80.31	85	5.1
$80,000 to $99,999	138.22	146	12.2
$100,000 or more	330.84	350	60.1
HOUSEHOLD TYPE			
Average household	**94.41**	**100**	**100.0**
Married couples	155.18	164	81.1
Married couples, no children	28.67	30	6.5
Married couples, with children	273.11	289	67.3
Oldest child under age 6	136.97	145	6.2
Oldest child aged 6 to 17	422.86	448	52.7
Oldest child aged 18 or older	109.95	116	8.4
Single parent with child under age 18	81.57	86	5.1
Single person	21.22	22	6.6
RACE AND HISPANIC ORIGIN			
Average household	**94.41**	**100**	**100.0**
Asian	285.54	302	12.9
Black	40.11	42	5.2
Hispanic	58.47	62	7.5
Non-Hispanic white and other	109.09	116	87.6
REGION			
Average household	**94.41**	**100**	**100.0**
Northeast	149.47	158	29.1
Midwest	83.25	88	19.7
South	56.13	59	21.8
West	122.82	130	29.5
EDUCATION			
Average household	**94.41**	**100**	**100.0**
Less than high school graduate	8.19	9	1.2
High school graduate	37.67	40	10.2
Some college	59.57	63	13.3
Associate's degree	79.05	84	7.9
Bachelor's degree or more	214.18	227	67.4
Bachelor's degree	176.45	187	35.3
Master's, professional, doctoral degree	280.05	297	32.1

Note: Market shares may not sum to 100.0 because of rounding and missing categories by household type. "Asian" and "black" include Hispanics and non-Hispanics who identify themselves as being of the respective race alone. "Hispanic" includes people of any race who identify themselves as Hispanic. "Other" includes people who identify themselves as non-Hispanic and as Alaska Native, American Indian, Asian (who are also included in the "Asian" row), or Native Hawaiian or other Pacific Islander as well as non-Hispanics reporting more than one race.

Source: Calculations by New Strategist based on the Bureau of Labor Statistics' 2010 Consumer Expenditure Survey

Film

Best customers: Householders aged 45 to 54 and 65 to 74
                             Married couples with school-aged children
                             Asians
                             Households in the Northeast and Midwest

Customer trends: Average household spending on film will disappear as digital cameras make film obsolete.

Married couples with school-aged children at home spend 58 percent more than the average household on film as they photograph the milestones in their children's lives the old-fashioned way. Householders aged 45 to 54 (many with children) and 65 to 74 (many with grandchildren) spend, respectively, 50 and 32 percent more than average on film.Asian householders spend 33 percent more than average on film. Households in the Northeast and Midwest spend, respectively, 49 and 30 percent more than average on this item.

Average household spending on film fell by an enormous 95 percent between 2000 and 2010, after adjusting for inflation. Behind the decline was the shift to digital photography, rendering film obsolete. This trend should continue as virtually all households replace their film cameras with digital models.

Table 5.11 Film

Total household spending $148,961,610.00
Average household spends   1.23

	AVERAGE HOUSEHOLD SPENDING	BEST CUSTOMERS (index)	BIGGEST CUSTOMERS (market share)
AGE OF HOUSEHOLDER			
Average household	**$1.23**	**100**	**100.0%**
Under age 25	0.51	41	2.8
Aged 25 to 34	0.82	67	11.1
Aged 35 to 44	1.44	117	21.2
Aged 45 to 54	1.85	150	31.1
Aged 55 to 64	1.12	91	16.1
Aged 65 to 74	1.62	132	14.2
Aged 75 or older	0.50	41	3.9

	AVERAGE HOUSEHOLD SPENDING	BEST CUSTOMERS (index)	BIGGEST CUSTOMERS (market share)
HOUSEHOLD INCOME			
Average household	**$1.23**	**100**	**100.0%**
Under $20,000	0.64	52	11.4
$20,000 to $39,999	0.87	71	16.3
$40,000 to $49,999	0.88	72	6.8
$50,000 to $69,999	0.96	78	11.2
$70,000 to $79,999	1.90	154	9.2
$80,000 to $99,999	1.35	110	9.2
$100,000 or more	2.61	212	36.4
HOUSEHOLD TYPE			
Average household	**1.23**	**100**	**100.0**
Married couples	1.49	121	59.8
Married couples, no children	1.25	102	21.6
Married couples, with children	1.60	130	30.3
Oldest child under age 6	1.18	96	4.1
Oldest child aged 6 to 17	1.94	158	18.5
Oldest child aged 18 or older	1.28	104	7.5
Single parent with child under age 18	1.17	95	5.6
Single person	0.83	67	19.8
RACE AND HISPANIC ORIGIN			
Average household	**1.23**	**100**	**100.0**
Asian	1.64	133	5.7
Black	1.02	83	10.1
Hispanic	0.95	77	9.4
Non-Hispanic white and other	1.31	107	80.7
REGION			
Average household	**1.23**	**100**	**100.0**
Northeast	1.83	149	27.3
Midwest	1.60	130	29.0
South	0.86	70	25.7
West	1.00	81	18.4
EDUCATION			
Average household	**1.23**	**100**	**100.0**
Less than high school graduate	0.77	63	8.9
High school graduate	0.92	75	19.1
Some college	1.00	81	17.1
Associate's degree	1.31	107	10.1
Bachelor's degree or more	1.87	152	45.2
Bachelor's degree	2.17	176	33.3
Master's, professional, doctoral degree	1.35	110	11.9

Note: Market shares may not sum to 100.0 because of rounding and missing categories by household type. "Asian" and "black" include Hispanics and non-Hispanics who identify themselves as being of the respective race alone. "Hispanic" includes people of any race who identify themselves as Hispanic. "Other" includes people who identify themselves as non-Hispanic and as Alaska Native, American Indian, Asian (who are also included in the "Asian" row), or Native Hawaiian or other Pacific Islander as well as non-Hispanics reporting more than one race.

Source: Calculations by New Strategist based on the Bureau of Labor Statistics' 2010 Consumer Expenditure Survey

Hunting and Fishing Equipment

Best customers: **Householders aged 25 to 34 and 55 to 74**
Married couples without children at home
Married couples with school-aged or older children at home
Non-Hispanic whites
Households in the South

Customer trends: **Average household spending on hunting and fishing equipment is likely to**
continue to decline as a growing share of the American population lives in
metropolitan areas.

Non-Hispanic white householders living in the South are the best customers of hunting and fishing equipment. Whites control 90 percent of the market for hunting and fishing equipment and households in the South spend 62 percent above average on this item. By age, young and old spend on hunting and fishing equipment. Householders aged 25 to 34 spend 19 percent more than average, householders aged 55 to 64, 23 percent more, and householders aged 65 to 74, 84 percent more than average on this item. Married couples without children at home spend 46 percent more than average on hunting and fishing equipment. Couples with adult children at home spend nearly two-and-one-half times the average on this item, and those with school-aged children spend one-quarter more than average.

Average household spending on hunting and fishing equipment has been in decline since 2000, falling 20 percent over the decade after adjusting for inflation. Behind the spending decline is the growing urbanization of the American population, with more than 80 percent of the population now living in a metropolitan area. Spending on hunting and fishing equipment is likely to continue to decline as this trend continues.

Table 5.12 Hunting and fishing equipment

Total household spending $3,169,370,190.00
Average household spends   26.17

	AVERAGE HOUSEHOLD SPENDING	BEST CUSTOMERS (index)	BIGGEST CUSTOMERS (market share)
AGE OF HOUSEHOLDER			
Average household	**$26.17**	**100**	**100.0%**
Under age 25	9.34	36	2.4
Aged 25 to 34	31.03	119	19.7
Aged 35 to 44	18.01	69	12.5
Aged 45 to 54	26.65	102	21.1
Aged 55 to 64	32.17	123	21.7
Aged 65 to 74	48.03	184	19.7
Aged 75 or older	7.17	27	2.6

	AVERAGE HOUSEHOLD SPENDING	BEST CUSTOMERS (index)	BIGGEST CUSTOMERS (market share)
HOUSEHOLD INCOME			
Average household	**$26.17**	**100**	**100.0%**
Under $20,000	7.99	31	6.7
$20,000 to $39,999	27.15	104	23.8
$40,000 to $49,999	12.76	49	4.6
$50,000 to $69,999	19.81	76	10.9
$70,000 to $79,999	17.27	66	4.0
$80,000 to $99,999	50.12	192	16.0
$100,000 or more	52.79	202	34.6
HOUSEHOLD TYPE			
Average household	**26.17**	**100**	**100.0**
Married couples	36.47	139	68.7
Married couples, no children	38.12	146	30.9
Married couples, with children	39.34	150	35.0
Oldest child under age 6	14.80	57	2.4
Oldest child aged 6 to 17	32.08	123	14.4
Oldest child aged 18 or older	62.73	240	17.3
Single parent with child under age 18	3.84	15	0.9
Single person	20.70	79	23.2
RACE AND HISPANIC ORIGIN			
Average household	**26.17**	**100**	**100.0**
Asian	5.83	22	0.9
Black	6.20	24	2.9
Hispanic	15.94	61	7.4
Non-Hispanic white and other	30.93	118	89.6
REGION			
Average household	**26.17**	**100**	**100.0**
Northeast	14.69	56	10.3
Midwest	24.78	95	21.1
South	42.36	162	59.4
West	10.33	39	8.9
EDUCATION			
Average household	**26.17**	**100**	**100.0**
Less than high school graduate	18.12	69	9.9
High school graduate	24.05	92	23.5
Some college	25.94	99	20.8
Associate's degree	21.34	82	7.7
Bachelor's degree or more	33.40	128	37.9
Bachelor's degree	27.84	106	20.1
Master's, professional, doctoral degree	44.35	169	18.3

Note: Market shares may not sum to 100.0 because of rounding and missing categories by household type. "Asian" and "black" include Hispanics and non-Hispanics who identify themselves as being of the respective race alone. "Hispanic" includes people of any race who identify themselves as Hispanic. "Other" includes people who identify themselves as non-Hispanic and as Alaska Native, American Indian, Asian (who are also included in the "Asian" row), or Native Hawaiian or other Pacific Islander as well as non-Hispanics reporting more than one race.

Source: Calculations by New Strategist based on the Bureau of Labor Statistics' 2010 Consumer Expenditure Survey

Live Entertainment for Catered Affairs

Best customers: Householders aged 25 to 34 and 45 to 54
High-income households
Asians and Hispanics
Households in the Northeast

Customer trends: Average household spending on live entertainment for catered affairs is likely to decline in the years ahead as households tighten their belts.

The best customers of live entertainment for catered affairs are affluent householders whose children are marrying. Households with incomes of $100,000 or more spend three-and-one-half times the average on live entertainment, as do Asian householders, a relatively well-to-do demographic. Hispanic householders spend nearly twice the average, and households in the Northeast spend over twice the average on this item. Householders aged 25 to 34 outspend the average by two-thirds and those aged 45 to 54 do so by three-quarters.

Live entertainment for catered affairs is a relatively new item in the Consumer Expenditure Survey, and comparable data from 2000 or 2006 do not exist. Average household spending on this item is likely to decline in the years ahead as households tighten their belts.

Table 5.13 Live entertainment for catered affairs

Total household spending — $1,252,246,380.00
Average household spends — 10.34

	AVERAGE HOUSEHOLD SPENDING	BEST CUSTOMERS (index)	BIGGEST CUSTOMERS (market share)
AGE OF HOUSEHOLDER			
Average household	**$10.34**	**100**	**100.0%**
Under age 25	10.68	103	6.9
Aged 25 to 34	17.03	165	27.4
Aged 35 to 44	7.50	73	13.1
Aged 45 to 54	17.83	172	35.7
Aged 55 to 64	8.26	80	14.1
Aged 65 to 74	1.02	10	1.1
Aged 75 or older	1.94	19	1.8

	AVERAGE HOUSEHOLD SPENDING	BEST CUSTOMERS (index)	BIGGEST CUSTOMERS (market share)
HOUSEHOLD INCOME			
Average household	**$10.34**	**100**	**100.0%**
Under $20,000	0.23	2	0.5
$20,000 to $39,999	3.90	38	8.7
$40,000 to $49,999	6.61	64	6.0
$50,000 to $69,999	5.77	56	8.0
$70,000 to $79,999	14.16	137	8.2
$80,000 to $99,999	8.58	83	6.9
$100,000 or more	37.36	361	62.0
HOUSEHOLD TYPE			
Average household	**10.34**	**100**	**100.0**
Married couples	13.62	132	65.0
Married couples, no children	12.36	120	25.4
Married couples, with children	9.91	96	22.3
Oldest child under age 6	1.27	12	0.5
Oldest child aged 6 to 17	11.65	113	13.2
Oldest child aged 18 or older	12.18	118	8.5
Single parent with child under age 18	7.06	68	4.0
Single person	3.10	30	8.8
RACE AND HISPANIC ORIGIN			
Average household	**10.34**	**100**	**100.0**
Asian	37.56	363	15.4
Black	4.55	44	5.4
Hispanic	19.65	190	23.2
Non-Hispanic white and other	9.75	94	71.5
REGION			
Average household	**10.34**	**100**	**100.0**
Northeast	22.62	219	40.1
Midwest	10.15	98	21.9
South	4.34	42	15.4
West	10.31	100	22.6
EDUCATION			
Average household	**10.34**	**100**	**100.0**
Less than high school graduate	5.71	55	7.9
High school graduate	8.65	84	21.4
Some college	3.70	36	7.5
Associate's degree	11.86	115	10.8
Bachelor's degree or more	18.24	176	52.4
Bachelor's degree	11.97	116	21.9
Master's, professional, doctoral degree	29.18	282	30.5

Note: Market shares may not sum to 100.0 because of rounding and missing categories by household type. "Asian" and "black" include Hispanics and non-Hispanics who identify themselves as being of the respective race alone. "Hispanic" includes people of any race who identify themselves as Hispanic. "Other" includes people who identify themselves as non-Hispanic and as Alaska Native, American Indian, Asian (who are also included in the "Asian" row), or Native Hawaiian or other Pacific Islander as well as non-Hispanics reporting more than one race.

Source: Calculations by New Strategist based on the Bureau of Labor Statistics' 2010 Consumer Expenditure Survey

Movie, Theater, Amusement Park, and Other Admissions (Including on Trips)

Best customers:

Householders aged 35 to 54
Married couples with school-aged or older children at home
Households in the West

Customer trends:

Average household spending on movie, theater, and amusement park tickets may continue to decline as households tighten their belts and the small generation X occupies the best-customer lifestage.

Spending on movie tickets dominates this item, which is the fourth-largest entertainment spending category. The best customers of movie, theater, amusement park, and other admissions are teenagers, which explains why householders aged 35 to 54 spend 24 to 25 percent more than average on this item—many have teenagers at home. Married couples with school-aged children spend 88 percent more than average on movie, theater, amusement park, and other admissions, and those with adult children at home, 31 percent. Households in the West spend 30 percent more than average on admissions.

Average household spending on movie, theater, amusement park and other admissions fell 9 percent between 2000 and 2010, after adjusting for inflation. Behind the decline in spending was changing technology, as DVDs and pay-per-view streaming allowed consumers to see movies at home rather than in a theater, as well as belt-tightening in response to the Great Recession. Spending on this category is likely to decline during the next few years as households continue to economize and the small generation X occupies the best-customer lifestage.

Table 5.14 Movie, theater, amusement park, and other admissions (including on trips)

Total household spending	$18,771,585,000.00
Average household spends	155.00

	AVERAGE HOUSEHOLD SPENDING	BEST CUSTOMERS (index)	BIGGEST CUSTOMERS (market share)
AGE OF HOUSEHOLDER			
Average household	**$155.00**	**100**	**100.0%**
Under age 25	91.84	59	3.9
Aged 25 to 34	141.89	92	15.2
Aged 35 to 44	191.95	124	22.4
Aged 45 to 54	193.75	125	25.9
Aged 55 to 64	161.28	104	18.4
Aged 65 to 74	138.83	90	9.6
Aged 75 or older	74.26	48	4.6

	AVERAGE HOUSEHOLD SPENDING	BEST CUSTOMERS (index)	BIGGEST CUSTOMERS (market share)
HOUSEHOLD INCOME			
Average household	$155.00	100	100.0%
Under $20,000	43.01	28	6.1
$20,000 to $39,999	78.76	51	11.6
$40,000 to $49,999	100.87	65	6.2
$50,000 to $69,999	139.76	90	12.9
$70,000 to $79,999	170.64	110	6.6
$80,000 to $99,999	223.44	144	12.0
$100,000 or more	403.24	260	44.6
HOUSEHOLD TYPE			
Average household	155.00	100	100.0
Married couples	208.10	134	66.2
Married couples, no children	185.63	120	25.4
Married couples, with children	237.10	153	35.6
Oldest child under age 6	144.26	93	4.0
Oldest child aged 6 to 17	291.42	188	22.1
Oldest child aged 18 or older	203.68	131	9.5
Single parent with child under age 18	132.72	86	5.0
Single person	89.41	58	16.9
RACE AND HISPANIC ORIGIN			
Average household	155.00	100	100.0
Asian	162.04	105	4.4
Black	68.59	44	5.4
Hispanic	125.41	81	9.9
Non-Hispanic white and other	173.84	112	85.0
REGION			
Average household	155.00	100	100.0
Northeast	170.42	110	20.2
Midwest	145.69	94	21.0
South	124.22	80	29.4
West	201.53	130	29.5
EDUCATION			
Average household	155.00	100	100.0
Less than high school graduate	39.41	25	3.6
High school graduate	82.01	53	13.5
Some college	145.49	94	19.7
Associate's degree	153.87	99	9.4
Bachelor's degree or more	280.40	181	53.7
Bachelor's degree	257.42	166	31.4
Master's, professional, doctoral degree	320.50	207	22.4

Note: Market shares may not sum to 100.0 because of rounding and missing categories by household type. "Asian" and "black" include Hispanics and non-Hispanics who identify themselves as being of the respective race alone. "Hispanic" includes people of any race who identify themselves as Hispanic. "Other" includes people who identify themselves as non-Hispanic and as Alaska Native, American Indian, Asian (who are also included in the "Asian" row), or Native Hawaiian or other Pacific Islander as well as non-Hispanics reporting more than one race.

Source: Calculations by New Strategist based on the Bureau of Labor Statistics' 2010 Consumer Expenditure Survey

Musical Instruments and Accessories, Purchase, Rental, and Repair

Best customers: Householders under age 25 and aged 45 to 64
High-income households
Married couples with school-aged or older children at home
Households in the West and Northeast
College graduates

Customer trends: Average household spending on the purchase, rental, and repair of musical instruments and accessories is likely to decline further in the years ahead as households and school districts tighten their belts.

The best customers of purchase, rental, and repair of musical instruments and accessories are families with children. Married couples with school-aged children spend over twice the average, while couples with adult children at home spend 55 percent more than average on musical instruments and their rental and repair. Householders under age 25 and those aged 45 to 54 outspend the average on this item by 24 percent, whereas householders aged 55 to 64 do so by 37 percent. High-income households spend three times the average on musical instruments. Households in the West and Northeast spend, respectively, 46 and 34 percent more than average on musical instruments and account for a 58 percent share of the market. College graduates, the most affluent demographic, spend twice the average on this item.

Average household spending on the purchase, rental, and repair of musical instruments and accessories fell by a steep 60 percent between 2000 and 2010, after adjusting for inflation. Behind the decline are school budget woes, which make fewer music programs available to schoolchildren. Spending on this item is likely to decline further in the years ahead as households and school districts tighten their belts.

Table 5.15 Musical Instruments and Accessories, Purchase, Rental, and Repair

Total household spending $2,020,064,760.00
Average household spends 16.68

	AVERAGE HOUSEHOLD SPENDING	BEST CUSTOMERS (index)	BIGGEST CUSTOMERS (market share)
AGE OF HOUSEHOLDER			
Average household	**$16.68**	**100**	**100.0%**
Under age 25	20.72	124	8.2
Aged 25 to 34	18.34	110	18.3
Aged 35 to 44	17.36	104	18.8
Aged 45 to 54	20.63	124	25.6
Aged 55 to 64	22.78	137	24.1
Aged 65 to 74	6.85	41	4.4
Aged 75 or older	0.96	6	0.5

	AVERAGE HOUSEHOLD SPENDING	BEST CUSTOMERS (index)	BIGGEST CUSTOMERS (market share)
HOUSEHOLD INCOME			
Average household	**$16.68**	**100**	**100.0%**
Under $20,000	7.95	48	10.4
$20,000 to $39,999	6.41	38	8.8
$40,000 to $49,999	11.79	71	6.7
$50,000 to $69,999	7.50	45	6.4
$70,000 to $79,999	12.95	78	4.6
$80,000 to $99,999	20.96	126	10.5
$100,000 or more	51.20	307	52.6
HOUSEHOLD TYPE			
Average household	**16.68**	**100**	**100.0**
Married couples	22.17	133	65.6
Married couples, no children	18.08	108	23.0
Married couples, with children	27.87	167	38.9
Oldest child under age 6	9.88	59	2.5
Oldest child aged 6 to 17	35.66	214	25.1
Oldest child aged 18 or older	25.83	155	11.2
Single parent with child under age 18	8.34	50	2.9
Single person	12.65	76	22.2
RACE AND HISPANIC ORIGIN			
Average household	**16.68**	**100**	**100.0**
Asian	16.37	98	4.2
Black	9.82	59	7.2
Hispanic	7.03	42	5.1
Non-Hispanic white and other	19.40	116	88.2
REGION			
Average household	**16.68**	**100**	**100.0**
Northeast	22.41	134	24.7
Midwest	17.49	105	23.4
South	8.57	51	18.9
West	24.40	146	33.1
EDUCATION			
Average household	**16.68**	**100**	**100.0**
Less than high school graduate	2.53	15	2.2
High school graduate	6.44	39	9.9
Some college	14.15	85	17.8
Associate's degree	17.53	105	9.9
Bachelor's degree or more	33.82	203	60.2
Bachelor's degree	37.67	226	42.7
Master's, professional, doctoral degree	27.10	162	17.6

Note: Market shares may not sum to 100.0 because of rounding and missing categories by household type. "Asian" and "black" include Hispanics and non-Hispanics who identify themselves as being of the respective race alone. "Hispanic" includes people of any race who identify themselves as Hispanic. "Other" includes people who identify themselves as non-Hispanic and as Alaska Native, American Indian, Asian (who are also included in the "Asian" row), or Native Hawaiian or other Pacific Islander as well as non-Hispanics reporting more than one race.

Source: Calculations by New Strategist based on the Bureau of Labor Statistics' 2010 Consumer Expenditure Survey

Personal Digital Audio Players

Best customers: **Householders aged 35 to 54**
Married couples with school-aged or older children at home
Households in the Northeast

Customer trends: **Average household spending on personal digital audio players may continue to decline in the years ahead as digital players wither in the competition with smartphones that offer music functions.**

Apple's sleek iPods have created such a demand for personal digital audio players that the Bureau of Labor Statistics added them as a new expenditure category in 2005. The best customers of these devices are married couples with children. Married couples with school-aged children spend almost three times the average on this item, while those with adult children at home spend 38 percent more than average. Householders aged 35 to 54, many of them with children at home, spend 26 to 86 percent more than average on personal digital audio players. Households in the Northeast outspend the average for personal digital audio players by 24 percent.

There are no decade-long spending trends for this new product category. Between 2006 and 2010, spending on personal digital audio players declined by a stunning 39 percent. Behind the decline was price discounting as less expensive products entered the market. Average household spending on personal digital audio players may continue to decline in the years ahead as this product competes with smartphones that offer music functions.

Table 5.16 Personal digital audio players

Total household spending	$1,383,041,940.00
Average household spends	11.42

	AVERAGE HOUSEHOLD SPENDING	BEST CUSTOMERS (index)	BIGGEST CUSTOMERS (market share)
AGE OF HOUSEHOLDER			
Average household	**$11.42**	**100**	**100.0%**
Under age 25	8.65	76	5.0
Aged 25 to 34	12.66	111	18.5
Aged 35 to 44	21.26	186	33.7
Aged 45 to 54	14.37	126	26.0
Aged 55 to 64	7.99	70	12.3
Aged 65 to 74	3.56	31	3.4
Aged 75 or older	1.35	12	1.1

	AVERAGE HOUSEHOLD SPENDING	BEST CUSTOMERS (index)	BIGGEST CUSTOMERS (market share)
HOUSEHOLD INCOME			
Average household	**$11.42**	**100**	**100.0%**
Under $20,000	3.27	29	6.2
$20,000 to $39,999	5.03	44	10.1
$40,000 to $49,999	10.52	92	8.7
$50,000 to $69,999	10.87	95	13.7
$70,000 to $79,999	12.36	108	6.5
$80,000 to $99,999	24.85	218	18.1
$100,000 or more	24.44	214	36.7
HOUSEHOLD TYPE			
Average household	**11.42**	**100**	**100.0**
Married couples	15.75	138	68.0
Married couples, no children	7.04	62	13.1
Married couples, with children	23.02	202	46.9
Oldest child under age 6	7.95	70	3.0
Oldest child aged 6 to 17	32.98	289	34.0
Oldest child aged 18 or older	15.73	138	9.9
Single parent with child under age 18	10.31	90	5.3
Single person	6.60	58	16.9
RACE AND HISPANIC ORIGIN			
Average household	**11.42**	**100**	**100.0**
Asian	5.62	49	2.1
Black	5.05	44	5.4
Hispanic	11.61	102	12.4
Non-Hispanic white and other	12.44	109	82.6
REGION			
Average household	**11.42**	**100**	**100.0**
Northeast	14.11	124	22.7
Midwest	11.37	100	22.2
South	9.85	86	31.7
West	11.84	104	23.5
EDUCATION			
Average household	**11.42**	**100**	**100.0**
Less than high school graduate	4.84	42	6.1
High school graduate	7.61	67	17.0
Some college	13.01	114	23.9
Associate's degree	10.27	90	8.5
Bachelor's degree or more	17.11	150	44.5
Bachelor's degree	14.86	130	24.6
Master's, professional, doctoral degree	21.02	184	19.9

Note: Market shares may not sum to 100.0 because of rounding and missing categories by household type. "Asian" and "black" include Hispanics and non-Hispanics who identify themselves as being of the respective race alone. "Hispanic" includes people of any race who identify themselves as Hispanic. "Other" includes people who identify themselves as non-Hispanic and as Alaska Native, American Indian, Asian (who are also included in the "Asian" row), or Native Hawaiian or other Pacific Islander as well as non-Hispanics reporting more than one race.

Source: Calculations by New Strategist based on the Bureau of Labor Statistics' 2010 Consumer Expenditure Survey

Pet Food

Best customers: **Householders aged 35 to 74**
Married couples
Non-Hispanic whites

Customer trends: **Average household spending on pet food could stabilize or even decline in the years ahead as households forego pet ownership because of the sharply higher expense.**

Middle-aged and older married couples spend the most on pets. Many acquire pets when their children are young and care for them long after their children have grown and left home. Pet food accounts for the largest share of pet expenses and ranks second in dollar terms among entertainment items. Householders aged 35 to 74 spend 10 to 48 percent more than the average household on pet food. Married couples spend 26 percent more than average, with the figure peaking at 34 percent among those without children at home (most of them empty-nesters). Non-Hispanic whites spend 19 percent more than the average on pet food and control 90 percent of the market

Average household spending on pet food rose by a steep 52 percent between 2000 and 2010, after adjusting for inflation. Between 2009 and 2010, however, spending on pet food fell 4 percent (not shown in table) as consumers reacted to the shock of higher pet costs. Spending on pet food could stabilize or even decline in the years ahead as households forego pet ownership because of the sharply higher expense.

Table 5.17 Pet food

Total household spending $20,006,876,400.00
Average household spends 165.20

	AVERAGE HOUSEHOLD SPENDING	BEST CUSTOMERS (index)	BIGGEST CUSTOMERS (market share)
AGE OF HOUSEHOLDER			
Average household	**$165.20**	**100**	**100.0%**
Under age 25	57.47	35	2.3
Aged 25 to 34	120.58	73	12.2
Aged 35 to 44	181.35	110	19.9
Aged 45 to 54	193.61	117	24.2
Aged 55 to 64	187.74	114	20.0
Aged 65 to 74	244.11	148	15.9
Aged 75 or older	91.67	55	5.3

	AVERAGE HOUSEHOLD SPENDING	BEST CUSTOMERS (index)	BIGGEST CUSTOMERS (market share)
HOUSEHOLD INCOME			
Average household	$165.20	100	100.0%
Under $20,000	81.53	49	10.8
$20,000 to $39,999	146.37	89	20.3
$40,000 to $49,999	153.83	93	8.8
$50,000 to $69,999	160.12	97	13.9
$70,000 to $79,999	236.40	143	8.6
$80,000 to $99,999	206.96	125	10.4
$100,000 or more	262.45	159	27.2
HOUSEHOLD TYPE			
Average household	165.20	100	100.0
Married couples	207.59	126	62.0
Married couples, no children	220.57	134	28.4
Married couples, with children	197.23	119	27.8
Oldest child under age 6	183.25	111	4.7
Oldest child aged 6 to 17	193.69	117	13.8
Oldest child aged 18 or older	209.66	127	9.2
Single parent with child under age 18	81.02	49	2.9
Single person	100.51	61	17.8
RACE AND HISPANIC ORIGIN			
Average household	165.20	100	100.0
Asian	47.96	29	1.2
Black	36.39	22	2.7
Hispanic	93.57	57	6.9
Non-Hispanic white and other	196.93	119	90.4
REGION			
Average household	165.20	100	100.0
Northeast	146.24	89	16.2
Midwest	153.26	93	20.7
South	178.94	108	39.8
West	170.18	103	23.3
EDUCATION			
Average household	165.20	100	100.0
Less than high school graduate	109.36	66	9.5
High school graduate	156.81	95	24.2
Some college	171.24	104	21.8
Associate's degree	169.79	103	9.7
Bachelor's degree or more	191.37	116	34.4
Bachelor's degree	196.72	119	22.5
Master's, professional, doctoral degree	180.83	109	11.8

Note: Market shares may not sum to 100.0 because of rounding and missing categories by household type. "Asian" and "black" include Hispanics and non-Hispanics who identify themselves as being of the respective race alone. "Hispanic" includes people of any race who identify themselves as Hispanic. "Other" includes people who identify themselves as non-Hispanic and as Alaska Native, American Indian, Asian (who are also included in the "Asian" row), or Native Hawaiian or other Pacific Islander as well as non-Hispanics reporting more than one race.

Source: Calculations by New Strategist based on the Bureau of Labor Statistics' 2010 Consumer Expenditure Survey

Pet Purchase, Supplies, and Medicines

Best customers: **Householders aged 35 to 64**
Married couples without children at home
Married couples with school-aged or older children at home
Non-Hispanic whites

Customer trends: **Average household spending on pet purchases, supplies, and medicines could**
stabilize or even decline in the years ahead as households forego pet ownership
because of the sharply higher expense.

Pets are so popular in the United States that spending on pet purchase, supplies, and medicines does not vary much by demographic characteristic, except by race and Hispanic origin. Householders ranging in age from 35 to 64 spend 15 to 32 percent more than average on pet purchase, supplies, and medicines. Married couples spend 23 percent more, the figure peaking at 43 percent among couples with adult children at home. To understand the market, it is almost more helpful to know who is least likely to spend on pets—single parents, single persons, householders with the lowest incomes, the youngest and the oldest householders, and minority householders all spend considerably less than average on pet purchase, supplies, and medicines.

Average household spending on pet purchase, supplies, and medicines more than doubled between 2000 and 2010, after adjusting for inflation, as pharmaceutical companies offered a growing variety of pricey medications. Between 2009 and 2010, however, spending on this category fell 4 percent (not shown in table) as consumers reacted to the shock of higher pet costs. This category, which now ranks third among entertainment items in dollar terms, could stabilize or even decline in the years ahead as households forego pet ownership because of the sharply higher expense.

Table 5.18 Pet purchase, supplies, and medicines

| Total household spending | $19,681,098,570.00 |
| Average household spends | 162.51 |

	AVERAGE HOUSEHOLD SPENDING	BEST CUSTOMERS (index)	BIGGEST CUSTOMERS (market share)
AGE OF HOUSEHOLDER			
Average household	**$162.51**	**100**	**100.0%**
Under age 25	79.31	49	3.2
Aged 25 to 34	148.72	92	15.2
Aged 35 to 44	187.06	115	20.8
Aged 45 to 54	214.59	132	27.3
Aged 55 to 64	186.53	115	20.2
Aged 65 to 74	138.51	85	9.2
Aged 75 or older	67.57	42	4.0

	AVERAGE HOUSEHOLD SPENDING	BEST CUSTOMERS (index)	BIGGEST CUSTOMERS (market share)
HOUSEHOLD INCOME			
Average household	**$162.51**	**100**	**100.0%**
Under $20,000	86.65	53	11.6
$20,000 to $39,999	123.49	76	17.4
$40,000 to $49,999	159.04	98	9.2
$50,000 to $69,999	183.28	113	16.2
$70,000 to $79,999	227.39	140	8.4
$80,000 to $99,999	207.67	128	10.7
$100,000 or more	251.12	155	26.5
HOUSEHOLD TYPE			
Average household	**162.51**	**100**	**100.0**
Married couples	199.85	123	60.7
Married couples, no children	200.85	124	26.3
Married couples, with children	197.12	121	28.2
Oldest child under age 6	128.45	79	3.4
Oldest child aged 6 to 17	200.67	123	14.5
Oldest child aged 18 or older	232.07	143	10.3
Single parent with child under age 18	100.61	62	3.7
Single person	111.83	69	20.2
RACE AND HISPANIC ORIGIN			
Average household	**162.51**	**100**	**100.0**
Asian	59.09	36	1.5
Black	53.28	33	4.0
Hispanic	116.98	72	8.8
Non-Hispanic white and other	187.32	115	87.4
REGION			
Average household	**162.51**	**100**	**100.0**
Northeast	144.06	89	16.3
Midwest	143.03	88	19.6
South	183.63	113	41.5
West	162.39	100	22.6
EDUCATION			
Average household	**162.51**	**100**	**100.0**
Less than high school graduate	108.94	67	9.6
High school graduate	149.51	92	23.5
Some college	152.47	94	19.7
Associate's degree	201.14	124	11.7
Bachelor's degree or more	194.26	120	35.5
Bachelor's degree	189.48	117	22.0
Master's, professional, doctoral degree	202.60	125	13.5

Note: Market shares may not sum to 100.0 because of rounding and missing categories by household type. "Asian" and "black" include Hispanics and non-Hispanics who identify themselves as being of the respective race alone. "Hispanic" includes people of any race who identify themselves as Hispanic. "Other" includes people who identify themselves as non-Hispanic and as Alaska Native, American Indian, Asian (who are also included in the "Asian" row), or Native Hawaiian or other Pacific Islander as well as non-Hispanics reporting more than one race.

Source: Calculations by New Strategist based on the Bureau of Labor Statistics' 2010 Consumer Expenditure Survey

Pet Services

Best customers: **Householders aged 35 to 64**
Married couples without children at home
Married couples with school-aged or older children at home
Non-Hispanic whites
Households in the West

Customer trends: **Average household spending on pet services could stabilize or even decline in the years ahead as households forego pet ownership because of the sharply higher expense.**

The best customers of pet services—such as grooming and day care—are middle-aged and older married couples. Householders ranging in age from 35 to 64 spend 23 to 44 percent more than average on this item. Married couples with adult children at home spend 50 percent more than average on pet services and those without children at home (most of them empty-nesters) spend 59 percent more than average. The spending of couples with school-aged children exceeds the average by 28 percent. Non-Hispanic whites outspend minorities by a large margin and account for 91 percent of the market. Households in the West spend 38 percent more than average on pet services.

Average household spending on pet services rose 59 percent between 2000 and 2010, after adjusting for inflation. Between 2009 and 2010, however, spending on pet services fell 12 percent (not shown in table) as consumers reacted to the shock of higher pet costs. Spending on pet services could stabilize or even decline in the years ahead as households forego pet ownership because of the sharply higher expense.

Table 5.19 Pet services

Total household spending $4,707,429,090.00
Average household spends   38.87

	AVERAGE HOUSEHOLD SPENDING	BEST CUSTOMERS (index)	BIGGEST CUSTOMERS (market share)
AGE OF HOUSEHOLDER			
Average household	**$38.87**	**100**	**100.0%**
Under age 25	11.43	29	2.0
Aged 25 to 34	20.36	52	8.7
Aged 35 to 44	47.92	123	22.3
Aged 45 to 54	55.97	144	29.8
Aged 55 to 64	52.08	134	23.6
Aged 65 to 74	31.97	82	8.8
Aged 75 or older	19.34	50	4.7

	AVERAGE HOUSEHOLD SPENDING	BEST CUSTOMERS (index)	BIGGEST CUSTOMERS (market share)
HOUSEHOLD INCOME			
Average household	**$38.87**	**100**	**100.0%**
Under $20,000	11.61	30	6.5
$20,000 to $39,999	16.01	41	9.4
$40,000 to $49,999	22.26	57	5.4
$50,000 to $69,999	36.46	94	13.5
$70,000 to $79,999	38.75	100	6.0
$80,000 to $99,999	63.61	164	13.6
$100,000 or more	103.29	266	45.6
HOUSEHOLD TYPE			
Average household	**38.87**	**100**	**100.0**
Married couples	53.16	137	67.5
Married couples, no children	61.62	159	33.7
Married couples, with children	50.94	131	30.5
Oldest child under age 6	41.34	106	4.6
Oldest child aged 6 to 17	49.85	128	15.1
Oldest child aged 18 or older	58.42	150	10.9
Single parent with child under age 18	6.81	18	1.0
Single person	30.78	79	23.2
RACE AND HISPANIC ORIGIN			
Average household	**38.87**	**100**	**100.0**
Asian	16.66	43	1.8
Black	13.34	34	4.2
Hispanic	21.22	55	6.7
Non-Hispanic white and other	46.85	121	91.4
REGION			
Average household	**38.87**	**100**	**100.0**
Northeast	39.05	100	18.4
Midwest	36.42	94	20.9
South	31.05	80	29.3
West	53.81	138	31.4
EDUCATION			
Average household	**38.87**	**100**	**100.0**
Less than high school graduate	10.38	27	3.8
High school graduate	21.29	55	14.0
Some college	27.42	71	14.8
Associate's degree	63.27	163	15.4
Bachelor's degree or more	68.01	175	52.0
Bachelor's degree	69.66	179	33.9
Master's, professional, doctoral degree	65.12	168	18.1

Note: Market shares may not sum to 100.0 because of rounding and missing categories by household type. "Asian" and "black" include Hispanics and non-Hispanics who identify themselves as being of the respective race alone. "Hispanic" includes people of any race who identify themselves as Hispanic. "Other" includes people who identify themselves as non-Hispanic and as Alaska Native, American Indian, Asian (who are also included in the "Asian" row), or Native Hawaiian or other Pacific Islander as well as non-Hispanics reporting more than one race.

Source: Calculations by New Strategist based on the Bureau of Labor Statistics' 2010 Consumer Expenditure Survey

Photographer's Fees

Best customers:	**Householders aged 25 to 54** **Married couples with children under age 18** **Single parents** **Hispanics** **Households in the West**
Customer trends:	**Average household spending on photographer's fees is likely to decline in the years ahead as households tighten their belts and professional photographers lose ground in the competition with digital technology.**

Average household spending on photographer's fees is all about children, and the best customers of this item are parents. Householders ranging in age from 25 to 54 spend 52 to 63 percent more than average on this item because most are parents. Married couples with preschoolers spend almost four times the average, while those with school-aged children spend three times the average on photographer's fees. Single parents outspend the average by 64 percent. Hispanics spend 30 percent more than average on photographer's fees, and average spending on this item by households in the West, where many Hispanics reside, tops the average by 54 percent.

Average household spending on photographer's fees dropped by a substantial 35 percent between 2000 and 2010, almost all of the decline coming since 2006. Spending on this category is likely to continue to decline in the years ahead as households tighten their belts and professional photographers lose ground in the competition with digital technology.

Table 5.20 Photographer's fees

Total household spending	$2,012,798,340.00
Average household spends	16.62

	AVERAGE HOUSEHOLD SPENDING	BEST CUSTOMERS (index)	BIGGEST CUSTOMERS (market share)
AGE OF HOUSEHOLDER			
Average household	**$16.62**	**100**	**100.0%**
Under age 25	18.69	112	7.5
Aged 25 to 34	25.79	155	25.8
Aged 35 to 44	25.22	152	27.5
Aged 45 to 54	27.13	163	33.8
Aged 55 to 64	3.81	23	4.0
Aged 65 to 74	2.09	13	1.4
Aged 75 or older	–	–	–

	AVERAGE HOUSEHOLD SPENDING	BEST CUSTOMERS (index)	BIGGEST CUSTOMERS (market share)
HOUSEHOLD INCOME			
Average household	**$16.62**	**100**	**100.0%**
Under $20,000	5.28	32	6.9
$20,000 to $39,999	8.82	53	12.2
$40,000 to $49,999	8.49	51	4.8
$50,000 to $69,999	7.51	45	6.5
$70,000 to $79,999	32.41	195	11.7
$80,000 to $99,999	31.75	191	15.9
$100,000 or more	44.36	267	45.8
HOUSEHOLD TYPE			
Average household	**16.62**	**100**	**100.0**
Married couples	24.37	147	72.3
Married couples, no children	3.24	19	4.1
Married couples, with children	40.27	242	56.4
Oldest child under age 6	63.91	385	16.5
Oldest child aged 6 to 17	50.43	303	35.7
Oldest child aged 18 or older	13.03	78	5.7
Single parent with child under age 18	27.29	164	9.7
Single person	7.33	44	12.9
RACE AND HISPANIC ORIGIN			
Average household	**16.62**	**100**	**100.0**
Asian	15.64	94	4.0
Black	17.64	106	13.0
Hispanic	21.56	130	15.8
Non-Hispanic white and other	15.64	94	71.3
REGION			
Average household	**16.62**	**100**	**100.0**
Northeast	7.67	46	8.5
Midwest	16.48	99	22.1
South	15.76	95	34.8
West	25.52	154	34.8
EDUCATION			
Average household	**16.62**	**100**	**100.0**
Less than high school graduate	8.23	50	7.1
High school graduate	3.66	22	5.6
Some college	33.00	199	41.7
Associate's degree	27.99	168	15.9
Bachelor's degree or more	15.98	96	28.6
Bachelor's degree	9.00	54	10.2
Master's, professional, doctoral degree	29.75	179	19.4

Note: Market shares may not sum to 100.0 because of rounding and missing categories by household type. "Asian" and "black" include Hispanics and non-Hispanics who identify themselves as being of the respective race alone. "Hispanic" includes people of any race who identify themselves as Hispanic. "Other" includes people who identify themselves as non-Hispanic and as Alaska Native, American Indian, Asian (who are also included in the Asian column), or Native Hawaiian or other Pacific Islander as well as non-Hispanics reporting more than one race. "–" means sample is too small to make a reliable estimate.

Source: Calculations by New Strategist based on the Bureau of Labor Statistics' 2010 Consumer Expenditure Survey

Photographic Equipment

Best customers: **Householders under age 55**
High-income households
Married couples
Asians
Households in the West

Customer trends: **Average household spending on photographic equipment is likely to continue to decline now that digital cameras have replaced film cameras in most homes and smartphones with cameras are dampening demand for stand-alone equipment.**

Household spending on digital cameras is the driving force in this category. The best customers of photographic equipment are well-to-do households and married couples with children under age 18. The parents of toddlers spend 36 percent more than average on photographic equipment, and couples with school-aged children spend twice the average. Households with incomes of $100,000 or more spend three times the average on photographic equipment. The spending on this item by Asian householders, a relatively affluent group, exceeds the average by 30 percent, and households in the West, where many Asians reside, top average spending by 43 percent.

Average household spending on photographic equipment fell 5 percent between 2000 and 2010, after adjusting for inflation. Between 2000 and 2006 (the year household spending peaked), spending on photographic equipment grew 38 percent, but between 2006 and 2010 spending on this item fell 31 percent. The replacement of film cameras with digital cameras was behind the increase earlier in the decade—a substitution that is largely complete. Behind the more-recent decline is the substitution of smartphone cameras for digital cameras. Spending on photographic equipment is likely to continue this decline in the years ahead as smartphone cameras dampen demand for stand-alone equipment.

Table 5.21 Photographic equipment

Total household spending $2,936,844,750.00
Average household spends   24.25

	AVERAGE HOUSEHOLD SPENDING	BEST CUSTOMERS (index)	BIGGEST CUSTOMERS (market share)
AGE OF HOUSEHOLDER			
Average household	**$24.25**	**100**	**100.0%**
Under age 25	36.48	150	10.0
Aged 25 to 34	28.16	116	19.3
Aged 35 to 44	28.11	116	21.0
Aged 45 to 54	26.99	111	23.0
Aged 55 to 64	21.60	89	15.7
Aged 65 to 74	19.37	80	8.6
Aged 75 or older	6.09	25	2.4

	AVERAGE HOUSEHOLD SPENDING	BEST CUSTOMERS (index)	BIGGEST CUSTOMERS (market share)
HOUSEHOLD INCOME			
Average household	**$24.25**	**100**	**100.0%**
Under $20,000	5.43	22	4.9
$20,000 to $39,999	11.17	46	10.6
$40,000 to $49,999	16.46	68	6.4
$50,000 to $69,999	14.76	61	8.7
$70,000 to $79,999	25.16	104	6.2
$80,000 to $99,999	32.82	135	11.3
$100,000 or more	73.45	303	51.9
HOUSEHOLD TYPE			
Average household	**24.25**	**100**	**100.0**
Married couples	34.93	144	71.1
Married couples, no children	33.23	137	29.1
Married couples, with children	38.24	158	36.7
Oldest child under age 6	33.02	136	5.8
Oldest child aged 6 to 17	48.32	199	23.4
Oldest child aged 18 or older	24.92	103	7.4
Single parent with child under age 18	9.10	38	2.2
Single person	10.16	42	12.3
RACE AND HISPANIC ORIGIN			
Average household	**24.25**	**100**	**100.0**
Asian	31.52	130	5.5
Black	13.36	55	6.7
Hispanic	20.42	84	10.3
Non-Hispanic white and other	26.76	110	83.7
REGION			
Average household	**24.25**	**100**	**100.0**
Northeast	24.30	100	18.4
Midwest	24.17	100	22.2
South	17.84	74	27.0
West	34.68	143	32.4
EDUCATION			
Average household	**24.25**	**100**	**100.0**
Less than high school graduate	7.18	30	4.2
High school graduate	14.30	59	15.1
Some college	21.49	89	18.6
Associate's degree	18.64	77	7.3
Bachelor's degree or more	44.76	185	54.8
Bachelor's degree	44.68	184	34.8
Master's, professional, doctoral degree	44.90	185	20.0

Note: Market shares may not sum to 100.0 because of rounding and missing categories by household type. "Asian" and "black" include Hispanics and non-Hispanics who identify themselves as being of the respective race alone. "Hispanic" includes people of any race who identify themselves as Hispanic. "Other" includes people who identify themselves as non-Hispanic and as Alaska Native, American Indian, Asian (who are also included in the "Asian" row), or Native Hawaiian or other Pacific Islander as well as non-Hispanics reporting more than one race.

Source: Calculations by New Strategist based on the Bureau of Labor Statistics' 2010 Consumer Expenditure Survey

Photographic Processing

Best customers:	Householders aged 35 to 54 and 65 to 74
	Married couples
	Non-Hispanic whites
	Households in the Midwest and West
Customer trends:	Average household spending on photo processing will continue to slip as home printers reduce processing needs.

The best customers of photographic processing are married couples with children. Couples with preschoolers spend well over twice the average on photographic processing as they get digital pictures of their children processed into prints. Couples with school-aged or older children at home spend 37 to 69 percent more than average on this item. Householders aged 35 to 54, many of them parents, spend 17 to 24 percent more than average on photographic processing. Householders aged 65 to 74, many of them grandparents, spend 18 percent more than average, and married couples without children at home (most of them older empty-nesters) spend 35 percent more than average on photographic processing. Households in the Midwest spend 26 percent more on photographic processing than the average household, and those in the West spend 19 percent more. Non-Hispanic whites spend 19 percent more than average on this item and account for 90 percent of the market.

Average household spending on photographic processing fell by an enormous 71 percent between 2000 and 2010, after adjusting for inflation. Behind the decline was the shift to digital photography, which allows families to process pictures on their computers and printers at home. Spending on photographic processing will continue to decline as this trend continues.

Table 5.22 Photographic processing

| Total household spending | $1,383,041,940.00 |
| Average household spends | 11.42 |

	AVERAGE HOUSEHOLD SPENDING	BEST CUSTOMERS (index)	BIGGEST CUSTOMERS (market share)
AGE OF HOUSEHOLDER			
Average household	**$11.42**	**100**	**100.0%**
Under age 25	6.41	56	3.7
Aged 25 to 34	10.93	96	15.9
Aged 35 to 44	13.38	117	21.2
Aged 45 to 54	14.14	124	25.6
Aged 55 to 64	11.09	97	17.1
Aged 65 to 74	13.49	118	12.7
Aged 75 or older	4.39	38	3.7

	AVERAGE HOUSEHOLD SPENDING	BEST CUSTOMERS (index)	BIGGEST CUSTOMERS (market share)
HOUSEHOLD INCOME			
Average household	**$11.42**	**100**	**100.0%**
Under $20,000	3.05	27	5.8
$20,000 to $39,999	5.97	52	12.0
$40,000 to $49,999	8.22	72	6.8
$50,000 to $69,999	12.93	113	16.2
$70,000 to $79,999	11.74	103	6.2
$80,000 to $99,999	14.54	127	10.6
$100,000 or more	28.22	247	42.4
HOUSEHOLD TYPE			
Average household	**11.42**	**100**	**100.0**
Married couples	17.01	149	73.5
Married couples, no children	15.41	135	28.7
Married couples, with children	19.56	171	39.8
Oldest child under age 6	26.77	234	10.0
Oldest child aged 6 to 17	19.30	169	19.9
Oldest child aged 18 or older	15.70	137	9.9
Single parent with child under age 18	6.18	54	3.2
Single person	4.94	43	12.7
RACE AND HISPANIC ORIGIN			
Average household	**11.42**	**100**	**100.0**
Asian	11.67	102	4.3
Black	3.78	33	4.1
Hispanic	5.37	47	5.7
Non-Hispanic white and other	13.61	119	90.4
REGION			
Average household	**11.42**	**100**	**100.0**
Northeast	10.59	93	17.0
Midwest	14.43	126	28.2
South	8.63	76	27.7
West	13.64	119	27.1
EDUCATION			
Average household	**11.42**	**100**	**100.0**
Less than high school graduate	3.37	30	4.2
High school graduate	7.51	66	16.8
Some college	9.62	84	17.7
Associate's degree	10.28	90	8.5
Bachelor's degree or more	20.28	178	52.8
Bachelor's degree	19.68	172	32.6
Master's, professional, doctoral degree	21.33	187	20.2

Note: Market shares may not sum to 100.0 because of rounding and missing categories by household type. "Asian" and "black" include Hispanics and non-Hispanics who identify themselves as being of the respective race alone. "Hispanic" includes people of any race who identify themselves as Hispanic. "Other" includes people who identify themselves as non-Hispanic and as Alaska Native, American Indian, Asian (who are also included in the "Asian" row), or Native Hawaiian or other Pacific Islander as well as non-Hispanics reporting more than one race.

Source: Calculations by New Strategist based on the Bureau of Labor Statistics' 2010 Consumer Expenditure Survey

Recreational Vehicles (Boats, Campers, Trailers), Purchase and Rental

Best customers:	**Householders aged 45 to 64** **High-income households** **Married couples without children at home** **Married couples with children under age 18** **Non-Hispanic whites** **Households in the Midwest**
Customer trends:	**Average household spending on the purchase and rental of recreational vehicles is likely to continue its decline as households tighten their belts and early retirement becomes less common.**

Middle-aged and older householders are the best customers of the purchase and rental of recreational vehicles—such as boats, trailers, and campers. Householders aged 45 to 64 spend 36 to 94 percent more than average on this item. Households with incomes of $100,000 or more spend over four times the average on the purchase and rental of recreational vehicles. Married couples without children at home (most of them empty-nesters) spend 81 percent more than average on recreational vehicles. Married couples with children under age 18 spend 31 to 46 percent more than average on this item. Non-Hispanic whites completely dominate the recreational vehicle market and account for nearly 100 percent of spending in this category. Households in the Midwest outspend the average by 82 percent.

Average household spending on the purchase and rental of recreational vehicles, the fifth-largest entertainment category, declined 17 percent between 2000 and 2010, after adjusting for inflation. The spending increase on this category in the earlier part of the decade was more than canceled out by a 41 percent decline in spending since 2006, the overall peak spending year. Behind the earlier increase were low-interest loans available during the time period, spurring many retirees to buy recreational vehicles. Behind the later decline is belt-tightening in the face of the Great Recession. Spending in this category is likely to continue its decline in the years ahead as households further curtail discretionary spending and early retirement becomes less common.

Table 5.23 Recreational Vehicles (Boats, Campers, Trailers), Purchase and Rental

Total household spending	$16,872,627,240.00
Average household spends	139.32

	AVERAGE HOUSEHOLD SPENDING	BEST CUSTOMERS (index)	BIGGEST CUSTOMERS (market share)
AGE OF HOUSEHOLDER			
Average household	**$139.32**	**100**	**100.0%**
Under age 25	8.05	6	0.4
Aged 25 to 34	101.48	73	12.1
Aged 35 to 44	109.86	79	14.3
Aged 45 to 54	270.34	194	40.1
Aged 55 to 64	189.76	136	24.0
Aged 65 to 74	80.06	57	6.2
Aged 75 or older	41.95	30	2.9

	AVERAGE HOUSEHOLD SPENDING	BEST CUSTOMERS (index)	BIGGEST CUSTOMERS (market share)
HOUSEHOLD INCOME			
Average household	**$139.32**	**100**	**100.0%**
Under $20,000	27.99	20	4.4
$20,000 to $39,999	16.24	12	2.7
$40,000 to $49,999	35.77	26	2.4
$50,000 to $69,999	122.20	88	12.6
$70,000 to $79,999	45.86	33	2.0
$80,000 to $99,999	82.81	59	5.0
$100,000 or more	584.11	419	71.9
HOUSEHOLD TYPE			
Average household	**139.32**	**100**	**100.0**
Married couples	239.51	172	84.8
Married couples, no children	252.32	181	38.5
Married couples, with children	159.36	114	26.6
Oldest child under age 6	203.83	146	6.3
Oldest child aged 6 to 17	182.89	131	15.4
Oldest child aged 18 or older	94.66	68	4.9
Single parent with child under age 18	–	–	–
Single person	42.86	31	9.0
RACE AND HISPANIC ORIGIN			
Average household	**139.32**	**100**	**100.0**
Asian	–	–	–
Black	–	–	–
Hispanic	2.76	2	0.2
Non-Hispanic white and other	182.76	131	99.5
REGION			
Average household	**139.32**	**100**	**100.0**
Northeast	174.03	125	22.9
Midwest	253.67	182	40.6
South	88.43	63	23.3
West	81.12	58	13.2
EDUCATION			
Average household	**139.32**	**100**	**100.0**
Less than high school graduate	10.62	8	1.1
High school graduate	49.35	35	9.0
Some college	194.01	139	29.3
Associate's degree	279.31	200	18.9
Bachelor's degree or more	195.31	140	41.6
Bachelor's degree	131.97	95	17.9
Master's, professional, doctoral degree	305.90	220	23.8

Note: Market shares may not sum to 100.0 because of rounding and missing categories by household type. "Asian" and "black" include Hispanics and non-Hispanics who identify themselves as being of the respective race alone. "Hispanic" includes people of any race who identify themselves as Hispanic. "Other" includes people who identify themselves as non-Hispanic and as Alaska Native, American Indian, Asian (who are also included in the Asian column), or Native Hawaiian or other Pacific Islander as well as non-Hispanics reporting more than one race. "–" means sample is too small to make a reliable estimate.

Source: Calculations by New Strategist based on the Bureau of Labor Statistics' 2010 Consumer Expenditure Survey.

Rental of Party Supplies for Catered Affairs

Best customers:
Householders aged 25 to 34 and 45 to 54
High-income households
Married couples with school-aged or older children at home
Asians and Hispanics
Households in the Northeast

Customer trends:
Average household spending on the rental of party supplies for catered affairs is likely to decline in the years ahead as households tighten their belts.

The best customers of rental of party supplies for catered affairs are affluent householders. Households with incomes of $100,000 or more spend three-and-one-half times the average on party supplies rental, as do Asian householders, a relatively well-off demographic. Hispanic householders spend 56 percent more than average on this item, and households in the Northeast spend 71 percent more. Householders aged 25 to 34 outspend the average by three-quarters and those aged 45 to 54 do so by one-half. Married couples with school-aged children spend 58 percent more than average on rental of party supplies for catered affairs, while couples with adult children at home spend more than twice the average on this item.

Rental of party supplies for catered affairs is a relatively new item in the Consumer Expenditure Survey, and comparable data from 2000 or 2006 do not exist. Average household spending on this item is likely to decline in the years ahead as households tighten their belts.

Table 5.24 **Rental of party supplies for catered affairs**

Total household spending: $1,541,692,110.00
Average household spends: 12.73

	AVERAGE HOUSEHOLD SPENDING	BEST CUSTOMERS (index)	BIGGEST CUSTOMERS (market share)
AGE OF HOUSEHOLDER			
Average household	**$12.73**	**100**	**100.0%**
Under age 25	11.48	90	6.0
Aged 25 to 34	22.15	174	29.0
Aged 35 to 44	11.85	93	16.8
Aged 45 to 54	19.78	155	32.1
Aged 55 to 64	9.44	74	13.1
Aged 65 to 74	3.28	26	2.8
Aged 75 or older	0.28	2	0.2

	AVERAGE HOUSEHOLD SPENDING	BEST CUSTOMERS (index)	BIGGEST CUSTOMERS (market share)
HOUSEHOLD INCOME			
Average household	**$12.73**	**100**	**100.0%**
Under $20,000	2.05	16	3.5
$20,000 to $39,999	1.91	15	3.4
$40,000 to $49,999	5.15	40	3.8
$50,000 to $69,999	3.70	29	4.2
$70,000 to $79,999	12.90	101	6.1
$80,000 to $99,999	26.51	208	17.4
$100,000 or more	45.77	360	61.7
HOUSEHOLD TYPE			
Average household	**12.73**	**100**	**100.0**
Married couples	18.53	146	71.8
Married couples, no children	15.02	118	25.1
Married couples, with children	20.39	160	37.3
Oldest child under age 6	7.59	60	2.6
Oldest child aged 6 to 17	20.14	158	18.6
Oldest child aged 18 or older	28.39	223	16.1
Single parent with child under age 18	3.03	24	1.4
Single person	0.71	6	1.6
RACE AND HISPANIC ORIGIN			
Average household	**12.73**	**100**	**100.0**
Asian	47.47	373	15.9
Black	5.04	40	4.8
Hispanic	19.91	156	19.1
Non-Hispanic white and other	12.78	100	76.1
REGION			
Average household	**12.73**	**100**	**100.0**
Northeast	21.75	171	31.4
Midwest	11.21	88	19.6
South	6.97	55	20.1
West	16.24	128	28.9
EDUCATION			
Average household	**12.73**	**100**	**100.0**
Less than high school graduate	6.75	53	7.6
High school graduate	5.97	47	12.0
Some college	6.20	49	10.2
Associate's degree	17.40	137	12.9
Bachelor's degree or more	24.55	193	57.3
Bachelor's degree	20.42	160	30.3
Master's, professional, doctoral degree	31.77	250	27.0

Note: Market shares may not sum to 100.0 because of rounding and missing categories by household type. "Asian" and "black" include Hispanics and non-Hispanics who identify themselves as being of the respective race alone. "Hispanic" includes people of any race who identify themselves as Hispanic. "Other" includes people who identify themselves as non-Hispanic and as Alaska Native, American Indian, Asian (who are also included in the "Asian" row), or Native Hawaiian or other Pacific Islander as well as non-Hispanics reporting more than one race.

Source: Calculations by New Strategist based on the Bureau of Labor Statistics' 2010 Consumer Expenditure Survey

Repair of Television, Radio, and Sound Equipment

Best customers: **Householders aged 65 or older**
Married couples without children at home
Married couples with adult children at home
Households in the Midwest

Customer trends: **Average household spending on repair of television, radio, and sound equipment**
could stabilize or even grow in the years ahead because it is more economical to
repair rather than replace expensive high-definition television sets.

The best customers of television, radio, and sound equipment repair are the oldest householders. Householders aged 65 or older spend 37 to 56 percent more than the average household on television, radio, and sound equipment repairs. Married couples with adult children at home spend 47 percent more than the average on this item. Married couples without children at home, most of them older empty-nesters, spend 31 percent more than average on the repair of television sets. Households in the Midwest spend 30 percent more than average on such repairs.

Average household spending on repair of television, radio, and sound equipment grew 46 percent between 2000 and 2006 after adjusting for inflation, then fell 55 percent between 2006 and 2010. One factor behind the recent decline is the relatively new inventory of television sets in the nation's households. Average household spending on this category could stabilize or even grow in the years ahead because it is more economical to repair rather than replace expensive high-definition television sets.

Table 5.25 Repair of television, radio, and sound equipment

Total household spending $325,777,830.00
Average household spends   2.69

	AVERAGE HOUSEHOLD SPENDING	BEST CUSTOMERS (index)	BIGGEST CUSTOMERS (market share)
AGE OF HOUSEHOLDER			
Average household	**$2.69**	**100**	**100.0%**
Under age 25	1.76	65	4.3
Aged 25 to 34	1.14	42	7.1
Aged 35 to 44	2.70	100	18.2
Aged 45 to 54	3.43	128	26.4
Aged 55 to 64	2.17	81	14.2
Aged 65 to 74	4.19	156	16.8
Aged 75 or older	3.68	137	13.0

	AVERAGE HOUSEHOLD SPENDING	BEST CUSTOMERS (index)	BIGGEST CUSTOMERS (market share)
HOUSEHOLD INCOME			
Average household	**$2.69**	**100**	**100.0%**
Under $20,000	0.66	25	5.4
$20,000 to $39,999	3.00	112	25.6
$40,000 to $49,999	3.09	115	10.9
$50,000 to $69,999	1.92	71	10.2
$70,000 to $79,999	5.12	190	11.4
$80,000 to $99,999	0.69	26	2.1
$100,000 or more	5.39	200	34.4
HOUSEHOLD TYPE			
Average household	**2.69**	**100**	**100.0**
Married couples	3.12	116	57.2
Married couples, no children	3.52	131	27.8
Married couples, with children	2.83	105	24.5
Oldest child under age 6	2.05	76	3.3
Oldest child aged 6 to 17	2.42	90	10.6
Oldest child aged 18 or older	3.95	147	10.6
Single parent with child under age 18	1.65	61	3.6
Single person	1.16	43	12.6
RACE AND HISPANIC ORIGIN			
Average household	**2.69**	**100**	**100.0**
Asian	0.17	6	0.3
Black	1.93	72	8.8
Hispanic	1.98	74	9.0
Non-Hispanic white and other	2.93	109	82.6
REGION			
Average household	**2.69**	**100**	**100.0**
Northeast	2.80	104	19.1
Midwest	3.50	130	29.0
South	2.37	88	32.3
West	2.31	86	19.5
EDUCATION			
Average household	**2.69**	**100**	**100.0**
Less than high school graduate	1.57	58	8.3
High school graduate	2.24	83	21.3
Some college	2.79	104	21.8
Associate's degree	3.16	117	11.1
Bachelor's degree or more	3.39	126	37.4
Bachelor's degree	2.50	93	17.6
Master's, professional, doctoral degree	4.95	184	19.9

Note: Market shares may not sum to 100.0 because of rounding and missing categories by household type. "Asian" and "black" include Hispanics and non-Hispanics who identify themselves as being of the respective race alone. "Hispanic" includes people of any race who identify themselves as Hispanic. "Other" includes people who identify themselves as non-Hispanic and as Alaska Native, American Indian, Asian (who are also included in the "Asian" row), or Native Hawaiian or other Pacific Islander as well as non-Hispanics reporting more than one race.

Source: Calculations by New Strategist based on the Bureau of Labor Statistics' 2010 Consumer Expenditure Survey

Satellite Radio Service

Best customers: **Householders aged 35 to 64**
Married couples without children at home
Married couples with school-aged or older children at home

Customer trends: **Average household spending on satellite radio service will depend more on trends**
in technology than on demographic change in the years ahead.

Householders aged 35 to 64 spend 19 to 28 percent more than average on satellite radio service and control 70 percent of the market. Married couples without children at home, most of them empty-nesters, spend 58 percent more than average on this item. Couples with school-aged or older children at home spend 31 to 47 percent more than average on satellite radio service.

Satellite radio service is a relatively new item in the Consumer Expenditure Survey, and comparable data from 2000 or 2006 do not exist. Average household spending on satellite radio service in the years ahead will depend more on trends in technology than on demographic change.

Table 5.26 Satellite radio service

Total household spending	$1,764,528,990.00
Average household spends	14.57

	AVERAGE HOUSEHOLD SPENDING	BEST CUSTOMERS (index)	BIGGEST CUSTOMERS (market share)
AGE OF HOUSEHOLDER			
Average household	**$14.57**	**100**	**100.0%**
Under age 25	5.94	41	2.7
Aged 25 to 34	9.66	66	11.0
Aged 35 to 44	17.29	119	21.5
Aged 45 to 54	17.93	123	25.5
Aged 55 to 64	18.71	128	22.6
Aged 65 to 74	15.11	104	11.2
Aged 75 or older	8.45	58	5.5

	AVERAGE HOUSEHOLD SPENDING	BEST CUSTOMERS (index)	BIGGEST CUSTOMERS (market share)
HOUSEHOLD INCOME			
Average household	**$14.57**	**100**	**100.0%**
Under $20,000	5.64	39	8.4
$20,000 to $39,999	9.50	65	14.9
$40,000 to $49,999	9.21	63	6.0
$50,000 to $69,999	19.16	132	18.9
$70,000 to $79,999	14.85	102	6.1
$80,000 to $99,999	21.00	144	12.0
$100,000 or more	28.61	196	33.7
HOUSEHOLD TYPE			
Average household	**14.57**	**100**	**100.0**
Married couples	20.62	142	69.8
Married couples, no children	23.02	158	33.6
Married couples, with children	18.82	129	30.0
Oldest child under age 6	13.78	95	4.0
Oldest child aged 6 to 17	19.08	131	15.4
Oldest child aged 18 or older	21.37	147	10.6
Single parent with child under age 18	5.60	38	2.3
Single person	7.21	49	14.5
RACE AND HISPANIC ORIGIN			
Average household	**14.57**	**100**	**100.0**
Asian	5.39	37	1.6
Black	10.74	74	9.0
Hispanic	12.39	85	10.4
Non-Hispanic white and other	15.54	107	80.9
REGION			
Average household	**14.57**	**100**	**100.0**
Northeast	13.20	91	16.6
Midwest	11.74	81	18.0
South	17.22	118	43.4
West	14.17	97	22.0
EDUCATION			
Average household	**14.57**	**100**	**100.0**
Less than high school graduate	8.31	57	8.1
High school graduate	12.98	89	22.7
Some college	13.89	95	20.0
Associate's degree	19.16	132	12.4
Bachelor's degree or more	17.98	123	36.7
Bachelor's degree	14.36	99	18.6
Master's, professional, doctoral degree	24.29	167	18.0

Note: Market shares may not sum to 100.0 because of rounding and missing categories by household type. "Asian" and "black" include Hispanics and non-Hispanics who identify themselves as being of the respective race alone. "Hispanic" includes people of any race who identify themselves as Hispanic. "Other" includes people who identify themselves as non-Hispanic and as Alaska Native, American Indian, Asian (who are also included in the "Asian" row), or Native Hawaiian or other Pacific Islander as well as non-Hispanics reporting more than one race.

Source: Calculations by New Strategist based on the Bureau of Labor Statistics' 2010 Consumer Expenditure Survey

Sound Components, Equipment, and Accessories (Includes Radios and Tape Recorders)

Best customers:	**Householders aged 25 to 34** **High-income households** **Married couples with children at home** **Asians** **Households in the Northeast**
Customer trends:	**Average household spending on sound components, equipment, and accessories is unlikely to rise in the years ahead because of continued price discounting and product substitution.**

The best customers of sound components, equipment, and accessories are families with children at home. Married couples with children at home spend 74 percent more than average on sound components, equipment, and accessories, the number peaking among those with adult children at home at well over twice the average. Households with incomes of $100,000 or more spend three-and-one-third times the average on sound equipment and accessories. Asian householders, a relatively well-to-do demographic, spend nearly four times the average amount on sound equipment. Householders aged 25 to 34 spend 77 percent more than average on this item as they outfit their homes.

Average household spending on sound components, equipment, and accessories fell by half between 2000 and 2010, after adjusting for inflation. Behind the decline is the substitution of personal digital audio equipment (such as iPods) for larger systems. Average household spending on this category is unlikely to rise in the years ahead because of continued price discounting and product substitution.

Table 5.27 Sound components, equipment, and accessories (includes radios and tape recorders)

Total household spending	$3,351,030,690.00
Average household spends	27.67

	AVERAGE HOUSEHOLD SPENDING	BEST CUSTOMERS (index)	BIGGEST CUSTOMERS (market share)
AGE OF HOUSEHOLDER			
Average household	**$27.67**	**100**	**100.0%**
Under age 25	10.75	39	2.6
Aged 25 to 34	49.08	177	29.5
Aged 35 to 44	30.84	111	20.2
Aged 45 to 54	25.85	93	19.3
Aged 55 to 64	34.37	124	21.9
Aged 65 to 74	10.77	39	4.2
Aged 75 or older	6.98	25	2.4

	AVERAGE HOUSEHOLD SPENDING	BEST CUSTOMERS (index)	BIGGEST CUSTOMERS (market share)
HOUSEHOLD INCOME			
Average household	**$27.67**	**100**	**100.0%**
Under $20,000	8.08	29	6.4
$20,000 to $39,999	9.36	34	7.7
$40,000 to $49,999	16.14	58	5.5
$50,000 to $69,999	26.38	95	13.7
$70,000 to $79,999	16.46	59	3.6
$80,000 to $99,999	25.55	92	7.7
$100,000 or more	92.62	335	57.4
HOUSEHOLD TYPE			
Average household	**27.67**	**100**	**100.0**
Married couples	32.85	119	58.6
Married couples, no children	21.41	77	16.4
Married couples, with children	48.03	174	40.4
Oldest child under age 6	41.30	149	6.4
Oldest child aged 6 to 17	39.31	142	16.7
Oldest child aged 18 or older	64.87	234	16.9
Single parent with child under age 18	10.41	38	2.2
Single person	13.50	49	14.3
RACE AND HISPANIC ORIGIN			
Average household	**27.67**	**100**	**100.0**
Asian	109.54	396	16.8
Black	12.57	45	5.6
Hispanic	14.20	51	6.3
Non-Hispanic white and other	32.39	117	88.7
REGION			
Average household	**27.67**	**100**	**100.0**
Northeast	34.56	125	22.9
Midwest	30.73	111	24.8
South	23.84	86	31.6
West	25.33	92	20.7
EDUCATION			
Average household	**27.67**	**100**	**100.0**
Less than high school graduate	11.26	41	5.8
High school graduate	14.72	53	13.6
Some college	23.46	85	17.8
Associate's degree	56.06	203	19.1
Bachelor's degree or more	40.04	145	43.0
Bachelor's degree	36.31	131	24.8
Master's, professional, doctoral degree	48.35	175	18.9

Note: Market shares may not sum to 100.0 because of rounding and missing categories by household type. "Asian" and "black" include Hispanics and non-Hispanics who identify themselves as being of the respective race alone. "Hispanic" includes people of any race who identify themselves as Hispanic. "Other" includes people who identify themselves as non-Hispanic and as Alaska Native, American Indian, Asian (who are also included in the "Asian" row), or Native Hawaiian or other Pacific Islander as well as non-Hispanics reporting more than one race.

Source: Calculations by New Strategist based on the Bureau of Labor Statistics' 2010 Consumer Expenditure Survey

Stamp and Coin Collecting

Best customers: **Householders aged 55 to 74**
Married couples without children at home
Married couples with preschoolers
People who live alone
Non-Hispanic whites
Households in the West

Customer trends: **Average household spending on stamp and coin collecting is likely to decline as younger cohorts move into the best-customer age groups.**

The best customers for stamp and coin collecting are older householders. Householders aged 55 to 64 spend well more than twice the average on stamp and coin collecting, and those aged 65 to 74 spend 58 percent more. Married couples without children at home (most of them older) spend 53 percent more than average on these hobbies, while those with preschoolers spend almost twice the average. Stamp and coin collecting is the extremely rare category on which people who live alone spend more than the average household, 22 percent more. Households in the West spend 70 percent more than average on stamp and coin collecting. Non-Hispanic whites completely dominate spending in this category and represent 98 percent of the market for stamp and coin collecting.

Stamp and coin collecting is a relatively new item in the Consumer Expenditure Survey, and comparable data from 2000 do not exist. From 2006 to 2010, spending on this category declined by a sharp 54 percent. Average household spending on stamp and coin collecting is likely to decline further in the years ahead as younger cohorts with no history of collecting move into the best-customer age groups.

Table 5.28 Stamp and coin collecting

Total household spending $335,466,390.00
Average household spends 2.77

	AVERAGE HOUSEHOLD SPENDING	BEST CUSTOMERS (index)	BIGGEST CUSTOMERS (market share)
AGE OF HOUSEHOLDER			
Average household	**$2.77**	**100**	**100.0%**
Under age 25	0.03	1	0.1
Aged 25 to 34	0.16	6	1.0
Aged 35 to 44	2.05	74	13.4
Aged 45 to 54	2.43	88	18.1
Aged 55 to 64	6.48	234	41.3
Aged 65 to 74	4.37	158	17.0
Aged 75 or older	2.63	95	9.1

	AVERAGE HOUSEHOLD SPENDING	BEST CUSTOMERS (index)	BIGGEST CUSTOMERS (market share)
HOUSEHOLD INCOME			
Average household	**$2.77**	**100**	**100.0%**
Under $20,000	2.24	81	17.7
$20,000 to $39,999	2.55	92	21.1
$40,000 to $49,999	1.75	63	6.0
$50,000 to $69,999	2.62	95	13.6
$70,000 to $79,999	2.93	106	6.3
$80,000 to $99,999	1.61	58	4.8
$100,000 or more	4.91	177	30.4
HOUSEHOLD TYPE			
Average household	**2.77**	**100**	**100.0**
Married couples	3.01	109	53.6
Married couples, no children	4.24	153	32.5
Married couples, with children	2.22	80	18.6
Oldest child under age 6	5.28	191	8.2
Oldest child aged 6 to 17	0.30	11	1.3
Oldest child aged 18 or older	3.53	127	9.2
Single parent with child under age 18	1.80	65	3.8
Single person	3.37	122	35.6
RACE AND HISPANIC ORIGIN			
Average household	**2.77**	**100**	**100.0**
Asian	1.33	48	2.0
Black	0.19	7	0.8
Hispanic	0.31	11	1.4
Non-Hispanic white and other	3.57	129	97.7
REGION			
Average household	**2.77**	**100**	**100.0**
Northeast	2.21	80	14.6
Midwest	2.34	84	18.8
South	2.10	76	27.8
West	4.71	170	38.5
EDUCATION			
Average household	**2.77**	**100**	**100.0**
Less than high school graduate	0.71	26	3.7
High school graduate	3.35	121	30.9
Some college	1.16	42	8.8
Associate's degree	4.11	148	14.0
Bachelor's degree or more	3.95	143	42.4
Bachelor's degree	2.97	107	20.3
Master's, professional, doctoral degree	5.68	205	22.2

Note: Market shares may not sum to 100.0 because of rounding and missing categories by household type. "Asian" and "black" include Hispanics and non-Hispanics who identify themselves as being of the respective race alone. "Hispanic" includes people of any race who identify themselves as Hispanic. "Other" includes people who identify themselves as non-Hispanic and as Alaska Native, American Indian, Asian (who are also included in the "Asian" row), or Native Hawaiian or other Pacific Islander as well as non-Hispanics reporting more than one race.

Source: Calculations by New Strategist based on the Bureau of Labor Statistics' 2010 Consumer Expenditure Survey

Streamed and Downloaded Audio

Best customers:	**Householders aged 25 to 54** **High-income households** **Married couples with children at home**
Customer trends:	**Average household spending on streamed and downloaded audio should rise in the years ahead as downloads become the norm for buying music.**

Streamed and downloaded audio is a spending category newly added to the Consumer Expenditure Survey in 2005. It captures spending on music downloads from sites such as iTunes and pay-per-listen programming. The best customers of audio downloads are households with school-aged children, which spend nearly two-and-one-half times the average on this item. Those with preschoolers spend 45 percent more than average on streamed and downloaded audio. Householders aged 25 to 54, many with children, spend 21 to 61 percent more than average on this item. Households with incomes of $100,000 or more spend three times the average on this item.

Spending on streamed and downloaded audio grew 71 percent between 2006 and 2010, making it the third-fastest growing entertainment category for that time period. In light of soaring sales of personal digital audio players, and with this capability being built into a growing number of cell phones, average household spending on music downloads should increase greatly in the years ahead.

Table 5.29 Streamed and downloaded audio

Total household spending $811,416,900.00
Average household spends   6.70

	AVERAGE HOUSEHOLD SPENDING	BEST CUSTOMERS (index)	BIGGEST CUSTOMERS (market share)
AGE OF HOUSEHOLDER			
Average household	**$6.70**	**100**	**100.0%**
Under age 25	6.39	95	6.3
Aged 25 to 34	8.14	121	20.2
Aged 35 to 44	10.81	161	29.2
Aged 45 to 54	9.64	144	29.8
Aged 55 to 64	4.06	61	10.7
Aged 65 to 74	1.88	28	3.0
Aged 75 or older	0.55	8	0.8

	AVERAGE HOUSEHOLD SPENDING	BEST CUSTOMERS (index)	BIGGEST CUSTOMERS (market share)
HOUSEHOLD INCOME			
Average household	**$6.70**	**100**	**100.0%**
Under $20,000	1.90	28	6.2
$20,000 to $39,999	2.71	40	9.3
$40,000 to $49,999	3.34	50	4.7
$50,000 to $69,999	4.20	63	9.0
$70,000 to $79,999	7.80	116	7.0
$80,000 to $99,999	9.52	142	11.8
$100,000 or more	20.33	303	52.0
HOUSEHOLD TYPE			
Average household	**6.70**	**100**	**100.0**
Married couples	8.65	129	63.7
Married couples, no children	4.74	71	15.0
Married couples, with children	12.70	190	44.1
Oldest child under age 6	9.72	145	6.2
Oldest child aged 6 to 17	16.15	241	28.3
Oldest child aged 18 or older	8.85	132	9.5
Single parent with child under age 18	2.38	36	2.1
Single person	4.23	63	18.5
RACE AND HISPANIC ORIGIN			
Average household	**6.70**	**100**	**100.0**
Asian	5.21	78	3.3
Black	4.24	63	7.7
Hispanic	4.69	70	8.5
Non-Hispanic white and other	7.44	111	84.2
REGION			
Average household	**6.70**	**100**	**100.0**
Northeast	6.36	95	17.4
Midwest	8.33	124	27.7
South	5.12	76	28.0
West	7.92	118	26.8
EDUCATION			
Average household	**6.70**	**100**	**100.0**
Less than high school graduate	0.87	13	1.9
High school graduate	3.35	50	12.8
Some college	5.66	84	17.8
Associate's degree	7.17	107	10.1
Bachelor's degree or more	12.97	194	57.5
Bachelor's degree	11.13	166	31.4
Master's, professional, doctoral degree	16.18	241	26.1

Note: Market shares may not sum to 100.0 because of rounding and missing categories by household type. "Asian" and "black" include Hispanics and non-Hispanics who identify themselves as being of the respective race alone. "Hispanic" includes people of any race who identify themselves as Hispanic. "Other" includes people who identify themselves as non-Hispanic and as Alaska Native, American Indian, Asian (who are also included in the "Asian" row), or Native Hawaiian or other Pacific Islander as well as non-Hispanics reporting more than one race.

Source: Calculations by New Strategist based on the Bureau of Labor Statistics' 2010 Consumer Expenditure Survey

Streamed and Downloaded Video

Best customers: **Householders under age 55**
                                    Married couples with children under age 18
                                    Asians
                                    Households in the West

Customer trends: **Average household spending on streamed and downloaded video should rise in the years ahead as Internet equipped televisions become the norm.**

Streamed and downloaded video is a spending category newly added to the Consumer Expenditure Survey in 2005. It captures spending on streaming services such as Netflix as well as pay-per-view programming for computers and Internet equipped televisions. The best customers of video downloads are households with school-aged children, which spend 57 percent more than average on this item. Couples with preschoolers outspend the average by 30 percent. Householders under age 55, many with children, spend 18 to 42 percent more than average on streamed and downloaded video. Asian householders spend 47 percent more than average on streamed video. Households in the West, where many Asians reside, spend 42 percent more than average on this item.

Streamed and downloaded video is a relatively new item in the Consumer Expenditure Survey and comparable data from 2000 do not exist. Between 2006 and 2010 average household spending in this category increased 74 percent. Average household spending on streamed and downloaded video should continue to increase greatly in the years ahead.

Table 5.30 Streamed and downloaded video

Total household spending   **$234,947,580.00**
Average household spends   **1.94**

	AVERAGE HOUSEHOLD SPENDING	BEST CUSTOMERS (index)	BIGGEST CUSTOMERS (market share)
AGE OF HOUSEHOLDER			
Average household	**$1.94**	**100**	**100.0%**
Under age 25	2.76	142	9.4
Aged 25 to 34	2.28	118	19.6
Aged 35 to 44	2.64	136	24.6
Aged 45 to 54	2.39	123	25.5
Aged 55 to 64	1.48	76	13.5
Aged 65 to 74	1.12	58	6.2
Aged 75 or older	0.21	11	1.0

	AVERAGE HOUSEHOLD SPENDING	BEST CUSTOMERS (index)	BIGGEST CUSTOMERS (market share)
HOUSEHOLD INCOME			
Average household	$1.94	100	100.0%
Under $20,000	0.57	29	6.4
$20,000 to $39,999	1.11	57	13.1
$40,000 to $49,999	1.37	71	6.7
$50,000 to $69,999	1.24	64	9.2
$70,000 to $79,999	2.10	108	6.5
$80,000 to $99,999	3.23	166	13.9
$100,000 or more	4.98	257	44.0
HOUSEHOLD TYPE			
Average household	1.94	100	100.0
Married couples	2.27	117	57.7
Married couples, no children	2.04	105	22.3
Married couples, with children	2.65	137	31.8
Oldest child under age 6	2.52	130	5.6
Oldest child aged 6 to 17	3.04	157	18.4
Oldest child aged 18 or older	2.08	107	7.7
Single parent with child under age 18	0.80	41	2.4
Single person	1.64	85	24.8
RACE AND HISPANIC ORIGIN			
Average household	1.94	100	100.0
Asian	2.86	147	6.3
Black	0.80	41	5.0
Hispanic	2.06	106	12.9
Non-Hispanic white and other	2.11	109	82.5
REGION			
Average household	1.94	100	100.0
Northeast	2.20	113	20.8
Midwest	1.60	82	18.4
South	1.51	78	28.6
West	2.75	142	32.1
EDUCATION			
Average household	1.94	100	100.0
Less than high school graduate	0.34	18	2.5
High school graduate	0.97	50	12.8
Some college	1.98	102	21.5
Associate's degree	2.01	104	9.8
Bachelor's degree or more	3.48	179	53.3
Bachelor's degree	2.85	147	27.8
Master's, professional, doctoral degree	4.59	237	25.6

Note: Market shares may not sum to 100.0 because of rounding and missing categories by household type. "Asian" and "black" include Hispanics and non-Hispanics who identify themselves as being of the respective race alone. "Hispanic" includes people of any race who identify themselves as Hispanic. "Other" includes people who identify themselves as non-Hispanic and as Alaska Native, American Indian, Asian (who are also included in the "Asian" row), or Native Hawaiian or other Pacific Islander as well as non-Hispanics reporting more than one race.

Source: Calculations by New Strategist based on the Bureau of Labor Statistics' 2010 Consumer Expenditure Survey

Television Sets

Best customers: **Married couples without children at home**
Married couples with children under age 18

Customer trends: **Average household spending on television sets is likely to continue to decline because most households have replaced their old sets with high-definition versions.**

The best customers of television sets are married couples with school-aged or younger children at home. Married couples with school-aged children spend 30 percent more than average on television sets, and those with preschoolers spend 66 percent more. Married couples without children at home spend 40 percent more than average on this item.

Average household spending on television sets grew 44 percent between 2000 and 2010. Spending grew 71 percent from 2000 to 2006 (the year overall household spending peaked) as high-definition sets became *de rigueur.* Then growth turned to decline and average household spending on television sets fell 16 percent between 2006 and 2010. Average household spending on television sets is likely to continue to decline now that most households have replaced their old sets with HD versions.

Table 5.31 Television sets

Total household spending $14,379,034,110.00
Average household spends   118.73

	AVERAGE HOUSEHOLD SPENDING	BEST CUSTOMERS (index)	BIGGEST CUSTOMERS (market share)
AGE OF HOUSEHOLDER			
Average household	**$118.73**	**100**	**100.0%**
Under age 25	86.37	73	4.8
Aged 25 to 34	132.80	112	18.6
Aged 35 to 44	128.44	108	19.6
Aged 45 to 54	121.38	102	21.1
Aged 55 to 64	147.14	124	21.9
Aged 65 to 74	81.93	69	7.4
Aged 75 or older	81.47	69	6.5

	AVERAGE HOUSEHOLD SPENDING	BEST CUSTOMERS (index)	BIGGEST CUSTOMERS (market share)
HOUSEHOLD INCOME			
Average household	**$118.73**	**100**	**100.0%**
Under $20,000	48.15	41	8.8
$20,000 to $39,999	85.49	72	16.5
$40,000 to $49,999	106.66	90	8.5
$50,000 to $69,999	131.54	111	15.9
$70,000 to $79,999	155.33	131	7.8
$80,000 to $99,999	162.73	137	11.4
$100,000 or more	214.74	181	31.0
HOUSEHOLD TYPE			
Average household	**118.73**	**100**	**100.0**
Married couples	156.50	132	65.0
Married couples, no children	165.75	140	29.7
Married couples, with children	152.53	128	29.9
Oldest child under age 6	197.66	166	7.1
Oldest child aged 6 to 17	153.88	130	15.2
Oldest child aged 18 or older	123.56	104	7.5
Single parent with child under age 18	87.92	74	4.4
Single person	69.82	59	17.2
RACE AND HISPANIC ORIGIN			
Average household	**118.73**	**100**	**100.0**
Asian	118.54	100	4.2
Black	89.77	76	9.3
Hispanic	130.05	110	13.3
Non-Hispanic white and other	122.71	103	78.4
REGION			
Average household	**118.73**	**100**	**100.0**
Northeast	107.57	91	16.6
Midwest	132.05	111	24.8
South	117.02	99	36.2
West	117.42	99	22.4
EDUCATION			
Average household	**118.73**	**100**	**100.0**
Less than high school graduate	57.02	48	6.9
High school graduate	107.38	90	23.1
Some college	134.97	114	23.9
Associate's degree	102.10	86	8.1
Bachelor's degree or more	151.96	128	38.0
Bachelor's degree	166.82	141	26.5
Master's, professional, doctoral degree	126.00	106	11.5

Note: Market shares may not sum to 100.0 because of rounding and missing categories by household type. "Asian" and "black" include Hispanics and non-Hispanics who identify themselves as being of the respective race alone. "Hispanic" includes people of any race who identify themselves as Hispanic. "Other" includes people who identify themselves as non-Hispanic and as Alaska Native, American Indian, Asian (who are also included in the "Asian" row), or Native Hawaiian or other Pacific Islander as well as non-Hispanics reporting more than one race.

Source: Calculations by New Strategist based on the Bureau of Labor Statistics' 2010 Consumer Expenditure Survey

Toys, Games, Hobbies, and Tricycles

Best customers:	**Householders aged 35 to 44** **Married couples with children under age 18**
Customer trends:	**Average household spending on toys, games, hobbies, and tricycles may continue to rise in the years ahead as the large millennial generation fills the best-customer lifestage.**

The best customers of toys, games, hobbies, and tricycles are parents with children under age 18. This explains why householders aged 35 to 44, many of them parents, spend 47 percent more than average on this item. Married couples with preschoolers spend twice the average on toys, and those with school-aged children spend more than twice the average.

Average household spending on toys, games, hobbies, and tricycles fell 39 percent between 2000 and 2006, after adjusting for inflation. Spending then climbed by a substantial 26 percent between 2006 and 2010. Spending on toys, games, hobbies, and tricycles may continue to rise in the years ahead as the large millennial generation fills the best-customer lifestage.

Table 5.32 Toys, games, hobbies, and tricycles

Total household spending	$14,263,982,460.00
Average household spends	117.78

	AVERAGE HOUSEHOLD SPENDING	BEST CUSTOMERS (index)	BIGGEST CUSTOMERS (market share)
AGE OF HOUSEHOLDER			
Average household	**$117.78**	**100**	**100.0%**
Under age 25	60.72	52	3.4
Aged 25 to 34	111.59	95	15.8
Aged 35 to 44	173.70	147	26.7
Aged 45 to 54	129.95	110	22.8
Aged 55 to 64	130.64	111	19.6
Aged 65 to 74	98.61	84	9.0
Aged 75 or older	33.78	29	2.7

	AVERAGE HOUSEHOLD SPENDING	BEST CUSTOMERS (index)	BIGGEST CUSTOMERS (market share)
HOUSEHOLD INCOME			
Average household	**$117.78**	**100**	**100.0%**
Under $20,000	49.51	42	9.2
$20,000 to $39,999	66.52	56	12.9
$40,000 to $49,999	91.19	77	7.3
$50,000 to $69,999	108.69	92	13.2
$70,000 to $79,999	141.91	120	7.2
$80,000 to $99,999	162.17	138	11.5
$100,000 or more	273.92	233	39.9
HOUSEHOLD TYPE			
Average household	**117.78**	**100**	**100.0**
Married couples	168.92	143	70.7
Married couples, no children	92.68	79	16.7
Married couples, with children	223.58	190	44.2
Oldest child under age 6	234.09	199	8.5
Oldest child aged 6 to 17	268.89	228	26.8
Oldest child aged 18 or older	150.65	128	9.2
Single parent with child under age 18	106.60	91	5.3
Single person	42.25	36	10.5
RACE AND HISPANIC ORIGIN			
Average household	**117.78**	**100**	**100.0**
Asian	111.91	95	4.0
Black	71.93	61	7.5
Hispanic	91.88	78	9.5
Non-Hispanic white and other	129.16	110	83.1
REGION			
Average household	**117.78**	**100**	**100.0**
Northeast	156.04	132	24.3
Midwest	122.49	104	23.2
South	99.55	85	31.0
West	111.67	95	21.5
EDUCATION			
Average household	**117.78**	**100**	**100.0**
Less than high school graduate	45.43	39	5.5
High school graduate	102.28	87	22.2
Some college	129.22	110	23.1
Associate's degree	140.29	119	11.3
Bachelor's degree or more	147.57	125	37.2
Bachelor's degree	138.31	117	22.2
Master's, professional, doctoral degree	165.82	141	15.2

Note: Market shares may not sum to 100.0 because of rounding and missing categories by household type. "Asian" and "black" include Hispanics and non-Hispanics who identify themselves as being of the respective race alone. "Hispanic" includes people of any race who identify themselves as Hispanic. "Other" includes people who identify themselves as non-Hispanic and as Alaska Native, American Indian, Asian (who are also included in the "Asian" row), or Native Hawaiian or other Pacific Islander as well as non-Hispanics reporting more than one race.

Source: Calculations by New Strategist based on the Bureau of Labor Statistics' 2010 Consumer Expenditure Survey

VCRs and Video Disc Players

Best customers:	**Householders aged 25 to 44**
	Married couples with children at home
	Asians
	Households in the West
Customer trends:	**Average household spending on video cassette recorders and video disc players will continue to decline because of technological change.**

The best customers of video cassette recorders and video disc players are parents with children buying equipment for their family's enjoyment. Householders ranging in age from 25 to 44 spend 26 to 32 percent more than average on video players and control 45 percent of the market. Married couples with children at home spend 56 percent more than average on video players, the figure peaking at nearly twice the average among householders with preschoolers. Asian householders outspend the average household by 90 percent. Households in the West, where many Asians reside, spend 52 percent more than average on this item.

Average household spending on video cassette recorders and video disc players fell by a steep 66 percent between 2000 and 2010, after adjusting for inflation. Changing technology and falling prices were behind the decline as VCRs became obsolete, cheaper imports reduced costs, and high-definition television sets allowed users to download movies. Technological change, coupled with the fact that the small generation X is in the best-customer lifestage, suggest that average household spending on this category will continue to decline.

Table 5.33 VCRs and Video Disc Players

Total household spending	$1,223,180,700.00
Average household spends	10.10

	AVERAGE HOUSEHOLD SPENDING	BEST CUSTOMERS (index)	BIGGEST CUSTOMERS (market share)
AGE OF HOUSEHOLDER			
Average household	**$10.10**	**100**	**100.0%**
Under age 25	6.62	66	4.3
Aged 25 to 34	12.73	126	21.0
Aged 35 to 44	13.37	132	24.0
Aged 45 to 54	10.02	99	20.5
Aged 55 to 64	10.86	108	19.0
Aged 65 to 74	6.23	62	6.6
Aged 75 or older	4.89	48	4.6

	AVERAGE HOUSEHOLD SPENDING	BEST CUSTOMERS (index)	BIGGEST CUSTOMERS (market share)
HOUSEHOLD INCOME			
Average household	**$10.10**	**100**	**100.0%**
Under $20,000	4.92	49	10.6
$20,000 to $39,999	4.62	46	10.5
$40,000 to $49,999	8.56	85	8.0
$50,000 to $69,999	10.67	106	15.2
$70,000 to $79,999	18.28	181	10.8
$80,000 to $99,999	15.43	153	12.7
$100,000 or more	18.94	188	32.2
HOUSEHOLD TYPE			
Average household	**10.10**	**100**	**100.0**
Married couples	13.75	136	67.2
Married couples, no children	11.89	118	25.0
Married couples, with children	15.71	156	36.2
Oldest child under age 6	19.27	191	8.2
Oldest child aged 6 to 17	16.31	161	19.0
Oldest child aged 18 or older	12.62	125	9.0
Single parent with child under age 18	8.52	84	5.0
Single person	5.78	57	16.8
RACE AND HISPANIC ORIGIN			
Average household	**10.10**	**100**	**100.0**
Asian	19.20	190	8.1
Black	6.47	64	7.8
Hispanic	11.80	117	14.2
Non-Hispanic white and other	10.47	104	78.6
REGION			
Average household	**10.10**	**100**	**100.0**
Northeast	7.72	76	14.0
Midwest	7.73	77	17.1
South	9.49	94	34.5
West	15.36	152	34.5
EDUCATION			
Average household	**10.10**	**100**	**100.0**
Less than high school graduate	5.41	54	7.7
High school graduate	7.37	73	18.6
Some college	8.22	81	17.1
Associate's degree	11.36	112	10.6
Bachelor's degree or more	15.63	155	46.0
Bachelor's degree	13.32	132	24.9
Master's, professional, doctoral degree	19.68	195	21.1

Note: Market shares may not sum to 100.0 because of rounding and missing categories by household type. "Asian" and "black" include Hispanics and non-Hispanics who identify themselves as being of the respective race alone. "Hispanic" includes people of any race who identify themselves as Hispanic. "Other" includes people who identify themselves as non-Hispanic and as Alaska Native, American Indian, Asian (who are also included in the "Asian" row), or Native Hawaiian or other Pacific Islander as well as non-Hispanics reporting more than one race.

Source: Calculations by New Strategist based on the Bureau of Labor Statistics' 2010 Consumer Expenditure Survey

Veterinary Services

Best customers: **Householders aged 45 to 74**
Married couples without children at home
Married couples with preschoolers
Married couples with adult children at home
Non-Hispanic whites
Households in the Northeast

Customer trends: **Average household spending on veterinary services could stabilize or even decline**
in the years ahead as households forego pet ownership because of the sharply
higher expense.

The best customers of veterinary services are older married couples, many of whom have older pets that require extensive veterinary care. Married couples with adult children at home spend 33 percent more than average on veterinary services, and couples without children at home (most of them older empty-nesters) outspend the average on this item by 38 percent. Couples with preschoolers—many acquiring their first pet—spend 58 percent more. Householders aged 45 to 74 spend 17 to 61 percent more than average on veterinary services. Non-Hispanic whites completely dominate spending on this category. They account for 96 percent of the market for veterinary services, spending 27 percent more than average. Households in the Northeast spend one-quarter more than the average household on this item.

Average household spending on veterinary services increased 36 percent between 2000 and 2010, after adjusting for inflation. Between 2009 and 2010, however, spending on veterinary services fell 32 percent (not shown in table) as consumers reacted to the shock of higher pet costs. Spending on veterinary services could stabilize or even decline in the years ahead as households forego pet ownership because of the sharply higher expense.

Table 5.34 Veterinary services

Total household spending $13,748,066,640.00
Average household spends   113.52

	AVERAGE HOUSEHOLD SPENDING	BEST CUSTOMERS (index)	BIGGEST CUSTOMERS (market share)
AGE OF HOUSEHOLDER			
Average household	**$113.52**	**100**	**100.0%**
Under age 25	21.96	19	1.3
Aged 25 to 34	71.16	63	10.4
Aged 35 to 44	117.42	103	18.7
Aged 45 to 54	135.94	120	24.8
Aged 55 to 64	132.82	117	20.6
Aged 65 to 74	182.33	161	17.3
Aged 75 or older	79.19	70	6.7

	AVERAGE HOUSEHOLD SPENDING	BEST CUSTOMERS (index)	BIGGEST CUSTOMERS (market share)
HOUSEHOLD INCOME			
Average household	**$113.52**	**100**	**100.0%**
Under $20,000	39.12	34	7.5
$20,000 to $39,999	54.70	48	11.0
$40,000 to $49,999	79.47	70	6.6
$50,000 to $69,999	109.19	96	13.8
$70,000 to $79,999	223.53	197	11.8
$80,000 to $99,999	98.68	87	7.2
$100,000 or more	285.73	252	43.2
HOUSEHOLD TYPE			
Average household	**113.52**	**100**	**100.0**
Married couples	135.05	119	58.7
Married couples, no children	156.67	138	29.3
Married couples, with children	125.83	111	25.8
Oldest child under age 6	179.71	158	6.8
Oldest child aged 6 to 17	90.71	80	9.4
Oldest child aged 18 or older	150.61	133	9.6
Single parent with child under age 18	32.19	28	1.7
Single person	62.30	55	16.1
RACE AND HISPANIC ORIGIN			
Average household	**113.52**	**100**	**100.0**
Asian	29.88	26	1.1
Black	15.58	14	1.7
Hispanic	17.42	15	1.9
Non-Hispanic white and other	144.29	127	96.4
REGION			
Average household	**113.52**	**100**	**100.0**
Northeast	141.96	125	23.0
Midwest	125.16	110	24.6
South	109.82	97	35.5
West	84.49	74	16.9
EDUCATION			
Average household	**113.52**	**100**	**100.0**
Less than high school graduate	32.19	28	4.1
High school graduate	66.31	58	14.9
Some college	160.21	141	29.7
Associate's degree	95.52	84	8.0
Bachelor's degree or more	163.02	144	42.7
Bachelor's degree	146.20	129	24.3
Master's, professional, doctoral degree	196.14	173	18.7

Note: Market shares may not sum to 100.0 because of rounding and missing categories by household type. "Asian" and "black" include Hispanics and non-Hispanics who identify themselves as being of the respective race alone. "Hispanic" includes people of any race who identify themselves as Hispanic. "Other" includes people who identify themselves as non-Hispanic and as Alaska Native, American Indian, Asian (who are also included in the "Asian" row), or Native Hawaiian or other Pacific Islander as well as non-Hispanics reporting more than one race.

Source: Calculations by New Strategist based on the Bureau of Labor Statistics' 2010 Consumer Expenditure Survey

Video Cassettes, Tapes, and Discs

Best customers:	**Householders aged 25 to 44** **Married couples with children at home** **Single parents** **Households in the West**
Customer trends:	**Average household spending on video cassettes, tapes, and discs is likely to continue to fall as these items are replaced by streamed video.**

The best customers of video cassettes, tapes, and discs are married couples with children, many of them buying children's programming to keep the kids entertained. Householders aged 25 to 44 spend 26 to 33 percent more than average on videos and DVDs and account for 45 percent of the market. Married couples with children at home spend 36 percent more than average on this item, the figure peaking among those with preschoolers, who spend 62 percent more than average. Single parents, whose spending is below average on most items, spend an average amount on video cassettes, tapes, and discs. Households in the West outspend the average by 22 percent.

Average household spending on video cassettes, tapes, and discs rose 4 percent between 2000 and 2010, after adjusting for inflation. Spending on this item had grown vigorously between 2000 and 2006 (the year household spending peaked), increasing 69 percent. Between 2006 and 2010, spending on this category fell by 39 percent. Behind the earlier increase was the substitution of DVDs for videos as DVD players replaced VCRs. Average household spending on video cassettes, tapes, and discs is likely to continue to fall as these items are replaced by streamed video.

Table 5.35 Video cassettes, tapes, and discs

Total household spending	$3,315,909,660.00
Average household spends	27.38

	AVERAGE HOUSEHOLD SPENDING	BEST CUSTOMERS (index)	BIGGEST CUSTOMERS (market share)
AGE OF HOUSEHOLDER			
Average household	**$27.38**	**100**	**100.0%**
Under age 25	30.18	110	7.3
Aged 25 to 34	36.40	133	22.1
Aged 35 to 44	34.38	126	22.7
Aged 45 to 54	28.94	106	21.9
Aged 55 to 64	27.27	100	17.6
Aged 65 to 74	15.53	57	6.1
Aged 75 or older	6.58	24	2.3

	AVERAGE HOUSEHOLD SPENDING	BEST CUSTOMERS (index)	BIGGEST CUSTOMERS (market share)
HOUSEHOLD INCOME			
Average household	**$27.38**	**100**	**100.0%**
Under $20,000	13.15	48	10.5
$20,000 to $39,999	19.88	73	16.6
$40,000 to $49,999	30.34	111	10.5
$50,000 to $69,999	32.46	119	17.0
$70,000 to $79,999	31.13	114	6.8
$80,000 to $99,999	36.18	132	11.0
$100,000 or more	44.03	161	27.6
HOUSEHOLD TYPE			
Average household	**27.38**	**100**	**100.0**
Married couples	31.57	115	56.9
Married couples, no children	24.20	88	18.8
Married couples, with children	37.16	136	31.6
Oldest child under age 6	44.25	162	6.9
Oldest child aged 6 to 17	37.79	138	16.2
Oldest child aged 18 or older	31.94	117	8.4
Single parent with child under age 18	27.72	101	6.0
Single person	19.24	70	20.6
RACE AND HISPANIC ORIGIN			
Average household	**27.38**	**100**	**100.0**
Asian	17.87	65	2.8
Black	20.04	73	9.0
Hispanic	21.25	78	9.5
Non-Hispanic white and other	29.48	108	81.6
REGION			
Average household	**27.38**	**100**	**100.0**
Northeast	20.55	75	13.8
Midwest	27.15	99	22.1
South	27.20	99	36.5
West	33.42	122	27.6
EDUCATION			
Average household	**27.38**	**100**	**100.0**
Less than high school graduate	13.46	49	7.0
High school graduate	22.48	82	21.0
Some college	33.17	121	25.5
Associate's degree	31.06	113	10.7
Bachelor's degree or more	33.01	121	35.8
Bachelor's degree	33.51	122	23.1
Master's, professional, doctoral degree	32.15	117	12.7

Note: Market shares may not sum to 100.0 because of rounding and missing categories by household type. "Asian" and "black" include Hispanics and non-Hispanics who identify themselves as being of the respective race alone. "Hispanic" includes people of any race who identify themselves as Hispanic. "Other" includes people who identify themselves as non-Hispanic and as Alaska Native, American Indian, Asian (who are also included in the "Asian" row), or Native Hawaiian or other Pacific Islander as well as non-Hispanics reporting more than one race.

Source: Calculations by New Strategist based on the Bureau of Labor Statistics' 2010 Consumer Expenditure Survey

Video Game Hardware and Software

Best customers: Householders aged 25 to 44
Married couples with school-aged children
Asians

Customer trends: Average household spending on video game hardware and software will continue to rise as younger generations, raised on video games, become a larger share of the overall population.

Children and teenagers are the best customers of video game hardware and software. That explains why householders aged 25 to 44—most having children at home—spend more than others on this item. Together the 25-to-44 age groups control 55 percent of household spending in this market. Married couples with school-aged children spend well over twice the average on video game hardware and software. Asians are some of the best customers of video game hardware and software, spending 48 percent more than the average household on this item.

Average household spending on video game hardware and software more than doubled between 2000 and 2010, after adjusting for inflation, with nary a sign of belt-tightening because of the Great Recession. Behind the increase were powerful new game players and a host of exciting new games. Average household spending on video game hardware and software should continue to rise as younger generations, raised on video games, become a larger share of the overall population.

Table 5.36 Video game hardware and software

| Total household spending | $6,152,235,600.00 |
| Average household spends | 50.80 |

	AVERAGE HOUSEHOLD SPENDING	BEST CUSTOMERS (index)	BIGGEST CUSTOMERS (market share)
AGE OF HOUSEHOLDER			
Average household	**$50.80**	**100**	**100.0%**
Under age 25	53.88	106	7.0
Aged 25 to 34	71.32	140	23.4
Aged 35 to 44	88.23	174	31.4
Aged 45 to 54	45.53	90	18.5
Aged 55 to 64	47.61	94	16.5
Aged 65 to 74	12.56	25	2.7
Aged 75 or older	3.66	7	0.7

	AVERAGE HOUSEHOLD SPENDING	BEST CUSTOMERS (index)	BIGGEST CUSTOMERS (market share)
HOUSEHOLD INCOME			
Average household	**$50.80**	**100**	**100.0%**
Under $20,000	24.38	48	10.5
$20,000 to $39,999	25.03	49	11.3
$40,000 to $49,999	44.59	88	8.3
$50,000 to $69,999	69.72	137	19.7
$70,000 to $79,999	90.14	177	10.6
$80,000 to $99,999	87.47	172	14.4
$100,000 or more	76.08	150	25.7
HOUSEHOLD TYPE			
Average household	**50.80**	**100**	**100.0**
Married couples	63.49	125	61.6
Married couples, no children	45.27	89	18.9
Married couples, with children	80.31	158	36.8
Oldest child under age 6	9.77	19	0.8
Oldest child aged 6 to 17	121.22	239	28.1
Oldest child aged 18 or older	55.43	109	7.9
Single parent with child under age 18	49.56	98	5.8
Single person	20.85	41	12.0
RACE AND HISPANIC ORIGIN			
Average household	**50.80**	**100**	**100.0**
Asian	75.17	148	6.3
Black	23.30	46	5.6
Hispanic	44.86	88	10.8
Non-Hispanic white and other	56.04	110	83.6
REGION			
Average household	**50.80**	**100**	**100.0**
Northeast	47.83	94	17.3
Midwest	44.95	88	19.7
South	51.35	101	37.1
West	58.27	115	26.0
EDUCATION			
Average household	**50.80**	**100**	**100.0**
Less than high school graduate	21.51	42	6.0
High school graduate	44.92	88	22.6
Some college	51.56	101	21.3
Associate's degree	59.82	118	11.1
Bachelor's degree or more	65.38	129	38.2
Bachelor's degree	56.44	111	21.0
Master's, professional, doctoral degree	82.98	163	17.7

Note: Market shares may not sum to 100.0 because of rounding and missing categories by household type. "Asian" and "black" include Hispanics and non-Hispanics who identify themselves as being of the respective race alone. "Hispanic" includes people of any race who identify themselves as Hispanic. "Other" includes people who identify themselves as non-Hispanic and as Alaska Native, American Indian, Asian (who are also included in the "Asian" row), or Native Hawaiian or other Pacific Islander as well as non-Hispanics reporting more than one race.

Source: Calculations by New Strategist based on the Bureau of Labor Statistics' 2010 Consumer Expenditure Survey

Video Tape, Disc, and Film Rental

Best customers: Householders aged 25 to 44
Married couples with children at home
Single parents
Households in the West

Customer trends: Average household spending on video rentals will continue to decline as streamed video becomes more popular.

Parents are the best customers of video rentals. This explains why householders aged 25 to 44—many of whom are parents—spend 39 to 46 percent more than the average household on this item. Married couples with children at home spend 63 percent more than average on video rentals, the figure peaking at 76 percent among those with school-aged children. Single parents, whose spending approaches average on only a few items, spend 7 percent more than average on video rentals. Households in the West spend 38 percent more than average on this item.

Average household spending on video and DVD rentals fell 59 percent between 2000 and 2010, after adjusting for inflation. Falling prices and changing technology are behind the drop as competition in the rental market reduced fees and more households opted for downloads or streaming video. Average household spending is likely to continue to decline as streamed video becomes more popular.

Table 5.37 Video tape, disc, and film rental

| Total household spending | $2,605,011,570.00 |
| Average household spends | 21.51 |

	AVERAGE HOUSEHOLD SPENDING	BEST CUSTOMERS (index)	BIGGEST CUSTOMERS (market share)
AGE OF HOUSEHOLDER			
Average household	$21.51	100	100.0%
Under age 25	18.60	86	5.7
Aged 25 to 34	31.49	146	24.4
Aged 35 to 44	29.80	139	25.1
Aged 45 to 54	25.16	117	24.2
Aged 55 to 64	16.92	79	13.9
Aged 65 to 74	9.74	45	4.9
Aged 75 or older	4.23	20	1.9

	AVERAGE HOUSEHOLD SPENDING	BEST CUSTOMERS (index)	BIGGEST CUSTOMERS (market share)
HOUSEHOLD INCOME			
Average household	$21.51	100	100.0%
Under $20,000	8.56	40	8.7
$20,000 to $39,999	14.08	65	15.0
$40,000 to $49,999	20.01	93	8.8
$50,000 to $69,999	22.71	106	15.1
$70,000 to $79,999	25.49	119	7.1
$80,000 to $99,999	33.91	158	13.1
$100,000 or more	40.31	187	32.1
HOUSEHOLD TYPE			
Average household	21.51	100	100.0
Married couples	27.04	126	62.0
Married couples, no children	18.73	87	18.5
Married couples, with children	35.00	163	37.9
Oldest child under age 6	35.54	165	7.1
Oldest child aged 6 to 17	37.87	176	20.7
Oldest child aged 18 or older	30.00	139	10.1
Single parent with child under age 18	22.97	107	6.3
Single person	12.15	56	16.5
RACE AND HISPANIC ORIGIN			
Average household	21.51	100	100.0
Asian	15.32	71	3.0
Black	12.78	59	7.3
Hispanic	20.06	93	11.4
Non-Hispanic white and other	23.13	108	81.5
REGION			
Average household	21.51	100	100.0
Northeast	17.01	79	14.5
Midwest	21.96	102	22.8
South	18.46	86	31.5
West	29.64	138	31.2
EDUCATION			
Average household	21.51	100	100.0
Less than high school graduate	9.09	42	6.0
High school graduate	15.64	73	18.6
Some college	23.18	108	22.7
Associate's degree	24.88	116	10.9
Bachelor's degree or more	30.27	141	41.8
Bachelor's degree	30.35	141	26.7
Master's, professional, doctoral degree	30.14	140	15.2

Note: Market shares may not sum to 100.0 because of rounding and missing categories by household type. "Asian" and "black" include Hispanics and non-Hispanics who identify themselves as being of the respective race alone. "Hispanic" includes people of any race who identify themselves as Hispanic. "Other" includes people who identify themselves as non-Hispanic and as Alaska Native, American Indian, Asian (who are also included in the "Asian" row), or Native Hawaiian or other Pacific Islander as well as non-Hispanics reporting more than one race.

Source: Calculations by New Strategist based on the Bureau of Labor Statistics' 2010 Consumer Expenditure Survey

Chapter 6.

Financial Services

Household Spending on Financial Services, 2010

Average household spending on financial services and miscellaneous items fell 7 percent between 2000 and 2010, after adjusting for inflation. Mixed trends, including less spending on taxes and more spending on charitable contributions, were behind the small overall decline in spending.

Average household spending on federal income tax declined by a substantial 63 percent between 2000 and 2010 because of tax cuts and layoffs. Spending on state and local income taxes fell 32 percent. Other losing categories include credit card membership fees (down 71 percent), occupational expenses (down 58 percent), finance charges except for mortgages and vehicles (down 42 percent), safe deposit box rental (down 37 percent), life and other personal insurance except health (down 37 percent), and funeral expenses as well as cemetery lots, vaults, and maintenance fee (down 11 percent).

Average household spending on cash contributions increased strongly between 2000 and 2006 (the year household spending peaked), climbing by 34 percent after adjusting for inflation (see Appendix D). But from 2006 to 2010, cash contributions fell 19 percent as households tightened their belts. Despite the decline between 2006 and 2010, the average household spent 17 percent more on contributions to religious organizations in 2010 than in 2000. It spent 42 percent more on cash contributions to educational institutions and 52 percent more on contributions to political organizations. In contrast, average household spending on contributions to charitable organizations fell 10 percent between 2000 and 2010. The average household's lottery and gambling losses were 49 percent larger in 2010 than in 2000, after adjusting for inflation. Almost all the increase occurred between 2000 and 2006, however.

Cash contributions to religious organizations

(average annual spending of households on cash contributions to religious organizations, 2000, 2006, and 2010; in 2010 dollars)

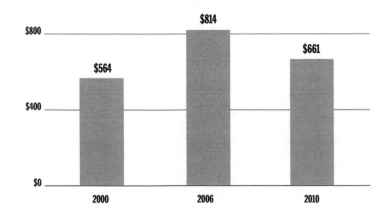

Table 6.1 Financial spending, 2000 to 2010

(average annual household spending on financial products and services and cash contributions, 2000 to 2010; percent change and percentage point change in spending, 2000–06, 2006–10, and 2000–10; in 2010 dollars; ranked by amount spent)

	2010 average household spending	2006 average household spending (in 2010$)	2000 average household spending (in 2010$)	percent change		
				2006–10	2000–06	2000–10
AVERAGE ANNUAL SPENDING						
Average household spending on financial products and services	**$9,265.37**	**$10,832.99**	**$9,973.39**	**−14.5%**	**8.6%**	**−7.1%**
Deductions for Social Security	3,902.53	4,121.65	2,710.39	−5.3	*	*
Tax, federal income (net, after refund)	1,135.67	1,850.90	3,050.92	−38.6	−39.3	−62.8
Cash contributions to religious organizations	661.03	814.29	564.30	−18.8	44.3	17.1
Deductions for private pensions (payroll deductions)	588.76	657.00	459.21	−10.4	*	*
Tax, state and local income (net, after refund)	482.45	561.46	711.40	−14.1	−21.1	−32.2
Contributions to retirement accounts (nonpayroll deposits)	469.09	484.31	493.41	−3.1	−1.8	−4.9
Cash gifts	398.06	442.06	–	−10.0	–	–
Insurance, life and other personal except health	318.12	348.44	504.76	−8.7	−31.0	−37.0
Child support	220.09	233.40	–	−5.7	–	–
Finance charges, except mortgage and vehicle	185.98	219.20	320.84	−15.2	−31.7	−42.0
Cash contributions to charitable organizations	159.51	207.89	177.12	−23.3	17.4	−9.9
Legal fees	128.73	171.95	131.64	−25.1	30.6	−2.2
Support for college students	97.78	102.05	–	−4.2	–	–
Deductions for government retirement	90.40	83.26	89.05	8.6	−6.5	1.5
Funeral expenses	79.36	62.16	89.51	27.7	−30.6	−11.3
Lottery and gambling losses	78.72	76.78	52.68	2.5	45.8	49.4
Accounting fees	65.52	67.44	69.87	−2.8	−3.5	−6.2
Occupational expenses	51.64	48.16	121.87	7.2	−60.5	−57.6
Alimony expenses	37.52	49.93	–	−24.9	–	–
Cash contributions to educational institutions	35.86	121.48	25.28	−70.5	380.6	41.9
Bank service charges	22.44	22.88	25.19	−1.9	−9.2	−10.9
Cemetery lots, vaults, maintenance fees	15.12	20.96	17.06	−27.9	22.9	−11.4
Cash contributions to political organizations	12.80	24.00	8.42	−46.7	185.0	52.0
Gifts to members of other households of stocks, bonds, and mutual funds	10.59	26.28	338.71	−59.7	−92.2	−96.9
Shopping club membership fees	8.50	8.19	–	3.8	–	–
Safe deposit box rental	3.65	4.03	5.80	−9.5	−30.4	−37.1
Vacation clubs	3.41	–	–	–	–	–
Credit card membership fees	1.72	2.04	5.96	−15.9	−65.7	−71.2
Dating services	0.32	0.78	–	−58.9	–	–

	2006–10	2000–06	2000–10	percentage point change		
				2006–10	2000–06	2000–10
PERCENT DISTRIBUTION OF SPENDING						
Average household spending on financial products and services	**100.0%**	**100.0%**	**100.0%**	–	–	–
Deductions for Social Security	42.1	38.1	27.2	4.1	*	*
Tax, federal income (net, after refund)	12.3	17.1	30.6	–4.8	–13.5	–18.3
Cash contributions to religious organizations	7.1	7.5	5.7	–0.4	1.9	1.5
Deductions for private pensions (payroll deductions)	6.4	6.1	4.6	0.3	*	*
Tax, state and local income (net, after refund)	5.2	5.2	7.1	0.0	–2.0	–1.9
Contributions to retirement accounts (nonpayroll deposits)	5.1	4.5	4.9	0.6	–0.5	0.1
Cash gifts	4.3	4.1	–	0.2	–	–
Insurance, life and other personal except health	3.4	3.2	5.1	0.2	–1.8	–1.6
Child support	2.4	2.2	–	0.2	–	–
Finance charges, except mortgage and vehicle	2.0	2.0	3.2	–0.0	–1.2	–1.2
Cash contributions to charitable organizations	1.7	1.9	1.8	–0.2	0.1	–0.1
Legal fees	1.4	1.6	1.3	–0.2	0.3	0.1
Support for college students	1.1	0.9	–	0.1	–	–
Deductions for government retirement	1.0	0.8	0.9	0.2	–0.1	0.1
Funeral expenses	0.9	0.6	0.9	0.3	–0.3	–0.0
Lottery and gambling losses	0.8	0.7	0.5	0.1	0.2	0.3
Accounting fees	0.7	0.6	0.7	0.1	–0.1	0.0
Occupational expenses	0.6	0.4	1.2	0.1	–0.8	–0.7
Alimony expenses	0.4	0.5	–	–0.1	–	–
Cash contributions to educational institutions	0.4	1.1	0.3	–0.7	0.9	0.1
Bank service charges	0.2	0.2	0.3	0.0	–0.0	–0.0
Cemetery lots, vaults, maintenance fees	0.2	0.2	0.2	–0.0	0.0	–0.0
Cash contributions to political organizations	0.1	0.2	0.1	–0.1	0.1	0.1
Gifts to members of other households of stocks, bonds, and mutual funds	0.1	0.2	3.4	–0.1	–3.2	–3.3
Shopping club membership fees	0.1	0.1	–	0.0	–	–
Safe deposit box rental	0.0	0.0	0.1	0.0	–0.0	–0.0
Vacation clubs	0.0	–	–	–	–	–
Credit card membership fees	0.0	0.0	0.1	–0.0	–0.0	–0.0
Dating services	0.0	0.0	–	–0.0	–	–

*Recent spending on pensions and Social Security is not comparable with 2000 because of changes in methodology.

Note: "–" means not applicable or data are unavailable.

Source: Bureau of Labor Statistics, 2000, 2006, and 2010 Consumer Expenditure Surveys; calculations by New Strategist

Accounting Fees

Best customers: **Householders aged 55 to 74**
Married couples without children at home
Married couples with school-aged or older children at home
Non-Hispanic whites

Customer trends: **Average household spending on accounting fees may continue to fall in the years ahead as better tax and estate planning software programs allow boomers to handle their finances without the help of a professional.**

The best customers of accountants are households with the most-complex financial matters. Householders with the highest incomes (45 to 54) and those of pre–retirement age (55 to 64), spend 26 percent more than average on accounting fees, and householders aged 65 to 74 spend 30 percent more. Married couples without children at home (most of them older empty-nesters) spend 59 percent more than average. Not only are these households less likely to be computer savvy, but they often have complex financial circumstances as they settle their parents' estates and attempt to simplify their own. Married couples with school-aged or older children at home outspend the average by 24 to 49 percent. Non-Hispanic whites dominate spending on this category and account for 90 percent of the accounting fees market.

Average household spending on accounting fees fell 6 percent between 2000 and 2010, after adjusting for inflation. Behind the small decline was the recession, which forced some households to tighten their belts and buy software rather than services to handle their finances. Spending on accounting fees may continue to fall in the years ahead as better tax and estate planning software programs allow boomers to handle their finances without the help of a professional.

Table 6.2 Accounting fees

Total household spending $7,934,930,640.00
Average household spends   65.52

	AVERAGE HOUSEHOLD SPENDING	BEST CUSTOMERS (index)	BIGGEST CUSTOMERS (market share)
AGE OF HOUSEHOLDER			
Average household	**$65.52**	**100**	**100.0%**
Under age 25	13.07	20	1.3
Aged 25 to 34	37.97	58	9.6
Aged 35 to 44	60.82	93	16.8
Aged 45 to 54	82.30	126	26.0
Aged 55 to 64	82.51	126	22.2
Aged 65 to 74	85.42	130	14.0
Aged 75 or older	68.71	105	10.0

	AVERAGE HOUSEHOLD SPENDING	BEST CUSTOMERS (index)	BIGGEST CUSTOMERS (market share)
HOUSEHOLD INCOME			
Average household	**$65.52**	**100**	**100.0%**
Under $20,000	28.19	43	9.4
$20,000 to $39,999	35.41	54	12.4
$40,000 to $49,999	51.65	79	7.5
$50,000 to $69,999	61.98	95	13.6
$70,000 to $79,999	77.18	118	7.1
$80,000 to $99,999	76.04	116	9.7
$100,000 or more	154.66	236	40.5
HOUSEHOLD TYPE			
Average household	**65.52**	**100**	**100.0**
Married couples	89.77	137	67.6
Married couples, no children	103.97	159	33.7
Married couples, with children	85.92	131	30.5
Oldest child under age 6	60.47	92	4.0
Oldest child aged 6 to 17	97.87	149	17.6
Oldest child aged 18 or older	81.54	124	9.0
Single parent with child under age 18	29.29	45	2.6
Single person	47.19	72	21.1
RACE AND HISPANIC ORIGIN			
Average household	**65.52**	**100**	**100.0**
Asian	56.30	86	3.7
Black	21.78	33	4.1
Hispanic	32.87	50	6.1
Non-Hispanic white and other	77.66	119	89.9
REGION			
Average household	**65.52**	**100**	**100.0**
Northeast	76.60	117	21.5
Midwest	50.71	77	17.3
South	56.80	87	31.8
West	85.22	130	29.5
EDUCATION			
Average household	**65.52**	**100**	**100.0**
Less than high school graduate	30.68	47	6.7
High school graduate	44.07	67	17.2
Some college	55.80	85	17.9
Associate's degree	64.41	98	9.3
Bachelor's degree or more	107.93	165	48.9
Bachelor's degree	86.13	131	24.8
Master's, professional, doctoral degree	146.00	223	24.1

Note: Market shares may not sum to 100.0 because of rounding and missing categories by household type. "Asian" and "black" include Hispanics and non-Hispanics who identify themselves as being of the respective race alone. "Hispanic" includes people of any race who identify themselves as Hispanic. "Other" includes people who identify themselves as non-Hispanic and as Alaska Native, American Indian, Asian (who are also included in the "Asian" row), or Native Hawaiian or other Pacific Islander as well as non-Hispanics reporting more than one race.

Source: Calculations by New Strategist based on the Bureau of Labor Statistics' 2010 Consumer Expenditure Survey

Bank Service Charges

Best customers: Householders aged 35 to 54
Married couples with children under age 18
Single parents
Households in the West

Customer trends: Average household spending on bank service charges may rise in the years ahead
if federal regulations tighten standards and force banks to make money the old-
fashioned way.

The biggest spenders on bank service charges are householders who cannot maintain the larger
bank balances necessary to receive free checking and other services. Householders aged 35 to 54
spend 20 to 29 percent more than the average household on bank service charges and account for
48 percent of the market. Married couples with children under age 18, many of them struggling
to make ends meet, spend 36 to 40 percent more than average on this item. Single parents, whose
spending on most items is well below average, spend an average amount on bank fees. Households
in the West spend 23 percent more than average on this item.

Average household spending on bank service charges fell 11 percent between 2000 and 2010,
after adjusting for inflation. Behind the decline was the elimination of fees as banks competed for
customers. Average household spending on bank service charges may rise in the years ahead if
federal regulations tighten standards and force banks to make money the old-fashioned way.

Table 6.3 Bank service charges

Total household spending $2,717,641,080.00
Average household spends   22.44

	AVERAGE HOUSEHOLD SPENDING	BEST CUSTOMERS (index)	BIGGEST CUSTOMERS (market share)
AGE OF HOUSEHOLDER			
Average household	**$22.44**	**100**	**100.0%**
Under age 25	21.96	98	6.5
Aged 25 to 34	24.50	109	18.2
Aged 35 to 44	28.92	129	23.3
Aged 45 to 54	26.91	120	24.8
Aged 55 to 64	22.21	99	17.5
Aged 65 to 74	16.11	72	7.7
Aged 75 or older	4.73	21	2.0

	AVERAGE HOUSEHOLD SPENDING	BEST CUSTOMERS (index)	BIGGEST CUSTOMERS (market share)
HOUSEHOLD INCOME			
Average household	**$22.44**	**100**	**100.0%**
Under $20,000	16.19	72	15.7
$20,000 to $39,999	19.06	85	19.5
$40,000 to $49,999	14.10	63	5.9
$50,000 to $69,999	24.29	108	15.5
$70,000 to $79,999	27.43	122	7.3
$80,000 to $99,999	29.38	131	10.9
$100,000 or more	32.84	146	25.1
HOUSEHOLD TYPE			
Average household	**22.44**	**100**	**100.0**
Married couples	24.27	108	53.4
Married couples, no children	17.34	77	16.4
Married couples, with children	28.32	126	29.4
Oldest child under age 6	30.44	136	5.8
Oldest child aged 6 to 17	31.51	140	16.5
Oldest child aged 18 or older	21.88	98	7.0
Single parent with child under age 18	22.41	100	5.9
Single person	18.10	81	23.6
RACE AND HISPANIC ORIGIN			
Average household	**22.44**	**100**	**100.0**
Asian	10.35	46	2.0
Black	24.49	109	13.4
Hispanic	21.38	95	11.6
Non-Hispanic white and other	22.54	100	76.2
REGION			
Average household	**22.44**	**100**	**100.0**
Northeast	22.77	101	18.6
Midwest	19.88	89	19.7
South	20.64	92	33.8
West	27.60	123	27.9
EDUCATION			
Average household	**22.44**	**100**	**100.0**
Less than high school graduate	13.26	59	8.4
High school graduate	16.87	75	19.2
Some college	22.86	102	21.4
Associate's degree	24.87	111	10.5
Bachelor's degree or more	30.56	136	40.5
Bachelor's degree	30.23	135	25.4
Master's, professional, doctoral degree	31.15	139	15.0

Note: Market shares may not sum to 100.0 because of rounding and missing categories by household type. "Asian" and "black" include Hispanics and non-Hispanics who identify themselves as being of the respective race alone. "Hispanic" includes people of any race who identify themselves as Hispanic. "Other" includes people who identify themselves as non-Hispanic and as Alaska Native, American Indian, Asian (who are also included in the "Asian" row), or Native Hawaiian or other Pacific Islander as well as non-Hispanics reporting more than one race.

Source: Calculations by New Strategist based on the Bureau of Labor Statistics' 2010 Consumer Expenditure Survey

Cash Contributions to Charitable Organizations

Best customers: **Householders aged 55 or older**
Married couples without children at home
Non-Hispanic whites
College graduates

Customer trends: **The average household is likely to spend less on cash contributions to charitable organizations until discretionary income rebounds.**

The biggest cash donors to charitable organizations are households with the greatest amount of discretionary income—older, educated, white, married couples. Householders aged 55 to 74 spend 31 to 45 percent more than average on this item, and those aged 75 or older spend nearly twice the average. Together 55-or-older householders account for 57 percent of charitable giving. Married couples without children at home (most of them empty-nesters) spend 87 percent more than average on cash gifts to charities and account for 40 percent of all charitable giving. Non-Hispanic whites account for 92 percent of all cash contributions to charitable organizations as they give 22 percent more than average. College graduates (who dominate the affluent) give well more than twice the average to charitable organizations.

Average household giving to charitable organizations grew 17 percent between 2000 and 2006, after adjusting for inflation, then fell 23 percent in the ensuing four years. Behind the decline was household belt tightening in financially distressed times. Expect to see spending on cash gifts to charities to decline further in the coming years unless discretionary income rises.

Table 6.4 Cash contributions to charitable organizations

| Total household spending | $19,317,777,570.00 |
| Average household spends | 159.51 |

	AVERAGE HOUSEHOLD SPENDING	BEST CUSTOMERS (index)	BIGGEST CUSTOMERS (market share)
AGE OF HOUSEHOLDER			
Average household	**$159.51**	**100**	**100.0%**
Under age 25	17.91	11	0.7
Aged 25 to 34	67.40	42	7.0
Aged 35 to 44	125.58	79	14.2
Aged 45 to 54	163.66	103	21.2
Aged 55 to 64	208.51	131	23.1
Aged 65 to 74	231.06	145	15.6
Aged 75 or older	302.85	190	18.1

	AVERAGE HOUSEHOLD SPENDING	BEST CUSTOMERS (index)	BIGGEST CUSTOMERS (market share)
HOUSEHOLD INCOME			
Average household	$159.51	100	100.0%
Under $20,000	48.36	30	6.6
$20,000 to $39,999	76.08	48	10.9
$40,000 to $49,999	84.97	53	5.0
$50,000 to $69,999	159.61	100	14.4
$70,000 to $79,999	127.00	80	4.8
$80,000 to $99,999	224.89	141	11.8
$100,000 or more	433.02	271	46.5
HOUSEHOLD TYPE			
Average household	159.51	100	100.0
Married couples	216.82	136	67.1
Married couples, no children	297.75	187	39.6
Married couples, with children	166.38	104	24.3
Oldest child under age 6	93.84	59	2.5
Oldest child aged 6 to 17	187.54	118	13.8
Oldest child aged 18 or older	174.94	110	7.9
Single parent with child under age 18	24.74	16	0.9
Single person	121.68	76	22.3
RACE AND HISPANIC ORIGIN			
Average household	159.51	100	100.0
Asian	132.14	83	3.5
Black	52.17	33	4.0
Hispanic	51.36	32	3.9
Non-Hispanic white and other	194.61	122	92.5
REGION			
Average household	159.51	100	100.0
Northeast	202.31	127	23.3
Midwest	180.55	113	25.2
South	115.08	72	26.5
West	176.11	110	25.0
EDUCATION			
Average household	159.51	100	100.0
Less than high school graduate	37.46	23	3.4
High school graduate	66.05	41	10.6
Some college	103.93	65	13.7
Associate's degree	124.81	78	7.4
Bachelor's degree or more	348.89	219	65.0
Bachelor's degree	277.23	174	32.8
Master's, professional, doctoral degree	474.02	297	32.2

Note: Market shares may not sum to 100.0 because of rounding and missing categories by household type. "Asian" and "black" include Hispanics and non-Hispanics who identify themselves as being of the respective race alone. "Hispanic" includes people of any race who identify themselves as Hispanic. "Other" includes people who identify themselves as non-Hispanic and as Alaska Native, American Indian, Asian (who are also included in the "Asian" row), or Native Hawaiian or other Pacific Islander as well as non-Hispanics reporting more than one race.

Source: Calculations by New Strategist based on the Bureau of Labor Statistics' 2010 Consumer Expenditure Survey

Cash Contributions to Educational Organizations

Best customers: Householders aged 45 to 54 and 75 or older
High-income households
Married couples without children at home
Married couples with school-aged children
Asians and non-Hispanic whites
Households in the Northeast and West
College graduates

Customer trends: Average household spending on cash contributions to educational organizations is likely to continue to decline in the years ahead as the economic downturn limits discretionary spending.

The biggest spenders on educational contributions are affluent, white, and educated. These are the households with the discretionary income to spend on their alma mater. Householders aged 75 or older spend two-and-one-half times the average on contributions to educational organizations, and those aged 45 to 54 give 17 percent more than average. Households with incomes of $100,000 and more contribute over three times the average amount to educational organizations and are responsible for 57 percent of giving. Married couples without children at home give 79 percent more than average to educational organizations, and couples with school-aged children give 55 percent more. Asians give 27 percent more than average to educational institutions, but non-Hispanic whites dominate donations to educational organizations and account for 91 percent of all such giving. Households in the Northeast and West donate two-thirds more than average to schools and universities. College graduates spend nearly three times the average on this item.

Average household spending on donations to educational organizations, which had increased enormously between 2000 and 2006, dropped by 70 percent between 2006 and 2010. Spending on contributions to educational organizations is likely to continue to decline in the years ahead as the economic downturn limits discretionary spending.

Table 6.5 Cash contributions to educational org\anizations

Total household spending $4,342,897,020.00
Average household spends   35.86

	AVERAGE HOUSEHOLD SPENDING	BEST CUSTOMERS (index)	BIGGEST CUSTOMERS (market share)
AGE OF HOUSEHOLDER			
Average household	**$35.86**	**100**	**100.0%**
Under age 25	1.50	4	0.3
Aged 25 to 34	14.23	40	6.6
Aged 35 to 44	31.02	87	15.7
Aged 45 to 54	41.87	117	24.2
Aged 55 to 64	38.36	107	18.9
Aged 65 to 74	36.21	101	10.9
Aged 75 or older	88.64	247	23.6

	AVERAGE HOUSEHOLD SPENDING	BEST CUSTOMERS (index)	BIGGEST CUSTOMERS (market share)
HOUSEHOLD INCOME			
Average household	**$35.86**	**100**	**100.0%**
Under $20,000	17.99	50	10.9
$20,000 to $39,999	8.64	24	5.5
$40,000 to $49,999	43.46	121	11.5
$50,000 to $69,999	13.82	39	5.5
$70,000 to $79,999	16.63	46	2.8
$80,000 to $99,999	27.46	77	6.4
$100,000 or more	120.02	335	57.4
HOUSEHOLD TYPE			
Average household	**35.86**	**100**	**100.0**
Married couples	50.00	139	68.8
Married couples, no children	64.14	179	38.0
Married couples, with children	38.54	107	25.0
Oldest child under age 6	14.56	41	1.7
Oldest child aged 6 to 17	55.47	155	18.2
Oldest child aged 18 or older	25.19	70	5.1
Single parent with child under age 18	3.67	10	0.6
Single person	21.05	59	17.2
RACE AND HISPANIC ORIGIN			
Average household	**35.86**	**100**	**100.0**
Asian	45.58	127	5.4
Black	14.91	42	5.1
Hispanic	11.63	32	4.0
Non-Hispanic white and other	43.27	121	91.5
REGION			
Average household	**35.86**	**100**	**100.0**
Northeast	61.04	170	31.2
Midwest	24.32	68	15.1
South	15.63	44	16.0
West	59.60	166	37.6
EDUCATION			
Average household	**35.86**	**100**	**100.0**
Less than high school graduate	1.21	3	0.5
High school graduate	3.06	9	2.2
Some college	20.17	56	11.8
Associate's degree	16.35	46	4.3
Bachelor's degree or more	98.02	273	81.2
Bachelor's degree	49.35	138	26.0
Master's, professional, doctoral degree	182.99	510	55.2

Note: Market shares may not sum to 100.0 because of rounding and missing categories by household type. "Asian" and "black" include Hispanics and non-Hispanics who identify themselves as being of the respective race alone. "Hispanic" includes people of any race who identify themselves as Hispanic. "Other" includes people who identify themselves as non-Hispanic and as Alaska Native, American Indian, Asian (who are also included in the "Asian" row), or Native Hawaiian or other Pacific Islander as well as non-Hispanics reporting more than one race.

Source: Calculations by New Strategist based on the Bureau of Labor Statistics' 2010 Consumer Expenditure Survey

Cash Contributions to Political Organizations

Best customers:

Householders aged 55 to 64
High-income households
Married couples without children at home
Married couples with children under age 18
Non-Hispanic whites
Households in the Northeast
College graduates

Customer trends:

Average household spending on cash contributions to political organizations is driven by the degree of political divisiveness among voters. Unless the political divide shrinks, contributions may be even greater in presidential election year 2012.

The biggest spenders on political contributions are older, affluent, white, and educated. These are the households with the discretionary income to devote to political causes. Householders aged 55 to 64 spend 71 percent more than average on contributions to political organizations. Householders with incomes of $100,000 or more give four times the average to political causes. Married couples without children at home (most of them empty-nesters) give 54 percent more, and those children under age 18 also give much more than average. Non-Hispanic whites account for 93 percent of all political donations. Households in the Northeast spend 50 percent more than average on this item. College graduates, who dominate the affluent, spend almost two-and-one-half times the average on this item.

Average household spending on donations to political organizations, which had grown rapidly between 2000 and 2006, after adjusting for inflation, declined by 47 percent in the four ensuing years. Behind the earlier increase was growing political polarization, driving both right and left to give money to organizations promoting their candidate. Then the Great Recession reduced spending on most discretionary items, including political donations. Unless the political divide shrinks, however, contributions may grow again in presidential election year 2012.

Table 6.6 Cash contributions to political organizations

Total household spending	$1,550,169,600.00
Average household spends	12.80

	AVERAGE HOUSEHOLD SPENDING	BEST CUSTOMERS (index)	BIGGEST CUSTOMERS (market share)
AGE OF HOUSEHOLDER			
Average household	**$12.80**	**100**	**100.0%**
Under age 25	0.53	4	0.3
Aged 25 to 34	2.09	16	2.7
Aged 35 to 44	17.09	134	24.2
Aged 45 to 54	11.45	89	18.5
Aged 55 to 64	21.84	171	30.1
Aged 65 to 74	14.20	111	11.9
Aged 75 or older	16.53	129	12.3

	AVERAGE HOUSEHOLD SPENDING	BEST CUSTOMERS (index)	BIGGEST CUSTOMERS (market share)
HOUSEHOLD INCOME			
Average household	**$12.80**	**100**	**100.0%**
Under $20,000	2.67	21	4.6
$20,000 to $39,999	3.56	28	6.4
$40,000 to $49,999	8.23	64	6.1
$50,000 to $69,999	8.05	63	9.0
$70,000 to $79,999	3.80	30	1.8
$80,000 to $99,999	5.29	41	3.4
$100,000 or more	51.31	401	68.7
HOUSEHOLD TYPE			
Average household	**12.80**	**100**	**100.0**
Married couples	19.22	150	74.1
Married couples, no children	19.72	154	32.7
Married couples, with children	20.63	161	37.5
Oldest child under age 6	42.68	333	14.3
Oldest child aged 6 to 17	17.62	138	16.2
Oldest child aged 18 or older	12.48	98	7.0
Single parent with child under age 18	0.32	3	0.1
Single person	9.88	77	22.6
RACE AND HISPANIC ORIGIN			
Average household	**12.80**	**100**	**100.0**
Asian	11.16	87	3.7
Black	2.84	22	2.7
Hispanic	5.26	41	5.0
Non-Hispanic white and other	15.75	123	93.3
REGION			
Average household	**12.80**	**100**	**100.0**
Northeast	19.15	150	27.5
Midwest	14.69	115	25.6
South	10.13	79	29.0
West	10.12	79	17.9
EDUCATION			
Average household	**12.80**	**100**	**100.0**
Less than high school graduate	1.92	15	2.1
High school graduate	5.81	45	11.6
Some college	5.98	47	9.8
Associate's degree	5.22	41	3.9
Bachelor's degree or more	31.28	244	72.6
Bachelor's degree	29.25	229	43.2
Master's, professional, doctoral degree	34.82	272	29.4

Note: Market shares may not sum to 100.0 because of rounding and missing categories by household type. "Asian" and "black" include Hispanics and non-Hispanics who identify themselves as being of the respective race alone. "Hispanic" includes people of any race who identify themselves as Hispanic. "Other" includes people who identify themselves as non-Hispanic and as Alaska Native, American Indian, Asian (who are also included in the "Asian" row), or Native Hawaiian or other Pacific Islander as well as non-Hispanics reporting more than one race.

Source: Calculations by New Strategist based on the Bureau of Labor Statistics' 2010 Consumer Expenditure Survey

Cash Contributions to Religious Organizations

Best customers:
Householders aged 55 or older
Married couples without children at home
Married couples with school-aged or older children at home
Blacks
Households in the South

Customer trends:
Average household spending on cash contributions to religious organizations may renew its climb as boomers enter the lifestage of increased giving.

Contributions to religious organizations are one of the most-important items in the household budget, ranking 17th among the items on which households spend the most. Those donating the most to religious organizations are older married couples. Householders aged 55 or older spend 21 to 51 percent more than the average household on cash contributions to churches and religious organizations. Married couples without children at home (most of them empty-nesters) spend 64 percent more than average, while couples with school-aged or older children at home spend 47 to 49 percent more. Blacks, whose spending is below average on most items, contribute 16 percent more than the average cash amount to religious institutions, and households in the South, where many blacks reside, donate 20 percent more than average.

Average household giving to religious organizations rose 44 percent between 2000 and 2006, after adjusting for inflation, then dropped 19 percent in the four ensuing years as the Great Recession reduced discretionary spending. The aging of the population into the lifestage when giving is greatest suggests renewed growth in this category.

Table 6.7 Cash contributions to religious organizations

Total household spending $80,055,360,210.00
Average household spends 661.03

	AVERAGE HOUSEHOLD SPENDING	BEST CUSTOMERS (index)	BIGGEST CUSTOMERS (market share)
AGE OF HOUSEHOLDER			
Average household	**$661.03**	**100**	**100.0%**
Under age 25	149.20	23	1.5
Aged 25 to 34	417.71	63	10.5
Aged 35 to 44	575.42	87	15.7
Aged 45 to 54	692.40	105	21.7
Aged 55 to 64	852.14	129	22.7
Aged 65 to 74	1,001.34	151	16.3
Aged 75 or older	798.91	121	11.5

	AVERAGE HOUSEHOLD SPENDING	BEST CUSTOMERS (index)	BIGGEST CUSTOMERS (market share)
HOUSEHOLD INCOME			
Average household	$661.03	100	100.0%
Under $20,000	239.15	36	7.9
$20,000 to $39,999	388.76	59	13.5
$40,000 to $49,999	571.64	86	8.2
$50,000 to $69,999	675.85	102	14.7
$70,000 to $79,999	827.96	125	7.5
$80,000 to $99,999	973.07	147	12.3
$100,000 or more	1,388.72	210	36.0
HOUSEHOLD TYPE			
Average household	661.03	100	100.0
Married couples	993.43	150	74.1
Married couples, no children	1,083.64	164	34.8
Married couples, with children	920.03	139	32.4
Oldest child under age 6	649.18	98	4.2
Oldest child aged 6 to 17	988.11	149	17.6
Oldest child aged 18 or older	969.77	147	10.6
Single parent with child under age 18	321.82	49	2.9
Single person	355.47	54	15.8
RACE AND HISPANIC ORIGIN			
Average household	661.03	100	100.0
Asian	517.51	78	3.3
Black	764.02	116	14.1
Hispanic	298.95	45	5.5
Non-Hispanic white and other	701.42	106	80.4
REGION			
Average household	661.03	100	100.0
Northeast	366.76	55	10.2
Midwest	654.39	99	22.1
South	795.08	120	44.1
West	688.81	104	23.6
EDUCATION			
Average household	661.03	100	100.0
Less than high school graduate	285.03	43	6.2
High school graduate	479.97	73	18.5
Some college	613.18	93	19.5
Associate's degree	711.49	108	10.2
Bachelor's degree or more	1,015.29	154	45.6
Bachelor's degree	899.18	136	25.7
Master's, professional, doctoral degree	1,218.00	184	19.9

Note: Market shares may not sum to 100.0 because of rounding and missing categories by household type. "Asian" and "black" include Hispanics and non-Hispanics who identify themselves as being of the respective race alone. "Hispanic" includes people of any race who identify themselves as Hispanic. "Other" includes people who identify themselves as non-Hispanic and as Alaska Native, American Indian, Asian (who are also included in the "Asian" row), or Native Hawaiian or other Pacific Islander as well as non-Hispanics reporting more than one race.

Source: Calculations by New Strategist based on the Bureau of Labor Statistics' 2010 Consumer Expenditure Survey

Cash Gifts, Other than Charitable, Educational, Political, or Religious

Best customers: **Householders aged 65 or older**
                                   Married couples without children at home

Customer trends: **Average household spending on cash gifts is likely to grow in the years ahead as aging boomers attempt to help their struggling adult children.**

Many older parents give money to their adult children to help them make a down payment on a home, to defray a grandchild's college expenses, or to cover necessities like health insurance and day care. Householders aged 75 or older spend nearly two-and-one-half times the average on such cash gifts, and householders aged 65 to 74 give twice the average amount in cash gifts. Married couples without children at home (most of them empty-nesters) give 91 percent more than average in cash gifts.

Average household spending on cash gifts fell 10 percent between 2006 and 2010, after adjusting for inflation, as the Great Recession reduced discretionary income. As millions of boomers move into the best-customer lifestage in the years ahead—many with struggling adult children—average household spending on cash gifts may grow.

Table 6.8 Cash gifts, other than charitable, educational, political, or religious

Total household spending $48,207,852,420.00
Average household spends   398.06

	AVERAGE HOUSEHOLD SPENDING	BEST CUSTOMERS (index)	BIGGEST CUSTOMERS (market share)
AGE OF HOUSEHOLDER			
Average household	**$398.06**	**100**	**100.0%**
Under age 25	85.24	21	1.4
Aged 25 to 34	238.53	60	10.0
Aged 35 to 44	231.15	58	10.5
Aged 45 to 54	259.40	65	13.5
Aged 55 to 64	450.09	113	19.9
Aged 65 to 74	798.62	201	21.6
Aged 75 or older	963.42	242	23.1

	AVERAGE HOUSEHOLD SPENDING	BEST CUSTOMERS (index)	BIGGEST CUSTOMERS (market share)
HOUSEHOLD INCOME			
Average household	**$398.06**	**100**	**100.0%**
Under $20,000	181.69	46	10.0
$20,000 to $39,999	366.33	92	21.1
$40,000 to $49,999	319.22	80	7.6
$50,000 to $69,999	405.05	102	14.6
$70,000 to $79,999	410.31	103	6.2
$80,000 to $99,999	548.63	138	11.5
$100,000 or more	675.96	170	29.1
HOUSEHOLD TYPE			
Average household	**398.06**	**100**	**100.0**
Married couples	475.14	119	58.9
Married couples, no children	762.01	191	40.7
Married couples, with children	232.32	58	13.6
Oldest child under age 6	170.73	43	1.8
Oldest child aged 6 to 17	191.85	48	5.7
Oldest child aged 18 or older	334.76	84	6.1
Single parent with child under age 18	66.68	17	1.0
Single person	370.59	93	27.3
RACE AND HISPANIC ORIGIN			
Average household	**398.06**	**100**	**100.0**
Asian	276.26	69	3.0
Black	187.58	47	5.8
Hispanic	373.22	94	11.4
Non-Hispanic white and other	435.35	109	82.9
REGION			
Average household	**398.06**	**100**	**100.0**
Northeast	456.58	115	21.1
Midwest	363.87	91	20.4
South	335.53	84	30.9
West	485.60	122	27.6
EDUCATION			
Average household	**398.06**	**100**	**100.0**
Less than high school graduate	304.47	76	10.9
High school graduate	279.48	70	17.9
Some college	397.44	100	21.0
Associate's degree	374.92	94	8.9
Bachelor's degree or more	552.77	139	41.3
Bachelor's degree	548.19	138	26.0
Master's, professional, doctoral degree	560.75	141	15.2

Note: Market shares may not sum to 100.0 because of rounding and missing categories by household type. "Asian" and "black" include Hispanics and non-Hispanics who identify themselves as being of the respective race alone. "Hispanic" includes people of any race who identify themselves as Hispanic. "Other" includes people who identify themselves as non-Hispanic and as Alaska Native, American Indian, Asian (who are also included in the "Asian" row), or Native Hawaiian or other Pacific Islander as well as non-Hispanics reporting more than one race.

Source: Calculations by New Strategist based on the Bureau of Labor Statistics' 2010 Consumer Expenditure Survey

Cemetery Lots, Vaults, Maintenance Fees

Best customers: Householders aged 55 to 64 and 75 or older
People who live alone

Customer trends: Average household spending on cemetery lots, vaults, and maintenance fees
should rise as the population ages unless more choose cremation.

Not surprisingly, the biggest spenders on cemetery lots, vaults, and maintenance fees are older Americans. Householders aged 55 to 64 and 75 or older spend two-and-one-half times the average on cemetery lots as they bury their parents and spouses, respectively. People who live alone, whose spending approaches average on only a few items, spend 27 percent above average on cemetery lots and maintenance.

Average household spending on cemetery lots, vaults, and maintenance fees rose 23 percent between 2000 and 2006, after adjusting for inflation, then declined 28 percent between 2006 and 2010 as households were forced to cut costs in the face of the Great Recession. Spending on cemetery lots, vaults, and maintenance fees should rise with the aging of the population unless more choose cremation.

Table 6.9 Cemetery lots, vaults, maintenance fees

Total household spending $1,831,137,840.00
Average household spends   15.12

	AVERAGE HOUSEHOLD SPENDING	BEST CUSTOMERS (index)	BIGGEST CUSTOMERS (market share)
AGE OF HOUSEHOLDER			
Average household	**$15.12**	**100**	**100.0%**
Under age 25	–	–	–
Aged 25 to 34	0.09	1	0.1
Aged 35 to 44	3.56	24	4.3
Aged 45 to 54	10.67	71	14.6
Aged 55 to 64	39.35	260	45.9
Aged 65 to 74	16.45	109	11.7
Aged 75 or older	37.16	246	23.4

	AVERAGE HOUSEHOLD SPENDING	BEST CUSTOMERS (index)	BIGGEST CUSTOMERS (market share)
HOUSEHOLD INCOME			
Average household	**$15.12**	**100**	**100.0%**
Under $20,000	9.38	62	13.5
$20,000 to $39,999	13.26	88	20.1
$40,000 to $49,999	15.19	100	9.5
$50,000 to $69,999	19.06	126	18.1
$70,000 to $79,999	6.10	40	2.4
$80,000 to $99,999	25.77	170	14.2
$100,000 or more	19.54	129	22.2
HOUSEHOLD TYPE			
Average household	**15.12**	**100**	**100.0**
Married couples	13.93	92	45.4
Married couples, no children	17.73	117	24.9
Married couples, with children	3.91	26	6.0
Oldest child under age 6	–	–	–
Oldest child aged 6 to 17	6.14	41	4.8
Oldest child aged 18 or older	2.59	17	1.2
Single parent with child under age 18	7.30	48	2.8
Single person	19.27	127	37.3
RACE AND HISPANIC ORIGIN			
Average household	**15.12**	**100**	**100.0**
Asian	30.52	202	8.6
Black	12.14	80	9.8
Hispanic	5.15	34	4.1
Non-Hispanic white and other	17.16	113	86.0
REGION			
Average household	**15.12**	**100**	**100.0**
Northeast	14.33	95	17.4
Midwest	16.04	106	23.6
South	14.69	97	35.7
West	15.55	103	23.3
EDUCATION			
Average household	**15.12**	**100**	**100.0**
Less than high school graduate	11.72	78	11.1
High school graduate	12.17	80	20.6
Some college	8.38	55	11.7
Associate's degree	9.87	65	6.2
Bachelor's degree or more	25.74	170	50.6
Bachelor's degree	18.72	124	23.4
Master's, professional, doctoral degree	37.99	251	27.2

Note: Market shares may not sum to 100.0 because of rounding and missing categories by household type. "Asian" and "black" include Hispanics and non-Hispanics who identify themselves as being of the respective race alone. "Hispanic" includes people of any race who identify themselves as Hispanic. "Other" includes people who identify themselves as non-Hispanic and as Alaska Native, American Indian, Asian (who are also included in the Asian column), or Native Hawaiian or other Pacific Islander as well as non-Hispanics reporting more than one race. "–" means sample is too small to make a reliable estimate.

Source: Calculations by New Strategist based on the Bureau of Labor Statistics' 2010 Consumer Expenditure Survey

Child Support

Best customers: **Householders aged 35 to 44**
                                Single parents
                                Hispanics and blacks

Customer trends: **Average household spending on child support is likely to decline as divorce becomes less common and the small generation X fills the most-divorce-prone age group.**

The biggest spenders on child support are householders aged 35 to 44, who spend twice the average on this item. Single parents outspend the average by 45 percent. Hispanics and blacks spend, respectively, 23 and 16 percent more than average on child support.

Child support payments are a relatively new item in the Consumer Expenditure Survey and comparable data for 2000 do not exist. Average household spending on child support declined 6 percent between 2006 and 2010, after adjusting for inflation. With the divorce rate declining and the much smaller generation X now in the most-divorce-prone 35-to-44 age group, average household spending on child support should continue to decline.

Table 6.10 Child support

Total household spending $26,654,439,630.00
Average household spends   220.09

	AVERAGE HOUSEHOLD SPENDING	BEST CUSTOMERS (index)	BIGGEST CUSTOMERS (market share)
AGE OF HOUSEHOLDER			
Average household	**$220.09**	**100**	**100.0%**
Under age 25	55.22	25	1.7
Aged 25 to 34	300.91	137	22.8
Aged 35 to 44	446.98	203	36.7
Aged 45 to 54	299.14	136	28.1
Aged 55 to 64	84.60	38	6.8
Aged 65 to 74	59.22	27	2.9
Aged 75 or older	23.82	11	1.0

	AVERAGE HOUSEHOLD SPENDING	BEST CUSTOMERS (index)	BIGGEST CUSTOMERS (market share)
HOUSEHOLD INCOME			
Average household	**$220.09**	**100**	**100.0%**
Under $20,000	74.10	34	7.3
$20,000 to $39,999	133.49	61	13.9
$40,000 to $49,999	296.80	135	12.7
$50,000 to $69,999	261.07	119	17.0
$70,000 to $79,999	378.13	172	10.3
$80,000 to $99,999	313.71	143	11.9
$100,000 or more	344.38	156	26.8
HOUSEHOLD TYPE			
Average household	**220.09**	**100**	**100.0**
Married couples	165.19	75	37.0
Married couples, no children	99.04	45	9.6
Married couples, with children	221.14	100	23.4
Oldest child under age 6	224.21	102	4.4
Oldest child aged 6 to 17	256.69	117	13.7
Oldest child aged 18 or older	161.42	73	5.3
Single parent with child under age 18	318.78	145	8.5
Single person	255.77	116	34.0
RACE AND HISPANIC ORIGIN			
Average household	**220.09**	**100**	**100.0**
Asian	33.17	15	0.6
Black	254.70	116	14.2
Hispanic	270.93	123	15.0
Non-Hispanic white and other	205.75	93	70.9
REGION			
Average household	**220.09**	**100**	**100.0**
Northeast	194.09	88	16.2
Midwest	239.35	109	24.2
South	230.44	105	38.4
West	205.43	93	21.1
EDUCATION			
Average household	**220.09**	**100**	**100.0**
Less than high school graduate	201.59	92	13.1
High school graduate	219.29	100	25.4
Some college	218.59	99	20.9
Associate's degree	313.40	142	13.5
Bachelor's degree or more	201.06	91	27.1
Bachelor's degree	219.63	100	18.9
Master's, professional, doctoral degree	168.64	77	8.3

Note: Market shares may not sum to 100.0 because of rounding and missing categories by household type. "Asian" and "black" include Hispanics and non-Hispanics who identify themselves as being of the respective race alone. "Hispanic" includes people of any race who identify themselves as Hispanic. "Other" includes people who identify themselves as non-Hispanic and as Alaska Native, American Indian, Asian (who are also included in the "Asian" row), or Native Hawaiian or other Pacific Islander as well as non-Hispanics reporting more than one race.

Source: Calculations by New Strategist based on the Bureau of Labor Statistics' 2010 Consumer Expenditure Survey

Contributions to Retirement Accounts (Nonpayroll Deposits)

Best customers: **Householders aged 45 to 64**
High-income households
Married couples without children at home
Married couples with children under age 18
Asians and non-Hispanic whites
Households in the Northeast and West
College graduates

Customer trends: **Average household spending on nonpayroll contributions to retirement accounts**
should grow as aging boomers attempt to save more for retirement—but only if
households can afford to save.

Affluent householders approaching retirement make the largest nonpayroll deposits to retirement accounts. Householders aged 45 to 64 spent 36 to 70 percent more than average on such accounts in 2010 and accounted for 58 percent of all such contributions. Households with incomes of $100,000 or more squirrel away three-and-three-quarter times the average and account for 64 percent of the market. Married couples without children at home (most of them empty-nesters) spend 83 percent more than average on contributions to retirement accounts, while couples with children under age 18 manage to save between 49 and 90 percent more than average for retirement. Asians spend 19 percent and non-Hispanic whites 23 percent more than average on nonpayroll contributions. Households in the West and Northeast spend, respectively, 48 and 22 percent more than average on nonpayroll deposits to retirement accounts. College graduates, who dominate the affluent, contribute twice the average to their retirement portfolios.

Average household spending on contributions to retirement accounts fell 5 percent between 2000 and 2010, after adjusting for inflation. As aging boomers attempt to save more for retirement, spending on contributions to retirement accounts may rise—but only if households can afford to save.

Table 6.11 Contributions to retirement accounts (nonpayroll deposits)

Total household spending   **$56,810,082,630.00**
Average household spends   **469.09**

	AVERAGE HOUSEHOLD SPENDING	BEST CUSTOMERS (index)	BIGGEST CUSTOMERS (market share)
AGE OF HOUSEHOLDER			
Average household	**$469.09**	**100**	**100.0%**
Under age 25	39.97	9	0.6
Aged 25 to 34	228.71	49	8.1
Aged 35 to 44	530.65	113	20.5
Aged 45 to 54	639.18	136	28.2
Aged 55 to 64	795.20	170	29.9
Aged 65 to 74	401.15	86	9.2
Aged 75 or older	175.17	37	3.6

	AVERAGE HOUSEHOLD SPENDING	BEST CUSTOMERS (index)	BIGGEST CUSTOMERS (market share)
HOUSEHOLD INCOME			
Average household	**$469.09**	**100**	**100.0%**
Under $20,000	39.37	8	1.8
$20,000 to $39,999	91.72	20	4.5
$40,000 to $49,999	232.61	50	4.7
$50,000 to $69,999	266.89	57	8.2
$70,000 to $79,999	406.92	87	5.2
$80,000 to $99,999	653.50	139	11.6
$100,000 or more	1,751.79	373	64.0
HOUSEHOLD TYPE			
Average household	**469.09**	**100**	**100.0**
Married couples	715.41	153	75.2
Married couples, no children	857.82	183	38.8
Married couples, with children	642.41	137	31.9
Oldest child under age 6	892.21	190	8.1
Oldest child aged 6 to 17	698.40	149	17.5
Oldest child aged 18 or older	403.11	86	6.2
Single parent with child under age 18	174.29	37	2.2
Single person	249.70	53	15.6
RACE AND HISPANIC ORIGIN			
Average household	**469.09**	**100**	**100.0**
Asian	557.55	119	5.1
Black	135.76	29	3.5
Hispanic	127.08	27	3.3
Non-Hispanic white and other	578.21	123	93.4
REGION			
Average household	**469.09**	**100**	**100.0**
Northeast	574.53	122	22.5
Midwest	499.36	106	23.7
South	258.04	55	20.2
West	695.82	148	33.6
EDUCATION			
Average household	**469.09**	**100**	**100.0**
Less than high school graduate	50.92	11	1.6
High school graduate	290.56	62	15.8
Some college	268.96	57	12.1
Associate's degree	479.91	102	9.7
Bachelor's degree or more	961.80	205	60.9
Bachelor's degree	741.94	158	29.9
Master's, professional, doctoral degree	1,345.68	287	31.0

Note: Market shares may not sum to 100.0 because of rounding and missing categories by household type. "Asian" and "black" include Hispanics and non-Hispanics who identify themselves as being of the respective race alone. "Hispanic" includes people of any race who identify themselves as Hispanic. "Other" includes people who identify themselves as non-Hispanic and as Alaska Native, American Indian, Asian (who are also included in the "Asian" row), or Native Hawaiian or other Pacific Islander as well as non-Hispanics reporting more than one race.

Source: Calculations by New Strategist based on the Bureau of Labor Statistics' 2010 Consumer Expenditure Survey

Credit Card Membership Fees

Best customers: Householders aged 55 to 74
Married couples without children at home
Married couples with preschoolers
Asians
Households in the Northeast and West
College graduates

Customer trends: Average household spending on credit card membership fees may rise as new
financial regulations tighten lending standards.

The biggest spenders on credit card memberships are households that carry the largest number of cards—older married couples. Householders aged 55 to 74 spend 28 to 31 percent more than the average household on credit card membership fees. Married couples without children at home, most empty-nesters, spend 53 percent more than average, and couples with preschoolers, 67 percent. Asians spend twice the average on credit card membership fees, but non-Hispanic whites account for 90 percent of the market. Households in the Northeast and West spend, respectively, 38 and 39 percent more than average on credit card membership fees. College graduates pay two-and-one-quarter times the average in credit card membership fees.

As competition among credit cards has grown, fees have fallen or disappeared entirely. Consequently, average household spending on credit card memberships has plummeted—down 71 percent between 2000 and 2010, after adjusting for inflation. Spending on this item may increase as new financial regulations tighten lending standards.

Table 6.12 Credit card membership fees

Total household spending $208,304,040.00
Average household spends   1.72

	AVERAGE HOUSEHOLD SPENDING	BEST CUSTOMERS (index)	BIGGEST CUSTOMERS (market share)
AGE OF HOUSEHOLDER			
Average household	**$1.72**	**100**	**100.0%**
Under age 25	0.68	40	2.6
Aged 25 to 34	1.61	94	15.6
Aged 35 to 44	1.89	110	19.9
Aged 45 to 54	1.59	92	19.1
Aged 55 to 64	2.20	128	22.6
Aged 65 to 74	2.25	131	14.1
Aged 75 or older	1.15	67	6.4

	AVERAGE HOUSEHOLD SPENDING	BEST CUSTOMERS (index)	BIGGEST CUSTOMERS (market share)
HOUSEHOLD INCOME			
Average household	**$1.72**	**100**	**100.0%**
Under $20,000	0.31	18	3.9
$20,000 to $39,999	1.12	65	14.9
$40,000 to $49,999	0.79	46	4.3
$50,000 to $69,999	1.74	101	14.5
$70,000 to $79,999	2.24	130	7.8
$80,000 to $99,999	1.34	78	6.5
$100,000 or more	4.96	288	49.4
HOUSEHOLD TYPE			
Average household	**1.72**	**100**	**100.0**
Married couples	2.04	119	58.5
Married couples, no children	2.63	153	32.5
Married couples, with children	1.73	101	23.4
Oldest child under age 6	2.88	167	7.2
Oldest child aged 6 to 17	1.50	87	10.3
Oldest child aged 18 or older	1.42	83	6.0
Single parent with child under age 18	0.78	45	2.7
Single person	1.39	81	23.7
RACE AND HISPANIC ORIGIN			
Average household	**1.72**	**100**	**100.0**
Asian	3.55	206	8.8
Black	1.08	63	7.7
Hispanic	0.34	20	2.4
Non-Hispanic white and other	2.05	119	90.4
REGION			
Average household	**1.72**	**100**	**100.0**
Northeast	2.38	138	25.4
Midwest	1.51	88	19.6
South	1.11	65	23.7
West	2.39	139	31.5
EDUCATION			
Average household	**1.72**	**100**	**100.0**
Less than high school graduate	0.27	16	2.2
High school graduate	0.70	41	10.4
Some college	1.31	76	16.0
Associate's degree	0.89	52	4.9
Bachelor's degree or more	3.85	224	66.5
Bachelor's degree	2.86	166	31.4
Master's, professional, doctoral degree	5.59	325	35.2

Note: Market shares may not sum to 100.0 because of rounding and missing categories by household type. "Asian" and "black" include Hispanics and non-Hispanics who identify themselves as being of the respective race alone. "Hispanic" includes people of any race who identify themselves as Hispanic. "Other" includes people who identify themselves as non-Hispanic and as Alaska Native, American Indian, Asian (who are also included in the "Asian" row), or Native Hawaiian or other Pacific Islander as well as non-Hispanics reporting more than one race.

Source: Calculations by New Strategist based on the Bureau of Labor Statistics' 2010 Consumer Expenditure Survey

Deductions for Government Retirement

Best customers:	**Householders aged 45 to 64** **Married couples without children at home** **Married couples with children under age 18** **College graduates**
Customer trends:	**Average household spending on deductions for government retirement may decline** **in the years ahead if federal, state, and local governments reduce their workforce.**

Affluent middle-aged or older married couples spend the most on government retirement plans. Householders aged 45 to 64 spend 54 to 57 percent more than average on deductions for government retirement. Married couples without children at home (most of them empty-nesters) spend 56 percent more than average on deductions for government retirement, and those with children under age 18 spend 34 to 61 percent more. College graduates, an affluent demographic, spend over twice the average on this item.

Average household spending on deductions for government retirement declined 6 percent between 2000 and 2006, after adjusting for inflation, then rose 9 percent in the ensuing four years for an overall 2 percent gain. Spending on this item may decline in the years ahead if job cuts in federal, state, and local government eliminate workers.

Table 6.13 Deductions for government retirement

Total household spending	$10,948,072,800.00
Average household spends	90.40

	AVERAGE HOUSEHOLD SPENDING	BEST CUSTOMERS (index)	BIGGEST CUSTOMERS (market share)
AGE OF HOUSEHOLDER			
Average household	**$90.40**	**100**	**100.0%**
Under age 25	25.56	28	1.9
Aged 25 to 34	81.38	90	15.0
Aged 35 to 44	90.89	101	18.2
Aged 45 to 54	141.83	157	32.5
Aged 55 to 64	139.59	154	27.2
Aged 65 to 74	39.45	44	4.7
Aged 75 or older	5.26	6	0.6

	AVERAGE HOUSEHOLD SPENDING	BEST CUSTOMERS (index)	BIGGEST CUSTOMERS (market share)
HOUSEHOLD INCOME			
Average household	**$90.40**	**100**	**100.0%**
Under $20,000	1.43	2	0.3
$20,000 to $39,999	16.14	18	4.1
$40,000 to $49,999	43.64	48	4.6
$50,000 to $69,999	102.11	113	16.2
$70,000 to $79,999	112.21	124	7.4
$80,000 to $99,999	181.55	201	16.7
$100,000 or more	266.90	295	50.6
HOUSEHOLD TYPE			
Average household	**90.40**	**100**	**100.0**
Married couples	126.35	140	68.9
Married couples, no children	141.28	156	33.2
Married couples, with children	127.37	141	32.8
Oldest child under age 6	121.12	134	5.7
Oldest child aged 6 to 17	145.36	161	18.9
Oldest child aged 18 or older	101.78	113	8.1
Single parent with child under age 18	49.63	55	3.2
Single person	54.24	60	17.6
RACE AND HISPANIC ORIGIN			
Average household	**90.40**	**100**	**100.0**
Asian	71.92	80	3.4
Black	80.62	89	10.9
Hispanic	54.77	61	7.4
Non-Hispanic white and other	97.42	108	81.7
REGION			
Average household	**90.40**	**100**	**100.0**
Northeast	61.04	68	12.4
Midwest	88.99	98	21.9
South	97.13	107	39.4
West	104.66	116	26.2
EDUCATION			
Average household	**90.40**	**100**	**100.0**
Less than high school graduate	12.02	13	1.9
High school graduate	44.90	50	12.7
Some college	71.93	80	16.7
Associate's degree	54.25	60	5.7
Bachelor's degree or more	191.76	212	63.0
Bachelor's degree	129.11	143	27.0
Master's, professional, doctoral degree	301.15	333	36.0

Note: Market shares may not sum to 100.0 because of rounding and missing categories by household type. "Asian" and "black" include Hispanics and non-Hispanics who identify themselves as being of the respective race alone. "Hispanic" includes people of any race who identify themselves as Hispanic. "Other" includes people who identify themselves as non-Hispanic and as Alaska Native, American Indian, Asian (who are also included in the "Asian" row), or Native Hawaiian or other Pacific Islander as well as non-Hispanics reporting more than one race.

Source: Calculations by New Strategist based on the Bureau of Labor Statistics' 2010 Consumer Expenditure Survey

Deductions for Private Pensions (Payroll Deductions)

Best customers:	**Householders aged 35 to 64** **High-income households** **Married couples** **Asians** **College graduates**
Customer trends:	**Average household spending on payroll deductions for private pensions may grow as aging boomers attempt to save more for retirement, but only if households can afford to save.**

Affluent middle-aged and older married couples are the biggest spenders on deductions for private pensions. Households with incomes of $100,000 or more spend nearly four times the average on this item and control 66 percent of the market. Householders aged 35 to 64, who have the highest incomes, spend 23 to 64 percent more than average. Married couples—many of them two-earner—spend 41 percent more than average on this item, the figure peaking at 83 percent above average for households that include preschoolers. Asians spend twice the average on this item. Households headed by college graduates spend more than twice the average on deductions for private pensions.

Average household spending on deductions for private pensions fell 10 percent between 2006 and 2010, after adjusting for inflation. (Because of a change in methodology, the 2000 figure is not directly comparable with the more-recent spending figures.) Spending on this item may grow as aging boomers attempt to save more for retirement, but only if households can afford to save.

Table 6.14 Deductions for private pensions (payroll deductions)

Total household spending	$71,302,957,320.00
Average household spends	588.76

	AVERAGE HOUSEHOLD SPENDING	BEST CUSTOMERS (index)	BIGGEST CUSTOMERS (market share)
AGE OF HOUSEHOLDER			
Average household	**$588.76**	**100**	**100.0%**
Under age 25	78.45	13	0.9
Aged 25 to 34	555.48	94	15.7
Aged 35 to 44	726.34	123	22.3
Aged 45 to 54	966.62	164	34.0
Aged 55 to 64	751.75	128	22.5
Aged 65 to 74	219.38	37	4.0
Aged 75 or older	36.63	6	0.6

	AVERAGE HOUSEHOLD SPENDING	BEST CUSTOMERS (index)	BIGGEST CUSTOMERS (market share)
HOUSEHOLD INCOME			
Average household	**$588.76**	**100**	**100.0%**
Under $20,000	8.00	1	0.3
$20,000 to $39,999	60.90	10	2.4
$40,000 to $49,999	152.75	26	2.5
$50,000 to $69,999	360.49	61	8.8
$70,000 to $79,999	720.78	122	7.3
$80,000 to $99,999	895.48	152	12.7
$100,000 or more	2,269.35	385	66.1
HOUSEHOLD TYPE			
Average household	**588.76**	**100**	**100.0**
Married couples	832.56	141	69.8
Married couples, no children	806.53	137	29.1
Married couples, with children	917.87	156	36.3
Oldest child under age 6	1,076.22	183	7.8
Oldest child aged 6 to 17	944.66	160	18.9
Oldest child aged 18 or older	780.34	133	9.6
Single parent with child under age 18	313.97	53	3.1
Single person	342.27	58	17.0
RACE AND HISPANIC ORIGIN			
Average household	**588.76**	**100**	**100.0**
Asian	1,192.32	203	8.6
Black	192.59	33	4.0
Hispanic	206.95	35	4.3
Non-Hispanic white and other	713.52	121	91.9
REGION			
Average household	**588.76**	**100**	**100.0**
Northeast	560.75	95	17.5
Midwest	686.53	117	26.0
South	494.88	84	30.8
West	667.38	113	25.7
EDUCATION			
Average household	**588.76**	**100**	**100.0**
Less than high school graduate	77.50	13	1.9
High school graduate	229.96	39	10.0
Some college	365.98	62	13.1
Associate's degree	601.65	102	9.7
Bachelor's degree or more	1,296.55	220	65.4
Bachelor's degree	1,084.49	184	34.8
Master's, professional, doctoral degree	1,666.81	283	30.6

Note: Market shares may not sum to 100.0 because of rounding and missing categories by household type. "Asian" and "black" include Hispanics and non-Hispanics who identify themselves as being of the respective race alone. "Hispanic" includes people of any race who identify themselves as Hispanic. "Other" includes people who identify themselves as non-Hispanic and as Alaska Native, American Indian, Asian (who are also included in the "Asian" row), or Native Hawaiian or other Pacific Islander as well as non-Hispanics reporting more than one race.

Source: Calculations by New Strategist based on the Bureau of Labor Statistics' 2010 Consumer Expenditure Survey

Deductions for Social Security

Best customers: **Householders aged 35 to 54**
Married couples with children at home
Asians

Customer trends: **Average household spending on deductions for Social Security should grow until more boomers retire, but temporary cuts in Social Security withholding may limit the rise.**

Since Social Security deductions are a percentage of earnings, households with workers in their peak earning years are the ones that have the most deducted from their paychecks for Social Security. Householders aged 35 to 54, who are in their peak earning years, spend 36 to 40 percent more than the average household on Social Security deductions. Married couples with children at home, many of them at the height of their career, spend 66 percent more than the average on this item. Asians, who have the highest average income among racial and ethnic groups, spend 41 percent more than the average on Social Security deductions.

The average household spends well over twice as much on Social Security deductions as on federal, state, and local income taxes combined—an average of $3,903 in 2010. Spending on this item may continue to grow until large numbers of boomers retire, but temporary cuts in Social Security withholding may limit the rise.

Table 6.15 Deductions for Social Security

Total household spending $472,623,700,710.00
Average household spends   3,902.53

	AVERAGE HOUSEHOLD SPENDING	BEST CUSTOMERS (index)	BIGGEST CUSTOMERS (market share)
AGE OF HOUSEHOLDER			
Average household	**$3,902.53**	**100**	**100.0%**
Under age 25	1,869.47	48	3.2
Aged 25 to 34	4,284.52	110	18.3
Aged 35 to 44	5,314.19	136	24.6
Aged 45 to 54	5,469.33	140	29.0
Aged 55 to 64	4,239.68	109	19.2
Aged 65 to 74	1,601.46	41	4.4
Aged 75 or older	546.06	14	1.3

	AVERAGE HOUSEHOLD SPENDING	BEST CUSTOMERS (index)	BIGGEST CUSTOMERS (market share)
HOUSEHOLD INCOME			
Average household	**$3,902.53**	**100**	**100.0%**
Under $20,000	346.62	9	1.9
$20,000 to $39,999	1,489.65	38	8.7
$40,000 to $49,999	2,702.10	69	6.5
$50,000 to $69,999	3,872.93	99	14.2
$70,000 to $79,999	5,227.28	134	8.0
$80,000 to $99,999	6,417.10	164	13.7
$100,000 or more	10,653.96	273	46.8
HOUSEHOLD TYPE			
Average household	**3,902.53**	**100**	**100.0**
Married couples	5,438.14	139	68.7
Married couples, no children	4,307.51	110	23.4
Married couples, with children	6,485.83	166	38.7
Oldest child under age 6	6,006.43	154	6.6
Oldest child aged 6 to 17	6,615.34	170	19.9
Oldest child aged 18 or older	6,559.17	168	12.1
Single parent with child under age 18	2,238.50	57	3.4
Single person	1,774.91	45	13.3
RACE AND HISPANIC ORIGIN			
Average household	**3,902.53**	**100**	**100.0**
Asian	5,484.56	141	6.0
Black	2,778.56	71	8.7
Hispanic	3,475.90	89	10.9
Non-Hispanic white and other	4,152.16	106	80.7
REGION			
Average household	**3,902.53**	**100**	**100.0**
Northeast	4,208.56	108	19.8
Midwest	3,705.55	95	21.2
South	3,639.42	93	34.2
West	4,274.73	110	24.8
EDUCATION			
Average household	**3,902.53**	**100**	**100.0**
Less than high school graduate	1,958.53	50	7.2
High school graduate	2,866.87	73	18.8
Some college	3,331.95	85	17.9
Associate's degree	4,220.50	108	10.2
Bachelor's degree or more	6,030.13	155	45.9
Bachelor's degree	5,581.91	143	27.0
Master's, professional, doctoral degree	6,812.71	175	18.9

Note: Market shares may not sum to 100.0 because of rounding and missing categories by household type. "Asian" and "black" include Hispanics and non-Hispanics who identify themselves as being of the respective race alone. "Hispanic" includes people of any race who identify themselves as Hispanic. "Other" includes people who identify themselves as non-Hispanic and as Alaska Native, American Indian, Asian (who are also included in the "Asian" row), or Native Hawaiian or other Pacific Islander as well as non-Hispanics reporting more than one race.

Source: Calculations by New Strategist based on the Bureau of Labor Statistics' 2010 Consumer Expenditure Survey

Finance Charges, except Mortgage and Vehicle

Best customers:	Householders aged 35 to 54
	Married couples with children at home
	Households in the West
Customer trends:	Average household spending on finance charges (except mortgage and vehicle)
	may fall as households cut their debt.

The biggest spenders on finance charges (except mortgage and vehicle) are the households most likely to carry credit card debt. These are families with children—many of them outfitting their homes for expanding families. Householders ranging in age from 35 to 54 spend 24 to 41 percent more than average on finance charges and account for 52 percent of the market. Married couples with children at home spend 42 percent more, the figure peaking at 63 percent above average among couples with preschoolers.

Average household spending on finance charges fell 42 percent between 2000 and 2010, after adjusting for inflation. Falling interest rates were one factor behind the decline. As households cut their debt in the years ahead, average household spending on finance charges may continue to decline.

Table 6.16 **Finance charges, except mortgage and vehicle**

Total household spending $22,523,479,860.00
Average household spends 185.98

	AVERAGE HOUSEHOLD SPENDING	BEST CUSTOMERS (index)	BIGGEST CUSTOMERS (market share)
AGE OF HOUSEHOLDER			
Average household	**$185.98**	**100**	**100.0%**
Under age 25	76.67	41	2.7
Aged 25 to 34	201.95	109	18.1
Aged 35 to 44	230.49	124	22.4
Aged 45 to 54	262.46	141	29.2
Aged 55 to 64	205.01	110	19.4
Aged 65 to 74	102.95	55	6.0
Aged 75 or older	42.32	23	2.2

	AVERAGE HOUSEHOLD SPENDING	BEST CUSTOMERS (index)	BIGGEST CUSTOMERS (market share)
HOUSEHOLD INCOME			
Average household	**$185.98**	**100**	**100.0%**
Under $20,000	65.24	35	7.7
$20,000 to $39,999	114.47	62	14.1
$40,000 to $49,999	204.13	110	10.4
$50,000 to $69,999	217.59	117	16.8
$70,000 to $79,999	314.48	169	10.1
$80,000 to $99,999	310.98	167	13.9
$100,000 or more	293.17	158	27.0
HOUSEHOLD TYPE			
Average household	**185.98**	**100**	**100.0**
Married couples	228.84	123	60.7
Married couples, no children	194.89	105	22.3
Married couples, with children	264.35	142	33.1
Oldest child under age 6	303.01	163	7.0
Oldest child aged 6 to 17	244.36	131	15.5
Oldest child aged 18 or older	273.98	147	10.6
Single parent with child under age 18	159.07	86	5.0
Single person	120.47	65	19.0
RACE AND HISPANIC ORIGIN			
Average household	**185.98**	**100**	**100.0**
Asian	96.00	52	2.2
Black	178.01	96	11.7
Hispanic	143.40	77	9.4
Non-Hispanic white and other	193.74	104	79.0
REGION			
Average household	**185.98**	**100**	**100.0**
Northeast	134.88	73	13.3
Midwest	149.50	80	17.9
South	186.14	100	36.7
West	263.03	141	32.0
EDUCATION			
Average household	**185.98**	**100**	**100.0**
Less than high school graduate	72.70	39	5.6
High school graduate	141.52	76	19.4
Some college	210.42	113	23.8
Associate's degree	220.88	119	11.2
Bachelor's degree or more	250.29	135	40.0
Bachelor's degree	266.81	143	27.1
Master's, professional, doctoral degree	221.44	119	12.9

Note: Market shares may not sum to 100.0 because of rounding and missing categories by household type. "Asian" and "black" include Hispanics and non-Hispanics who identify themselves as being of the respective race alone. "Hispanic" includes people of any race who identify themselves as Hispanic. "Other" includes people who identify themselves as non-Hispanic and as Alaska Native, American Indian, Asian (who are also included in the "Asian" row), or Native Hawaiian or other Pacific Islander as well as non-Hispanics reporting more than one race.

Source: Calculations by New Strategist based on the Bureau of Labor Statistics' 2010 Consumer Expenditure Survey

Funeral Expenses

Best customers: Householders aged 65 or older
Married couples without children at home
Married couples with adult children at home
Blacks
Households in the Northeast and South

Customer trends: Average household spending on funerals should rise as the population ages unless more choose cremation or other less-expensive options.

Not surprisingly, the biggest spenders on funeral expenses are older Americans. Householders aged 65 to 74 spend twice the average, and those aged 75 or older spend two-and-three-quarters times the average on funeral costs as they bury parents or spouses. Married couples without children at home (most of them older) spend 33 percent more than average on funeral costs, whereas couples with adult children at home spend 89 percent more than average on funeral costs. Black householders spend 39 percent more than average on funerals. Households in the Northeast and South outspend the average by, respectively, 24 and 37 percent.

Average household spending on funeral expenses fell 31 percent between 2000 and 2006, after adjusting for inflation, then grew 28 percent in the ensuing four years, for an overall drop of 11 percent. This decline occurred despite the aging of the population and could be due to price discounting on caskets and other funeral costs. Spending on funeral expenses should rise with the aging of the population, unless more choose cremation or other less-expensive options when laying to rest their loved ones' remains.

Table 6.17 Funeral expenses

Total household spending		$9,611,051,520.00	
Average household spends		79.36	
	AVERAGE HOUSEHOLD SPENDING	**BEST CUSTOMERS (index)**	**BIGGEST CUSTOMERS (market share)**
AGE OF HOUSEHOLDER			
Average household	**$79.36**	**100**	**100.0%**
Under age 25	5.73	7	0.5
Aged 25 to 34	7.10	9	1.5
Aged 35 to 44	80.32	101	18.3
Aged 45 to 54	54.44	69	14.2
Aged 55 to 64	79.44	100	17.7
Aged 65 to 74	160.91	203	21.8
Aged 75 or older	216.79	273	26.1

	AVERAGE HOUSEHOLD SPENDING	BEST CUSTOMERS (index)	BIGGEST CUSTOMERS (market share)
HOUSEHOLD INCOME			
Average household	$79.36	100	100.0%
Under $20,000	100.72	127	27.7
$20,000 to $39,999	81.12	102	23.4
$40,000 to $49,999	49.80	63	5.9
$50,000 to $69,999	55.98	71	10.1
$70,000 to $79,999	86.28	109	6.5
$80,000 to $99,999	119.43	150	12.5
$100,000 or more	63.76	80	13.8
HOUSEHOLD TYPE			
Average household	79.36	100	100.0
Married couples	93.79	118	58.3
Married couples, no children	105.45	133	28.2
Married couples, with children	76.51	96	22.4
Oldest child under age 6	24.74	31	1.3
Oldest child aged 6 to 17	50.42	64	7.5
Oldest child aged 18 or older	149.69	189	13.6
Single parent with child under age 18	47.27	60	3.5
Single person	64.65	81	23.9
RACE AND HISPANIC ORIGIN			
Average household	79.36	100	100.0
Asian	26.70	34	1.4
Black	110.59	139	17.1
Hispanic	48.55	61	7.5
Non-Hispanic white and other	79.04	100	75.5
REGION			
Average household	79.36	100	100.0
Northeast	98.02	124	22.7
Midwest	54.63	69	15.3
South	108.79	137	50.3
West	40.90	52	11.7
EDUCATION			
Average household	79.36	100	100.0
Less than high school graduate	107.11	135	19.3
High school graduate	76.04	96	24.5
Some college	77.63	98	20.6
Associate's degree	47.03	59	5.6
Bachelor's degree or more	80.37	101	30.1
Bachelor's degree	54.16	68	12.9
Master's, professional, doctoral degree	126.12	159	17.2

Note: Market shares may not sum to 100.0 because of rounding and missing categories by household type. "Asian" and "black" include Hispanics and non-Hispanics who identify themselves as being of the respective race alone. "Hispanic" includes people of any race who identify themselves as Hispanic. "Other" includes people who identify themselves as non-Hispanic and as Alaska Native, American Indian, Asian (who are also included in the "Asian" row), or Native Hawaiian or other Pacific Islander as well as non-Hispanics reporting more than one race.

Source: Calculations by New Strategist based on the Bureau of Labor Statistics' 2010 Consumer Expenditure Survey

Insurance, Life and Other Personal except Health

Best customers: **Householders aged 45 to 74**
                             Married couples

Customer trends: **Average household spending on life and other personal insurance (except health)**
                             may continue to decline as boomers become empty-nesters.

The biggest spenders on life and other personal insurance are older married couples with children and assets to protect. Householders ranging in age from 45 to 74 spend 21 to 48 percent more than the average household on life and other personal insurance and control more than two-thirds of the market. Married couples without children at home, most of them empty-nesters, spend 55 percent more than average on such insurance. Those with children at home spend 66 percent more, the figure peaking among couples with adult children at home at 81 percent.

Average household spending on life and other personal insurance fell 37 percent between 2000 and 2010, after adjusting for inflation. The declining popularity of life insurance as an investment vehicle is one factor behind the decline. As more boomers become empty-nesters and their children no longer need financial protection, spending on life and other personal insurance may continue to decline.

Table 6.18 Insurance, life and other personal except health

Total household spending $38,526,558,840.00
Average household spends   318.12

	AVERAGE HOUSEHOLD SPENDING	BEST CUSTOMERS (index)	BIGGEST CUSTOMERS (market share)
AGE OF HOUSEHOLDER			
Average household	**$318.12**	**100**	**100.0%**
Under age 25	22.13	7	0.5
Aged 25 to 34	167.04	53	8.7
Aged 35 to 44	280.15	88	15.9
Aged 45 to 54	441.20	139	28.7
Aged 55 to 64	471.16	148	26.1
Aged 65 to 74	386.33	121	13.1
Aged 75 or older	232.91	73	7.0

	AVERAGE HOUSEHOLD SPENDING	BEST CUSTOMERS (index)	BIGGEST CUSTOMERS (market share)
HOUSEHOLD INCOME			
Average household	**$318.12**	**100**	**100.0%**
Under $20,000	93.85	30	6.4
$20,000 to $39,999	159.74	50	11.5
$40,000 to $49,999	203.27	64	6.0
$50,000 to $69,999	292.07	92	13.2
$70,000 to $79,999	375.71	118	7.1
$80,000 to $99,999	423.57	133	11.1
$100,000 or more	828.93	261	44.7
HOUSEHOLD TYPE			
Average household	**318.12**	**100**	**100.0**
Married couples	494.72	156	76.7
Married couples, no children	494.28	155	33.0
Married couples, with children	528.79	166	38.7
Oldest child under age 6	467.92	147	6.3
Oldest child aged 6 to 17	521.22	164	19.3
Oldest child aged 18 or older	577.21	181	13.1
Single parent with child under age 18	130.42	41	2.4
Single person	143.01	45	13.2
RACE AND HISPANIC ORIGIN			
Average household	**318.12**	**100**	**100.0**
Asian	333.28	105	4.5
Black	212.26	67	8.2
Hispanic	149.46	47	5.7
Non-Hispanic white and other	362.08	114	86.3
REGION			
Average household	**318.12**	**100**	**100.0**
Northeast	349.77	110	20.2
Midwest	384.33	121	26.9
South	286.10	90	33.0
West	279.20	88	19.9
EDUCATION			
Average household	**318.12**	**100**	**100.0**
Less than high school graduate	136.17	43	6.1
High school graduate	227.95	72	18.3
Some college	248.51	78	16.4
Associate's degree	340.33	107	10.1
Bachelor's degree or more	525.31	165	49.1
Bachelor's degree	408.43	128	24.3
Master's, professional, doctoral degree	729.38	229	24.8

Note: Market shares may not sum to 100.0 because of rounding and missing categories by household type. "Asian" and "black" include Hispanics and non-Hispanics who identify themselves as being of the respective race alone. "Hispanic" includes people of any race who identify themselves as Hispanic. "Other" includes people who identify themselves as non-Hispanic and as Alaska Native, American Indian, Asian (who are also included in the "Asian" row), or Native Hawaiian or other Pacific Islander as well as non-Hispanics reporting more than one race.

Source: Calculations by New Strategist based on the Bureau of Labor Statistics' 2010 Consumer Expenditure Survey

Legal Fees

Best customers:

Householders aged 45 to 64
Married couples with preschoolers
Single parents
Households in the West

Customer trends:

Average household spending on legal fees may continue to decline because of the slump in the housing market.

People who are divorcing or buying and selling homes are the biggest spenders on legal fees. Householders aged 45 to 64 spend 30 percent more than average on legal fees as they hire attorneys to negotiate divorce, child custody, and home sales. Married couples with preschoolers spend nearly three times the average on this item. Single parents, whose spending approaches average on only a few items, spend one-fifth more than average on legal fees. Western households spend 53 percent more than average on this item.

Average household spending on legal fees grew 31 percent between 2000 and 2006, after adjusting for inflation, then fell 25 percent between 2006 and 2010. The increased number of real estate transactions during the housing boom is one factor behind the earlier rise. Average household spending on legal fees may continue to decline in the years ahead because of the slump in the housing market.

Table 6.19 Legal fees

Total household spending $15,590,104,110.00
Average household spends   128.73

	AVERAGE HOUSEHOLD SPENDING	BEST CUSTOMERS (index)	BIGGEST CUSTOMERS (market share)
AGE OF HOUSEHOLDER			
Average household	**$128.73**	**100**	**100.0%**
Under age 25	36.88	29	1.9
Aged 25 to 34	125.46	97	16.2
Aged 35 to 44	119.34	93	16.8
Aged 45 to 54	167.63	130	26.9
Aged 55 to 64	167.78	130	23.0
Aged 65 to 74	116.30	90	9.7
Aged 75 or older	73.56	57	5.5

	AVERAGE HOUSEHOLD SPENDING	BEST CUSTOMERS (index)	BIGGEST CUSTOMERS (market share)
HOUSEHOLD INCOME			
Average household	**$128.73**	**100**	**100.0%**
Under $20,000	50.02	39	8.5
$20,000 to $39,999	81.63	63	14.5
$40,000 to $49,999	83.91	65	6.2
$50,000 to $69,999	199.12	155	22.2
$70,000 to $79,999	140.52	109	6.5
$80,000 to $99,999	141.99	110	9.2
$100,000 or more	247.11	192	32.9
HOUSEHOLD TYPE			
Average household	**128.73**	**100**	**100.0**
Married couples	132.23	103	50.7
Married couples, no children	102.66	80	16.9
Married couples, with children	161.91	126	29.3
Oldest child under age 6	360.17	280	12.0
Oldest child aged 6 to 17	97.38	76	8.9
Oldest child aged 18 or older	149.45	116	8.4
Single parent with child under age 18	154.71	120	7.1
Single person	117.26	91	26.7
RACE AND HISPANIC ORIGIN			
Average household	**128.73**	**100**	**100.0**
Asian	61.18	48	2.0
Black	47.44	37	4.5
Hispanic	96.74	75	9.2
Non-Hispanic white and other	146.81	114	86.5
REGION			
Average household	**128.73**	**100**	**100.0**
Northeast	147.99	115	21.1
Midwest	99.36	77	17.2
South	94.49	73	26.9
West	197.50	153	34.8
EDUCATION			
Average household	**128.73**	**100**	**100.0**
Less than high school graduate	80.52	63	8.9
High school graduate	114.85	89	22.8
Some college	110.95	86	18.1
Associate's degree	184.98	144	13.6
Bachelor's degree or more	158.53	123	36.6
Bachelor's degree	149.30	116	21.9
Master's, professional, doctoral degree	174.65	136	14.7

Note: Market shares may not sum to 100.0 because of rounding and missing categories by household type. "Asian" and "black" include Hispanics and non-Hispanics who identify themselves as being of the respective race alone. "Hispanic" includes people of any race who identify themselves as Hispanic. "Other" includes people who identify themselves as non-Hispanic and as Alaska Native, American Indian, Asian (who are also included in the "Asian" row), or Native Hawaiian or other Pacific Islander as well as non-Hispanics reporting more than one race.

Source: Calculations by New Strategist based on the Bureau of Labor Statistics' 2010 Consumer Expenditure Survey

Lottery and Gambling Losses

Best customers: **Householders aged 55 to 64**
People who live alone
Households in the West

Customer trends: **Average household spending on lotteries and gambling will rise as more boomers become empty-nesters and casinos become more widespread.**

The biggest spenders (losers) on lotteries and gambling are households with discretionary time and income. Hoping to strike it rich they buy lottery tickets, travel to Las Vegas, or visit Indian reservations to try their luck. Householders aged 55 to 64 lose three times the average and represent the only age group to gamble away significant sums of money. People who live alone, who generally spend far less than average on most items, lose 86 percent more than the average amount on lotteries and gambling. Households in the West gamble away over twice the average amount.

Average household losses on lotteries and gambling rose by 46 percent between 2000 and 2006, after adjusting or inflation, and has held essentially steady since then. Spending on this item will continue to rise in the years ahead as casinos become more widespread and more boomers become empty-nesters.

Table 6.20 **Lottery and gambling losses**

Total household spending $9,533,543,040.00
Average household spends 78.72

	AVERAGE HOUSEHOLD SPENDING	BEST CUSTOMERS (index)	BIGGEST CUSTOMERS (market share)
AGE OF HOUSEHOLDER			
Average household	**$78.72**	**100**	**100.0%**
Under age 25	11.71	15	1.0
Aged 25 to 34	36.73	47	7.8
Aged 35 to 44	38.87	49	8.9
Aged 45 to 54	59.92	76	15.7
Aged 55 to 64	239.97	305	53.8
Aged 65 to 74	70.93	90	9.7
Aged 75 or older	22.84	29	2.8

	AVERAGE HOUSEHOLD SPENDING	BEST CUSTOMERS (index)	BIGGEST CUSTOMERS (market share)
HOUSEHOLD INCOME			
Average household	**$78.72**	**100**	**100.0%**
Under $20,000	34.29	44	9.5
$20,000 to $39,999	36.05	46	10.5
$40,000 to $49,999	26.95	34	3.2
$50,000 to $69,999	246.39	313	44.9
$70,000 to $79,999	78.76	100	6.0
$80,000 to $99,999	56.41	72	6.0
$100,000 or more	87.81	112	19.1
HOUSEHOLD TYPE			
Average household	**78.72**	**100**	**100.0**
Married couples	58.75	75	36.8
Married couples, no children	52.30	66	14.1
Married couples, with children	38.50	49	11.4
Oldest child under age 6	23.37	30	1.3
Oldest child aged 6 to 17	31.02	39	4.6
Oldest child aged 18 or older	57.38	73	5.3
Single parent with child under age 18	3.51	4	0.3
Single person	146.79	186	54.6
RACE AND HISPANIC ORIGIN			
Average household	**78.72**	**100**	**100.0**
Asian	16.32	21	0.9
Black	53.76	68	8.4
Hispanic	26.34	33	4.1
Non-Hispanic white and other	90.82	115	87.5
REGION			
Average household	**78.72**	**100**	**100.0**
Northeast	87.00	111	20.3
Midwest	50.01	64	14.2
South	38.30	49	17.9
West	167.60	213	48.2
EDUCATION			
Average household	**78.72**	**100**	**100.0**
Less than high school graduate	30.53	39	5.5
High school graduate	51.30	65	16.6
Some college	52.26	66	14.0
Associate's degree	48.60	62	5.8
Bachelor's degree or more	153.46	195	57.9
Bachelor's degree	177.58	226	42.6
Master's, professional, doctoral degree	105.96	135	14.6

Note: Market shares may not sum to 100.0 because of rounding and missing categories by household type. "Asian" and "black" include Hispanics and non-Hispanics who identify themselves as being of the respective race alone. "Hispanic" includes people of any race who identify themselves as Hispanic. "Other" includes people who identify themselves as non-Hispanic and as Alaska Native, American Indian, Asian (who are also included in the "Asian" row), or Native Hawaiian or other Pacific Islander as well as non-Hispanics reporting more than one race.

Source: Calculations by New Strategist based on the Bureau of Labor Statistics' 2010 Consumer Expenditure Survey

Occupational Expenses

Best customers: **Householders aged 25 to 64**
Married couples with children at home
Asians
Households in the West

Customer trends: **Average household spending on occupational expenses may decline in the years**
ahead unless manufacturing employment begins to grow.

The biggest spenders on occupational expenses are households with workers, particularly union members and licensed professionals such as social workers. Householders ranging in age from 25 to 64 spent 19 to 36 percent more than average on this item. Married couples with children at home, most of them dual earners, spend 48 percent more than average on occupational expenses. Asians spend 51 percent more than average on this item. Households in the West spend 63 percent more than average on occupational expenses.

Average household spending on occupational expenses fell steeply between 2000 and 2006, down 60 percent after adjusting for inflation, then rose 7 percent in the ensuing four years. Behind the decline was the loss of union jobs as manufacturing employment fell over the years. Spending on occupational expenses may decline in the years ahead unless manufacturing employment begins to grow.

Table 6.21 Occupational expenses

Total household spending $6,253,965,480.00
Average household spends   51.64

	AVERAGE HOUSEHOLD SPENDING	BEST CUSTOMERS (index)	BIGGEST CUSTOMERS (market share)
AGE OF HOUSEHOLDER			
Average household	**$51.64**	**100**	**100.0%**
Under age 25	16.68	32	2.1
Aged 25 to 34	61.59	119	19.9
Aged 35 to 44	61.75	120	21.6
Aged 45 to 54	66.33	128	26.6
Aged 55 to 64	69.99	136	23.9
Aged 65 to 74	21.14	41	4.4
Aged 75 or older	8.08	16	1.5

	AVERAGE HOUSEHOLD SPENDING	BEST CUSTOMERS (index)	BIGGEST CUSTOMERS (market share)
HOUSEHOLD INCOME			
Average household	**$51.64**	**100**	**100.0%**
Under $20,000	5.89	11	2.5
$20,000 to $39,999	20.52	40	9.1
$40,000 to $49,999	32.55	63	6.0
$50,000 to $69,999	49.52	96	13.8
$70,000 to $79,999	72.32	140	8.4
$80,000 to $99,999	98.45	191	15.9
$100,000 or more	133.80	259	44.4
HOUSEHOLD TYPE			
Average household	**51.64**	**100**	**100.0**
Married couples	66.90	130	63.9
Married couples, no children	57.67	112	23.7
Married couples, with children	76.49	148	34.5
Oldest child under age 6	86.81	168	7.2
Oldest child aged 6 to 17	71.88	139	16.4
Oldest child aged 18 or older	77.87	151	10.9
Single parent with child under age 18	33.81	65	3.9
Single person	31.21	60	17.7
RACE AND HISPANIC ORIGIN			
Average household	**51.64**	**100**	**100.0**
Asian	78.06	151	6.4
Black	28.91	56	6.9
Hispanic	36.01	70	8.5
Non-Hispanic white and other	57.92	112	85.0
REGION			
Average household	**51.64**	**100**	**100.0**
Northeast	54.12	105	19.2
Midwest	55.98	108	24.2
South	27.85	54	19.8
West	83.93	163	36.8
EDUCATION			
Average household	**51.64**	**100**	**100.0**
Less than high school graduate	15.47	30	4.3
High school graduate	33.32	65	16.5
Some college	48.32	94	19.7
Associate's degree	60.06	116	11.0
Bachelor's degree or more	84.47	164	48.6
Bachelor's degree	68.02	132	24.9
Master's, professional, doctoral degree	113.19	219	23.7

Note: Market shares may not sum to 100.0 because of rounding and missing categories by household type. "Asian" and "black" include Hispanics and non-Hispanics who identify themselves as being of the respective race alone. "Hispanic" includes people of any race who identify themselves as Hispanic. "Other" includes people who identify themselves as non-Hispanic and as Alaska Native, American Indian, Asian (who are also included in the "Asian" row), or Native Hawaiian or other Pacific Islander as well as non-Hispanics reporting more than one race.

Source: Calculations by New Strategist based on the Bureau of Labor Statistics' 2010 Consumer Expenditure Survey

Safe Deposit Box Rental

Best customers: **Householders aged 55 or older**
Married couples without children at home
Asians and non-Hispanic whites

Customer trends: **Average household spending on safe deposit box rentals will continue to decline as paper documents give way to electronic records.**

Older Americans are the best customers of safe deposit box rentals because they grew up in an era when only a single paper copy of many important documents existed. Householders aged 55 to 64 spend 26 percent more than average on safe deposit boxes, householders aged 75 or older spend 69 percent more, and householders aged 65 to 74 spend more than two times the average. Together, householders aged 55 or older control 62 percent of the market for safe deposit box rentals. Married couples without children at home, many of them empty-nesters, spend 84 percent more than average on this item. Asians spend two-and-three-quarter times the average and non-Hispanic whites 23 percent more.

Average household spending on safe deposit boxes plummeted between 2000 and 2010, falling by 37 percent after adjusting for inflation. Electronic record keeping and high-tech home security systems are reducing the need for safe deposit boxes, which should limit spending on this item in the future.

Table 6.22 Safe deposit box rental

Total household spending $442,040,550.00
Average household spends   3.65

	AVERAGE HOUSEHOLD SPENDING	BEST CUSTOMERS (index)	BIGGEST CUSTOMERS (market share)
AGE OF HOUSEHOLDER			
Average household	**$3.65**	**100**	**100.0%**
Under age 25	1.03	28	1.9
Aged 25 to 34	1.39	38	6.3
Aged 35 to 44	1.32	36	6.5
Aged 45 to 54	4.11	113	23.3
Aged 55 to 64	4.60	126	22.2
Aged 65 to 74	7.99	219	23.6
Aged 75 or older	6.17	169	16.1

	AVERAGE HOUSEHOLD SPENDING	BEST CUSTOMERS (index)	BIGGEST CUSTOMERS (market share)
HOUSEHOLD INCOME			
Average household	**$3.65**	**100**	**100.0%**
Under $20,000	1.48	40	8.8
$20,000 to $39,999	2.19	60	13.8
$40,000 to $49,999	3.44	94	8.9
$50,000 to $69,999	4.29	118	16.9
$70,000 to $79,999	2.99	82	4.9
$80,000 to $99,999	4.47	122	10.2
$100,000 or more	7.76	213	36.5
HOUSEHOLD TYPE			
Average household	**3.65**	**100**	**100.0**
Married couples	4.74	130	64.1
Married couples, no children	6.72	184	39.1
Married couples, with children	3.35	92	21.4
Oldest child under age 6	4.52	124	5.3
Oldest child aged 6 to 17	2.55	70	8.2
Oldest child aged 18 or older	3.96	108	7.8
Single parent with child under age 18	0.94	26	1.5
Single person	2.91	80	23.4
RACE AND HISPANIC ORIGIN			
Average household	**3.65**	**100**	**100.0**
Asian	9.96	273	11.6
Black	1.11	30	3.7
Hispanic	0.94	26	3.1
Non-Hispanic white and other	4.48	123	93.1
REGION			
Average household	**3.65**	**100**	**100.0**
Northeast	3.14	86	15.8
Midwest	3.50	96	21.4
South	3.67	101	36.9
West	4.17	114	25.9
EDUCATION			
Average household	**3.65**	**100**	**100.0**
Less than high school graduate	1.40	38	5.5
High school graduate	2.76	76	19.3
Some college	3.20	88	18.4
Associate's degree	3.59	98	9.3
Bachelor's degree or more	5.83	160	47.5
Bachelor's degree	5.11	140	26.4
Master's, professional, doctoral degree	7.07	194	21.0

Note: Market shares may not sum to 100.0 because of rounding and missing categories by household type. "Asian" and "black" include Hispanics and non-Hispanics who identify themselves as being of the respective race alone. "Hispanic" includes people of any race who identify themselves as Hispanic. "Other" includes people who identify themselves as non-Hispanic and as Alaska Native, American Indian, Asian (who are also included in the "Asian" row), or Native Hawaiian or other Pacific Islander as well as non-Hispanics reporting more than one race.

Source: Calculations by New Strategist based on the Bureau of Labor Statistics' 2010 Consumer Expenditure Survey

Shopping Club Membership Fees

Best customers: **Householders aged 35 to 74**
Married couples
Asians
Households in the West

Customer trends: **Average household spending on shopping club membership fees may decline as competition among discounters heats up.**

Middle-aged and older married couples, many with children at home, are the best customers of shopping club memberships. Householders ranging in age from 35 to 74 spend more than average on this item. Married couples spend 47 percent more than average on shopping club memberships, the figure peaking at 63 percent among those with preschoolers. Households in the West spend 87 percent more than average on this item. Asians, many of whom live in the West, spend two-thirds more than average on shopping club memberships.

Average household spending on shopping club memberships is minimal and may fall in the years ahead as competition among discounters reduces the need to join the club for savings.

Table 6.23 **Shopping club membership fees**

Total household spending $1,029,409,500.00
Average household spends   8.50

	AVERAGE HOUSEHOLD SPENDING	BEST CUSTOMERS (index)	BIGGEST CUSTOMERS (market share)
AGE OF HOUSEHOLDER			
Average household	**$8.50**	**100**	**100.0%**
Under age 25	2.36	28	1.8
Aged 25 to 34	7.19	85	14.1
Aged 35 to 44	9.97	117	21.2
Aged 45 to 54	9.64	113	23.5
Aged 55 to 64	9.88	116	20.5
Aged 65 to 74	10.37	122	13.1
Aged 75 or older	5.20	61	5.8

	AVERAGE HOUSEHOLD SPENDING	BEST CUSTOMERS (index)	BIGGEST CUSTOMERS (market share)
HOUSEHOLD INCOME			
Average household	**$8.50**	**100**	**100.0%**
Under $20,000	2.38	28	6.1
$20,000 to $39,999	5.52	65	14.9
$40,000 to $49,999	8.20	96	9.1
$50,000 to $69,999	8.90	105	15.0
$70,000 to $79,999	11.26	132	7.9
$80,000 to $99,999	13.42	158	13.2
$100,000 or more	16.79	198	33.9
HOUSEHOLD TYPE			
Average household	**8.50**	**100**	**100.0**
Married couples	12.53	147	72.7
Married couples, no children	12.65	149	31.6
Married couples, with children	12.76	150	34.9
Oldest child under age 6	13.87	163	7.0
Oldest child aged 6 to 17	12.84	151	17.8
Oldest child aged 18 or older	11.97	141	10.2
Single parent with child under age 18	4.16	49	2.9
Single person	3.66	43	12.6
RACE AND HISPANIC ORIGIN			
Average household	**8.50**	**100**	**100.0**
Asian	14.18	167	7.1
Black	4.65	55	6.7
Hispanic	9.88	116	14.2
Non-Hispanic white and other	8.90	105	79.4
REGION			
Average household	**8.50**	**100**	**100.0**
Northeast	6.97	82	15.0
Midwest	5.63	66	14.8
South	6.44	76	27.8
West	15.93	187	42.5
EDUCATION			
Average household	**8.50**	**100**	**100.0**
Less than high school graduate	6.03	71	10.1
High school graduate	6.06	71	18.2
Some college	7.79	92	19.3
Associate's degree	9.05	106	10.1
Bachelor's degree or more	12.12	143	42.4
Bachelor's degree	11.81	139	26.2
Master's, professional, doctoral degree	12.67	149	16.1

Note: Market shares may not sum to 100.0 because of rounding and missing categories by household type. "Asian" and "black" include Hispanics and non-Hispanics who identify themselves as being of the respective race alone. "Hispanic" includes people of any race who identify themselves as Hispanic. "Other" includes people who identify themselves as non-Hispanic and as Alaska Native, American Indian, Asian (who are also included in the "Asian" row), or Native Hawaiian or other Pacific Islander as well as non-Hispanics reporting more than one race.

Source: Calculations by New Strategist based on the Bureau of Labor Statistics' 2010 Consumer Expenditure Survey

Support for College Students

Best customers:	**Householders aged 45 to 64**
	High-income households
	Married couples without children at home
	Married couples with adult children at home
	Asians
Customer trends:	**Average household spending on support for college students is likely to grow as boomers help their children through college.**

Many parents give money to their college-bound children for living expenses and other items. Householders aged 45 to 54 spend over twice the average on such support and account for 49 percent of spending. Those aged 55 to 64 spend 35 percent more than average and account for another 24 percent of spending. Married couples without children at home (most of them empty-nesters) spend 97 percent more than average, and those with adult children at home spend two-and-one-quarter times the average on support for college students. Asians, who tend to more educated and prosperous than average, spend 41 percent more than average on student support.

Average household spending on support for college students is likely to grow as boomers help their children through college.

Table 6.24 **Support for college students**

Total household spending	$11,841,842,460.00
Average household spends	97.78

	AVERAGE HOUSEHOLD SPENDING	BEST CUSTOMERS (index)	BIGGEST CUSTOMERS (market share)
AGE OF HOUSEHOLDER			
Average household	**$97.78**	**100**	**100.0%**
Under age 25	4.03	4	0.3
Aged 25 to 34	9.24	9	1.6
Aged 35 to 44	40.24	41	7.4
Aged 45 to 54	230.12	235	48.7
Aged 55 to 64	132.18	135	23.8
Aged 65 to 74	109.33	112	12.0
Aged 75 or older	63.01	64	6.1

	AVERAGE HOUSEHOLD SPENDING	BEST CUSTOMERS (index)	BIGGEST CUSTOMERS (market share)
HOUSEHOLD INCOME			
Average household	**$97.78**	**100**	**100.0%**
Under $20,000	20.23	21	4.5
$20,000 to $39,999	28.72	29	6.7
$40,000 to $49,999	83.05	85	8.0
$50,000 to $69,999	67.80	69	9.9
$70,000 to $79,999	73.69	75	4.5
$80,000 to $99,999	80.62	82	6.9
$100,000 or more	338.70	346	59.4
HOUSEHOLD TYPE			
Average household	**97.78**	**100**	**100.0**
Married couples	154.13	158	77.8
Married couples, no children	192.63	197	41.8
Married couples, with children	135.62	139	32.3
Oldest child under age 6	7.19	7	0.3
Oldest child aged 6 to 17	130.18	133	15.7
Oldest child aged 18 or older	220.64	226	16.3
Single parent with child under age 18	42.13	43	2.5
Single person	42.54	44	12.7
RACE AND HISPANIC ORIGIN			
Average household	**97.78**	**100**	**100.0**
Asian	138.27	141	6.0
Black	41.99	43	5.3
Hispanic	51.55	53	6.4
Non-Hispanic white and other	115.30	118	89.4
REGION			
Average household	**97.78**	**100**	**100.0**
Northeast	116.28	119	21.8
Midwest	93.13	95	21.2
South	92.89	95	34.9
West	95.28	97	22.1
EDUCATION			
Average household	**97.78**	**100**	**100.0**
Less than high school graduate	48.50	50	7.1
High school graduate	49.80	51	13.0
Some college	62.05	63	13.3
Associate's degree	85.92	88	8.3
Bachelor's degree or more	191.76	196	58.3
Bachelor's degree	151.68	155	29.3
Master's, professional, doctoral degree	261.75	268	29.0

Note: Market shares may not sum to 100.0 because of rounding and missing categories by household type. "Asian" and "black" include Hispanics and non-Hispanics who identify themselves as being of the respective race alone. "Hispanic" includes people of any race who identify themselves as Hispanic. "Other" includes people who identify themselves as non-Hispanic and as Alaska Native, American Indian, Asian (who are also included in the "Asian" row), or Native Hawaiian or other Pacific Islander as well as non-Hispanics reporting more than one race.

Source: Calculations by New Strategist based on the Bureau of Labor Statistics' 2010 Consumer Expenditure Survey

Tax, Federal Income (Net, after Refund)

Best customers:	**Householders aged 45 to 64** **High-income households** **Married couples** **Asians and non-Hispanics whites** **Households in the Northeast and West** **College graduates**
Customer trends:	**Average household spending on federal income taxes is likely to climb as tax rates increase to pay for services demanded by the middle class.**

Households with the highest incomes pay the most in federal income tax. Eighty-seven percent of federal income taxes are paid by households with incomes of $100,000 or more. Householders aged 45 to 64, who have the highest incomes, pay 34 to 103 percent more than average in federal taxes. Married couples, the most-affluent household type, pay 51 percent more than average in federal income taxes, the figure peaking at 66 percent above average among couples without children at home, most of them empty-nesters. Asians pay over three times the average in federal income taxes, and non-Hispanics whites pay 28 percent more. Households in the West pay 22 percent and those in the Northeast 19 percent more than average in federal income tax. Households headed by college graduates, who dominate the nation's affluent, spend over two-and-one-half times the average on federal income taxes.

The average household paid $1,136 in federal income taxes in 2010—a substantial amount, but less than one-third of what the average household devotes to Social Security contributions. Average household spending on federal income taxes fell by a significant 63 percent between 2000 and 2010, after adjusting for inflation. In the years ahead, spending on this item is likely to rise as the aging middle class demands more services.

Table 6.25 Tax, federal income (net, after refund)

Total household spending	$137,537,586,690.00
Average household spends	1,135.67

	AVERAGE HOUSEHOLD SPENDING	BEST CUSTOMERS (index)	BIGGEST CUSTOMERS (market share)
AGE OF HOUSEHOLDER			
Average household	**$1,135.67**	**100**	**100.0%**
Under age 25	−47.21	−4	−0.3
Aged 25 to 34	521.01	46	7.6
Aged 35 to 44	1,241.80	109	19.8
Aged 45 to 54	2,309.23	203	42.1
Aged 55 to 64	1,519.62	134	23.6
Aged 65 to 74	739.33	65	7.0
Aged 75 or older	21.95	2	0.2

	AVERAGE HOUSEHOLD SPENDING	BEST CUSTOMERS (index)	BIGGEST CUSTOMERS (market share)
HOUSEHOLD INCOME			
Average household	$1,135.67	100	100.0%
Under $20,000	−185.96	−16	−3.6
$20,000 to $39,999	−287.35	−25	−5.8
$40,000 to $49,999	−49.88	−4	−0.4
$50,000 to $69,999	485.07	43	6.1
$70,000 to $79,999	1,070.29	94	5.6
$80,000 to $99,999	1,447.47	127	10.6
$100,000 or more	5,788.25	510	87.4
HOUSEHOLD TYPE			
Average household	1,135.67	100	100.0
Married couples	1,716.48	151	74.6
Married couples, no children	1,888.64	166	35.3
Married couples, with children	1,583.39	139	32.4
Oldest child under age 6	1,437.08	127	5.4
Oldest child aged 6 to 17	1,617.23	142	16.7
Oldest child aged 18 or older	1,615.03	142	10.3
Single parent with child under age 18	−762.64	−67	−4.0
Single person	730.03	64	18.8
RACE AND HISPANIC ORIGIN			
Average household	1,135.67	100	100.0
Asian	3,594.32	316	13.5
Black	122.08	11	1.3
Hispanic	190.16	17	2.0
Non-Hispanic white and other	1,450.94	128	96.9
REGION			
Average household	1,135.67	100	100.0
Northeast	1,348.75	119	21.8
Midwest	922.79	81	18.1
South	1,002.20	88	32.4
West	1,388.77	122	27.7
EDUCATION			
Average household	1,135.67	100	100.0
Less than high school graduate	−136.26	−12	−1.7
High school graduate	191.26	17	4.3
Some college	582.22	51	10.8
Associate's degree	829.12	73	6.9
Bachelor's degree or more	3,048.15	268	79.7
Bachelor's degree	2,257.00	199	37.5
Master's, professional, doctoral degree	4,429.49	390	42.2

Note: Market shares may not sum to 100.0 because of rounding and missing categories by household type. "Asian" and "black" include Hispanics and non-Hispanics who identify themselves as being of the respective race alone. "Hispanic" includes people of any race who identify themselves as Hispanic. "Other" includes people who identify themselves as non-Hispanic and as Alaska Native, American Indian, Asian (who are also included in the "Asian" row), or Native Hawaiian or other Pacific Islander as well as non-Hispanics reporting more than one race.

Source: Calculations by New Strategist based on the Bureau of Labor Statistics' 2010 Consumer Expenditure Survey

Tax, State and Local Income (Net, after Refund)

Best customers: **Householders aged 35 to 54**
High-income households
Married couples with children at home
Asians and non-Hispanic whites
Households in the Northeast and West
College graduates

Customer trends: **Average household spending on state and local income taxes will rise as states and localities, squeezed for cash, raise taxes to pay for necessary services.**

Households with the highest incomes pay the most in state and local income taxes. Sixty-three percent of state and local income taxes are paid by households with incomes of $100,000 or more. Householders aged 35 to 54, who have the highest incomes, spend 35 to 72 percent more than average on this item. Married couples, the most-affluent household type, pay 43 percent more than average in state and local income taxes, the figure peaking at 85 percent among those with school-aged children. Asians, who as a group are relatively affluent, pay well more than twice the average in state and local income taxes, and non-Hispanic whites pay 18 percent more. Households in the Northeast pay 45 percent more than average on these taxes, while those in the West pay 21 percent more. College graduates pay twice the average on this item.

Average household spending on state and local income taxes fell by a significant 32 percent between 2000 and 2010, after adjusting for inflation. Now states and localities are squeezed for cash, and the pendulum is likely to swing the other way. Look for average household spending on state and local income taxes to rise.

Table 6.26 Tax, state and local income (net, after refund)

Total household spending $58,428,072,150.00
Average household spends   482.45

	AVERAGE HOUSEHOLD SPENDING	BEST CUSTOMERS (index)	BIGGEST CUSTOMERS (market share)
AGE OF HOUSEHOLDER			
Average household	**$482.45**	**100**	**100.0%**
Under age 25	144.97	30	2.0
Aged 25 to 34	463.29	96	16.0
Aged 35 to 44	650.25	135	24.4
Aged 45 to 54	830.53	172	35.6
Aged 55 to 64	529.18	110	19.3
Aged 65 to 74	122.17	25	2.7
Aged 75 or older	−2.62	−1	−0.1

	AVERAGE HOUSEHOLD SPENDING	BEST CUSTOMERS (index)	BIGGEST CUSTOMERS (market share)
HOUSEHOLD INCOME			
Average household	**$482.45**	**100**	**100.0%**
Under $20,000	0.13	0	0.0
$20,000 to $39,999	83.25	17	4.0
$40,000 to $49,999	197.24	41	3.9
$50,000 to $69,999	352.60	73	10.5
$70,000 to $79,999	571.69	118	7.1
$80,000 to $99,999	657.92	136	11.4
$100,000 or more	1,779.11	369	63.2
HOUSEHOLD TYPE			
Average household	**482.45**	**100**	**100.0**
Married couples	691.63	143	70.7
Married couples, no children	576.47	119	25.4
Married couples, with children	807.42	167	38.9
Oldest child under age 6	690.87	143	6.1
Oldest child aged 6 to 17	890.93	185	21.7
Oldest child aged 18 or older	740.53	153	11.1
Single parent with child under age 18	140.97	29	1.7
Single person	290.60	60	17.6
RACE AND HISPANIC ORIGIN			
Average household	**482.45**	**100**	**100.0**
Asian	1,143.20	237	10.1
Black	222.98	46	5.7
Hispanic	201.85	42	5.1
Non-Hispanic white and other	568.95	118	89.4
REGION			
Average household	**482.45**	**100**	**100.0**
Northeast	699.52	145	26.6
Midwest	455.51	94	21.0
South	328.94	68	25.0
West	581.80	121	27.3
EDUCATION			
Average household	**482.45**	**100**	**100.0**
Less than high school graduate	108.88	23	3.2
High school graduate	224.82	47	11.9
Some college	347.80	72	15.2
Associate's degree	476.19	99	9.3
Bachelor's degree or more	980.79	203	60.4
Bachelor's degree	866.65	180	33.9
Master's, professional, doctoral degree	1,180.06	245	26.5

Note: Market shares may not sum to 100.0 because of rounding and missing categories by household type. "Asian" and "black" include Hispanics and non-Hispanics who identify themselves as being of the respective race alone. "Hispanic" includes people of any race who identify themselves as Hispanic. "Other" includes people who identify themselves as non-Hispanic and as Alaska Native, American Indian, Asian (who are also included in the "Asian" row), or Native Hawaiian or other Pacific Islander as well as non-Hispanics reporting more than one race.

Source: Calculations by New Strategist based on the Bureau of Labor Statistics' 2010 Consumer Expenditure Survey

Chapter 7.

Furnishings and Equipment

Household Spending on Furnishings and Equipment, 2010

In 2010 the average household spent $1,172 on home furnishings and equipment. Average household spending on everything from major appliances to indoor plants and outdoor furniture declined 22 percent since the overall peak spending year of 2006, after adjusting for inflation. Household spending on home furnishings had been stable between 2000 and 2006, along with increased spending on housing itself during the housing boom years. Behind the considerable recent decline in spending on furnishings was the economic downturn, which brought foreclosures and curtailed discretionary spending.

The largest home furnishings category, major appliances (such as refrigerators and washing machines), accounts for 18 percent of the dollars spent on home furnishings and equipment. Average household spending on major appliances, which had grown by 9 percent between 2000 and 2006, fell 20 percent between 2006 and 2010, after adjusting for inflation. Some categories experienced even larger declines. Average household spending on bedroom linens dropped 44 percent over the latter time period; wall units, cabinets, and other furniture experienced a 40 percent decline; and kitchen and dining room furniture as well as linens saw a 37 percent decrease, to name just the four biggest losing categories.

Other categories saw gains, some quite large. Average household spending on portable heating and cooling equipment tripled from 2006 to 2010, after adjusting for inflation. Spending on outdoor furniture increased by a whopping 56 percent, and spending on power and hand tools grew 53 percent since 2006. Closet and storage items witnessed the second-largest swing, jumping from an 88 percent gain between 2000 and 2006 to a 17 percent loss from 2006 to 2010. Small electric kitchen appliances, slipcovers and decorative pillows, and nonpermanent floor coverings (rugs) were among the most stable home furnishings and equipment categories during the 2000-to-2010 time period.

Average household spending on home furnishings may increase in the years ahead as millions of boomers become empty-nesters and redecorate their homes, but only if discretionary income grows.

Spending on furnishings and equipment

(average annual spending of households on furnishings and equipment, 2000, 2006, and 2010; in 2010 dollars)

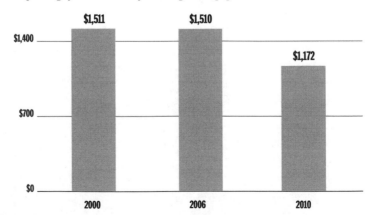

Table 7.1 Household furnishings and equipment spending, 2000 to 2010

(average annual household spending on household furnishings and equipment by category, 2000 to 2010; percent change and percentage point change in spending, 2000–06, 2006–10, and 2000–10; in 2010 dollars; ranked by amount spent)

	2010 average household spending	2006 average household spending (in 2010$)	2000 average household spending (in 2010$)	percent change		
				2006–10	2000–06	2000–10
AVERAGE ANNUAL SPENDING						
Average annual household spending on furnishings and equipment	**$1,172.35**	**$1,510.49**	**$1,510.74**	**–22.4%**	**–0.0%**	**–22.4%**
Appliances, major	209.19	260.95	239.28	–19.8	9.1	–12.6
Decorative items for the home	101.37	149.13	224.51	–32.0	–33.6	–54.8
Sofas	84.27	125.52	112.89	–32.9	11.2	–25.4
Housewares	65.92	90.69	82.14	–27.3	10.4	–19.8
Bedroom furniture, except mattresses and springs	62.56	91.92	87.51	–31.9	5.0	–28.5
Power and hand tools	52.99	34.53	36.19	53.5	–4.6	46.4
Living room chairs and tables	52.63	68.99	77.28	–23.7	–10.7	–31.9
Mattresses and springs	48.62	70.60	67.09	–31.1	5.2	–27.5
Bedroom linens	45.95	81.60	56.38	–43.7	44.7	–18.5
Plants and fresh flowers, indoor	42.60	49.94	72.19	–14.7	–30.8	–41.0
Wall units, cabinets, and other furniture	40.97	68.43	64.09	–40.1	6.8	–36.1
Lawn and garden equipment	37.06	53.74	59.29	–31.0	–9.4	–37.5
Outdoor equipment	34.74	31.00	23.29	12.1	33.1	49.2
Kitchen and dining room furniture	31.79	50.23	58.83	–36.7	–14.6	–46.0
Outdoor furniture	26.39	16.95	19.20	55.7	–11.7	37.5
Infants' equipment and furniture	24.55	26.16	18.02	–6.2	45.2	36.2
Window coverings	22.96	28.85	16.49	–20.4	75.0	39.3
Lamps and lighting fixtures	21.93	18.26	13.68	20.1	33.5	60.4
Kitchen appliances, small electric	21.85	20.64	21.58	5.9	–4.4	1.3
Portable heating and cooling equipment	18.73	6.23	6.93	200.6	–10.1	170.4
Floor coverings, wall-to-wall	18.69	23.74	35.18	–21.3	–32.5	–46.9
Bathroom linens	18.68	28.96	22.22	–35.5	30.3	–15.9
Laundry and cleaning equipment	17.83	16.57	12.76	7.6	29.8	39.7
Curtains and draperies	17.69	26.45	26.67	–33.1	–0.8	–33.7
Floor coverings, nonpermanent	17.38	23.60	19.27	–26.4	22.5	–9.8
Closet and storage items	15.85	19.14	10.17	–17.2	88.3	55.9
Sewing materials for household items	9.53	13.03	12.35	–26.9	5.6	–22.8
Kitchen and dining room linens	5.92	9.35	11.79	–36.7	–20.7	–49.8
Slipcovers and decorative pillows	3.71	5.30	3.48	–30.0	52.2	6.5

	2006–10	2000–06	2000–10	percentage point change		
				2006–10	2000–06	2000–10
PERCENT DISTRIBUTION OF SPENDING						
Average annual household spending on furnishings and equipment	**100.0%**	**100.0%**	**100.0%**	–	–	–
Appliances, major	17.8	17.3	15.8	0.6	1.4	2.0
Decorative items for the home	8.6	9.9	14.9	−1.2	−5.0	−6.2
Sofas	7.2	8.3	7.5	−1.1	0.8	−0.3
Housewares	5.6	6.0	5.4	−0.4	0.6	0.2
Bedroom furniture, except mattresses and springs	5.3	6.1	5.8	−0.7	0.3	−0.5
Power and hand tools	4.5	2.3	2.4	2.2	−0.1	2.1
Living room chairs and tables	4.5	4.6	5.1	−0.1	−0.5	−0.6
Mattresses and springs	4.1	4.7	4.4	−0.5	0.2	−0.3
Bedroom linens	3.9	5.4	3.7	−1.5	1.7	0.2
Plants and fresh flowers, indoor	3.6	3.3	4.8	0.3	−1.5	−1.1
Wall units, cabinets, and other furniture	3.5	4.5	4.2	−1.0	0.3	−0.7
Lawn and garden equipment	3.2	3.6	3.9	−0.4	−0.4	−0.8
Outdoor equipment	3.0	2.1	1.5	0.9	0.5	1.4
Kitchen and dining room furniture	2.7	3.3	3.9	−0.6	−0.6	−1.2
Outdoor furniture	2.3	1.1	1.3	1.1	−0.1	1.0
Infants' equipment and furniture	2.1	1.7	1.2	0.4	0.5	0.9
Window coverings	2.0	1.9	1.1	0.1	0.8	0.9
Lamps and lighting fixtures	1.9	1.2	0.9	0.7	0.3	1.0
Kitchen appliances, small electric	1.9	1.4	1.4	0.5	−0.1	0.4
Portable heating and cooling equipment	1.6	0.4	0.5	1.2	−0.1	1.1
Floor coverings, wall-to-wall	1.6	1.6	2.3	0.0	−0.8	−0.7
Bathroom linens	1.6	1.9	1.5	−0.3	0.4	0.1
Laundry and cleaning equipment	1.5	1.1	0.8	0.4	0.3	0.7
Curtains and draperies	1.5	1.8	1.8	−0.2	−0.0	−0.3
Floor coverings, nonpermanent	1.5	1.6	1.3	−0.1	0.3	0.2
Closet and storage items	1.4	1.3	0.7	0.1	0.6	0.7
Sewing materials for household items	0.8	0.9	0.8	−0.1	0.1	−0.0
Kitchen and dining room linens	0.5	0.6	0.8	−0.1	−0.2	−0.3
Slipcovers and decorative pillows	0.3	0.4	0.2	−0.0	0.1	0.1

Note: "–" means not applicable.

Source: Bureau of Labor Statistics, 2000, 2006, and 2010 Consumer Expenditure Surveys; calculations by New Strategist

Appliances, Kitchen, Small Electric

Best customers: Householders aged 55 to 64
Married couples without children at home
Married couples with preschoolers
Households in the Northeast and West

Customer trends: Average household spending on small electric kitchen appliances should continue
to grow as more boomers become empty nesters buying for their adult children,
but the economic downturn may limit the gains.

The category small electric kitchen appliances includes coffeemakers, food processors, bread makers, and so on. The best customers of small electric kitchen appliances are older married couples. Married couples without children at home (most of them older) spend 31 percent more than average on small electric kitchen appliances, many helping grown children outfit their first homes. Similarly, householders aged 55 to 64 spend 21 percent more than average on this item. Couples with preschoolers spend 62 percent more than average on small electric kitchen appliances as they establish their household. Households in the West spend one-quarter more than average on small electric kitchen appliances, and households in the Northeast spend 17 percent more.

Average household spending on small electric kitchen appliances grew 1 percent between 2000 and 2010, after adjusting for inflation. Behind the gain was the entry of the large baby-boom generation into one of the best customer lifestages. Spending on small electric kitchen appliances should continue to grow as more boomers become empty nesters buying for their adult children, but the economic downturn may limit the gains.

Table 7.2 Appliances, kitchen, small electric

Total household spending $2,646,187,950.00
Average household spends 21.85

	AVERAGE HOUSEHOLD SPENDING	BEST CUSTOMERS (index)	BIGGEST CUSTOMERS (market share)
AGE OF HOUSEHOLDER			
Average household	**$21.85**	**100**	**100.0%**
Under age 25	17.16	79	5.2
Aged 25 to 34	24.50	112	18.7
Aged 35 to 44	18.94	87	15.7
Aged 45 to 54	23.82	109	22.6
Aged 55 to 64	26.47	121	21.4
Aged 65 to 74	23.19	106	11.4
Aged 75 or older	11.67	53	5.1

	AVERAGE HOUSEHOLD SPENDING	BEST CUSTOMERS (index)	BIGGEST CUSTOMERS (market share)
HOUSEHOLD INCOME			
Average household	**$21.85**	**100**	**100.0%**
Under $20,000	12.09	55	12.1
$20,000 to $39,999	17.50	80	18.4
$40,000 to $49,999	15.68	72	6.8
$50,000 to $69,999	22.74	104	14.9
$70,000 to $79,999	24.71	113	6.8
$80,000 to $99,999	25.82	118	9.9
$100,000 or more	39.82	182	31.2
HOUSEHOLD TYPE			
Average household	**21.85**	**100**	**100.0**
Married couples	26.91	123	60.8
Married couples, no children	28.72	131	27.9
Married couples, with children	25.26	116	26.9
Oldest child under age 6	35.49	162	7.0
Oldest child aged 6 to 17	21.69	99	11.7
Oldest child aged 18 or older	25.01	114	8.3
Single parent with child under age 18	14.98	69	4.0
Single person	16.35	75	21.9
RACE AND HISPANIC ORIGIN			
Average household	**21.85**	**100**	**100.0**
Asian	23.81	109	4.6
Black	14.51	66	8.1
Hispanic	15.94	73	8.9
Non-Hispanic white and other	23.93	110	83.0
REGION			
Average household	**21.85**	**100**	**100.0**
Northeast	25.63	117	21.5
Midwest	21.38	98	21.8
South	16.67	76	28.0
West	27.65	127	28.7
EDUCATION			
Average household	**21.85**	**100**	**100.0**
Less than high school graduate	11.04	51	7.2
High school graduate	18.84	86	22.0
Some college	21.93	100	21.1
Associate's degree	25.93	119	11.2
Bachelor's degree or more	28.28	129	38.5
Bachelor's degree	25.73	118	22.2
Master's, professional, doctoral degree	32.73	150	16.2

Note: Market shares may not sum to 100.0 because of rounding and missing categories by household type. "Asian" and "black" include Hispanics and non-Hispanics who identify themselves as being of the respective race alone. "Hispanic" includes people of any race who identify themselves as Hispanic. "Other" includes people who identify themselves as non-Hispanic and as Alaska Native, American Indian, Asian (who are also included in the "Asian" row), or Native Hawaiian or other Pacific Islander as well as non-Hispanics reporting more than one race.

Source: Calculations by New Strategist based on the Bureau of Labor Statistics' 2010 Consumer Expenditure Survey

Appliances, Major

Best customers: **Householders aged 35 to 44 and 55 to 64**
Married couples

Customer trends: **Average household spending on major appliances may continue to fall as household formation slows and families tighten their belts.**

The biggest spenders on major appliances—the largest expense category among household furnishings and supplies—are married couples who are outfitting their home for expanding families and older couples who are upgrading appliances after their children have left home or buying them for grown children as they establish their own households. This explains why householders aged 35 to 44 spend 25 percent more than average on this item and those aged 55 to 64 spend 19 percent more. Married couples spend 34 percent more than average on major appliances, the figure peaking at 50 percent among those with adult children at home.

Average household spending on major appliances grew 9 percent between 2000 and 2006, then fell 20 percent from 2006 to 2010, after adjusting for inflation. The economic downturn is behind the decline. Average household spending on major appliances may continue to fall as household formation slows and families tighten their belts.

Table 7.3 Appliances, major

Total household spending $25,334,373,330.00
Average household spends   209.19

	AVERAGE HOUSEHOLD SPENDING	BEST CUSTOMERS (index)	BIGGEST CUSTOMERS (market share)
AGE OF HOUSEHOLDER			
Average household	**$209.19**	**100**	**100.0%**
Under age 25	91.72	44	2.9
Aged 25 to 34	159.82	76	12.7
Aged 35 to 44	261.87	125	22.6
Aged 45 to 54	220.29	105	21.8
Aged 55 to 64	248.76	119	21.0
Aged 65 to 74	180.74	86	9.3
Aged 75 or older	211.28	101	9.6

	AVERAGE HOUSEHOLD SPENDING	BEST CUSTOMERS (index)	BIGGEST CUSTOMERS (market share)
HOUSEHOLD INCOME			
Average household	**$209.19**	**100**	**100.0%**
Under $20,000	71.64	34	7.5
$20,000 to $39,999	132.50	63	14.5
$40,000 to $49,999	167.67	80	7.6
$50,000 to $69,999	242.55	116	16.6
$70,000 to $79,999	297.73	142	8.5
$80,000 to $99,999	302.70	145	12.1
$100,000 or more	406.06	194	33.3
HOUSEHOLD TYPE			
Average household	**209.19**	**100**	**100.0**
Married couples	279.99	134	66.0
Married couples, no children	270.84	129	27.5
Married couples, with children	292.92	140	32.6
Oldest child under age 6	302.14	144	6.2
Oldest child aged 6 to 17	274.27	131	15.4
Oldest child aged 18 or older	314.59	150	10.9
Single parent with child under age 18	141.03	67	4.0
Single person	102.19	49	14.3
RACE AND HISPANIC ORIGIN			
Average household	**209.19**	**100**	**100.0**
Asian	184.71	88	3.8
Black	173.41	83	10.1
Hispanic	152.69	73	8.9
Non-Hispanic white and other	224.08	107	81.2
REGION			
Average household	**209.19**	**100**	**100.0**
Northeast	197.17	94	17.3
Midwest	187.01	89	19.9
South	209.61	100	36.8
West	239.99	115	26.0
EDUCATION			
Average household	**209.19**	**100**	**100.0**
Less than high school graduate	93.56	45	6.4
High school graduate	184.53	88	22.5
Some college	195.18	93	19.6
Associate's degree	180.95	87	8.2
Bachelor's degree or more	304.80	146	43.3
Bachelor's degree	305.45	146	27.6
Master's, professional, doctoral degree	302.36	145	15.6

Note: Market shares may not sum to 100.0 because of rounding and missing categories by household type. "Asian" and "black" include Hispanics and non-Hispanics who identify themselves as being of the respective race alone. "Hispanic" includes people of any race who identify themselves as Hispanic. "Other" includes people who identify themselves as non-Hispanic and as Alaska Native, American Indian, Asian (who are also included in the "Asian" row), or Native Hawaiian or other Pacific Islander as well as non-Hispanics reporting more than one race.

Source: Calculations by New Strategist based on the Bureau of Labor Statistics' 2010 Consumer Expenditure Survey

Bathroom Linens

Best customers:	Householders aged 35 to 54
	Married couples with children at home
	Single parents
	Hispanics

Customer trends:	Average household spending on bathroom linens is likely to decline further because the small generation X is in the best-customer lifestage, and the economic downturn is limiting discretionary spending.

The biggest spenders on bathroom linens are families with children. Householders aged 35 to 54, most with children, spend 16 to 20 percent more than average on bathroom linens. Married couples with children at home spend 42 percent more than the average household on this item. Single parents, whose spending is well below average on most items, spend 3 percent above average on bathroom linens. Hispanics, who tend to have the largest families, outspend the average by 70 percent.

Average household spending on bathroom linens climbed 30 percent between 2000 and 2006 (the year overall household spending peaked), after adjusting for inflation. Spending on this item then sank 35 percent between 2006 and 2010. Spending on bathroom linens is likely to decline further because the small generation X is in the best-customer lifestage, and the economic downturn is limiting discretionary spending.

Table 7.4 Bathroom linens

Total household spending	$2,262,278,760.00
Average household spends	18.68

	AVERAGE HOUSEHOLD SPENDING	BEST CUSTOMERS (index)	BIGGEST CUSTOMERS (market share)
AGE OF HOUSEHOLDER			
Average household	**$18.68**	**100**	**100.0%**
Under age 25	12.82	69	4.6
Aged 25 to 34	14.77	79	13.2
Aged 35 to 44	21.73	116	21.0
Aged 45 to 54	22.46	120	24.9
Aged 55 to 64	17.80	95	16.8
Aged 65 to 74	16.79	90	9.7
Aged 75 or older	19.36	104	9.9

	AVERAGE HOUSEHOLD SPENDING	BEST CUSTOMERS (index)	BIGGEST CUSTOMERS (market share)
HOUSEHOLD INCOME			
Average household	**$18.68**	**100**	**100.0%**
Under $20,000	12.54	67	14.6
$20,000 to $39,999	14.72	79	18.1
$40,000 to $49,999	11.29	60	5.7
$50,000 to $69,999	17.29	93	13.3
$70,000 to $79,999	22.11	118	7.1
$80,000 to $99,999	34.04	182	15.2
$100,000 or more	29.09	156	26.7
HOUSEHOLD TYPE			
Average household	**18.68**	**100**	**100.0**
Married couples	22.80	122	60.2
Married couples, no children	20.43	109	23.2
Married couples, with children	26.61	142	33.1
Oldest child under age 6	26.74	143	6.1
Oldest child aged 6 to 17	25.48	136	16.0
Oldest child aged 18 or older	28.22	151	10.9
Single parent with child under age 18	19.28	103	6.1
Single person	10.93	59	17.1
RACE AND HISPANIC ORIGIN			
Average household	**18.68**	**100**	**100.0**
Asian	20.23	108	4.6
Black	14.70	79	9.6
Hispanic	31.82	170	20.8
Non-Hispanic white and other	17.22	92	69.9
REGION			
Average household	**18.68**	**100**	**100.0**
Northeast	18.58	99	18.3
Midwest	18.70	100	22.3
South	19.52	104	38.4
West	17.37	93	21.1
EDUCATION			
Average household	**18.68**	**100**	**100.0**
Less than high school graduate	25.36	136	19.4
High school graduate	17.55	94	24.0
Some college	14.90	80	16.8
Associate's degree	10.47	56	5.3
Bachelor's degree or more	22.22	119	35.3
Bachelor's degree	22.91	123	23.2
Master's, professional, doctoral degree	20.84	112	12.1

Note: Market shares may not sum to 100.0 because of rounding and missing categories by household type. "Asian" and "black" include Hispanics and non-Hispanics who identify themselves as being of the respective race alone. "Hispanic" includes people of any race who identify themselves as Hispanic. "Other" includes people who identify themselves as non-Hispanic and as Alaska Native, American Indian, Asian (who are also included in the "Asian" row), or Native Hawaiian or other Pacific Islander as well as non-Hispanics reporting more than one race.

Source: Calculations by New Strategist based on the Bureau of Labor Statistics' 2010 Consumer Expenditure Survey

Bedroom Furniture, except Mattresses and Springs

Best customers:	**Householders under age 45** **Married couples with children at home** **Hispanics and blacks**
Customer trends:	**Average household spending on bedroom furniture may rise in the years ahead as more of the large millennial generation enters the best-customer lifestage, but the economic downturn may limit any gains in this category.**

The best customers of bedroom furniture except mattresses and springs are households with children at home, outfitting their homes for their expanding families. Married couples with children spend 60 percent more than average on this item. Householders under age 45, many with children at home, spend 20 to 47 percent more than average on this item and account for 59 percent of the market. Hispanics and blacks spend one-quarter more than average on bedroom furniture and account for 31 percent of the market.

Average household spending on bedroom furniture except mattresses and springs fell 29 percent between 2000 and 2010, after adjusting for inflation. Behind the decline was the small generation X in the best-customer lifestage as well as the Great Recession. Average household spending on bedroom furniture may rise in the years ahead as more of the large millennial generation enters the best-customer lifestage, but the economic downturn may limit any gains in this category.

Table 7.5 Bedroom furniture, except mattresses and springs

Total household spending	$7,576,453,920.00
Average household spends	62.56

	AVERAGE HOUSEHOLD SPENDING	BEST CUSTOMERS (index)	BIGGEST CUSTOMERS (market share)
AGE OF HOUSEHOLDER			
Average household	**$62.56**	**100**	**100.0%**
Under age 25	75.07	120	8.0
Aged 25 to 34	92.24	147	24.6
Aged 35 to 44	90.45	145	26.2
Aged 45 to 54	47.01	75	15.5
Aged 55 to 64	60.60	97	17.1
Aged 65 to 74	28.27	45	4.9
Aged 75 or older	25.16	40	3.8

	AVERAGE HOUSEHOLD SPENDING	BEST CUSTOMERS (index)	BIGGEST CUSTOMERS (market share)
HOUSEHOLD INCOME			
Average household	**$62.56**	**100**	**100.0%**
Under $20,000	28.96	46	10.1
$20,000 to $39,999	29.02	46	10.6
$40,000 to $49,999	45.94	73	6.9
$50,000 to $69,999	67.55	108	15.5
$70,000 to $79,999	92.19	147	8.8
$80,000 to $99,999	72.14	115	9.6
$100,000 or more	140.11	224	38.4
HOUSEHOLD TYPE			
Average household	**62.56**	**100**	**100.0**
Married couples	78.74	126	62.1
Married couples, no children	57.10	91	19.4
Married couples, with children	100.00	160	37.2
Oldest child under age 6	148.37	237	10.2
Oldest child aged 6 to 17	88.00	141	16.5
Oldest child aged 18 or older	90.87	145	10.5
Single parent with child under age 18	55.00	88	5.2
Single person	37.95	61	17.8
RACE AND HISPANIC ORIGIN			
Average household	**62.56**	**100**	**100.0**
Asian	66.84	107	4.5
Black	77.55	124	15.2
Hispanic	78.85	126	15.4
Non-Hispanic white and other	57.88	93	70.1
REGION			
Average household	**62.56**	**100**	**100.0**
Northeast	61.61	98	18.1
Midwest	50.63	81	18.0
South	64.75	104	38.0
West	71.52	114	25.9
EDUCATION			
Average household	**62.56**	**100**	**100.0**
Less than high school graduate	34.44	55	7.9
High school graduate	42.96	69	17.5
Some college	54.50	87	18.3
Associate's degree	67.62	108	10.2
Bachelor's degree or more	97.02	155	46.1
Bachelor's degree	101.74	163	30.7
Master's, professional, doctoral degree	88.77	142	15.4

Note: Market shares may not sum to 100.0 because of rounding and missing categories by household type. "Asian" and "black" include Hispanics and non-Hispanics who identify themselves as being of the respective race alone. "Hispanic" includes people of any race who identify themselves as Hispanic. "Other" includes people who identify themselves as non-Hispanic and as Alaska Native, American Indian, Asian (who are also included in the "Asian" row), or Native Hawaiian or other Pacific Islander as well as non-Hispanics reporting more than one race.

Source: Calculations by New Strategist based on the Bureau of Labor Statistics' 2010 Consumer Expenditure Survey

Bedroom Linens

Best customers:
Householders aged 35 to 44 and 55 to 64
Married couples with school-aged or older children at home
Single parents

Customer trends:
Average household spending on bedroom linens may reverse its recent decline as the large millennial generation begins to enter one of the best-customer age groups, but only if discretionary income grows.

The biggest spenders on bedroom linens are the parents of school-aged or older children children. Married couples with school-aged children spend 48 percent more than average on this item and their counterparts with adult children at home spend 66 percent more. Single parents spend 60 percent more than average on bedroom linens despite their low incomes. Householders aged 35 to 44 spend 32 percent more than average on bedroom linens, and those aged 55 to 64 spend 29 percent more.

Average household spending on bedroom linens, which had risen strongly from 2000 to 2006, fell 44 percent between 2006 and 2010, after adjusting for inflation. Average household spending on bedroom linens may reverse its recent decline as the large millennial generation begins to enter one of the best-customer age group, but only if discretionary income grows.

Table 7.6 Bedroom linens

Total household spending $5,564,866,650.00
Average household spends 45.95

	AVERAGE HOUSEHOLD SPENDING	BEST CUSTOMERS (index)	BIGGEST CUSTOMERS (market share)
AGE OF HOUSEHOLDER			
Average household	**$45.95**	**100**	**100.0%**
Under age 25	28.70	62	4.1
Aged 25 to 34	37.79	82	13.7
Aged 35 to 44	60.69	132	23.9
Aged 45 to 54	44.30	96	19.9
Aged 55 to 64	59.44	129	22.8
Aged 65 to 74	46.94	102	11.0
Aged 75 or older	21.74	47	4.5

	AVERAGE HOUSEHOLD SPENDING	BEST CUSTOMERS (index)	BIGGEST CUSTOMERS (market share)
HOUSEHOLD INCOME			
Average household	**$45.95**	**100**	**100.0%**
Under $20,000	25.16	55	11.9
$20,000 to $39,999	19.18	42	9.6
$40,000 to $49,999	26.69	58	5.5
$50,000 to $69,999	37.45	82	11.7
$70,000 to $79,999	69.12	150	9.0
$80,000 to $99,999	80.18	174	14.5
$100,000 or more	104.60	228	39.0
HOUSEHOLD TYPE			
Average household	**45.95**	**100**	**100.0**
Married couples	61.06	133	65.5
Married couples, no children	54.77	119	25.3
Married couples, with children	67.57	147	34.2
Oldest child under age 6	48.31	105	4.5
Oldest child aged 6 to 17	68.21	148	17.5
Oldest child aged 18 or older	76.49	166	12.0
Single parent with child under age 18	73.65	160	9.5
Single person	21.86	48	13.9
RACE AND HISPANIC ORIGIN			
Average household	**45.95**	**100**	**100.0**
Asian	41.01	89	3.8
Black	37.21	81	9.9
Hispanic	36.33	79	9.6
Non-Hispanic white and other	48.77	106	80.5
REGION			
Average household	**45.95**	**100**	**100.0**
Northeast	47.57	104	19.0
Midwest	45.92	100	22.3
South	38.04	83	30.4
West	57.69	126	28.4
EDUCATION			
Average household	**45.95**	**100**	**100.0**
Less than high school graduate	22.52	49	7.0
High school graduate	43.20	94	24.0
Some college	43.81	95	20.0
Associate's degree	49.32	107	10.1
Bachelor's degree or more	59.17	129	38.3
Bachelor's degree	55.25	120	22.7
Master's, professional, doctoral degree	66.90	146	15.8

Note: Market shares may not sum to 100.0 because of rounding and missing categories by household type. "Asian" and "black" include Hispanics and non-Hispanics who identify themselves as being of the respective race alone. "Hispanic" includes people of any race who identify themselves as Hispanic. "Other" includes people who identify themselves as non-Hispanic and as Alaska Native, American Indian, Asian (who are also included in the "Asian" row), or Native Hawaiian or other Pacific Islander as well as non-Hispanics reporting more than one race.

Source: Calculations by New Strategist based on the Bureau of Labor Statistics' 2010 Consumer Expenditure Survey

Closet and Storage Items

Best customers:	**Householders aged 45 to 54** **Married couples** **Blacks and Asians** **Households in the South**
Customer trends:	**Average household spending on closet and storage items may rise again as Americans try to organize their burgeoning possessions, but only if discretionary income grows.**

Householders aged 45 to 54 are the best customers of closet and storage items, spending 58 percent more than average on this item. Married couples spend 53 percent more than average on closet and storage items, the number peaking at nearly 80 percent above average among couples with preschoolers or adult children at home. The spending on closet and storage items by blacks and Asians is, respectively, 43 and 22 percent above average. Households in the South, where many blacks reside, outspend the average by one-quarter.

Average household spending on closet and storage items grew by an enormous 88 percent between 2000 and 2006 (the year overall household spending peaked). Then the pattern reversed and spending on this item fell 17 percent between 2006 and 2010, after adjusting for inflation. Behind the earlier increase was the growing variety of closet and storage items available, while the decline is a result of belt-tightening among financially strapped householders. Spending on this item may rise again as Americans try to organize their burgeoning possessions, but only if discretionary income grows.

Table 7.7 Closet and storage items

Total household spending	$1,782,493,250.00
Average household spends	14.75

	AVERAGE HOUSEHOLD SPENDING	BEST CUSTOMERS (index)	BIGGEST CUSTOMERS (market share)
AGE OF HOUSEHOLDER			
Average household	**$14.75**	**100**	**100.0%**
Under age 25	9.45	64	4.2
Aged 25 to 34	18.03	122	20.3
Aged 35 to 44	14.60	99	18.2
Aged 45 to 54	16.69	113	23.8
Aged 55 to 64	16.97	115	19.7
Aged 65 to 74	11.98	81	8.6
Aged 75 or older	7.88	53	5.2

	AVERAGE HOUSEHOLD SPENDING	BEST CUSTOMERS (index)	BIGGEST CUSTOMERS (market share)
HOUSEHOLD INCOME			
Average household	$14.75	100	100.0%
Under $20,000	6.80	46	9.7
$20,000 to $39,999	10.37	70	16.3
$40,000 to $49,999	10.53	71	6.8
$50,000 to $69,999	9.72	66	9.7
$70,000 to $79,999	24.38	165	9.1
$80,000 to $99,999	24.49	166	13.7
$100,000 or more	28.33	192	34.3
HOUSEHOLD TYPE			
Average household	14.75	100	100.0
Married couples	19.63	133	67.5
Married couples, no children	18.48	125	27.8
Married couples, with children	20.72	140	34.3
Oldest child under age 6	32.79	222	9.5
Oldest child aged 6 to 17	15.92	108	13.4
Oldest child aged 18 or older	21.59	146	11.3
Single parent with child under age 18	6.88	47	2.6
Single person	10.31	70	20.1
RACE AND HISPANIC ORIGIN			
Average household	14.75	100	100.0
Asian	15.12	103	3.9
Black	7.96	54	6.5
Hispanic	13.85	94	11.1
Non-Hispanic white and other	15.98	108	82.6
REGION			
Average household	14.75	100	100.0
Northeast	18.95	128	23.8
Midwest	13.20	89	20.4
South	11.51	78	28.3
West	18.03	122	27.4
EDUCATION			
Average household	14.75	100	100.0
Less than high school graduate	7.48	51	7.0
High school graduate	10.75	73	18.7
Some college	16.40	111	23.5
Associate's degree	15.39	104	10.4
Bachelor's degree or more	19.83	134	39.6
Bachelor's degree	15.39	104	20.2
Master's, professional, doctoral degree	28.19	191	19.2

Note: Market shares may not sum to 100.0 because of rounding and missing categories by household type. "Asian" and "black" include Hispanics and non-Hispanics who identify themselves as being of the respective race alone. "Hispanic" includes people of any race who identify themselves as Hispanic. "Other" includes people who identify themselves as non-Hispanic and as Alaska Native, American Indian, Asian (who are also included in the "Asian" row), or Native Hawaiian or other Pacific Islander as well as non-Hispanics reporting more than one race.

Source: Calculations by New Strategist based on the Bureau of Labor Statistics' 2010 Consumer Expenditure Survey

Curtains and Draperies

Best customers:	**Householders aged 55 to 64** **Married couples without children at home** **Married couples with school-aged children** **Households in the Northeast**
Customer trends:	**Average household spending on curtains and draperies is likely to continue to fall as the economic downturn limits discretionary spending.**

The best customers of curtains and draperies, married couples with school-aged children, spend 88 percent more than average on this item. Couples without children at home, most older, spend 64 percent more than average on curtains and draperies, perhaps redecorating after their grown children have moved out. Householders aged 55 to 64 spend twice the average on curtains and draperies. The spending on curtains and drapes by households in the Northeast is 36 percent higher than average.

Average household spending on curtains and draperies was stable between 2000 and 2006 (the year overall household spending peaked), then fell 33 percent between 2006 and 2010, after adjusting for inflation. Behind the decline was belt tightening due to the Great Recession. Average household spending on curtains and draperies is likely to continue to fall as the economic downturn limits discretionary spending.

Table 7.8 Curtains and draperies

Total household spending	$2,142,382,830.00
Average household spends	17.69

	AVERAGE HOUSEHOLD SPENDING	BEST CUSTOMERS (index)	BIGGEST CUSTOMERS (market share)
AGE OF HOUSEHOLDER			
Average household	**$17.69**	**100**	**100.0%**
Under age 25	6.25	35	2.3
Aged 25 to 34	13.25	75	12.5
Aged 35 to 44	13.97	79	14.3
Aged 45 to 54	17.41	98	20.4
Aged 55 to 64	35.82	202	35.7
Aged 65 to 74	18.36	104	11.2
Aged 75 or older	6.78	38	3.7

	AVERAGE HOUSEHOLD SPENDING	BEST CUSTOMERS (index)	BIGGEST CUSTOMERS (market share)
HOUSEHOLD INCOME			
Average household	**$17.69**	**100**	**100.0%**
Under $20,000	5.75	32	7.1
$20,000 to $39,999	10.17	58	13.2
$40,000 to $49,999	14.36	81	7.7
$50,000 to $69,999	10.59	60	8.6
$70,000 to $79,999	35.44	200	12.0
$80,000 to $99,999	13.94	79	6.6
$100,000 or more	46.33	262	44.9
HOUSEHOLD TYPE			
Average household	**17.69**	**100**	**100.0**
Married couples	27.92	158	77.9
Married couples, no children	28.93	164	34.7
Married couples, with children	25.22	143	33.2
Oldest child under age 6	17.21	97	4.2
Oldest child aged 6 to 17	33.33	188	22.2
Oldest child aged 18 or older	16.77	95	6.8
Single parent with child under age 18	9.12	52	3.0
Single person	7.88	45	13.0
RACE AND HISPANIC ORIGIN			
Average household	**17.69**	**100**	**100.0**
Asian	15.95	90	3.8
Black	8.23	47	5.7
Hispanic	8.89	50	6.1
Non-Hispanic white and other	20.58	116	88.2
REGION			
Average household	**17.69**	**100**	**100.0**
Northeast	23.98	136	24.9
Midwest	10.25	58	12.9
South	18.67	106	38.7
West	18.32	104	23.5
EDUCATION			
Average household	**17.69**	**100**	**100.0**
Less than high school graduate	5.40	31	4.4
High school graduate	11.10	63	16.0
Some college	15.22	86	18.1
Associate's degree	27.99	158	15.0
Bachelor's degree or more	27.74	157	46.6
Bachelor's degree	24.83	140	26.5
Master's, professional, doctoral degree	32.80	185	20.1

Note: Market shares may not sum to 100.0 because of rounding and missing categories by household type. "Asian" and "black" include Hispanics and non-Hispanics who identify themselves as being of the respective race alone. "Hispanic" includes people of any race who identify themselves as Hispanic. "Other" includes people who identify themselves as non-Hispanic and as Alaska Native, American Indian, Asian (who are also included in the "Asian" row), or Native Hawaiian or other Pacific Islander as well as non-Hispanics reporting more than one race.

Source: Calculations by New Strategist based on the Bureau of Labor Statistics' 2010 Consumer Expenditure Survey

Decorative Items for the Home

Best customers: Householders aged 35 to 54
Married couples without children at home
Married couples with school-aged or older children at home
Non-Hispanic whites

Customer trends: Average household spending on decorative items is unlikely to grow much until
the millennial generation enters the best customer age group.

Decorative items for the home—a category that includes the many whimsical items of home decor—are the fourth-largest expense within the home furnishings category, behind major appliances; laundry and cleaning supplies; and cleansing and toilet tissue, paper towels, and napkins. The biggest spenders on decorative items for the home are middle-aged or older married couples. Householders ranging in age from 35 to 54 spend 28 to 29 percent more than the average household on this item. Married couples without children at home, most of them empty-nesters, spend 46 percent more than average on decorative items, while couples with school-aged or older children at home spend 31 to 83 percent more. Non-Hispanic whites outspend minorities by a wide margin.

Average household spending on decorative items for the home has declined throughout the decade, falling 55 percent between 2000 and 2010, after adjusting for inflation. Behind the decline is the baby-boom generation's exit from the best-customer age groups, as well as household belt tightening in face of the Great Recession. Average household spending on decorative items is unlikely to grow much until the millennial generation enters the best-customer age group.

Table 7.9 Decorative items for the home

Total household spending $12,276,616,590.00
Average household spends   101.37

	AVERAGE HOUSEHOLD SPENDING	BEST CUSTOMERS (index)	BIGGEST CUSTOMERS (market share)
AGE OF HOUSEHOLDER			
Average household	**$101.37**	**100**	**100.0%**
Under age 25	51.46	51	3.4
Aged 25 to 34	83.27	82	13.7
Aged 35 to 44	130.21	128	23.2
Aged 45 to 54	130.40	129	26.6
Aged 55 to 64	85.75	85	14.9
Aged 65 to 74	119.23	118	12.7
Aged 75 or older	57.50	57	5.4

	AVERAGE HOUSEHOLD SPENDING	BEST CUSTOMERS (index)	BIGGEST CUSTOMERS (market share)
HOUSEHOLD INCOME			
Average household	**$101.37**	**100**	**100.0%**
Under $20,000	36.25	36	7.8
$20,000 to $39,999	61.21	60	13.8
$40,000 to $49,999	47.58	47	4.4
$50,000 to $69,999	74.39	73	10.5
$70,000 to $79,999	99.36	98	5.9
$80,000 to $99,999	112.94	111	9.3
$100,000 or more	294.92	291	49.9
HOUSEHOLD TYPE			
Average household	**101.37**	**100**	**100.0**
Married couples	147.46	145	71.8
Married couples, no children	147.69	146	30.9
Married couples, with children	153.32	151	35.2
Oldest child under age 6	100.51	99	4.2
Oldest child aged 6 to 17	185.23	183	21.5
Oldest child aged 18 or older	132.78	131	9.5
Single parent with child under age 18	69.80	69	4.1
Single person	34.14	34	9.9
RACE AND HISPANIC ORIGIN			
Average household	**101.37**	**100**	**100.0**
Asian	38.66	38	1.6
Black	53.74	53	6.5
Hispanic	67.40	66	8.1
Non-Hispanic white and other	114.14	113	85.4
REGION			
Average household	**101.37**	**100**	**100.0**
Northeast	91.55	90	16.6
Midwest	83.98	83	18.5
South	111.70	110	40.4
West	109.99	109	24.6
EDUCATION			
Average household	**101.37**	**100**	**100.0**
Less than high school graduate	33.00	33	4.7
High school graduate	55.46	55	14.0
Some college	70.14	69	14.5
Associate's degree	109.19	108	10.2
Bachelor's degree or more	192.04	189	56.3
Bachelor's degree	138.41	137	25.8
Master's, professional, doctoral degree	297.66	294	31.8

Note: Market shares may not sum to 100.0 because of rounding and missing categories by household type. "Asian" and "black" include Hispanics and non-Hispanics who identify themselves as being of the respective race alone. "Hispanic" includes people of any race who identify themselves as Hispanic. "Other" includes people who identify themselves as non-Hispanic and as Alaska Native, American Indian, Asian (who are also included in the "Asian" row), or Native Hawaiian or other Pacific Islander as well as non-Hispanics reporting more than one race.

Source: Calculations by New Strategist based on the Bureau of Labor Statistics' 2010 Consumer Expenditure Survey

Floor Coverings, Nonpermanent

Best customers:	Householders aged 55 to 64
	High-income households
	Married couples without children at home
	Married couples with children under age 18
	Asians
	Households in the Northeast
	College graduates
Customer trends:	Average household spending on nonpermanent floor coverings should stabilize in the years ahead as more boomers become empty-nesters, but the economic downturn may limit any increase.

The biggest spenders on rugs are older well-to-do married couples, as well as those who are outfitting children's rooms. Married couples without children at home, most of them empty-nesters, spend 49 percent more than average on rugs. Householders aged 55 to 64 spend 74 percent more than average on this item and control 31 percent of the market. Married couples with preschoolers spend 53 percent more than average on nonpermanent floor coverings, while those with school-aged children spend over twice the average. Households with incomes of $100,000 or more spend more than three times the average on rugs. College graduates, who have relatively high incomes, spend double the average on this item. Asians spend 29 percent more than average on rugs. Households in the Northeast spend nearly twice the average on this item.

Average household spending on rugs and other nonpermanent floor coverings climbed 22 percent between 2000 and 2006 (the year overall household spending peaked), then fell 26 percent between 2006 and 2010, after adjusting for inflation. Spending on rugs should stabilize in the years ahead as more boomers become empty-nesters, but the economic downturn may limit any increase.

Table 7.10 Floor coverings, nonpermanent

Total household spending $2,104,839,660.00
Average household spends   17.38

	AVERAGE HOUSEHOLD SPENDING	BEST CUSTOMERS (index)	BIGGEST CUSTOMERS (market share)
AGE OF HOUSEHOLDER			
Average household	**$17.38**	**100**	**100.0%**
Under age 25	6.44	37	2.5
Aged 25 to 34	14.81	85	14.2
Aged 35 to 44	20.44	118	21.3
Aged 45 to 54	15.62	90	18.6
Aged 55 to 64	30.31	174	30.8
Aged 65 to 74	11.71	67	7.2
Aged 75 or older	10.02	58	5.5

	AVERAGE HOUSEHOLD SPENDING	BEST CUSTOMERS (index)	BIGGEST CUSTOMERS (market share)
HOUSEHOLD INCOME			
Average household	**$17.38**	**100**	**100.0%**
Under $20,000	3.97	23	5.0
$20,000 to $39,999	5.34	31	7.0
$40,000 to $49,999	7.65	44	4.2
$50,000 to $69,999	12.10	70	10.0
$70,000 to $79,999	23.52	135	8.1
$80,000 to $99,999	20.87	120	10.0
$100,000 or more	56.51	325	55.8
HOUSEHOLD TYPE			
Average household	**17.38**	**100**	**100.0**
Married couples	24.53	141	69.6
Married couples, no children	25.93	149	31.7
Married couples, with children	26.05	150	34.9
Oldest child under age 6	26.55	153	6.5
Oldest child aged 6 to 17	36.55	210	24.7
Oldest child aged 18 or older	8.67	50	3.6
Single parent with child under age 18	5.62	32	1.9
Single person	12.19	70	20.5
RACE AND HISPANIC ORIGIN			
Average household	**17.38**	**100**	**100.0**
Asian	22.41	129	5.5
Black	12.72	73	9.0
Hispanic	7.87	45	5.5
Non-Hispanic white and other	19.61	113	85.5
REGION			
Average household	**17.38**	**100**	**100.0**
Northeast	33.93	195	35.8
Midwest	15.62	90	20.0
South	12.60	72	26.6
West	13.46	77	17.5
EDUCATION			
Average household	**17.38**	**100**	**100.0**
Less than high school graduate	3.87	22	3.2
High school graduate	10.80	62	15.9
Some college	11.35	65	13.7
Associate's degree	13.43	77	7.3
Bachelor's degree or more	35.07	202	59.9
Bachelor's degree	24.10	139	26.2
Master's, professional, doctoral degree	54.23	312	33.8

Note: Market shares may not sum to 100.0 because of rounding and missing categories by household type. "Asian" and "black" include Hispanics and non-Hispanics who identify themselves as being of the respective race alone. "Hispanic" includes people of any race who identify themselves as Hispanic. "Other" includes people who identify themselves as non-Hispanic and as Alaska Native, American Indian, Asian (who are also included in the "Asian" row), or Native Hawaiian or other Pacific Islander as well as non-Hispanics reporting more than one race.

Source: Calculations by New Strategist based on the Bureau of Labor Statistics' 2010 Consumer Expenditure Survey

Floor Coverings, Wall-to-Wall

Best customers:

Householders aged 25 to 34
High-income households
Married couples without children at home
Married couples with children under age 18
Blacks
Households in the South

Customer trends:

Average household spending on wall-to-wall floor coverings is not likely to grow much until the housing market improves and discretionary income rises.

The best customers of wall-to-wall carpeting are young black couples living in the South and the well-to-do. Householders aged 25 to 34 spend 55 percent more than average on wall-to-wall carpeting, and married couples with children under age 18 spend 44 to 56 percent more. Householders with incomes of $100,000 or more spend more than triple the average. Married couples without children at home spend 38 percent more than average on wall-to-wall floor coverings. Black householders spend over twice the average on this item and control a sizeable 25 percent of the market. Households in the South, where many blacks reside, outspend the average by 37 percent.

Average household spending on wall-to-wall carpeting has been in a decade-long decline, falling by 49 percent between 2000 and 2010, after adjusting for inflation. Behind the decline was price discounting as well as household belt-tightening. Average household spending on wall-to-wall carpeting is not likely to grow much until the housing market improves and discretionary income rises.

Table 7.11 Floor coverings, wall-to-wall

Total household spending	$2,263,489,830.00
Average household spends	18.69

	AVERAGE HOUSEHOLD SPENDING	BEST CUSTOMERS (index)	BIGGEST CUSTOMERS (market share)
AGE OF HOUSEHOLDER			
Average household	**$18.69**	**100**	**100.0%**
Under age 25	1.46	8	0.5
Aged 25 to 34	29.05	155	25.9
Aged 35 to 44	21.43	115	20.7
Aged 45 to 54	20.91	112	23.1
Aged 55 to 64	20.71	111	19.5
Aged 65 to 74	7.98	43	4.6
Aged 75 or older	11.01	59	5.6

	AVERAGE HOUSEHOLD SPENDING	BEST CUSTOMERS (index)	BIGGEST CUSTOMERS (market share)
HOUSEHOLD INCOME			
Average household	**$18.69**	**100**	**100.0%**
Under $20,000	2.53	14	3.0
$20,000 to $39,999	4.74	25	5.8
$40,000 to $49,999	25.25	135	12.8
$50,000 to $69,999	22.09	118	16.9
$70,000 to $79,999	8.84	47	2.8
$80,000 to $99,999	8.35	45	3.7
$100,000 or more	59.96	321	55.0
HOUSEHOLD TYPE			
Average household	**18.69**	**100**	**100.0**
Married couples	25.48	136	67.2
Married couples, no children	25.73	138	29.2
Married couples, with children	26.14	140	32.5
Oldest child under age 6	26.98	144	6.2
Oldest child aged 6 to 17	29.13	156	18.3
Oldest child aged 18 or older	20.78	111	8.0
Single parent with child under age 18	0.34	2	0.1
Single person	19.74	106	30.9
RACE AND HISPANIC ORIGIN			
Average household	**18.69**	**100**	**100.0**
Asian	6.58	35	1.5
Black	38.82	208	25.4
Hispanic	15.28	82	10.0
Non-Hispanic white and other	17.15	92	69.6
REGION			
Average household	**18.69**	**100**	**100.0**
Northeast	11.30	60	11.1
Midwest	11.06	59	13.2
South	25.55	137	50.2
West	21.11	113	25.6
EDUCATION			
Average household	**18.69**	**100**	**100.0**
Less than high school graduate	7.53	40	5.8
High school graduate	7.73	41	10.6
Some college	20.41	109	23.0
Associate's degree	20.89	112	10.6
Bachelor's degree or more	31.59	169	50.2
Bachelor's degree	42.69	228	43.1
Master's, professional, doctoral degree	12.18	65	7.1

Note: Market shares may not sum to 100.0 because of rounding and missing categories by household type. "Asian" and "black" include Hispanics and non-Hispanics who identify themselves as being of the respective race alone. "Hispanic" includes people of any race who identify themselves as Hispanic. "Other" includes people who identify themselves as non-Hispanic and as Alaska Native, American Indian, Asian (who are also included in the "Asian" row), or Native Hawaiian or other Pacific Islander as well as non-Hispanics reporting more than one race.

Source: Calculations by New Strategist based on the Bureau of Labor Statistics' 2010 Consumer Expenditure Survey

Housewares

Best customers: **Married couples**
                                          Households in the Northeast and West

Customer trends: **Average household spending on housewares should rebound as boomers help their adult children outfit their homes, but only if discretionary income grows.**

Housewares is a category that includes dishes, glassware, flatware, and nonelectric cookware—all the things that fill our kitchen cupboards. The best customers of housewares are older married couples who are redecorating or helping grown children outfit their homes. Married couples without children at home (most of them empty-nesters) spend 32 percent more than average on this item, while married couples with children at home spend 50 percent more than average on housewares. Spending on this item by households in the Northeast and West is 23 percent higher than average.

After having grown 10 percent between 2000 and 2006 (the year overall household spending peaked), average household spending on housewares fell 27 percent between 2006 and 2010, after adjusting for inflation. Behind the decline was the economic downturn, which limited discretionary spending on many categories. Average household spending on housewares should rebound as boomers help their adult children outfit their homes, but only if discretionary income grows.

Table 7.12 Housewares

Total household spending   **$7,983,373,440.00**
Average household spends   **65.92**

	AVERAGE HOUSEHOLD SPENDING	BEST CUSTOMERS (index)	BIGGEST CUSTOMERS (market share)
AGE OF HOUSEHOLDER			
Average household	**$65.92**	**100**	**100.0%**
Under age 25	23.63	36	2.4
Aged 25 to 34	68.36	104	17.3
Aged 35 to 44	75.50	115	20.7
Aged 45 to 54	69.20	105	21.7
Aged 55 to 64	70.46	107	18.9
Aged 65 to 74	70.13	106	11.4
Aged 75 or older	52.79	80	7.6

	AVERAGE HOUSEHOLD SPENDING	BEST CUSTOMERS (index)	BIGGEST CUSTOMERS (market share)
HOUSEHOLD INCOME			
Average household	**$65.92**	**100**	**100.0%**
Under $20,000	31.48	48	10.4
$20,000 to $39,999	40.61	62	14.1
$40,000 to $49,999	35.53	54	5.1
$50,000 to $69,999	63.86	97	13.9
$70,000 to $79,999	78.33	119	7.1
$80,000 to $99,999	76.54	116	9.7
$100,000 or more	156.22	237	40.6
HOUSEHOLD TYPE			
Average household	**65.92**	**100**	**100.0**
Married couples	90.57	137	67.8
Married couples, no children	87.14	132	28.1
Married couples, with children	98.66	150	34.8
Oldest child under age 6	99.94	152	6.5
Oldest child aged 6 to 17	87.27	132	15.6
Oldest child aged 18 or older	115.09	175	12.6
Single parent with child under age 18	35.46	54	3.2
Single person	32.02	49	14.2
RACE AND HISPANIC ORIGIN			
Average household	**65.92**	**100**	**100.0**
Asian	69.51	105	4.5
Black	32.10	49	6.0
Hispanic	53.75	82	9.9
Non-Hispanic white and other	73.41	111	84.4
REGION			
Average household	**65.92**	**100**	**100.0**
Northeast	81.20	123	22.6
Midwest	54.68	83	18.5
South	56.11	85	31.2
West	80.94	123	27.8
EDUCATION			
Average household	**65.92**	**100**	**100.0**
Less than high school graduate	27.37	42	5.9
High school graduate	47.13	71	18.3
Some college	63.42	96	20.2
Associate's degree	79.65	121	11.4
Bachelor's degree or more	96.86	147	43.7
Bachelor's degree	81.31	123	23.3
Master's, professional, doctoral degree	127.22	193	20.9

Note: Market shares may not sum to 100.0 because of rounding and missing categories by household type. "Asian" and "black" include Hispanics and non-Hispanics who identify themselves as being of the respective race alone. "Hispanic" includes people of any race who identify themselves as Hispanic. "Other" includes people who identify themselves as non-Hispanic and as Alaska Native, American Indian, Asian (who are also included in the "Asian" row), or Native Hawaiian or other Pacific Islander as well as non-Hispanics reporting more than one race.

Source: Calculations by New Strategist based on the Bureau of Labor Statistics' 2010 Consumer Expenditure Survey

Infants' Equipment and Furniture

Best customers: **Householders under age 45**
Married couples without children at home
Married couples with preschoolers
Hispanics and Asians
Households in the Northeast

Customer trends: **Average household spending on infants' equipment and furniture should rebound
as the large millennial generation has children.**

The best customers of infants' equipment and furniture are young married couples with preschoolers. Married couples with preschoolers spend five times the average on this item. Householders under age 45 spend 51 to 82 percent more than average on infants' equipment and furniture and control two-thirds of the market. Hispanics, who tend to have more children than other racial and ethnic groups, spend 76 percent more than average on infants' equipment and furniture. The spending on this item by Asian householders is 38 percent above average. Households in the Northeast outspend the average by 63 percent.

Average household spending on infants' equipment and furniture was on an accelerated growth track early in the decade, but then came the Great Recession and the trend reversed. After growing 45 percent between 2000 and 2006 (the year overall household spending peaked), spending on infants' equipment and furniture fell 6 percent in the four years from 2006 to 2010, after adjusting for inflation. Behind the increase was the entrance of the large millennial generation into the family formation lifestage, which is why spending on infants' equipment and furniture should rebound in the years ahead.

Table 7.13 Infants' equipment and furniture

Total household spending $2,973,176,850.00
Average household spends   24.55

	AVERAGE HOUSEHOLD SPENDING	BEST CUSTOMERS (index)	BIGGEST CUSTOMERS (market share)
AGE OF HOUSEHOLDER			
Average household	**$24.55**	**100**	**100.0%**
Under age 25	44.60	182	12.1
Aged 25 to 34	40.07	163	27.2
Aged 35 to 44	36.95	151	27.2
Aged 45 to 54	14.55	59	12.3
Aged 55 to 64	20.18	82	14.5
Aged 65 to 74	12.63	51	5.5
Aged 75 or older	3.51	14	1.4

	AVERAGE HOUSEHOLD SPENDING	BEST CUSTOMERS (index)	BIGGEST CUSTOMERS (market share)
HOUSEHOLD INCOME			
Average household	**$24.55**	**100**	**100.0%**
Under $20,000	13.35	54	11.9
$20,000 to $39,999	11.21	46	10.5
$40,000 to $49,999	16.46	67	6.3
$50,000 to $69,999	19.48	79	11.4
$70,000 to $79,999	20.88	85	5.1
$80,000 to $99,999	32.33	132	11.0
$100,000 or more	64.38	262	45.0
HOUSEHOLD TYPE			
Average household	**24.55**	**100**	**100.0**
Married couples	36.22	148	72.8
Married couples, no children	35.70	145	30.9
Married couples, with children	37.38	152	35.4
Oldest child under age 6	121.83	496	21.2
Oldest child aged 6 to 17	21.57	88	10.3
Oldest child aged 18 or older	15.77	64	4.6
Single parent with child under age 18	18.44	75	4.4
Single person	2.31	9	2.8
RACE AND HISPANIC ORIGIN			
Average household	**24.55**	**100**	**100.0**
Asian	33.99	138	5.9
Black	11.24	46	5.6
Hispanic	43.09	176	21.4
Non-Hispanic white and other	23.71	97	73.2
REGION			
Average household	**24.55**	**100**	**100.0**
Northeast	39.95	163	29.9
Midwest	18.40	75	16.7
South	22.55	92	33.7
West	21.35	87	19.7
EDUCATION			
Average household	**24.55**	**100**	**100.0**
Less than high school graduate	25.10	102	14.6
High school graduate	17.44	71	18.1
Some college	18.76	76	16.1
Associate's degree	15.79	64	6.1
Bachelor's degree or more	37.69	154	45.6
Bachelor's degree	31.94	130	24.6
Master's, professional, doctoral degree	48.57	198	21.4

Note: Market shares may not sum to 100.0 because of rounding and missing categories by household type. "Asian" and "black" include Hispanics and non-Hispanics who identify themselves as being of the respective race alone. "Hispanic" includes people of any race who identify themselves as Hispanic. "Other" includes people who identify themselves as non-Hispanic and as Alaska Native, American Indian, Asian (who are also included in the "Asian" row), or Native Hawaiian or other Pacific Islander as well as non-Hispanics reporting more than one race.

Source: Calculations by New Strategist based on the Bureau of Labor Statistics' 2010 Consumer Expenditure Survey

Kitchen and Dining Room Furniture

Best customers: **Householders aged 35 to 44**
                       Married couples without children at home
                       Married couples with children under age 18
                       Hispanics and blacks

Customer trends: **Average household spending on kitchen and dining room furniture should stabilize as the large millennial generation has children—but only if discretionary income grows.**

The best customers of kitchen and dining room furniture are young married couples who are outfitting their first homes and empty-nesters redecorating after the children have moved out. Householders aged 35 to 44 spend 73 percent more than average on this item, while married couples without children at home (most of them empty-nesters) spend 33 percent more. Couples with preschoolers spend 54 percent more than average on this item, and those with school-aged children spend 65 percent more. Hispanics and blacks spend, respectively, 34 and 28 percent more than average on kitchen and dining room furniture.

Average household spending on kitchen and dining room furniture fell by a substantial 46 percent between 2000 and 2010, after adjusting for inflation. Behind the decline is the economic downturn, which reduced discretionary spending. Spending on kitchen and dining room furniture should stabilize as the large millennial generation has children—but only if discretionary income grows.

Table 7.14 **Kitchen and dining room furniture**

Total household spending $3,849,991,530.00
Average household spends   31.79

	AVERAGE HOUSEHOLD SPENDING	BEST CUSTOMERS (index)	BIGGEST CUSTOMERS (market share)
AGE OF HOUSEHOLDER			
Average household	**$31.79**	**100**	**100.0%**
Under age 25	18.55	58	3.9
Aged 25 to 34	34.97	110	18.3
Aged 35 to 44	55.00	173	31.3
Aged 45 to 54	24.53	77	16.0
Aged 55 to 64	32.88	103	18.2
Aged 65 to 74	31.94	100	10.8
Aged 75 or older	5.01	16	1.5

	AVERAGE HOUSEHOLD SPENDING	BEST CUSTOMERS (index)	BIGGEST CUSTOMERS (market share)
HOUSEHOLD INCOME			
Average household	$31.79	100	100.0%
Under $20,000	10.26	32	7.0
$20,000 to $39,999	13.17	41	9.5
$40,000 to $49,999	31.80	100	9.5
$50,000 to $69,999	24.67	78	11.1
$70,000 to $79,999	34.34	108	6.5
$80,000 to $99,999	47.33	149	12.4
$100,000 or more	81.61	257	44.0
HOUSEHOLD TYPE			
Average household	31.79	100	100.0
Married couples	42.52	134	66.0
Married couples, no children	42.42	133	28.3
Married couples, with children	46.50	146	34.0
Oldest child under age 6	48.99	154	6.6
Oldest child aged 6 to 17	52.59	165	19.5
Oldest child aged 18 or older	35.09	110	8.0
Single parent with child under age 18	16.88	53	3.1
Single person	23.01	72	21.2
RACE AND HISPANIC ORIGIN			
Average household	31.79	100	100.0
Asian	31.98	101	4.3
Black	40.61	128	15.6
Hispanic	42.59	134	16.3
Non-Hispanic white and other	30.47	96	72.7
REGION			
Average household	31.79	100	100.0
Northeast	29.20	92	16.9
Midwest	27.23	86	19.1
South	37.46	118	43.2
West	29.19	92	20.8
EDUCATION			
Average household	31.79	100	100.0
Less than high school graduate	24.20	76	10.9
High school graduate	16.42	52	13.2
Some college	21.51	68	14.2
Associate's degree	30.86	97	9.2
Bachelor's degree or more	56.23	177	52.5
Bachelor's degree	57.17	180	34.0
Master's, professional, doctoral degree	54.60	172	18.6

Note: Market shares may not sum to 100.0 because of rounding and missing categories by household type. "Asian" and "black" include Hispanics and non-Hispanics who identify themselves as being of the respective race alone. "Hispanic" includes people of any race who identify themselves as Hispanic. "Other" includes people who identify themselves as non-Hispanic and as Alaska Native, American Indian, Asian (who are also included in the "Asian" row), or Native Hawaiian or other Pacific Islander as well as non-Hispanics reporting more than one race.

Source: Calculations by New Strategist based on the Bureau of Labor Statistics' 2010 Consumer Expenditure Survey

Kitchen and Dining Room Linens

Best customers:	**Householders aged 45 to 54** **Married couples without children at home** **Married couples with school-aged or older children at home** **Households in the West**
Customer trends:	**Average household spending on kitchen and dining room linens may stabilize, but only if discretionary income grows.**

The best customers of kitchen and dining room linens are older married couples. Householders aged 45 to 54 spend 36 percent more than average on kitchen and dining room linens. Married couples without children at home, most of them empty-nesters, spend 61 percent more than average on kitchen and dining room linens. Married couples with school-aged or adult children at home spend 36 to 76 percent more than average on this item. Households in the West outspend the average by 56 percent.

Average household spending on kitchen and dining room linens, already the second-smallest of the household furnishings categories, fell by an enormous 50 percent between 2000 and 2010, after adjusting for inflation. Behind the decline is the substitution of paper products for linens as well as the economic downturn, which reduced discretionary spending. Spending on kitchen and dining room linens may stabilize, but only if discretionary income grows.

Table 7.15 Kitchen and dining room linens

Total household spending $716,953,440.00
Average household spends   5.92

	AVERAGE HOUSEHOLD SPENDING	BEST CUSTOMERS (index)	BIGGEST CUSTOMERS (market share)
AGE OF HOUSEHOLDER			
Average household	**$5.92**	**100**	**100.0%**
Under age 25	–	–	–
Aged 25 to 34	5.07	86	14.3
Aged 35 to 44	5.67	96	17.3
Aged 45 to 54	8.08	136	28.2
Aged 55 to 64	6.80	115	20.3
Aged 65 to 74	6.69	113	12.2
Aged 75 or older	4.74	80	7.6

	AVERAGE HOUSEHOLD SPENDING	BEST CUSTOMERS (index)	BIGGEST CUSTOMERS (market share)
HOUSEHOLD INCOME			
Average household	**$5.92**	**100**	**100.0%**
Under $20,000	1.41	24	5.2
$20,000 to $39,999	4.73	80	18.3
$40,000 to $49,999	5.16	87	8.2
$50,000 to $69,999	3.11	53	7.5
$70,000 to $79,999	4.65	79	4.7
$80,000 to $99,999	7.18	121	10.1
$100,000 or more	16.22	274	47.0
HOUSEHOLD TYPE			
Average household	**5.92**	**100**	**100.0**
Married couples	8.72	147	72.7
Married couples, no children	9.52	161	34.2
Married couples, with children	8.29	140	32.6
Oldest child under age 6	2.48	42	1.8
Oldest child aged 6 to 17	10.43	176	20.7
Oldest child aged 18 or older	8.08	136	9.9
Single parent with child under age 18	3.42	58	3.4
Single person	2.18	37	10.8
RACE AND HISPANIC ORIGIN			
Average household	**5.92**	**100**	**100.0**
Asian	1.37	23	1.0
Black	4.95	84	10.2
Hispanic	5.60	95	11.5
Non-Hispanic white and other	6.12	103	78.4
REGION			
Average household	**5.92**	**100**	**100.0**
Northeast	4.92	83	15.3
Midwest	4.33	73	16.3
South	5.38	91	33.4
West	9.24	156	35.4
EDUCATION			
Average household	**5.92**	**100**	**100.0**
Less than high school graduate	3.75	63	9.1
High school graduate	3.49	59	15.1
Some college	7.03	119	25.0
Associate's degree	8.22	139	13.1
Bachelor's degree or more	7.45	126	37.4
Bachelor's degree	7.05	119	22.5
Master's, professional, doctoral degree	8.24	139	15.1

Note: Market shares may not sum to 100.0 because of rounding and missing categories by household type. "Asian" and "black" include Hispanics and non-Hispanics who identify themselves as being of the respective race alone. "Hispanic" includes people of any race who identify themselves as Hispanic. "Other" includes people who identify themselves as non-Hispanic and as Alaska Native, American Indian, Asian (who are also included in the Asian column), or Native Hawaiian or other Pacific Islander as well as non-Hispanics reporting more than one race. "–" means sample is too small to make a reliable estimate.

Source: Calculations by New Strategist based on the Bureau of Labor Statistics' 2010 Consumer Expenditure Survey

Lamps and Lighting Fixtures

Best customers:	Householders aged 25 to 34 and 65 to 74
	Married couples without children at home
	Married couples with school-aged or older children at home
	Hispanics

Best customers:
Householders aged 25 to 34 and 65 to 74
Married couples without children at home
Married couples with school-aged or older children at home
Hispanics

Customer trends:
Average household spending on lamps and lighting fixtures should stabilize in the years ahead once light bulb replacement (of compact fluorescents for incandescents) is complete.

The best customers of lamps and lighting fixtures are older married couples without children at home. Householders aged 65 to 74 spend 55 percent more than average on lamps and lighting fixtures. Married couples without children at home spend 81 percent more than average on this item. Married couples with school-aged or older children at home spend 23 to 67 percent more than average on lamps and lighting fixtures. The spending on this item by Hispanic householders is 26 percent higher than average.

Average household spending on lamps and lighting fixtures climbed by an astonishing 60 percent between 2000 and 2010, after adjusting for inflation, despite the Great Recession. Behind the hefty increase was the switch to much more energy efficient compact fluorescent light bulbs. Average household spending on lamps and lighting fixtures should stabilize in the years ahead once light bulb replacement is complete.

Table 7.16 Lamps and lighting fixtures

Total household spending $2,655,876,510.00
Average household spends 21.93

	AVERAGE HOUSEHOLD SPENDING	BEST CUSTOMERS (index)	BIGGEST CUSTOMERS (market share)
AGE OF HOUSEHOLDER			
Average household	**$21.93**	**100**	**100.0%**
Under age 25	1.32	6	0.4
Aged 25 to 34	28.67	131	21.8
Aged 35 to 44	17.63	80	14.5
Aged 45 to 54	25.17	115	23.7
Aged 55 to 64	20.77	95	16.7
Aged 65 to 74	34.06	155	16.7
Aged 75 or older	13.64	62	5.9

	AVERAGE HOUSEHOLD SPENDING	BEST CUSTOMERS (index)	BIGGEST CUSTOMERS (market share)
HOUSEHOLD INCOME			
Average household	**$21.93**	**100**	**100.0%**
Under $20,000	4.86	22	4.8
$20,000 to $39,999	10.27	47	10.7
$40,000 to $49,999	18.14	83	7.8
$50,000 to $69,999	17.15	78	11.2
$70,000 to $79,999	47.88	218	13.1
$80,000 to $99,999	28.86	132	11.0
$100,000 or more	54.99	251	43.0
HOUSEHOLD TYPE			
Average household	**21.93**	**100**	**100.0**
Married couples	34.38	157	77.3
Married couples, no children	39.78	181	38.5
Married couples, with children	30.15	137	32.0
Oldest child under age 6	17.85	81	3.5
Oldest child aged 6 to 17	36.55	167	19.6
Oldest child aged 18 or older	26.91	123	8.9
Single parent with child under age 18	20.40	93	5.5
Single person	10.11	46	13.5
RACE AND HISPANIC ORIGIN			
Average household	**21.93**	**100**	**100.0**
Asian	10.77	49	2.1
Black	7.50	34	4.2
Hispanic	27.67	126	15.4
Non-Hispanic white and other	23.36	107	80.8
REGION			
Average household	**21.93**	**100**	**100.0**
Northeast	24.55	112	20.5
Midwest	23.23	106	23.6
South	23.16	106	38.8
West	16.44	75	17.0
EDUCATION			
Average household	**21.93**	**100**	**100.0**
Less than high school graduate	6.07	28	4.0
High school graduate	11.28	51	13.1
Some college	9.08	41	8.7
Associate's degree	41.64	190	17.9
Bachelor's degree or more	41.05	187	55.6
Bachelor's degree	51.00	233	43.9
Master's, professional, doctoral degree	21.45	98	10.6

Note: Market shares may not sum to 100.0 because of rounding and missing categories by household type. "Asian" and "black" include Hispanics and non-Hispanics who identify themselves as being of the respective race alone. "Hispanic" includes people of any race who identify themselves as Hispanic. "Other" includes people who identify themselves as non-Hispanic and as Alaska Native, American Indian, Asian (who are also included in the "Asian" row), or Native Hawaiian or other Pacific Islander as well as non-Hispanics reporting more than one race.

Source: Calculations by New Strategist based on the Bureau of Labor Statistics' 2010 Consumer Expenditure Survey

Laundry and Cleaning Equipment

Best customers:	**Householders aged 35 to 54** **Married couples without children at home** **Married couples with school-aged or older children at home** **Single parents**
Customer trends:	**Average household spending on laundry and cleaning equipment should continue to grow in the years ahead as the large millennial generation moves into the best-customer age group.**

The best customers of laundry and cleaning equipment are middle-aged married couples with children. Householders aged 35 to 54, most with children, spend 17 to 20 percent more than average. Married couples with school-aged children spend 40 percent more, and those with adult children at home spend 65 percent more than average on laundry and cleaning equipment. Married couples without children at home spend 19 percent more than average on this item. Despite their low incomes single parents spend an average amount on laundry and cleaning equipment.

Average household spending on laundry and cleaning equipment grew by 30 percent between 2000 and 2006 (the year overall household spending peaked), after adjusting for inflation, and then grew by another 8 percent between 2006 and 2010. Spending on this item should continue to grow in the years ahead as the large millennial generation moves into the best-customer age group.

Table 7.17 Laundry and cleaning equipment

Total household spending	$2,159,337,810.00
Average household spends	17.83

	AVERAGE HOUSEHOLD SPENDING	BEST CUSTOMERS (index)	BIGGEST CUSTOMERS (market share)
AGE OF HOUSEHOLDER			
Average household	**$17.83**	**100**	**100.0%**
Under age 25	10.16	57	3.8
Aged 25 to 34	16.28	91	15.2
Aged 35 to 44	20.90	117	21.2
Aged 45 to 54	21.34	120	24.8
Aged 55 to 64	16.67	93	16.5
Aged 65 to 74	19.22	108	11.6
Aged 75 or older	12.92	72	6.9

	AVERAGE HOUSEHOLD SPENDING	BEST CUSTOMERS (index)	BIGGEST CUSTOMERS (market share)
HOUSEHOLD INCOME			
Average household	$17.83	100	100.0%
Under $20,000	9.87	55	12.1
$20,000 to $39,999	16.22	91	20.8
$40,000 to $49,999	16.76	94	8.9
$50,000 to $69,999	17.90	100	14.4
$70,000 to $79,999	14.72	83	4.9
$80,000 to $99,999	23.37	131	10.9
$100,000 or more	29.40	165	28.3
HOUSEHOLD TYPE			
Average household	17.83	100	100.0
Married couples	23.06	129	63.8
Married couples, no children	21.24	119	25.3
Married couples, with children	24.38	137	31.8
Oldest child under age 6	13.00	73	3.1
Oldest child aged 6 to 17	24.91	140	16.4
Oldest child aged 18 or older	29.43	165	11.9
Single parent with child under age 18	17.98	101	5.9
Single person	10.58	59	17.4
RACE AND HISPANIC ORIGIN			
Average household	17.83	100	100.0
Asian	17.94	101	4.3
Black	13.02	73	8.9
Hispanic	19.15	107	13.1
Non-Hispanic white and other	18.39	103	78.2
REGION			
Average household	17.83	100	100.0
Northeast	19.22	108	19.8
Midwest	17.02	95	21.3
South	17.21	97	35.4
West	18.55	104	23.6
EDUCATION			
Average household	17.83	100	100.0
Less than high school graduate	15.13	85	12.1
High school graduate	15.61	88	22.4
Some college	15.02	84	17.7
Associate's degree	23.52	132	12.5
Bachelor's degree or more	21.12	118	35.2
Bachelor's degree	20.54	115	21.8
Master's, professional, doctoral degree	22.27	125	13.5

Note: Market shares may not sum to 100.0 because of rounding and missing categories by household type. "Asian" and "black" include Hispanics and non-Hispanics who identify themselves as being of the respective race alone. "Hispanic" includes people of any race who identify themselves as Hispanic. "Other" includes people who identify themselves as non-Hispanic and as Alaska Native, American Indian, Asian (who are also included in the "Asian" row), or Native Hawaiian or other Pacific Islander as well as non-Hispanics reporting more than one race.

Source: Calculations by New Strategist based on the Bureau of Labor Statistics' 2010 Consumer Expenditure Survey

Lawn and Garden Equipment

Best customers:
Householders aged 25 to 54
Married couples with children at home
Non-Hispanic whites
Households in the Northeast

Customer trends:
Average household spending on lawn and garden equipment may continue to decline because of the slump in the housing market and the arrival of the small generation X in the best-customer age group.

The best customers of lawn and garden equipment (such as lawnmowers, string trimmers, and blowers) are householders ranging in age from 25 to 54—many of them new homeowners. Married couples with school-aged children spend more than twice the average on this item. Non-Hispanic whites outspend the minorities by a wide margin on lawn and garden equipment. Households in the Northeast spend 49 percent more than average on this item.

Average household spending on lawn and garden equipment fell 37 percent between 2000 and 2010, after adjusting for inflation. Spending on lawn and garden equipment may continue to decline because of the slump in the housing market and the arrival of the small generation X in the best-customer lifestage.

Table 7.18 **Lawn and garden equipment**

Total household spending $4,488,225,420.00
Average household spends   37.06

	AVERAGE HOUSEHOLD SPENDING	BEST CUSTOMERS (index)	BIGGEST CUSTOMERS (market share)
AGE OF HOUSEHOLDER			
Average household	**$37.06**	**100**	**100.0%**
Under age 25	3.48	9	0.6
Aged 25 to 34	44.58	120	20.0
Aged 35 to 44	39.26	106	19.2
Aged 45 to 54	53.39	144	29.8
Aged 55 to 64	37.62	102	17.9
Aged 65 to 74	22.17	60	6.4
Aged 75 or older	23.09	62	5.9

	AVERAGE HOUSEHOLD SPENDING	BEST CUSTOMERS (index)	BIGGEST CUSTOMERS (market share)
HOUSEHOLD INCOME			
Average household	**$37.06**	**100**	**100.0%**
Under $20,000	10.29	28	6.1
$20,000 to $39,999	31.21	84	19.3
$40,000 to $49,999	44.47	120	11.3
$50,000 to $69,999	22.84	62	8.8
$70,000 to $79,999	47.33	128	7.6
$80,000 to $99,999	37.74	102	8.5
$100,000 or more	82.94	224	38.4
HOUSEHOLD TYPE			
Average household	**37.06**	**100**	**100.0**
Married couples	47.93	129	63.8
Married couples, no children	31.98	86	18.3
Married couples, with children	59.09	159	37.1
Oldest child under age 6	81.52	220	9.4
Oldest child aged 6 to 17	57.23	154	18.2
Oldest child aged 18 or older	50.37	136	9.8
Single parent with child under age 18	30.91	83	4.9
Single person	13.77	37	10.9
RACE AND HISPANIC ORIGIN			
Average household	**37.06**	**100**	**100.0**
Asian	10.83	29	1.2
Black	15.37	41	5.1
Hispanic	29.67	80	9.8
Non-Hispanic white and other	41.65	112	85.2
REGION			
Average household	**37.06**	**100**	**100.0**
Northeast	55.22	149	27.3
Midwest	29.47	80	17.7
South	37.74	102	37.4
West	28.74	78	17.6
EDUCATION			
Average household	**37.06**	**100**	**100.0**
Less than high school graduate	5.71	15	2.2
High school graduate	25.58	69	17.6
Some college	42.64	115	24.2
Associate's degree	46.62	126	11.9
Bachelor's degree or more	53.78	145	43.1
Bachelor's degree	55.10	149	28.1
Master's, professional, doctoral degree	51.17	138	14.9

Note: Market shares may not sum to 100.0 because of rounding and missing categories by household type. "Asian" and "black" include Hispanics and non-Hispanics who identify themselves as being of the respective race alone. "Hispanic" includes people of any race who identify themselves as Hispanic. "Other" includes people who identify themselves as non-Hispanic and as Alaska Native, American Indian, Asian (who are also included in the "Asian" row), or Native Hawaiian or other Pacific Islander as well as non-Hispanics reporting more than one race.

Source: Calculations by New Strategist based on the Bureau of Labor Statistics' 2010 Consumer Expenditure Survey

Living Room Chairs and Tables

Best customers: **Householders aged 55 to 64**
                             Married couples without children at home
                             Married couples with adult children at home

Customer trends: **Average household spending on living room chairs and tables is likely to continue**
                             to decline until the housing market recovers and discretionary income grows.

The best customers of living room chairs and tables are older married couples, redecorating their home as their children establish independent households. Married couples with adult children at home spend 36 percent more than the average household on this item, but those without children at home (mostly older empty-nesters) spend 77 percent more than average on this item. Householders aged 55 to 64 spend 51 percent more than average on living room chairs and tables.

Average household spending on living room tables and chairs fell 32 percent between 2000 and 2010, after adjusting for inflation. This category suffered the fate of most types of furniture, with less spending as mortgages grew in size followed by less spending because of the Great Recession. Spending on living room tables and chairs is likely to continue to decline until the housing market recovers and discretionary income grows.

Table 7.19 Living room chairs and tables

Total household spending $6,373,861,410.00
Average household spends   52.63

	AVERAGE HOUSEHOLD SPENDING	BEST CUSTOMERS (index)	BIGGEST CUSTOMERS (market share)
AGE OF HOUSEHOLDER			
Average household	**$52.63**	**100**	**100.0%**
Under age 25	40.57	77	5.1
Aged 25 to 34	47.02	89	14.9
Aged 35 to 44	55.73	106	19.2
Aged 45 to 54	41.58	79	16.3
Aged 55 to 64	79.57	151	26.7
Aged 65 to 74	46.79	89	9.6
Aged 75 or older	45.65	87	8.3

	AVERAGE HOUSEHOLD SPENDING	BEST CUSTOMERS (index)	BIGGEST CUSTOMERS (market share)
HOUSEHOLD INCOME			
Average household	**$52.63**	**100**	**100.0%**
Under $20,000	19.49	37	8.1
$20,000 to $39,999	33.72	64	14.7
$40,000 to $49,999	33.46	64	6.0
$50,000 to $69,999	54.69	104	14.9
$70,000 to $79,999	68.92	131	7.8
$80,000 to $99,999	56.59	108	9.0
$100,000 or more	121.28	230	39.5
HOUSEHOLD TYPE			
Average household	**52.63**	**100**	**100.0**
Married couples	72.61	138	68.1
Married couples, no children	93.34	177	37.7
Married couples, with children	63.15	120	27.9
Oldest child under age 6	51.13	97	4.2
Oldest child aged 6 to 17	62.29	118	13.9
Oldest child aged 18 or older	71.69	136	9.8
Single parent with child under age 18	21.56	41	2.4
Single person	32.83	62	18.3
RACE AND HISPANIC ORIGIN			
Average household	**52.63**	**100**	**100.0**
Asian	32.85	62	2.7
Black	42.60	81	9.9
Hispanic	30.24	57	7.0
Non-Hispanic white and other	57.69	110	83.1
REGION			
Average household	**52.63**	**100**	**100.0**
Northeast	43.92	83	15.3
Midwest	51.83	98	22.0
South	55.69	106	38.8
West	55.51	105	23.9
EDUCATION			
Average household	**52.63**	**100**	**100.0**
Less than high school graduate	22.60	43	6.1
High school graduate	53.61	102	26.0
Some college	43.31	82	17.3
Associate's degree	54.47	103	9.8
Bachelor's degree or more	72.22	137	40.8
Bachelor's degree	69.87	133	25.1
Master's, professional, doctoral degree	76.32	145	15.7

Note: Market shares may not sum to 100.0 because of rounding and missing categories by household type. "Asian" and "black" include Hispanics and non-Hispanics who identify themselves as being of the respective race alone. "Hispanic" includes people of any race who identify themselves as Hispanic. "Other" includes people who identify themselves as non-Hispanic and as Alaska Native, American Indian, Asian (who are also included in the "Asian" row), or Native Hawaiian or other Pacific Islander as well as non-Hispanics reporting more than one race.

Source: Calculations by New Strategist based on the Bureau of Labor Statistics' 2010 Consumer Expenditure Survey

Mattresses and Springs

Best customers: **Householders aged 35 to 44**
                                    Married couples
                                    Blacks

Customer trends: **Average household spending on mattresses and springs should at least stabilize in the years ahead as the large millennial generation enters the nest-building lifestage.**

The best customers of mattresses and springs are married couples purchasing mattresses for expanding families. Householders aged 35 to 44 spend 48 percent more than average on mattresses and springs. Married couples with children at home spend 50 percent more than average, the figure peaking at 68 percent above average among those with adult children at home. Blacks, whose spending approaches average on only a few items, spend 18 percent more than average on mattresses and springs.

After climbing moderately from 2000 to 2006 (the year overall household spending peaked), average household spending on mattresses and springs fell 31 percent between 2006 and 2010, after adjusting for inflation. Average household spending on mattresses and springs should at least stabilize in the years ahead as the large millennial generation enters the nest-building lifestage.

Table 7.20 Mattresses and springs

Total household spending	$5,888,222,340.00
Average household spends	48.62

	AVERAGE HOUSEHOLD SPENDING	BEST CUSTOMERS (index)	BIGGEST CUSTOMERS (market share)
AGE OF HOUSEHOLDER			
Average household	**$48.62**	**100**	**100.0%**
Under age 25	28.62	59	3.9
Aged 25 to 34	55.61	114	19.0
Aged 35 to 44	71.92	148	26.8
Aged 45 to 54	56.04	115	23.8
Aged 55 to 64	41.10	85	14.9
Aged 65 to 74	31.88	66	7.1
Aged 75 or older	22.80	47	4.5

	AVERAGE HOUSEHOLD SPENDING	BEST CUSTOMERS (index)	BIGGEST CUSTOMERS (market share)
HOUSEHOLD INCOME			
Average household	**$48.62**	**100**	**100.0%**
Under $20,000	16.94	35	7.6
$20,000 to $39,999	27.99	58	13.2
$40,000 to $49,999	41.94	86	8.2
$50,000 to $69,999	53.99	111	15.9
$70,000 to $79,999	70.70	145	8.7
$80,000 to $99,999	81.56	168	14.0
$100,000 or more	91.97	189	32.4
HOUSEHOLD TYPE			
Average household	**48.62**	**100**	**100.0**
Married couples	65.09	134	66.0
Married couples, no children	60.98	125	26.6
Married couples, with children	72.94	150	34.9
Oldest child under age 6	64.16	132	5.6
Oldest child aged 6 to 17	70.64	145	17.1
Oldest child aged 18 or older	81.91	168	12.2
Single parent with child under age 18	26.35	54	3.2
Single person	25.66	53	15.5
RACE AND HISPANIC ORIGIN			
Average household	**48.62**	**100**	**100.0**
Asian	50.76	104	4.4
Black	57.42	118	14.5
Hispanic	39.64	82	9.9
Non-Hispanic white and other	48.71	100	76.0
REGION			
Average household	**48.62**	**100**	**100.0**
Northeast	56.51	116	21.3
Midwest	36.67	75	16.8
South	44.75	92	33.8
West	60.25	124	28.1
EDUCATION			
Average household	**48.62**	**100**	**100.0**
Less than high school graduate	35.68	73	10.5
High school graduate	36.34	75	19.1
Some college	38.48	79	16.6
Associate's degree	53.82	111	10.5
Bachelor's degree or more	70.92	146	43.3
Bachelor's degree	68.51	141	26.6
Master's, professional, doctoral degree	75.14	155	16.7

Note: Market shares may not sum to 100.0 because of rounding and missing categories by household type. "Asian" and "black" include Hispanics and non-Hispanics who identify themselves as being of the respective race alone. "Hispanic" includes people of any race who identify themselves as Hispanic. "Other" includes people who identify themselves as non-Hispanic and as Alaska Native, American Indian, Asian (who are also included in the "Asian" row), or Native Hawaiian or other Pacific Islander as well as non-Hispanics reporting more than one race.

Source: Calculations by New Strategist based on the Bureau of Labor Statistics' 2010 Consumer Expenditure Survey

Outdoor Equipment

Best customers:
Householders aged 45 to 64
High-income households
Married couples without children at home
Married couples with school-aged or older children at home
Hispanics
Households in the West

Customer trends:
Average household spending on outdoor equipment is likely to decline in the years ahead because the economic downturn has reduced homeownership and discretionary income.

The best customers of outdoor equipment (such as grills) are older homeowners. Householders aged 45 to 64 spend 37 to 53 percent more than average on outdoor equipment. Married couples without children at home, most of them empty-nesters, spend 68 percent more than average on this item. Couples with school-aged or older children at home spend 39 to 72 percent more than average on outdoor equipment. Householders with incomes of $100,000 or more spend three-and-one-half times the average on this item. Hispanic householders outspend the average on outdoor equipment by 43 percent. Households in the West spend 55 percent more than average on outdoor equipment.

Average household spending on outdoor equipment grew by a hefty 49 percent between 2000 and 2010, after adjusting for inflation. The increase in homeownership during the early part of the decade is one factor behind the spending increase, as is the popularity of grilling and the introduction of high-end grills. Average household spending on outdoor equipment is likely to decline in the years ahead because the economic downturn has reduced homeownership and discretionary income.

Table 7.21 Outdoor equipment

Total household spending $4,207,257,180.00
Average household spends 34.74

	AVERAGE HOUSEHOLD SPENDING	BEST CUSTOMERS (index)	BIGGEST CUSTOMERS (market share)
AGE OF HOUSEHOLDER			
Average household	**$34.74**	**100**	**100.0%**
Under age 25	32.24	93	6.2
Aged 25 to 34	19.74	57	9.5
Aged 35 to 44	36.87	106	19.2
Aged 45 to 54	47.50	137	28.3
Aged 55 to 64	53.13	153	27.0
Aged 65 to 74	18.16	52	5.6
Aged 75 or older	14.73	42	4.0

	AVERAGE HOUSEHOLD SPENDING	BEST CUSTOMERS (index)	BIGGEST CUSTOMERS (market share)
HOUSEHOLD INCOME			
Average household	**$34.74**	**100**	**100.0%**
Under $20,000	10.61	31	6.7
$20,000 to $39,999	13.74	40	9.1
$40,000 to $49,999	20.33	59	5.5
$50,000 to $69,999	26.03	75	10.7
$70,000 to $79,999	20.99	60	3.6
$80,000 to $99,999	26.61	77	6.4
$100,000 or more	123.29	355	60.9
HOUSEHOLD TYPE			
Average household	**34.74**	**100**	**100.0**
Married couples	50.86	146	72.2
Married couples, no children	58.41	168	35.7
Married couples, with children	45.43	131	30.4
Oldest child under age 6	9.61	28	1.2
Oldest child aged 6 to 17	48.22	139	16.3
Oldest child aged 18 or older	59.61	172	12.4
Single parent with child under age 18	2.62	8	0.4
Single person	9.17	26	7.7
RACE AND HISPANIC ORIGIN			
Average household	**34.74**	**100**	**100.0**
Asian	10.87	31	1.3
Black	2.51	7	0.9
Hispanic	49.84	143	17.5
Non-Hispanic white and other	37.47	108	81.8
REGION			
Average household	**34.74**	**100**	**100.0**
Northeast	30.17	87	15.9
Midwest	42.05	121	27.0
South	20.86	60	22.0
West	53.97	155	35.2
EDUCATION			
Average household	**34.74**	**100**	**100.0**
Less than high school graduate	13.69	39	5.6
High school graduate	15.81	46	11.6
Some college	39.07	112	23.6
Associate's degree	39.05	112	10.6
Bachelor's degree or more	56.09	161	48.0
Bachelor's degree	66.77	192	36.3
Master's, professional, doctoral degree	35.05	101	10.9

Note: Market shares may not sum to 100.0 because of rounding and missing categories by household type. "Asian" and "black" include Hispanics and non-Hispanics who identify themselves as being of the respective race alone. "Hispanic" includes people of any race who identify themselves as Hispanic. "Other" includes people who identify themselves as non-Hispanic and as Alaska Native, American Indian, Asian (who are also included in the "Asian" row), or Native Hawaiian or other Pacific Islander as well as non-Hispanics reporting more than one race.

Source: Calculations by New Strategist based on the Bureau of Labor Statistics' 2010 Consumer Expenditure Survey

Outdoor Furniture

Best customers:
Householders aged 45 to 64
Married couples without children at home
Non-Hispanic whites
Households in the Northeast

Customer trends:
Average household spending on outdoor furniture may decline during the next few years because households are tightening their belts and devoting less money to many discretionary items.

The best customers of outdoor furniture are older married couples. Householders aged 45 to 64 spend 15 to 26 percent more than the average on this item. Married couples without children at home, most of them empty-nesters, spend 63 percent more than average on outdoor furniture. Non-Hispanic whites outspend minorities by a wide margin on this item and control 91 percent of the market. Households in the Northeast spend 82 percent more than average on outdoor furniture.

Average household spending on outdoor furniture seesawed between 2000 and 2010, falling 12 percent over the first six years of that period, after adjusting for inflation, then growing by 56 percent from 2006 to 2010. Spending on outdoor furniture may decline during the next few years because households are tightening their belts and devoting less money to many discretionary items.

Table 7.22 Outdoor furniture

| Total household spending | $3,196,013,730.00 |
| Average household spends | 26.39 |

	AVERAGE HOUSEHOLD SPENDING	BEST CUSTOMERS (index)	BIGGEST CUSTOMERS (market share)
AGE OF HOUSEHOLDER			
Average household	**$26.39**	**100**	**100.0%**
Under age 25	–	–	–
Aged 25 to 34	41.43	–	26.1
Aged 35 to 44	23.59	89	16.2
Aged 45 to 54	33.35	126	26.1
Aged 55 to 64	30.39	115	20.3
Aged 65 to 74	5.77	22	2.4
Aged 75 or older	24.72	94	8.9

	AVERAGE HOUSEHOLD SPENDING	BEST CUSTOMERS (index)	BIGGEST CUSTOMERS (market share)
HOUSEHOLD INCOME			
Average household	**$26.39**	**100**	**100.0%**
Under $20,000	–	–	–
$20,000 to $39,999	11.71	44	10.2
$40,000 to $49,999	34.41	130	12.3
$50,000 to $69,999	13.41	51	7.3
$70,000 to $79,999	20.26	77	4.6
$80,000 to $99,999	2.86	11	0.9
$100,000 or more	77.68	294	50.5
HOUSEHOLD TYPE			
Average household	**26.39**	**100**	**100.0**
Married couples	33.01	125	61.7
Married couples, no children	43.03	163	34.6
Married couples, with children	27.07	103	23.9
Oldest child under age 6	2.09	8	0.3
Oldest child aged 6 to 17	31.20	118	13.9
Oldest child aged 18 or older	33.69	128	9.2
Single parent with child under age 18	65.00	–	14.5
Single person	13.11	50	14.6
RACE AND HISPANIC ORIGIN			
Average household	**26.39**	**100**	**100.0**
Asian	5.93	22	1.0
Black	6.08	23	2.8
Hispanic	12.73	48	5.9
Non-Hispanic white and other	31.74	120	91.2
REGION			
Average household	**26.39**	**100**	**100.0**
Northeast	47.97	182	33.4
Midwest	31.73	120	26.8
South	17.82	68	24.8
West	17.41	66	14.9
EDUCATION			
Average household	**26.39**	**100**	**100.0**
Less than high school graduate	2.16	8	1.2
High school graduate	23.16	88	22.4
Some college	13.32	50	10.6
Associate's degree	26.57	101	9.5
Bachelor's degree or more	49.41	187	55.6
Bachelor's degree	48.80	185	34.9
Master's, professional, doctoral degree	50.61	192	20.7

Note: Market shares may not sum to 100.0 because of rounding and missing categories by household type. "Asian" and "black" include Hispanics and non-Hispanics who identify themselves as being of the respective race alone. "Hispanic" includes people of any race who identify themselves as Hispanic. "Other" includes people who identify themselves as non-Hispanic and as Alaska Native, American Indian, Asian (who are also included in the "Asian" row), or Native Hawaiian or other Pacific Islander as well as non-Hispanics reporting more than one race.

Source: Calculations by New Strategist based on the Bureau of Labor Statistics' 2010 Consumer Expenditure Survey

Plants and Fresh Flowers, Indoor

Best customers:　　　　　**Householders aged 45 to 54 and 65 to 74**
Married couples without children at home
Married couples with school-aged or older children at home
Households in the Northeast and West

Customer trends:　　　　　**Average household spending on indoor plants and fresh flowers should begin to**
stabilize, but only if discretionary income grows.

The best customers of indoor plants and fresh flowers are married couples. Many are buying flowers for anniversaries or for ailing friends and relatives. Married couples without children at home (most of them empty-nesters) spend 51 percent more than average on indoor plants and fresh flowers, while those with school-aged or adult children at home spend, respectively, 77 and 25 percent more. Householders aged 45 to 54 spend 38 percent more than average on this item, while those aged 65 to 74 spend 23 percent more. Households in the Northeast outspend the average by 35 percent, and those in the West by 21 percent.

Average household spending on indoor plants and fresh flowers fell 41 percent between 2000 and 2010, after adjusting for inflation. The lower prices offered by grocery stores and discounters such as Wal-Mart are behind the decline, as well as belt tightening in face of the economic downturn. Average household spending on indoor plants and fresh flowers should begin to stabilize, but only if discretionary income grows.

Table 7.23　**Plants and fresh flowers, indoor**

Total household spending　　　　　　　　　　　　　　$5,159,158,200.00
Average household spends　　　　　　　　　　　　　　42.60

	AVERAGE HOUSEHOLD SPENDING	BEST CUSTOMERS (index)	BIGGEST CUSTOMERS (market share)
AGE OF HOUSEHOLDER			
Average household	**$42.60**	**100**	**100.0%**
Under age 25	11.48	27	1.8
Aged 25 to 34	30.94	73	12.1
Aged 35 to 44	46.31	109	19.7
Aged 45 to 54	58.70	138	28.5
Aged 55 to 64	42.90	101	17.8
Aged 65 to 74	52.23	123	13.2
Aged 75 or older	30.34	71	6.8

	AVERAGE HOUSEHOLD SPENDING	BEST CUSTOMERS (index)	BIGGEST CUSTOMERS (market share)
HOUSEHOLD INCOME			
Average household	**$42.60**	**100**	**100.0%**
Under $20,000	17.48	41	9.0
$20,000 to $39,999	19.07	45	10.3
$40,000 to $49,999	39.78	93	8.8
$50,000 to $69,999	31.43	74	10.6
$70,000 to $79,999	51.10	120	7.2
$80,000 to $99,999	58.32	137	11.4
$100,000 or more	109.04	256	43.9
HOUSEHOLD TYPE			
Average household	**42.60**	**100**	**100.0**
Married couples	60.71	143	70.3
Married couples, no children	64.49	151	32.2
Married couples, with children	62.08	146	33.9
Oldest child under age 6	40.01	94	4.0
Oldest child aged 6 to 17	75.56	177	20.9
Oldest child aged 18 or older	53.29	125	9.0
Single parent with child under age 18	6.85	16	0.9
Single person	25.52	60	17.5
RACE AND HISPANIC ORIGIN			
Average household	**42.60**	**100**	**100.0**
Asian	51.44	121	5.1
Black	15.39	36	4.4
Hispanic	20.59	48	5.9
Non-Hispanic white and other	50.34	118	89.6
REGION			
Average household	**42.60**	**100**	**100.0**
Northeast	57.72	135	24.9
Midwest	43.42	102	22.7
South	29.22	69	25.2
West	51.44	121	27.4
EDUCATION			
Average household	**42.60**	**100**	**100.0**
Less than high school graduate	24.62	58	8.3
High school graduate	27.32	64	16.4
Some college	33.14	78	16.4
Associate's degree	40.73	96	9.0
Bachelor's degree or more	71.49	168	49.9
Bachelor's degree	69.33	163	30.7
Master's, professional, doctoral degree	75.75	178	19.2

Note: Market shares may not sum to 100.0 because of rounding and missing categories by household type. "Asian" and "black" include Hispanics and non-Hispanics who identify themselves as being of the respective race alone. "Hispanic" includes people of any race who identify themselves as Hispanic. "Other" includes people who identify themselves as non-Hispanic and as Alaska Native, American Indian, Asian (who are also included in the Asian column), or Native Hawaiian or other Pacific Islander as well as non-Hispanics reporting more than one race. "–" means sample is too small to make a reliable estimate.

Source: Calculations by New Strategist based on the Bureau of Labor Statistics' 2010 Consumer Expenditure Survey

Portable Heating and Cooling Equipment

Best customers: **Householders aged 55 to 74**
Married couples without children at home
Married couples with adult children at home
Households in the South

Customer trends: **Average household spending on portable heating and cooling equipment will**
continue to grow as global warming intensifies.

Older Americans are the biggest spenders on portable heating and cooling equipment, a category that includes window air conditioners. Householders aged 65 to 74 spend one-third more than average on this item, and those aged 55 to 64 spend nearly triple the average. Many older householders live in homes without central air conditioning, necessitating the purchase of window air conditioners as average temperatures rise. Married couples without children at home (most of them older) spend over twice the average on portable heating and cooling equipment. Couples with adult children at home spend two-and-two-third times the average on such equipment. Households in the South outspend the average for this item by 54 percent and control 57 percent of the market for portable heating and cooling equipment.

Average household spending on portable heating and cooling equipment tripled between 2000 and 2010, after adjusting for inflation. Behind the increase are rising average temperatures, driving purchases of window air conditioners. Spending on portable heating and cooling equipment will continue to grow as global warming intensifies.

Table 7.24 **Portable heating and cooling equipment**

Total household spending $2,268,334,110.00
Average household spends   18.73

	AVERAGE HOUSEHOLD SPENDING	BEST CUSTOMERS (index)	BIGGEST CUSTOMERS (market share)
AGE OF HOUSEHOLDER			
Average household	**$18.73**	**100**	**100.0%**
Under age 25	3.98	21	1.4
Aged 25 to 34	3.93	21	3.5
Aged 35 to 44	10.60	57	10.2
Aged 45 to 54	18.62	99	20.6
Aged 55 to 64	52.55	281	49.5
Aged 65 to 74	24.82	133	14.3
Aged 75 or older	–	–	–

	AVERAGE HOUSEHOLD SPENDING	BEST CUSTOMERS (index)	BIGGEST CUSTOMERS (market share)
HOUSEHOLD INCOME			
Average household	**$18.73**	**100**	**100.0%**
Under $20,000	2.54	14	3.0
$20,000 to $39,999	28.17	150	34.5
$40,000 to $49,999	22.70	121	11.5
$50,000 to $69,999	20.29	108	15.5
$70,000 to $79,999	8.00	43	2.6
$80,000 to $99,999	5.31	28	2.4
$100,000 or more	31.51	168	28.8
HOUSEHOLD TYPE			
Average household	**18.73**	**100**	**100.0**
Married couples	30.42	162	80.1
Married couples, no children	40.80	218	46.3
Married couples, with children	24.10	129	29.9
Oldest child under age 6	3.97	21	0.9
Oldest child aged 6 to 17	13.58	73	8.5
Oldest child aged 18 or older	50.09	267	19.3
Single parent with child under age 18	7.89	42	2.5
Single person	5.54	30	8.7
RACE AND HISPANIC ORIGIN			
Average household	**18.73**	**100**	**100.0**
Asian	9.15	49	2.1
Black	13.15	70	8.6
Hispanic	13.83	74	9.0
Non-Hispanic white and other	20.36	109	82.4
REGION			
Average household	**18.73**	**100**	**100.0**
Northeast	10.55	56	10.3
Midwest	19.44	104	23.1
South	28.86	154	56.6
West	8.04	43	9.7
EDUCATION			
Average household	**18.73**	**100**	**100.0**
Less than high school graduate	5.45	29	4.2
High school graduate	31.22	167	42.6
Some college	13.54	72	15.2
Associate's degree	9.59	51	4.8
Bachelor's degree or more	20.50	109	32.5
Bachelor's degree	18.22	97	18.4
Master's, professional, doctoral degree	25.00	133	14.4

Note: Market shares may not sum to 100.0 because of rounding and missing categories by household type. "Asian" and "black" include Hispanics and non-Hispanics who identify themselves as being of the respective race alone. "Hispanic" includes people of any race who identify themselves as Hispanic. "Other" includes people who identify themselves as non-Hispanic and as Alaska Native, American Indian, Asian (who are also included in the Asian column), or Native Hawaiian or other Pacific Islander as well as non-Hispanics reporting more than one race. "–" means sample is too small to make a reliable estimate.

Source: Calculations by New Strategist based on the Bureau of Labor Statistics' 2010 Consumer Expenditure Survey

Power and Hand Tools

Best customers:	Householders aged 45 to 64
	Married couples without children at home
	Married couples with school-aged or older children at home
	Hispanics
	Households in the West

| Customer trends: | Average household spending on power and hand tools may continue to increase in the years ahead as the large millennial generation enters the do-it-yourself lifestage. |

The best customers of power tools are homeowners tackling do-it-yourself projects. This explains why householders aged 45 to 64 spend 16 to 38 percent more than average on tools. Married couples without children at home spend 36 percent more than average on tools, while those with school-aged or older children at home spend 45 to 57 percent more than average on this item. Hispanics outspend the average for this item by 37 percent. Households in the West, where many Hispanics reside, spend 49 percent more than average on tools.

Average household spending on power and hand tools fell 5 percent between 2000 and 2006, after adjusting for inflation, but grew by 53 percent between 2006 and 2010. Behind the increase was the Great Recession, spurring more homeowners to tackle projects themselves rather than hire someone. Spending on tools may continue to increase in the years ahead as the large millennial generation enters the do-it-yourself lifestage.

Table 7.25 Power and hand tools

Total household spending $6,417,459,930.00
Average household spends 52.99

	AVERAGE HOUSEHOLD SPENDING	BEST CUSTOMERS (index)	BIGGEST CUSTOMERS (market share)
AGE OF HOUSEHOLDER			
Average household	**$52.99**	**100**	**100.0%**
Under age 25	32.72	62	4.1
Aged 25 to 34	48.71	92	15.3
Aged 35 to 44	45.58	86	15.6
Aged 45 to 54	61.61	116	24.1
Aged 55 to 64	73.24	138	24.4
Aged 65 to 74	51.16	97	10.4
Aged 75 or older	33.51	63	6.0

	AVERAGE HOUSEHOLD SPENDING	BEST CUSTOMERS (index)	BIGGEST CUSTOMERS (market share)
HOUSEHOLD INCOME			
Average household	**$52.99**	**100**	**100.0%**
Under $20,000	23.60	45	9.7
$20,000 to $39,999	46.46	88	20.1
$40,000 to $49,999	34.01	64	6.1
$50,000 to $69,999	65.56	124	17.7
$70,000 to $79,999	98.10	185	11.1
$80,000 to $99,999	79.77	151	12.6
$100,000 or more	71.45	135	23.1
HOUSEHOLD TYPE			
Average household	**52.99**	**100**	**100.0**
Married couples	74.22	140	69.1
Married couples, no children	72.14	136	28.9
Married couples, with children	73.31	138	32.2
Oldest child under age 6	37.21	70	3.0
Oldest child aged 6 to 17	83.45	157	18.5
Oldest child aged 18 or older	76.67	145	10.4
Single parent with child under age 18	7.87	15	0.9
Single person	23.82	45	13.2
RACE AND HISPANIC ORIGIN			
Average household	**52.99**	**100**	**100.0**
Asian	23.20	44	1.9
Black	17.98	34	4.2
Hispanic	72.53	137	16.7
Non-Hispanic white and other	55.71	105	79.7
REGION			
Average household	**52.99**	**100**	**100.0**
Northeast	49.78	94	17.2
Midwest	47.61	90	20.0
South	42.15	80	29.2
West	78.95	149	33.8
EDUCATION			
Average household	**52.99**	**100**	**100.0**
Less than high school graduate	50.69	96	13.7
High school graduate	58.70	111	28.3
Some college	53.35	101	21.2
Associate's degree	67.45	127	12.0
Bachelor's degree or more	43.93	83	24.6
Bachelor's degree	39.91	75	14.2
Master's, professional, doctoral degree	51.82	98	10.6

Note: Market shares may not sum to 100.0 because of rounding and missing categories by household type. "Asian" and "black" include Hispanics and non-Hispanics who identify themselves as being of the respective race alone. "Hispanic" includes people of any race who identify themselves as Hispanic. "Other" includes people who identify themselves as non-Hispanic and as Alaska Native, American Indian, Asian (who are also included in the "Asian" row), or Native Hawaiian or other Pacific Islander as well as non-Hispanics reporting more than one race.

Source: Calculations by New Strategist based on the Bureau of Labor Statistics' 2010 Consumer Expenditure Survey

Sewing Materials for Household Items

Best customers:
Householders aged 45 or older
Married couples without children at home
Married couples with adult children at home
Non-Hispanic whites
Households in the West

Customer trends:
Average household spending on sewing materials for household items may continue to fall in the years ahead as younger generations with little skill in sewing fill the best-customer age groups.

Sewing is becoming a lost art, and younger generations of women are much less knowledgeable about sewing than older women. The best customers of sewing materials for household items—such as slipcovers and curtains—are householders aged 45 or older. Those aged 45 to 64 spend 24 to 32 percent more than average on sewing materials, while householders aged 65 to 74 spend nearly double the average. Married couples without children at home (most of them older) also spend nearly twice the average on sewing materials, and those with adult children at home outspend the average by 55 percent. Non-Hispanic whites account for 91 percent of the market. Households in the West spend 77 percent more than average on sewing materials.

Average household spending on sewing materials for household items fell 23 percent between 2000 and 2010, after adjusting for inflation. Spending on sewing materials for household items may continue to fall in the years ahead as younger generations with little skill in sewing fill the best-customer age groups.

Table 7.26 Sewing materials for household items

Total household spending $1,154,149,710.00
Average household spends 9.53

	AVERAGE HOUSEHOLD SPENDING	BEST CUSTOMERS (index)	BIGGEST CUSTOMERS (market share)
AGE OF HOUSEHOLDER			
Average household	**$9.53**	**100**	**100.0%**
Under age 25	2.45	26	1.7
Aged 25 to 34	4.86	51	8.5
Aged 35 to 44	5.20	55	9.9
Aged 45 to 54	11.80	124	25.6
Aged 55 to 64	12.58	132	23.3
Aged 65 to 74	17.51	184	19.8
Aged 75 or older	11.23	118	11.2

	AVERAGE HOUSEHOLD SPENDING	BEST CUSTOMERS (index)	BIGGEST CUSTOMERS (market share)
HOUSEHOLD INCOME			
Average household	$9.53	100	100.0%
Under $20,000	4.53	48	10.4
$20,000 to $39,999	6.17	65	14.8
$40,000 to $49,999	10.36	109	10.3
$50,000 to $69,999	11.53	121	17.4
$70,000 to $79,999	13.88	146	8.7
$80,000 to $99,999	13.83	145	12.1
$100,000 or more	14.61	153	26.3
HOUSEHOLD TYPE			
Average household	9.53	100	100.0
Married couples	13.56	142	70.2
Married couples, no children	18.23	191	40.6
Married couples, with children	11.25	118	27.5
Oldest child under age 6	7.45	78	3.3
Oldest child aged 6 to 17	10.49	110	12.9
Oldest child aged 18 or older	14.74	155	11.2
Single parent with child under age 18	2.71	28	1.7
Single person	5.91	62	18.2
RACE AND HISPANIC ORIGIN			
Average household	9.53	100	100.0
Asian	5.04	53	2.2
Black	2.23	23	2.9
Hispanic	4.49	47	5.7
Non-Hispanic white and other	11.48	120	91.3
REGION			
Average household	9.53	100	100.0
Northeast	5.26	55	10.1
Midwest	10.53	110	24.6
South	6.50	68	25.0
West	16.89	177	40.1
EDUCATION			
Average household	9.53	100	100.0
Less than high school graduate	4.05	42	6.1
High school graduate	6.16	65	16.5
Some college	13.31	140	29.4
Associate's degree	6.95	73	6.9
Bachelor's degree or more	13.19	138	41.1
Bachelor's degree	10.35	109	20.5
Master's, professional, doctoral degree	18.15	190	20.6

Note: Market shares may not sum to 100.0 because of rounding and missing categories by household type. "Asian" and "black" include Hispanics and non-Hispanics who identify themselves as being of the respective race alone. "Hispanic" includes people of any race who identify themselves as Hispanic. "Other" includes people who identify themselves as non-Hispanic and as Alaska Native, American Indian, Asian (who are also included in the "Asian" row), or Native Hawaiian or other Pacific Islander as well as non-Hispanics reporting more than one race.

Source: Calculations by New Strategist based on the Bureau of Labor Statistics' 2010 Consumer Expenditure Survey

Slipcovers and Decorative Pillows

Best customers: **Householders aged 65 to 74**
Married couples without children at home
Married couples with adult children at home
Households in the Northeast

Customer trends: **Average household spending on slipcovers and decorative pillows is likely to**
continue to fall as the economic downturn limits discretionary spending.

The biggest spenders on slipcovers and decorative pillows are older married couples who redecorate their homes after their grown children have moved out. Householders aged 65 to 74 spend 76 percent more than the average household on slipcovers and decorative pillows. Married couples without children at home spend 65 percent more than average on this item, while those adult children at home spend 88 percent more than average. Households in the Northeast spend 62 percent more than average on slipcovers and decorative pillows.

After growing 52 percent between 2000 and 2006, average household spending on slipcovers and decorative pillows fell 30 percent between 2006 and 2010, after adjusting for inflation. Behind the decline was the end of the homeownership boom and belt tightening due to the Great Recession. Average household spending on slipcovers and decorative pillows is likely to continue to fall as the economic downturn limits discretionary spending.

Table 7.27 Slipcovers and decorative pillows

Total household spending $449,306,970.00
Average household spends   3.71

	AVERAGE HOUSEHOLD SPENDING	BEST CUSTOMERS (index)	BIGGEST CUSTOMERS (market share)
AGE OF HOUSEHOLDER			
Average household	**$3.71**	**100**	**100.0%**
Under age 25	1.51	41	2.7
Aged 25 to 34	3.01	81	13.5
Aged 35 to 44	3.52	95	17.2
Aged 45 to 54	4.16	112	23.2
Aged 55 to 64	4.24	114	20.2
Aged 65 to 74	6.54	176	19.0
Aged 75 or older	1.70	46	4.4

	AVERAGE HOUSEHOLD SPENDING	BEST CUSTOMERS (index)	BIGGEST CUSTOMERS (market share)
HOUSEHOLD INCOME			
Average household	**$3.71**	**100**	**100.0%**
Under $20,000	1.34	36	7.9
$20,000 to $39,999	2.00	54	12.4
$40,000 to $49,999	4.39	118	11.2
$50,000 to $69,999	3.19	86	12.3
$70,000 to $79,999	4.58	123	7.4
$80,000 to $99,999	8.39	226	18.9
$100,000 or more	6.50	175	30.0
HOUSEHOLD TYPE			
Average household	**3.71**	**100**	**100.0**
Married couples	5.12	138	68.1
Married couples, no children	6.14	165	35.2
Married couples, with children	4.77	129	29.9
Oldest child under age 6	3.62	98	4.2
Oldest child aged 6 to 17	3.84	104	12.2
Oldest child aged 18 or older	6.98	188	13.6
Single parent with child under age 18	1.98	53	3.1
Single person	2.27	61	17.9
RACE AND HISPANIC ORIGIN			
Average household	**3.71**	**100**	**100.0**
Asian	4.33	117	5.0
Black	2.47	67	8.1
Hispanic	2.89	78	9.5
Non-Hispanic white and other	4.05	109	82.8
REGION			
Average household	**3.71**	**100**	**100.0**
Northeast	6.01	162	29.7
Midwest	3.29	89	19.8
South	3.12	84	30.9
West	3.21	87	19.6
EDUCATION			
Average household	**3.71**	**100**	**100.0**
Less than high school graduate	2.00	54	7.7
High school graduate	2.51	68	17.3
Some college	4.36	118	24.7
Associate's degree	3.25	88	8.3
Bachelor's degree or more	5.26	142	42.1
Bachelor's degree	4.45	120	22.7
Master's, professional, doctoral degree	6.66	180	19.4

Note: Market shares may not sum to 100.0 because of rounding and missing categories by household type. "Asian" and "black" include Hispanics and non-Hispanics who identify themselves as being of the respective race alone. "Hispanic" includes people of any race who identify themselves as Hispanic. "Other" includes people who identify themselves as non-Hispanic and as Alaska Native, American Indian, Asian (who are also included in the "Asian" row), or Native Hawaiian or other Pacific Islander as well as non-Hispanics reporting more than one race.

Source: Calculations by New Strategist based on the Bureau of Labor Statistics' 2010 Consumer Expenditure Survey

Sofas

Best customers:

Householders aged 25 to 44
Married couples without children at home
Married couples with children under age 18
Asians

Customer trends:

Average household spending on sofas is likely to continue to fall in the years ahead because the economic downturn has slashed discretionary spending and household formation has slowed.

Sofas are the sixth-largest home furnishing expense for the average household and consume 5 percent of the average home furnishings budget. Householders aged 25 to 44, many outfitting their first home, spend 12 to 23 percent more than average on sofas. Married couples with children under age 18 spend 43 to 69 percent more than average on sofas, while couples without children at home outspend the average by 39 percent. Asian households spend 46 percent more than average on sofas.

After rising moderately between 2000 and 2006, average household spending on sofas declined 33 percent between 2006 and 2010, after adjusting for inflation. Behind the decline was the economic downturn and the collapse in the housing market. Average household spending on sofas is likely to continue to decline in the years ahead because the economic downturn has slashed discretionary spending and household formation has slowed.

Table 7.28 Sofas

Total household spending $10,205,686,890.00
Average household spends   84.27

	AVERAGE HOUSEHOLD SPENDING	BEST CUSTOMERS (index)	BIGGEST CUSTOMERS (market share)
AGE OF HOUSEHOLDER			
Average household	**$84.27**	**100**	**100.0%**
Under age 25	77.33	92	6.1
Aged 25 to 34	103.24	123	20.4
Aged 35 to 44	94.78	112	20.3
Aged 45 to 54	85.31	101	20.9
Aged 55 to 64	82.42	98	17.2
Aged 65 to 74	64.18	76	8.2
Aged 75 or older	59.90	71	6.8

	AVERAGE HOUSEHOLD SPENDING	BEST CUSTOMERS (index)	BIGGEST CUSTOMERS (market share)
HOUSEHOLD INCOME			
Average household	**$84.27**	**100**	**100.0%**
Under $20,000	38.54	46	10.0
$20,000 to $39,999	62.25	74	16.9
$40,000 to $49,999	57.50	68	6.4
$50,000 to $69,999	82.45	98	14.0
$70,000 to $79,999	88.51	105	6.3
$80,000 to $99,999	78.23	93	7.7
$100,000 or more	189.66	225	38.6
HOUSEHOLD TYPE			
Average household	**84.27**	**100**	**100.0**
Married couples	107.53	128	62.9
Married couples, no children	117.36	139	29.6
Married couples, with children	113.87	135	31.4
Oldest child under age 6	120.64	143	6.1
Oldest child aged 6 to 17	142.71	169	19.9
Oldest child aged 18 or older	62.90	75	5.4
Single parent with child under age 18	70.35	83	4.9
Single person	56.22	67	19.5
RACE AND HISPANIC ORIGIN			
Average household	**84.27**	**100**	**100.0**
Asian	123.34	146	6.2
Black	67.44	80	9.8
Hispanic	69.26	82	10.0
Non-Hispanic white and other	89.15	106	80.2
REGION			
Average household	**84.27**	**100**	**100.0**
Northeast	72.71	86	15.8
Midwest	87.10	103	23.0
South	78.40	93	34.1
West	100.38	119	27.0
EDUCATION			
Average household	**84.27**	**100**	**100.0**
Less than high school graduate	37.89	45	6.4
High school graduate	73.91	88	22.4
Some college	57.81	69	14.4
Associate's degree	96.69	115	10.8
Bachelor's degree or more	130.27	155	45.9
Bachelor's degree	105.22	125	23.6
Master's, professional, doctoral degree	174.00	206	22.3

Note: Market shares may not sum to 100.0 because of rounding and missing categories by household type. "Asian" and "black" include Hispanics and non-Hispanics who identify themselves as being of the respective race alone. "Hispanic" includes people of any race who identify themselves as Hispanic. "Other" includes people who identify themselves as non-Hispanic and as Alaska Native, American Indian, Asian (who are also included in the "Asian" row), or Native Hawaiian or other Pacific Islander as well as non-Hispanics reporting more than one race.

Source: Calculations by New Strategist based on the Bureau of Labor Statistics' 2010 Consumer Expenditure Survey

Wall Units, Cabinets, and Other Furniture

Best customers: **Householders aged 55 to 64**
Married couples without children at home
Married couples with school-aged children
Asians
Households in the Northeast

Customer trends: **Average household spending on wall units, cabinets, and other furniture**
may continue to decline in the years ahead as the economic downturn cuts
discretionary spending.

The biggest spenders on wall units, cabinets, and other furniture are older married couples. Householders aged 55 to 64 spend 79 percent more than the average household on this item. Married couples without children at home spend 35 percent more. Those with school-aged children spend twice the average. Asians outspend the average for wall units, cabinets, and other furniture by 23 percent. Spending on this item by households in the Northeast is 45 percent above average.

After growing moderately from 2000 to 2006 (the year when overall household spending peaked), average household spending on wall units, cabinets, and other furniture plunged 40 percent between 2006 and 2010, after adjusting for inflation. Average household spending on wall units may continue to decline in the years ahead as the economic downturn cuts discretionary spending.

Table 7.29 Wall units, cabinets, and other furniture

Total household spending $4,961,753,790.00
Average household spends   40.97

	AVERAGE HOUSEHOLD SPENDING	BEST CUSTOMERS (index)	BIGGEST CUSTOMERS (market share)
AGE OF HOUSEHOLDER			
Average household	**$40.97**	**100**	**100.0%**
Under age 25	20.31	50	3.3
Aged 25 to 34	39.91	97	16.2
Aged 35 to 44	40.51	99	17.9
Aged 45 to 54	30.65	75	15.5
Aged 55 to 64	73.50	179	31.6
Aged 65 to 74	41.37	101	10.9
Aged 75 or older	19.88	49	4.6

	AVERAGE HOUSEHOLD SPENDING	BEST CUSTOMERS (index)	BIGGEST CUSTOMERS (market share)
HOUSEHOLD INCOME			
Average household	**$40.97**	**100**	**100.0%**
Under $20,000	11.02	27	5.9
$20,000 to $39,999	19.76	48	11.0
$40,000 to $49,999	26.24	64	6.1
$50,000 to $69,999	32.02	78	11.2
$70,000 to $79,999	58.13	142	8.5
$80,000 to $99,999	43.71	107	8.9
$100,000 or more	115.75	283	48.4
HOUSEHOLD TYPE			
Average household	**40.97**	**100**	**100.0**
Married couples	56.85	139	68.4
Married couples, no children	55.28	135	28.7
Married couples, with children	62.38	152	35.4
Oldest child under age 6	44.62	109	4.7
Oldest child aged 6 to 17	82.14	200	23.6
Oldest child aged 18 or older	40.73	99	7.2
Single parent with child under age 18	14.17	35	2.0
Single person	28.78	70	20.6
RACE AND HISPANIC ORIGIN			
Average household	**40.97**	**100**	**100.0**
Asian	50.31	123	5.2
Black	25.92	63	7.7
Hispanic	21.48	52	6.4
Non-Hispanic white and other	46.48	113	86.0
REGION			
Average household	**40.97**	**100**	**100.0**
Northeast	59.44	145	26.6
Midwest	43.48	106	23.7
South	35.16	86	31.5
West	32.96	80	18.2
EDUCATION			
Average household	**40.97**	**100**	**100.0**
Less than high school graduate	16.84	41	5.9
High school graduate	25.32	62	15.8
Some college	26.92	66	13.8
Associate's degree	41.28	101	9.5
Bachelor's degree or more	75.88	185	55.0
Bachelor's degree	64.32	157	29.7
Master's, professional, doctoral degree	96.06	234	25.4

Note: Market shares may not sum to 100.0 because of rounding and missing categories by household type. "Asian" and "black" include Hispanics and non-Hispanics who identify themselves as being of the respective race alone. "Hispanic" includes people of any race who identify themselves as Hispanic. "Other" includes people who identify themselves as non-Hispanic and as Alaska Native, American Indian, Asian (who are also included in the "Asian" row), or Native Hawaiian or other Pacific Islander as well as non-Hispanics reporting more than one race.

Source: Calculations by New Strategist based on the Bureau of Labor Statistics' 2010 Consumer Expenditure Survey

Window Coverings

Best customers:

Householders aged 35 to 44
High-income households
Married couples without children at home
Married couples with school-aged children
Blacks
College graduates

Customer trends:

Average household spending on window coverings is likely to continue to fall as the economic downturn limits discretionary spending.

The biggest spenders on window coverings—a category that includes blinds and shutters, but not curtains or draperies—are middle-aged married couples as well as the most-affluent householders. Householders aged 35 to 44 spend 61 percent more than the average household on window coverings. Married couples with school-aged children spend two-and-one-half times the average on this item. Households with incomes of $100,000 or more spend three-and-one-half times the average on window coverings. Married couples without children at home spend two-thirds more than the average on window covering. Black householders outspend the average on window coverings by 37 percent. College graduates spend well over twice the average on this item.

After growing by 75 percent from 2000 to 2006, average household spending on window coverings fell 20 percent between 2006 and 2010, after adjusting for inflation. Behind the decline was the end of the homeownership boom and belt tightening due to the Great Recession. Average household spending on window coverings is likely to continue to fall as the economic downturn limits discretionary spending.

Table 7.30 Window coverings

Total household spending — $2,780,616,720.00
Average household spends — 22.96

	AVERAGE HOUSEHOLD SPENDING	BEST CUSTOMERS (index)	BIGGEST CUSTOMERS (market share)
AGE OF HOUSEHOLDER			
Average household	**$22.96**	**100**	**100.0%**
Under age 25	2.01	9	0.6
Aged 25 to 34	23.28	101	16.9
Aged 35 to 44	36.91	161	29.1
Aged 45 to 54	25.33	110	22.8
Aged 55 to 64	24.08	105	18.5
Aged 65 to 74	19.42	85	9.1
Aged 75 or older	7.34	32	3.0

	AVERAGE HOUSEHOLD SPENDING	BEST CUSTOMERS (index)	BIGGEST CUSTOMERS (market share)
HOUSEHOLD INCOME			
Average household	**$22.96**	**100**	**100.0%**
Under $20,000	2.84	12	2.7
$20,000 to $39,999	6.47	28	6.5
$40,000 to $49,999	16.31	71	6.7
$50,000 to $69,999	12.52	55	7.8
$70,000 to $79,999	11.15	49	2.9
$80,000 to $99,999	33.44	146	12.1
$100,000 or more	82.06	357	61.3
HOUSEHOLD TYPE			
Average household	**22.96**	**100**	**100.0**
Married couples	36.27	158	77.9
Married couples, no children	38.63	168	35.7
Married couples, with children	38.24	167	38.7
Oldest child under age 6	18.80	82	3.5
Oldest child aged 6 to 17	58.50	255	30.0
Oldest child aged 18 or older	16.78	73	5.3
Single parent with child under age 18	8.84	39	2.3
Single person	12.22	53	15.6
RACE AND HISPANIC ORIGIN			
Average household	**22.96**	**100**	**100.0**
Asian	14.83	65	2.7
Black	31.36	137	16.7
Hispanic	24.27	106	12.9
Non-Hispanic white and other	24.66	107	81.4
REGION			
Average household	**22.96**	**100**	**100.0**
Northeast	17.98	78	14.4
Midwest	26.94	117	26.2
South	21.26	93	34.0
West	25.85	113	25.5
EDUCATION			
Average household	**22.96**	**100**	**100.0**
Less than high school graduate	4.57	20	2.8
High school graduate	10.05	44	11.2
Some college	14.86	65	13.6
Associate's degree	11.78	51	4.8
Bachelor's degree or more	52.20	227	67.5
Bachelor's degree	51.03	222	42.0
Master's, professional, doctoral degree	54.25	236	25.6

Note: Market shares may not sum to 100.0 because of rounding and missing categories by household type. "Asian" and "black" include Hispanics and non-Hispanics who identify themselves as being of the respective race alone. "Hispanic" includes people of any race who identify themselves as Hispanic. "Other" includes people who identify themselves as non-Hispanic and as Alaska Native, American Indian, Asian (who are also included in the "Asian" row), or Native Hawaiian or other Pacific Islander as well as non-Hispanics reporting more than one race.

Source: Calculations by New Strategist based on the Bureau of Labor Statistics' 2010 Consumer Expenditure Survey

Chapter 8.

Gifts for People in Other Households

Household Spending on Gifts for People in Other Households, 2010

Average household spending on gifts for people in other households fell by one-quarter between 2000 and 2010, after adjusting for inflation. The most generous gift-givers are middle-aged and older Americans helping their children and grandchildren pay for college. Consequently, gifts of education expenses account for the largest share (21 percent) of gift giving and are the only gift category to see an increase in spending between 2000 and 2010. Spending on gifts of entertainment, the second-largest gift category with a 9 percent share, fell 20 percent during those years. Average household spending on gifts of food, the third-largest gift category, held almost steady between 2000 and 2010, although the overall stability masks a 43 percent decline from 2000 to 2006 and an ensuing 30 percent gain from 2006 to 2010.

Transportation, the second-biggest gift category in 2008, has slipped to fourth place and accounted for 8 percent of total gift spending in 2010. Average household spending on this category climbed 11 percent between 2006 and 2010, after adjusting for inflation, but because it had fallen 14 percent between 2000 and 2006, overall spending on gifts of transportation fell 5 percent during the decade. All other gift categories—with the exception of the relatively stable infants' apparel category—experienced double-digit declines in spending over the decade.

Spending on gifts for people in other households

(average annual spending of households on gifts for people in other households, 2000, 2006, and 2010; in 2010 dollars)

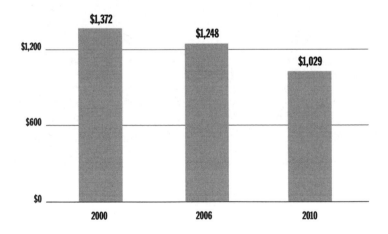

Table 8.1 Spending on gifts for people in other households, 2000 to 2010

(average annual household spending on gifts for people in other households, 2000, 2006, and 2010; percent change in spending, 2000–06, 2000–10, and 2006–10; in 2010 dollars; ranked by amount spent)

	2010 average household spending	2006 average household spending (in 2010$)	2000 average household spending (in 2010$)	percent change		
				2006–10	2000–06	2000–10
AVERAGE ANNUAL SPENDING						
Average household spending on gifts for people in other households	**$1,029.46**	**$1,248.27**	**$1,371.57**	**–17.5%**	**–9.0%**	**–24.9%**
Education expenses	220.95	227.09	191.21	–2.7	18.8	15.6
Entertainment	95.07	82.52	118.73	15.2	–30.5	–19.9
Food	88.57	126.58	88.75	–30.0	42.6	–0.2
Transportation	84.73	76.10	88.98	11.3	–14.5	–4.8
Women's and girls' apparel	73.29	90.24	107.99	–18.8	–16.4	–32.1
Men's and boys' apparel	49.59	64.41	85.54	–23.0	–24.7	–42.0
Infants' apparel	46.95	56.30	51.55	–16.6	9.2	–8.9
Household equipment	46.56	53.28	89.03	–12.6	–40.2	–47.7
Housekeeping supplies	25.13	30.03	49.51	–16.3	–39.4	–49.2
Appliances and housewares	22.27	27.38	35.63	–18.7	–23.2	–37.5
Health care expenses	21.06	44.01	48.22	–52.1	–8.7	–56.3
Jewelry and watches	17.15	25.92	21.34	–33.8	21.5	–19.6
Household textiles	8.39	12.35	16.72	–32.1	–26.1	–49.8

	2006–10	2000–06	2000–10	percentage point change		
				2006–10	2000–06	2000–10
PERCENT DISTRIBUTION OF SPENDING						
Average household spending on gifts for people in other households	**100.0%**	**100.0%**	**100.0%**	–	–	–
Education expenses	21.5	18.2	13.9	3.3	4.3	7.5
Entertainment	9.2	6.6	8.7	2.6	–2.1	0.6
Food	8.6	10.1	6.5	–1.5	3.7	2.1
Transportation	8.2	6.1	6.5	2.1	–0.4	1.7
Women's and girls' apparel	7.1	7.2	7.9	–0.1	–0.6	–0.8
Men's and boys' apparel	4.8	5.2	6.2	–0.3	–1.1	–1.4
Infants' apparel	4.6	4.5	3.8	0.1	0.8	0.8
Household equipment	4.5	4.3	6.5	0.3	–2.2	–2.0
Housekeeping supplies	2.4	2.4	3.6	0.0	–1.2	–1.2
Appliances and housewares	2.2	2.2	2.6	–0.0	–0.4	–0.4
Health care expenses	2.1	3.5	3.5	–1.5	0.0	–1.5
Jewelry and watches	1.7	2.1	1.6	–0.4	0.5	0.1
Household textiles	0.8	1.0	1.2	–0.2	–0.2	–0.4

Note: Numbers do not add to total because not all categories are shown. "–" means not applicable.

Source: Bureau of Labor Statistics, 2000, 2006, and 2010 Consumer Expenditure Surveys; calculations by New Strategist

Gifts of Appliances and Housewares

Best customers: **Householders aged 55 to 64 and 75 or older**
Married couples without children at home
Married couples with preschoolers
Married couples with adult children at home

Customer trends: **Average household spending on gifts of appliances and housewares may increase as more boomers become empty-nesters and help adult children outfit their homes.**

The biggest spenders on gifts of appliances and housewares for people in other households are older married couples, many of them empty-nesters. These households are buying appliances and housewares for grown children who live elsewhere. Householders aged 55 to 64 spend 58 percent more than average on this item and householders aged 75 or older, 30 percent. Married couples without children at home spend 61 percent more than average on appliances and housewares for people in other households. Couples with preschoolers spend 58 percent more than average and those with adult children at home, 85 percent more than average on this item.

Average household spending on gifts of appliances and housewares for people in other households fell a significant 38 percent between 2000 and 2010, after adjusting for inflation. Average household spending on this item may expand in the years ahead as millions more boomers become empty-nesters and help their children outfit their homes.

Table 8.2 Gifts of appliances and housewares

Total household spending $2,697,052,890.00
Average household spends   22.27

	AVERAGE HOUSEHOLD SPENDING	BEST CUSTOMERS (index)	BIGGEST CUSTOMERS (market share)
AGE OF HOUSEHOLDER			
Average household	**$22.27**	**100**	**100.0%**
Under age 25	6.58	30	2.0
Aged 25 to 34	14.67	66	11.0
Aged 35 to 44	19.27	87	15.7
Aged 45 to 54	22.57	101	21.0
Aged 55 to 64	35.16	158	27.8
Aged 65 to 74	21.40	96	10.3
Aged 75 or older	29.00	130	12.4

	AVERAGE HOUSEHOLD SPENDING	BEST CUSTOMERS (index)	BIGGEST CUSTOMERS (market share)
HOUSEHOLD INCOME			
Average household	**$22.27**	**100**	**100.0%**
Under $20,000	8.26	37	8.1
$20,000 to $39,999	17.29	78	17.8
$40,000 to $49,999	11.16	50	4.7
$50,000 to $69,999	24.50	110	15.8
$70,000 to $79,999	20.09	90	5.4
$80,000 to $99,999	26.12	117	9.8
$100,000 or more	50.01	225	38.5
HOUSEHOLD TYPE			
Average household	**22.27**	**100**	**100.0**
Married couples	29.30	132	64.9
Married couples, no children	35.94	161	34.3
Married couples, with children	26.76	120	28.0
Oldest child under age 6	35.29	158	6.8
Oldest child aged 6 to 17	14.40	65	7.6
Oldest child aged 18 or older	41.14	185	13.3
Single parent with child under age 18	6.42	29	1.7
Single person	15.98	72	21.0
RACE AND HISPANIC ORIGIN			
Average household	**22.27**	**100**	**100.0**
Asian	20.83	94	4.0
Black	7.31	33	4.0
Hispanic	11.88	53	6.5
Non-Hispanic white and other	26.28	118	89.5
REGION			
Average household	**22.27**	**100**	**100.0**
Northeast	26.23	118	21.6
Midwest	22.24	100	22.3
South	21.67	97	35.7
West	20.01	90	20.4
EDUCATION			
Average household	**22.27**	**100**	**100.0**
Less than high school graduate	2.88	13	1.8
High school graduate	19.59	88	22.5
Some college	18.61	84	17.6
Associate's degree	21.94	99	9.3
Bachelor's degree or more	36.11	162	48.2
Bachelor's degree	36.28	163	30.8
Master's, professional, doctoral degree	35.56	160	17.3

Note: Market shares may not sum to 100.0 because of rounding and missing categories by household type. "Asian" and "black" include Hispanics and non-Hispanics who identify themselves as being of the respective race alone. "Hispanic" includes people of any race who identify themselves as Hispanic. "Other" includes people who identify themselves as non-Hispanic and as Alaska Native, American Indian, Asian (who are also included in the "Asian" row), or Native Hawaiian or other Pacific Islander as well as non-Hispanics reporting more than one race.

Source: Calculations by New Strategist based on the Bureau of Labor Statistics' 2010 Consumer Expenditure Survey

Gifts of Education Expenses

Best customers:	Householders aged 45 to 64
	High-income households
	Married couples without children at home
	Married couples with school-aged or older children at home
	Asians
	Households in the Northeast and Midwest
	College graduates
Customer trends:	Average household spending on gifts of education expenses should continue to rise in the years ahead as grandparents help their grandchildren pay college bills.

The biggest spenders on gifts of education expenses for people in other households are affluent, educated, middle-aged or older married couples likely to have children in college. Households with incomes of $100,000 or more spend four-and-one-half times the average on gifts of education expenses. Married couples without children at home, most of them empty-nesters, spend 75 percent more than average on gifts of education expenses. Householders aged 45 to 54 and college graduates spend nearly three times the average on this item, and college graduates spend two-and-one-half times the average. Married couples with school-aged or older children at home spend 67 to 76 percent more than average on this item. Asians spend 55 percent more than average on gifts of education expenses. Households in the Northeast and Midwest outspend the average by 52 and 32 percent, respectively.

Average household spending on gifts of education expenses for people in other households rose by 16 percent between 2000 and 2010, after adjusting for inflation, as the children of boomers went to college. This increase is in contrast to the 25 percent decline in overall gift spending during those years. Average household spending on gifts of college tuition should continue to rise in the years ahead as growing numbers of grandparents help their grandchildren pay college bills.

Table 8.3 Gifts of education expenses

Total household spending $26,758,591,650.00
Average household spends 220.95

	AVERAGE HOUSEHOLD SPENDING	BEST CUSTOMERS (index)	BIGGEST CUSTOMERS (market share)
AGE OF HOUSEHOLDER			
Average household	**$220.95**	**100**	**100.0%**
Under age 25	16.76	8	0.5
Aged 25 to 34	19.15	9	1.4
Aged 35 to 44	128.25	58	10.5
Aged 45 to 54	611.44	277	57.2
Aged 55 to 64	309.07	140	24.7
Aged 65 to 74	62.64	28	3.1
Aged 75 or older	59.63	27	2.6

	AVERAGE HOUSEHOLD SPENDING	BEST CUSTOMERS (index)	BIGGEST CUSTOMERS (market share)
HOUSEHOLD INCOME			
Average household	**$220.95**	**100**	**100.0%**
Under $20,000	16.40	7	1.6
$20,000 to $39,999	45.29	20	4.7
$40,000 to $49,999	38.56	17	1.6
$50,000 to $69,999	76.38	35	5.0
$70,000 to $79,999	105.98	48	2.9
$80,000 to $99,999	179.17	81	6.8
$100,000 or more	998.75	452	77.5
HOUSEHOLD TYPE			
Average household	**220.95**	**100**	**100.0**
Married couples	342.43	155	76.4
Married couples, no children	385.58	175	37.1
Married couples, with children	311.94	141	32.8
Oldest child under age 6	7.65	3	0.1
Oldest child aged 6 to 17	388.11	176	20.7
Oldest child aged 18 or older	367.99	167	12.0
Single parent with child under age 18	13.79	6	0.4
Single person	93.23	42	12.4
RACE AND HISPANIC ORIGIN			
Average household	**220.95**	**100**	**100.0**
Asian	342.98	155	6.6
Black	67.94	31	3.8
Hispanic	177.64	80	9.8
Non-Hispanic white and other	252.95	114	86.8
REGION			
Average household	**220.95**	**100**	**100.0**
Northeast	336.71	152	28.0
Midwest	292.56	132	29.5
South	131.48	60	21.8
West	201.65	91	20.7
EDUCATION			
Average household	**220.95**	**100**	**100.0**
Less than high school graduate	15.73	7	1.0
High school graduate	75.46	34	8.7
Some college	86.28	39	8.2
Associate's degree	195.51	88	8.4
Bachelor's degree or more	547.93	248	73.7
Bachelor's degree	382.05	173	32.7
Master's, professional, doctoral degree	837.54	379	41.0

Note: Market shares may not sum to 100.0 because of rounding and missing categories by household type. "Asian" and "black" include Hispanics and non-Hispanics who identify themselves as being of the respective race alone. "Hispanic" includes people of any race who identify themselves as Hispanic. "Other" includes people who identify themselves as non-Hispanic and as Alaska Native, American Indian, Asian (who are also included in the "Asian" row), or Native Hawaiian or other Pacific Islander as well as non-Hispanics reporting more than one race.

Source: Calculations by New Strategist based on the Bureau of Labor Statistics' 2010 Consumer Expenditure Survey

Gifts of Entertainment

Best customers:	**Householders aged 45 to 74** **Married couples without children at home** **Married couples with school-aged children**
Customer trends:	**Average household spending on gifts of entertainment may continue to grow as aging boomers give their children and grandchildren the latest gadgets.**

The biggest spenders on gifts of entertainment (which includes items ranging from dance lessons to movie tickets, from iPods to video games) for people in other households are middle-aged and older married couples—most of them buying gifts for children and grandchildren living elsewhere. Householders ranging in age from 45 to 74 spend 20 to 71 percent more than average on this item. Married couples without children at home (most of them empty-nesters) spend 40 percent more than average on this item, while those with school-aged children spend 26 percent more.

Average household spending on gifts of entertainment for people in other households fell by a steep 30 percent between 2000 and 2006, after adjusting for inflation, but gained 15 percent in the ensuing four years. Average household spending on gifts of entertainment for people in other households may continue to grow as aging boomers give their children and grandchildren the latest gadgets.

Table 8.4 Gifts of entertainment

Total household spending $11,513,642,490.00
Average household spends   95.07

	AVERAGE HOUSEHOLD SPENDING	BEST CUSTOMERS (index)	BIGGEST CUSTOMERS (market share)
AGE OF HOUSEHOLDER			
Average household	**$95.07**	**100**	**100.0%**
Under age 25	34.65	36	2.4
Aged 25 to 34	56.41	59	9.9
Aged 35 to 44	65.81	69	12.5
Aged 45 to 54	114.36	120	24.9
Aged 55 to 64	161.29	170	29.9
Aged 65 to 74	115.48	121	13.1
Aged 75 or older	70.84	75	7.1

	AVERAGE HOUSEHOLD SPENDING	BEST CUSTOMERS (index)	BIGGEST CUSTOMERS (market share)
HOUSEHOLD INCOME			
Average household	**$95.07**	**100**	**100.0%**
Under $20,000	43.16	45	9.9
$20,000 to $39,999	52.59	55	12.7
$40,000 to $49,999	52.92	56	5.3
$50,000 to $69,999	104.65	110	15.8
$70,000 to $79,999	87.53	92	5.5
$80,000 to $99,999	95.68	101	8.4
$100,000 or more	238.66	251	43.0
HOUSEHOLD TYPE			
Average household	**95.07**	**100**	**100.0**
Married couples	117.75	124	61.1
Married couples, no children	132.78	140	29.7
Married couples, with children	97.82	103	23.9
Oldest child under age 6	37.43	39	1.7
Oldest child aged 6 to 17	119.88	126	14.8
Oldest child aged 18 or older	97.28	102	7.4
Single parent with child under age 18	36.66	39	2.3
Single person	79.14	83	24.4
RACE AND HISPANIC ORIGIN			
Average household	**95.07**	**100**	**100.0**
Asian	48.35	51	2.2
Black	43.70	46	5.6
Hispanic	41.92	44	5.4
Non-Hispanic white and other	111.55	117	89.0
REGION			
Average household	**95.07**	**100**	**100.0**
Northeast	113.05	119	21.8
Midwest	103.82	109	24.3
South	84.51	89	32.6
West	88.69	93	21.1
EDUCATION			
Average household	**95.07**	**100**	**100.0**
Less than high school graduate	20.39	21	3.1
High school graduate	80.02	84	21.5
Some college	91.48	96	20.2
Associate's degree	75.96	80	7.5
Bachelor's degree or more	150.79	159	47.1
Bachelor's degree	136.38	143	27.1
Master's, professional, doctoral degree	179.20	188	20.4

Note: Market shares may not sum to 100.0 because of rounding and missing categories by household type. "Asian" and "black" include Hispanics and non-Hispanics who identify themselves as being of the respective race alone. "Hispanic" includes people of any race who identify themselves as Hispanic. "Other" includes people who identify themselves as non-Hispanic and as Alaska Native, American Indian, Asian (who are also included in the "Asian" row), or Native Hawaiian or other Pacific Islander as well as non-Hispanics reporting more than one race.

Source: Calculations by New Strategist based on the Bureau of Labor Statistics' 2010 Consumer Expenditure Survey

Gifts of Food

Best customers: **Householders aged 45 to 64**
Married couples without children at home
Married couples with school-aged or older children at home

Customer trends: **Average household spending on gifts of food should rise again as more boomers become empty-nesters.**

The biggest spenders on gifts of food for people in other households are older empty-nesters. Many gift givers are buying food for grown children and grandchildren who live elsewhere. Householders aged 45 to 64 spend 78 to 83 percent more than average on gifts of food and control 69 percent of the market for this item. Married couples without children at home (most of them empty-nesters) spend 72 percent more than average on gifts of food for people in other households, while those with school-aged or older children at home outspend the average by 22 to 30 percent.

Average household spending on gifts of food for people in other households was the same in 2010 as in 2000, after adjusting for inflation. The overall level performance masks a 43 percent increase between 2000 and the overall peak-spending year of 2006 and a steep 30 percent decline in the ensuing four years. Behind the earlier growth was the entry of the baby-boom generation into the empty-nest lifestage. Average household spending on gifts of food should rise again as more boomers become empty-nesters.

Table 8.5 Gifts of food

| Total household spending | $10,726,446,990.00 |
| Average household spends | 88.57 |

	AVERAGE HOUSEHOLD SPENDING	BEST CUSTOMERS (index)	BIGGEST CUSTOMERS (market share)
AGE OF HOUSEHOLDER			
Average household	**$88.57**	**100**	**100.0%**
Under age 25	16.04	18	1.2
Aged 25 to 34	41.01	46	7.7
Aged 35 to 44	48.50	55	9.9
Aged 45 to 54	162.31	183	37.9
Aged 55 to 64	157.55	178	31.4
Aged 65 to 74	60.09	68	7.3
Aged 75 or older	41.12	46	4.4

	AVERAGE HOUSEHOLD SPENDING	BEST CUSTOMERS (index)	BIGGEST CUSTOMERS (market share)
HOUSEHOLD INCOME			
Average household	**$88.57**	**100**	**100.0%**
Under $20,000	26.57	30	6.5
$20,000 to $39,999	31.59	36	8.2
$40,000 to $49,999	63.94	72	6.8
$50,000 to $69,999	73.96	84	12.0
$70,000 to $79,999	114.93	130	7.8
$80,000 to $99,999	90.87	103	8.6
$100,000 or more	261.91	296	50.7
HOUSEHOLD TYPE			
Average household	**88.57**	**100**	**100.0**
Married couples	126.31	143	70.3
Married couples, no children	152.06	172	36.5
Married couples, with children	106.81	121	28.1
Oldest child under age 6	82.14	93	4.0
Oldest child aged 6 to 17	115.20	130	15.3
Oldest child aged 18 or older	107.95	122	8.8
Single parent with child under age 18	30.31	34	2.0
Single person	60.86	69	20.1
RACE AND HISPANIC ORIGIN			
Average household	**88.57**	**100**	**100.0**
Asian	87.93	99	4.2
Black	38.31	43	5.3
Hispanic	48.85	55	6.7
Non-Hispanic white and other	102.79	116	88.0
REGION			
Average household	**88.57**	**100**	**100.0**
Northeast	99.67	113	20.7
Midwest	91.65	103	23.1
South	77.29	87	32.0
West	94.89	107	24.3
EDUCATION			
Average household	**88.57**	**100**	**100.0**
Less than high school graduate	21.91	25	3.5
High school graduate	56.88	64	16.4
Some college	50.76	57	12.0
Associate's degree	84.14	95	9.0
Bachelor's degree or more	175.08	198	58.7
Bachelor's degree	162.76	184	34.7
Master's, professional, doctoral degree	198.41	224	24.2

Note: Market shares may not sum to 100.0 because of rounding and missing categories by household type. "Asian" and "black" include Hispanics and non-Hispanics who identify themselves as being of the respective race alone. "Hispanic" includes people of any race who identify themselves as Hispanic. "Other" includes people who identify themselves as non-Hispanic and as Alaska Native, American Indian, Asian (who are also included in the "Asian" row), or Native Hawaiian or other Pacific Islander as well as non-Hispanics reporting more than one race.

Source: Calculations by New Strategist based on the Bureau of Labor Statistics' 2010 Consumer Expenditure Survey

Gifts of Health Care Expenses

Best customers: **Householders aged 55 to 74**
Married couples with adult children at home
People who live alone
Non-Hispanic whites
Households in the Midwest and West

Customer trends: **Average household spending on gifts of health care expenses will continue to decline in the years ahead as a growing proportion of the population has access to health insurance.**

The biggest spenders on gifts of health care expenses for people in other households are middle-aged and older householders—many of them paying for the health care of their uninsured children or grandchildren. Householders aged 65 to 74 spend 41 percent more than average on this item, and those aged 55 to 64 spend more than twice the average. Together the two groups control over half the market. People who live alone, many of them elderly, spend 52 percent more than average on this item and account for 45 percent of the market although their share of consumer units is only 29 percent. Non-Hispanic whites greatly outspend minorities on this item and control 94 percent of the market. Households in the West and Midwest outspend the average by 77 and 31 percent, respectively.

Average household spending on gifts of health care expenses for people in other households fell by 56 between 2000 and 2010, after adjusting for inflation. Most of the decline came between 2006 and 2010, when spending on this item dropped 52 percent. Spending on gifts of health care expenses for people in other households will continue to decline in the years ahead as health insurance reform results in a growing proportion of the population with access to health insurance.

Table 8.6 Gifts of health care expenses

Total household spending $2,550,513,420.00
Average household spends   21.06

AGE OF HOUSEHOLDER	AVERAGE HOUSEHOLD SPENDING	BEST CUSTOMERS (index)	BIGGEST CUSTOMERS (market share)
Average household	**$21.06**	**100**	**100.0%**
Under age 25	4.38	21	1.4
Aged 25 to 34	6.63	31	5.2
Aged 35 to 44	17.23	82	14.8
Aged 45 to 54	22.42	106	22.0
Aged 55 to 64	44.93	213	37.6
Aged 65 to 74	29.59	141	15.1
Aged 75 or older	8.27	39	3.7

	AVERAGE HOUSEHOLD SPENDING	BEST CUSTOMERS (index)	BIGGEST CUSTOMERS (market share)
HOUSEHOLD INCOME			
Average household	$21.06	100	100.0%
Under $20,000	2.43	12	2.5
$20,000 to $39,999	11.94	57	13.0
$40,000 to $49,999	5.82	28	2.6
$50,000 to $69,999	32.66	155	22.2
$70,000 to $79,999	31.35	149	8.9
$80,000 to $99,999	30.07	143	11.9
$100,000 or more	48.31	229	39.3
HOUSEHOLD TYPE			
Average household	21.06	100	100.0
Married couples	21.43	102	50.2
Married couples, no children	25.43	121	25.6
Married couples, with children	20.21	96	22.3
Oldest child under age 6	23.32	111	4.7
Oldest child aged 6 to 17	10.14	48	5.7
Oldest child aged 18 or older	34.87	166	12.0
Single parent with child under age 18	2.65	13	0.7
Single person	32.02	152	44.5
RACE AND HISPANIC ORIGIN			
Average household	21.06	100	100.0
Asian	18.84	89	3.8
Black	4.11	20	2.4
Hispanic	5.63	27	3.3
Non-Hispanic white and other	26.20	124	94.3
REGION			
Average household	21.06	100	100.0
Northeast	16.46	78	14.3
Midwest	27.55	131	29.2
South	9.45	45	16.5
West	37.19	177	40.0
EDUCATION			
Average household	21.06	100	100.0
Less than high school graduate	5.21	25	3.5
High school graduate	11.21	53	13.6
Some college	19.01	90	19.0
Associate's degree	42.60	202	19.1
Bachelor's degree or more	31.65	150	44.6
Bachelor's degree	13.91	66	12.5
Master's, professional, doctoral degree	62.61	297	32.2

Note: Market shares may not sum to 100.0 because of rounding and missing categories by household type. "Asian" and "black" include Hispanics and non-Hispanics who identify themselves as being of the respective race alone. "Hispanic" includes people of any race who identify themselves as Hispanic. "Other" includes people who identify themselves as non-Hispanic and as Alaska Native, American Indian, Asian (who are also included in the "Asian" row), or Native Hawaiian or other Pacific Islander as well as non-Hispanics reporting more than one race.

Source: Calculations by New Strategist based on the Bureau of Labor Statistics' 2010 Consumer Expenditure Survey

Gifts of Household Equipment

Best customers: **Householders aged 55 to 74**
                             Married couples without children at home
                             Households in the Northeast

Customer trends: **Average household spending on gifts of household equipment for people in other**
                             households should rise as the children of boomers set up their own households.

The household equipment category includes many traditional gifts, such as infants' equipment, indoor plants and fresh flowers, and decorative household items. The biggest spenders on gifts of household equipment for people in other households are older married couples, many with grown children living elsewhere. Householders aged 55 to 74 spend 47 to 52 percent more than average on this item. Married couples without children at home (many of them empty-nesters) spend 86 percent more than average on gifts of household equipment. Households in the Northeast outspend the average by 56 percent.

Average household spending on gifts of household equipment fell by a significant 48 percent between 2000 and 2010, after adjusting for inflation. Spending on gifts of household equipment should rise as the children of boomers establish their own households.

Table 8.7 Gifts of household equipment

| Total household spending | $5,638,741,920.00 |
| Average household spends | 46.56 |

	AVERAGE HOUSEHOLD SPENDING	BEST CUSTOMERS (index)	BIGGEST CUSTOMERS (market share)
AGE OF HOUSEHOLDER			
Average household	**$46.56**	**100**	**100.0%**
Under age 25	35.15	75	5.0
Aged 25 to 34	26.59	57	9.5
Aged 35 to 44	39.21	84	15.2
Aged 45 to 54	44.35	95	19.7
Aged 55 to 64	70.91	152	26.9
Aged 65 to 74	68.47	147	15.8
Aged 75 or older	37.86	81	7.8

	AVERAGE HOUSEHOLD SPENDING	BEST CUSTOMERS (index)	BIGGEST CUSTOMERS (market share)
HOUSEHOLD INCOME			
Average household	**$46.56**	**100**	**100.0%**
Under $20,000	12.84	28	6.0
$20,000 to $39,999	29.91	64	14.7
$40,000 to $49,999	28.08	60	5.7
$50,000 to $69,999	42.48	91	13.1
$70,000 to $79,999	63.53	136	8.2
$80,000 to $99,999	48.41	104	8.7
$100,000 or more	120.95	260	44.5
HOUSEHOLD TYPE			
Average household	**46.56**	**100**	**100.0**
Married couples	57.56	124	61.0
Married couples, no children	86.80	186	39.6
Married couples, with children	37.79	81	18.9
Oldest child under age 6	29.33	63	2.7
Oldest child aged 6 to 17	45.46	98	11.5
Oldest child aged 18 or older	30.81	66	4.8
Single parent with child under age 18	23.39	50	3.0
Single person	35.36	76	22.2
RACE AND HISPANIC ORIGIN			
Average household	**46.56**	**100**	**100.0**
Asian	32.46	70	3.0
Black	21.56	46	5.7
Hispanic	36.31	78	9.5
Non-Hispanic white and other	52.09	112	84.8
REGION			
Average household	**46.56**	**100**	**100.0**
Northeast	72.85	156	28.7
Midwest	33.57	72	16.1
South	41.74	90	32.9
West	45.87	99	22.3
EDUCATION			
Average household	**46.56**	**100**	**100.0**
Less than high school graduate	17.04	37	5.2
High school graduate	23.93	51	13.1
Some college	33.49	72	15.1
Associate's degree	56.09	120	11.4
Bachelor's degree or more	85.98	185	54.9
Bachelor's degree	67.20	144	27.3
Master's, professional, doctoral degree	122.53	263	28.5

Note: Market shares may not sum to 100.0 because of rounding and missing categories by household type. "Asian" and "black" include Hispanics and non-Hispanics who identify themselves as being of the respective race alone. "Hispanic" includes people of any race who identify themselves as Hispanic. "Other" includes people who identify themselves as non-Hispanic and as Alaska Native, American Indian, Asian (who are also included in the "Asian" row), or Native Hawaiian or other Pacific Islander as well as non-Hispanics reporting more than one race.

Source: Calculations by New Strategist based on the Bureau of Labor Statistics' 2010 Consumer Expenditure Survey

Gifts of Household Textiles

Best customers: **Householders aged 55 to 74**
Married couples without children at home
Married couples with adult children at home
Asians
Households in the Northeast

Customer trends: **Average household spending on gifts of household textiles for people in other households may rise as boomers help their adult children outfit their homes.**

The biggest spenders on gifts of household textiles (such as towels and bed linens) for people in other households are older married couples, many of them empty-nesters giving this traditional gift to adult children who live elsewhere. Householders aged 55 to 74 spend 49 to 98 percent more than the average household on this item. Married couples without children at home spend 86 percent more than average and control a sizeable 40 percent of the market. Married couples with adult children at home spend 53 percent more than average on gifts of household textiles. Asian householders spend 44 percent more than average on this gift category. Northeastern households outspend the average by 87 percent.

Average household spending on gifts of household textiles for people in other households, already the smallest gift category, dropped by one-half between 2000 and 2010. Spending on gifts of household textiles may grow in the years ahead as millions of boomers help their adult children outfit their homes.

Table 8.8 Gifts of household textiles

| | Total household spending | $1,016,087,730.00 |
| | Average household spends | 8.39 |

	AVERAGE HOUSEHOLD SPENDING	BEST CUSTOMERS (index)	BIGGEST CUSTOMERS (market share)
AGE OF HOUSEHOLDER			
Average household	**$8.39**	**100**	**100.0%**
Under age 25	0.63	8	0.5
Aged 25 to 34	3.63	43	7.2
Aged 35 to 44	5.03	60	10.8
Aged 45 to 54	9.96	119	24.6
Aged 55 to 64	12.48	149	26.2
Aged 65 to 74	16.59	198	21.3
Aged 75 or older	7.93	95	9.0

	AVERAGE HOUSEHOLD SPENDING	BEST CUSTOMERS (index)	BIGGEST CUSTOMERS (market share)
HOUSEHOLD INCOME			
Average household	**$8.39**	**100**	**100.0%**
Under $20,000	2.94	35	7.7
$20,000 to $39,999	6.11	73	16.7
$40,000 to $49,999	7.20	86	8.1
$50,000 to $69,999	8.37	100	14.3
$70,000 to $79,999	15.04	179	10.7
$80,000 to $99,999	7.08	84	7.0
$100,000 or more	17.75	212	36.3
HOUSEHOLD TYPE			
Average household	**8.39**	**100**	**100.0**
Married couples	12.03	143	70.7
Married couples, no children	15.61	186	39.5
Married couples, with children	8.66	103	24.0
Oldest child under age 6	0.26	3	0.1
Oldest child aged 6 to 17	8.79	105	12.3
Oldest child aged 18 or older	12.80	153	11.0
Single parent with child under age 18	5.45	65	3.8
Single person	4.27	51	14.9
RACE AND HISPANIC ORIGIN			
Average household	**8.39**	**100**	**100.0**
Asian	12.09	144	6.1
Black	2.71	32	4.0
Hispanic	4.47	53	6.5
Non-Hispanic white and other	9.90	118	89.5
REGION			
Average household	**8.39**	**100**	**100.0**
Northeast	15.70	187	34.3
Midwest	6.76	81	18.0
South	5.57	66	24.4
West	8.64	103	23.3
EDUCATION			
Average household	**8.39**	**100**	**100.0**
Less than high school graduate	4.03	48	6.9
High school graduate	4.84	58	14.7
Some college	8.25	98	20.7
Associate's degree	10.73	128	12.1
Bachelor's degree or more	12.78	152	45.3
Bachelor's degree	13.71	163	30.9
Master's, professional, doctoral degree	11.24	134	14.5

Note: Market shares may not sum to 100.0 because of rounding and missing categories by household type. "Asian" and "black" include Hispanics and non-Hispanics who identify themselves as being of the respective race alone. "Hispanic" includes people of any race who identify themselves as Hispanic. "Other" includes people who identify themselves as non-Hispanic and as Alaska Native, American Indian, Asian (who are also included in the "Asian" row), or Native Hawaiian or other Pacific Islander as well as non-Hispanics reporting more than one race.

Source: Calculations by New Strategist based on the Bureau of Labor Statistics' 2010 Consumer Expenditure Survey

Gifts of Housekeeping Supplies

Best customers: | **Householders aged 45 to 74**
People who live alone
Households in the Midwest

Customer trends: | **Average household spending on gifts of housekeeping supplies for people in other households may begin to rise as boomers help their adult children outfit their homes.**

The category gifts of housekeeping supplies (such as laundry and cleaning supplies, lawn and garden supplies, postage, and stationery) shows relatively little variation by demographic category. Householders aged 45 to 54 spend 21 percent more than average on this item, and those aged 65 to 74 spend 49 percent more than average. People who live alone, whose spending is well below average for most items, spend slightly above average on gifts of housekeeping supplies. Households in the Midwest outspend the average by 19 percent.

Average household spending on gifts of housekeeping supplies for people in other households fell by an enormous 49 percent between 2000 and 2010, after adjusting for inflation. A large part of the loss came before the peak-spending year of 2006, but spending on gifts of housekeeping supplies decreased 16 percent between 2006 and 2010. Average household spending on gifts of housekeeping supplies may begin to rise in the years ahead as millions of boomers help their adult children outfit their homes.

Table 8.9 Gifts of housekeeping supplies

Total household spending | $3,043,418,910.00
Average household spends | 25.13

	AVERAGE HOUSEHOLD SPENDING	BEST CUSTOMERS (index)	BIGGEST CUSTOMERS (market share)
AGE OF HOUSEHOLDER			
Average household	**$25.13**	**100**	**100.0%**
Under age 25	13.52	54	3.6
Aged 25 to 34	19.97	79	13.2
Aged 35 to 44	19.49	78	14.0
Aged 45 to 54	30.29	121	24.9
Aged 55 to 64	26.85	107	18.8
Aged 65 to 74	37.43	149	16.0
Aged 75 or older	23.99	95	9.1

	AVERAGE HOUSEHOLD SPENDING	BEST CUSTOMERS (index)	BIGGEST CUSTOMERS (market share)
HOUSEHOLD INCOME			
Average household	**$25.13**	**100**	**100.0%**
Under $20,000	15.89	63	13.8
$20,000 to $39,999	18.12	72	16.5
$40,000 to $49,999	18.04	72	6.8
$50,000 to $69,999	31.01	123	17.7
$70,000 to $79,999	29.51	117	7.0
$80,000 to $99,999	26.20	104	8.7
$100,000 or more	43.29	172	29.5
HOUSEHOLD TYPE			
Average household	**25.13**	**100**	**100.0**
Married couples	26.49	105	52.0
Married couples, no children	28.68	114	24.2
Married couples, with children	25.13	100	23.3
Oldest child under age 6	23.32	93	4.0
Oldest child aged 6 to 17	29.11	116	13.6
Oldest child aged 18 or older	20.11	80	5.8
Single parent with child under age 18	3.84	15	0.9
Single person	25.80	103	30.1
RACE AND HISPANIC ORIGIN			
Average household	**25.13**	**100**	**100.0**
Asian	9.19	37	1.6
Black	18.87	75	9.2
Hispanic	9.57	38	4.6
Non-Hispanic white and other	28.53	114	86.1
REGION			
Average household	**25.13**	**100**	**100.0**
Northeast	22.61	90	16.5
Midwest	29.91	119	26.5
South	21.91	87	32.0
West	27.64	110	24.9
EDUCATION			
Average household	**25.13**	**100**	**100.0**
Less than high school graduate	14.08	56	8.0
High school graduate	16.79	67	17.1
Some college	29.32	117	24.5
Associate's degree	40.48	161	15.2
Bachelor's degree or more	29.14	116	34.4
Bachelor's degree	28.03	112	21.1
Master's, professional, doctoral degree	31.32	125	13.5

Note: Market shares may not sum to 100.0 because of rounding and missing categories by household type. "Asian" and "black" include Hispanics and non-Hispanics who identify themselves as being of the respective race alone. "Hispanic" includes people of any race who identify themselves as Hispanic. "Other" includes people who identify themselves as non-Hispanic and as Alaska Native, American Indian, Asian (who are also included in the "Asian" row), or Native Hawaiian or other Pacific Islander as well as non-Hispanics reporting more than one race.

Source: Calculations by New Strategist based on the Bureau of Labor Statistics' 2010 Consumer Expenditure Survey

Gifts of Infants' Apparel

Best customers:
Householders aged 25 to 34
Married couples with children at home
Single parents
Asians and Hispanics

Customer trends:
Average household spending on gifts of infants' apparel for people in other households should rise as the large millennial generation has children.

The biggest spenders on gifts of infants' apparel for people in other households are younger married couples with children. Many are buying gifts for friends and relatives who have recently had children. Householders aged 25 to 34 spend 58 percent more than average on this item. Married couples with children at home spend 54 percent more than average on gifts of infant apparel, the number peaking among couples with preschoolers at over two times the average. Single parents, whose spending approaches average on only a few categories, spend 12 percent more than average on this gift category. Asians and Hispanics spend, respectively, 61 and 41 percent more than average on gifts of infants' apparel.

Average household spending on gifts of infants' apparel for people in other households declined by 9 percent between 2000 and 2010, after adjusting for inflation. Spending on gifts of infants' apparel should increase as the millennial generation has children.

Table 8.10 Gifts of infants' apparel

Total household spending $5,685,973,650.00
Average household spends 46.95

	AVERAGE HOUSEHOLD SPENDING	BEST CUSTOMERS (index)	BIGGEST CUSTOMERS (market share)
AGE OF HOUSEHOLDER			
Average household	**$46.95**	**100**	**100.0%**
Under age 25	33.72	72	4.8
Aged 25 to 34	74.07	158	26.3
Aged 35 to 44	52.10	111	20.1
Aged 45 to 54	45.11	96	19.9
Aged 55 to 64	46.40	99	17.4
Aged 65 to 74	32.88	70	7.5
Aged 75 or older	20.79	44	4.2

	AVERAGE HOUSEHOLD SPENDING	BEST CUSTOMERS (index)	BIGGEST CUSTOMERS (market share)
HOUSEHOLD INCOME			
Average household	**$46.95**	**100**	**100.0%**
Under $20,000	21.54	46	10.0
$20,000 to $39,999	37.91	81	18.5
$40,000 to $49,999	47.71	102	9.6
$50,000 to $69,999	54.58	116	16.7
$70,000 to $79,999	57.18	122	7.3
$80,000 to $99,999	48.11	102	8.5
$100,000 or more	79.53	169	29.0
HOUSEHOLD TYPE			
Average household	**46.95**	**100**	**100.0**
Married couples	64.68	138	68.0
Married couples, no children	54.08	115	24.5
Married couples, with children	72.40	154	35.9
Oldest child under age 6	99.33	212	9.1
Oldest child aged 6 to 17	71.82	153	18.0
Oldest child aged 18 or older	60.51	129	9.3
Single parent with child under age 18	52.35	112	6.6
Single person	16.93	36	10.6
RACE AND HISPANIC ORIGIN			
Average household	**46.95**	**100**	**100.0**
Asian	75.75	161	6.9
Black	34.77	74	9.1
Hispanic	66.01	141	17.1
Non-Hispanic white and other	46.34	99	74.8
REGION			
Average household	**46.95**	**100**	**100.0**
Northeast	51.57	110	20.2
Midwest	42.03	90	20.0
South	45.05	96	35.2
West	51.22	109	24.7
EDUCATION			
Average household	**46.95**	**100**	**100.0**
Less than high school graduate	42.36	90	12.9
High school graduate	41.88	89	22.8
Some college	46.38	99	20.8
Associate's degree	43.07	92	8.7
Bachelor's degree or more	55.41	118	35.1
Bachelor's degree	49.25	105	19.8
Master's, professional, doctoral degree	66.90	142	15.4

Note: Market shares may not sum to 100.0 because of rounding and missing categories by household type. "Asian" and "black" include Hispanics and non-Hispanics who identify themselves as being of the respective race alone. "Hispanic" includes people of any race who identify themselves as Hispanic. "Other" includes people who identify themselves as non-Hispanic and as Alaska Native, American Indian, Asian (who are also included in the "Asian" row), or Native Hawaiian or other Pacific Islander as well as non-Hispanics reporting more than one race.

Source: Calculations by New Strategist based on the Bureau of Labor Statistics' 2010 Consumer Expenditure Survey

Gifts of Jewelry and Watches

Best customers: **Householders aged 25 to 34**
           People who live alone
           Asians

Customer trends: **Average household spending on gifts of jewelry and watches should continue to**
           decline because of the economic downturn and the loss of discretionary income.

The biggest spenders on gifts of jewelry and watches for people in other households are young adults who live alone, many buying engagement or wedding rings. Householders aged 25 to 34 spend nearly twice the average on gifts of jewelry and watches, accounting for 30 percent of the market. Single-person households—many headed by young adults—spend 41 percent more than average on this item. Asians spend 54 percent more than average on gifts of jewelry and watches.

Average household spending on gifts of jewelry and watches for people in other households had grown by 21 percent between 2000 and the overall peak-spending year of 2006, after adjusting for inflation. Then spending fell by an enormous 34 percent between 2006 and 2010. Spending on gifts of jewelry and watches should continue to decline because of the economic downturn and the loss of discretionary income.

Table 8.11 Gifts of jewelry and watches

Total household spending $2,076,985,050.00
Average household spends   17.15

	AVERAGE HOUSEHOLD SPENDING	BEST CUSTOMERS (index)	BIGGEST CUSTOMERS (market share)
AGE OF HOUSEHOLDER			
Average household	**$17.15**	**100**	**100.0%**
Under age 25	9.73	57	3.8
Aged 25 to 34	31.40	183	30.5
Aged 35 to 44	9.11	53	9.6
Aged 45 to 54	18.81	110	22.7
Aged 55 to 64	18.29	107	18.8
Aged 65 to 74	11.02	64	6.9
Aged 75 or older	13.83	81	7.7

	AVERAGE HOUSEHOLD SPENDING	BEST CUSTOMERS (index)	BIGGEST CUSTOMERS (market share)
HOUSEHOLD INCOME			
Average household	**$17.15**	**100**	**100.0%**
Under $20,000	6.85	40	8.7
$20,000 to $39,999	11.44	67	15.3
$40,000 to $49,999	20.41	119	11.2
$50,000 to $69,999	21.01	123	17.6
$70,000 to $79,999	15.83	92	5.5
$80,000 to $99,999	31.47	183	15.3
$100,000 or more	27.90	163	27.9
HOUSEHOLD TYPE			
Average household	**17.15**	**100**	**100.0**
Married couples	12.53	73	36.0
Married couples, no children	17.16	100	21.3
Married couples, with children	9.14	53	12.4
Oldest child under age 6	4.11	24	1.0
Oldest child aged 6 to 17	5.87	34	4.0
Oldest child aged 18 or older	16.52	96	7.0
Single parent with child under age 18	4.30	25	1.5
Single person	24.25	141	41.4
RACE AND HISPANIC ORIGIN			
Average household	**17.15**	**100**	**100.0**
Asian	26.34	154	6.5
Black	3.93	23	2.8
Hispanic	12.50	73	8.9
Non-Hispanic white and other	19.98	117	88.3
REGION			
Average household	**17.15**	**100**	**100.0**
Northeast	17.93	105	19.2
Midwest	18.73	109	24.3
South	16.28	95	34.8
West	16.43	96	21.7
EDUCATION			
Average household	**17.15**	**100**	**100.0**
Less than high school graduate	3.09	18	2.6
High school graduate	13.87	81	20.6
Some college	18.51	108	22.7
Associate's degree	20.91	122	11.5
Bachelor's degree or more	24.58	143	42.6
Bachelor's degree	30.57	178	33.7
Master's, professional, doctoral degree	13.38	78	8.4

Note: Market shares may not sum to 100.0 because of rounding and missing categories by household type. "Asian" and "black" include Hispanics and non-Hispanics who identify themselves as being of the respective race alone. "Hispanic" includes people of any race who identify themselves as Hispanic. "Other" includes people who identify themselves as non-Hispanic and as Alaska Native, American Indian, Asian (who are also included in the "Asian" row), or Native Hawaiian or other Pacific Islander as well as non-Hispanics reporting more than one race.

Source: Calculations by New Strategist based on the Bureau of Labor Statistics' 2010 Consumer Expenditure Survey

Gifts of Men's and Boys' Apparel

Best customers:
Householders aged 55 to 74
Married couples without children at home
Households in the Northeast

Customer trends:
Average household spending on gifts of men's and boys' apparel for people in other households will continue to decline as electronics trump apparel in gift giving to men and boys.

Apparel is one of the biggest gift-giving categories. In 2010, the average household spent a combined $170 on gifts of women's, men's, and children's apparel for people in other households. Older married couples dominate gifts of men's and boys' apparel, many of them buying clothes for adult children and grandchildren living elsewhere. Householders aged 55 to 74 spend 32 to 47 percent more than average on gifts of men's and boys' apparel. Married couples without children at home, most of them empty-nesters, spend 55 percent more than average on gifts of clothing for males. Households in the Northeast outspend the average by 62 percent.

Average household spending on gifts of men's and boys' apparel for people in other households fell by a substantial 42 percent between 2000 and 2010, after adjusting for inflation. Spending in this category will continue to decline as electronics trump apparel in gift giving to men and boys.

Table 8.12 Gifts of men's and boys' apparel

Total household spending $6,005,696,130.00
Average household spends   49.59

	AVERAGE HOUSEHOLD SPENDING	BEST CUSTOMERS (index)	BIGGEST CUSTOMERS (market share)
AGE OF HOUSEHOLDER			
Average household	**$49.59**	**100**	**100.0%**
Under age 25	37.20	75	5.0
Aged 25 to 34	35.96	73	12.1
Aged 35 to 44	44.50	90	16.2
Aged 45 to 54	46.24	93	19.3
Aged 55 to 64	72.87	147	25.9
Aged 65 to 74	65.22	132	14.2
Aged 75 or older	37.95	77	7.3

	AVERAGE HOUSEHOLD SPENDING	BEST CUSTOMERS (index)	BIGGEST CUSTOMERS (market share)
HOUSEHOLD INCOME			
Average household	**$49.59**	**100**	**100.0%**
Under $20,000	18.76	38	8.3
$20,000 to $39,999	40.27	81	18.6
$40,000 to $49,999	29.55	60	5.6
$50,000 to $69,999	37.06	75	10.7
$70,000 to $79,999	78.84	159	9.5
$80,000 to $99,999	74.71	151	12.6
$100,000 or more	104.01	210	36.0
HOUSEHOLD TYPE			
Average household	**49.59**	**100**	**100.0**
Married couples	59.97	121	59.7
Married couples, no children	76.94	155	33.0
Married couples, with children	47.85	96	22.4
Oldest child under age 6	34.82	70	3.0
Oldest child aged 6 to 17	54.50	110	12.9
Oldest child aged 18 or older	44.85	90	6.5
Single parent with child under age 18	21.54	43	2.6
Single person	41.60	84	24.6
RACE AND HISPANIC ORIGIN			
Average household	**49.59**	**100**	**100.0**
Asian	42.43	86	3.6
Black	32.47	65	8.0
Hispanic	35.82	72	8.8
Non-Hispanic white and other	54.40	110	83.2
REGION			
Average household	**49.59**	**100**	**100.0**
Northeast	80.57	162	29.8
Midwest	37.94	77	17.1
South	42.78	86	31.7
West	47.14	95	21.5
EDUCATION			
Average household	**49.59**	**100**	**100.0**
Less than high school graduate	21.89	44	6.3
High school graduate	39.68	80	20.4
Some college	50.59	102	21.4
Associate's degree	53.09	107	10.1
Bachelor's degree or more	68.82	139	41.2
Bachelor's degree	61.62	124	23.5
Master's, professional, doctoral degree	82.87	167	18.1

Note: Market shares may not sum to 100.0 because of rounding and missing categories by household type. "Asian" and "black" include Hispanics and non-Hispanics who identify themselves as being of the respective race alone. "Hispanic" includes people of any race who identify themselves as Hispanic. "Other" includes people who identify themselves as non-Hispanic and as Alaska Native, American Indian, Asian (who are also included in the "Asian" row), or Native Hawaiian or other Pacific Islander as well as non-Hispanics reporting more than one race.

Source: Calculations by New Strategist based on the Bureau of Labor Statistics' 2010 Consumer Expenditure Survey

Gifts of Transportation

Best customers: Householders aged 45 to 54 and 65 or older
                        Married couples without children at home
                        Asians

Customer trends: Average household spending on gifts of transportation may rise as growing
                        numbers of empty-nest boomers help their adult children come home for a visit.

The biggest spenders on gifts of transportation for people in other households are middle-aged and older people buying airline tickets for adult children or even helping grown children buy a car. Householders aged 65 to 74, most with adult children who live elsewhere, spend 21 percent more than average on this item, and those aged 45 to 54 spend 47 percent more on such gifts. But both groups are outspent by householders aged 75 or older, who spend 65 percent more than average on gifts of transportation. Married couples without children at home, most of them empty-nesters, spend 61 percent more than average on this item. Asians spend two-and-one-half times the average amount on gifts of transportation.

Average household spending on gifts of transportation for people in other households was relatively flat between 2000 and 2010, falling just 5 percent after adjusting for inflation. Things were not as stable as they may seem, however, as spending on gifts of transportation first dropped 14 percent between 2000 and 2006 and then increased by 11 percent over the ensuing four years. Average household spending on gifts of transportation may continue to rise as growing numbers of empty-nest boomers help their adult children come home for a visit.

Table 8.13 Gifts of transportation

Total household spending $10,261,396,110.00
Average household spends   84.73

	AVERAGE HOUSEHOLD SPENDING	BEST CUSTOMERS (index)	BIGGEST CUSTOMERS (market share)
AGE OF HOUSEHOLDER			
Average household	**$84.73**	**100**	**100.0%**
Under age 25	16.64	20	1.3
Aged 25 to 34	56.61	67	11.1
Aged 35 to 44	47.88	57	10.2
Aged 45 to 54	124.17	147	30.3
Aged 55 to 64	87.72	104	18.3
Aged 65 to 74	102.29	121	13.0
Aged 75 or older	140.14	165	15.8

	AVERAGE HOUSEHOLD SPENDING	BEST CUSTOMERS (index)	BIGGEST CUSTOMERS (market share)
HOUSEHOLD INCOME			
Average household	**$84.73**	**100**	**100.0%**
Under $20,000	15.93	19	4.1
$20,000 to $39,999	45.67	54	12.4
$40,000 to $49,999	93.40	110	10.4
$50,000 to $69,999	86.57	102	14.7
$70,000 to $79,999	208.58	246	14.7
$80,000 to $99,999	134.88	159	13.3
$100,000 or more	150.38	177	30.4
HOUSEHOLD TYPE			
Average household	**84.73**	**100**	**100.0**
Married couples	100.59	119	58.6
Married couples, no children	136.29	161	34.2
Married couples, with children	71.51	84	19.6
Oldest child under age 6	83.65	99	4.2
Oldest child aged 6 to 17	67.01	79	9.3
Oldest child aged 18 or older	71.63	85	6.1
Single parent with child under age 18	18.38	22	1.3
Single person	82.42	97	28.5
RACE AND HISPANIC ORIGIN			
Average household	**84.73**	**100**	**100.0**
Asian	207.88	245	10.4
Black	26.54	31	3.8
Hispanic	50.57	60	7.3
Non-Hispanic white and other	99.36	117	88.9
REGION			
Average household	**84.73**	**100**	**100.0**
Northeast	79.87	94	17.3
Midwest	71.66	85	18.9
South	85.43	101	37.0
West	100.42	119	26.8
EDUCATION			
Average household	**84.73**	**100**	**100.0**
Less than high school graduate	32.45	38	5.5
High school graduate	80.90	95	24.4
Some college	58.78	69	14.6
Associate's degree	74.94	88	8.4
Bachelor's degree or more	134.79	159	47.3
Bachelor's degree	98.93	117	22.1
Master's, professional, doctoral degree	197.33	233	25.2

Note: Market shares may not sum to 100.0 because of rounding and missing categories by household type. "Asian" and "black" include Hispanics and non-Hispanics who identify themselves as being of the respective race alone. "Hispanic" includes people of any race who identify themselves as Hispanic. "Other" includes people who identify themselves as non-Hispanic and as Alaska Native, American Indian, Asian (who are also included in the "Asian" row), or Native Hawaiian or other Pacific Islander as well as non-Hispanics reporting more than one race.

Source: Calculations by New Strategist based on the Bureau of Labor Statistics' 2010 Consumer Expenditure Survey

Gifts of Women's and Girls' Apparel

Best customers: **Householders aged 55 or older**
Married couples without children at home
Single parents
Households in the Northeast

Customer trends: **Average household spending on gifts of women's and girls' apparel may continue
to decline in the years ahead as electronics increasingly replace apparel as gift
items.**

Older householders dominate spending on gifts of women's and girls' apparel for people in other households, many of them buying clothes for adult children and grandchildren. Householders aged 55 or older spend 22 to 47 percent more than average on this item and account for 52 percent of the market. Married couples without children at home, many of them empty-nesters, spend 70 percent more than average on gifts of women's and girls' apparel. Single parents, whose spending is well below average on most categories, spend 21 percent more than average on gifts of female apparel. Households in the Northeast outspend the average by 40 percent.

Average household spending on gifts of women's and girls' apparel for people in other households fell by nearly one-third between 2000 and 2010, after adjusting for inflation. Price discounting is one factor behind the decline, as is the substitution of electronics for apparel as gifts. Average household spending on gifts of women's and girls' apparel may continue to decline in the years ahead as this trend continues.

Table 8.14 Gifts of women's and girls' apparel

Total household spending $8,875,932,030.00
Average household spends   73.29

	AVERAGE HOUSEHOLD SPENDING	BEST CUSTOMERS (index)	BIGGEST CUSTOMERS (market share)
AGE OF HOUSEHOLDER			
Average household	**$73.29**	**100**	**100.0%**
Under age 25	39.56	54	3.6
Aged 25 to 34	37.38	51	8.5
Aged 35 to 44	51.16	70	12.6
Aged 45 to 54	83.25	114	23.5
Aged 55 to 64	107.89	147	26.0
Aged 65 to 74	89.38	122	13.1
Aged 75 or older	96.55	132	12.6

	AVERAGE HOUSEHOLD SPENDING	BEST CUSTOMERS (index)	BIGGEST CUSTOMERS (market share)
HOUSEHOLD INCOME			
Average household	**$73.29**	**100**	**100.0%**
Under $20,000	30.88	42	9.2
$20,000 to $39,999	81.10	111	25.4
$40,000 to $49,999	76.33	104	9.8
$50,000 to $69,999	63.76	87	12.5
$70,000 to $79,999	91.63	125	7.5
$80,000 to $99,999	85.31	116	9.7
$100,000 or more	108.36	148	25.4
HOUSEHOLD TYPE			
Average household	**73.29**	**100**	**100.0**
Married couples	86.54	118	58.2
Married couples, no children	124.95	170	36.2
Married couples, with children	53.26	73	16.9
Oldest child under age 6	64.59	88	3.8
Oldest child aged 6 to 17	44.51	61	7.1
Oldest child aged 18 or older	60.83	83	6.0
Single parent with child under age 18	88.81	121	7.1
Single person	57.91	79	23.1
RACE AND HISPANIC ORIGIN			
Average household	**73.29**	**100**	**100.0**
Asian	61.44	84	3.6
Black	48.95	67	8.2
Hispanic	49.45	67	8.2
Non-Hispanic white and other	80.79	110	83.6
REGION			
Average household	**73.29**	**100**	**100.0**
Northeast	102.79	140	25.7
Midwest	75.83	103	23.1
South	61.58	84	30.8
West	65.85	90	20.4
EDUCATION			
Average household	**73.29**	**100**	**100.0**
Less than high school graduate	39.42	54	7.7
High school graduate	53.97	74	18.8
Some college	69.54	95	19.9
Associate's degree	95.22	130	12.3
Bachelor's degree or more	100.64	137	40.8
Bachelor's degree	108.91	149	28.1
Master's, professional, doctoral degree	84.40	115	12.5

Note: Market shares may not sum to 100.0 because of rounding and missing categories by household type. "Asian" and "black" include Hispanics and non-Hispanics who identify themselves as being of the respective race alone. "Hispanic" includes people of any race who identify themselves as Hispanic. "Other" includes people who identify themselves as non-Hispanic and as Alaska Native, American Indian, Asian (who are also included in the "Asian" row), or Native Hawaiian or other Pacific Islander as well as non-Hispanics reporting more than one race.

Source: Calculations by New Strategist based on the Bureau of Labor Statistics' 2010 Consumer Expenditure Survey

Chapter 9.

Groceries

Household Spending on Groceries, 2010

Not surprisingly, groceries are one of the largest household expenses. In 2010, the average household spent $3,624 on groceries (or what the Consumer Expenditure Survey calls "food at home"). Average household spending on groceries fell 3 percent between 2000 and 2006 (the year household spending peaked, see Appendix D) because people were devoting more money to eating out. Grocery spending fell another 2 percent between 2006 and 2010 as shoppers substituted private labels for branded products and bought less-expensive items in an attempt to cut costs because of the Great Recession.

Although many Americans cannot afford to eat out as frequently as they once did, they still want the convenience of prepared food. That explains why the grocery category "prepared foods (except salads, desserts, and frozen meals)," which did not crack the top-10 grocery spending categories in 2000, trailed only fresh fruit and fresh vegetables as the grocery category on which households spent the most in 2010. The average household devoted $147 to prepared foods in 2010, up 57 percent from the inflation-adjusted $94 in 2000. After fruit, vegetables, and prepared food households spend the most on sodas, fresh milk, cheese, chicken, and potato chips and other snacks. They devoted $121 to fresh milk in 2010, 20 percent less than the inflation-adjusted $151 in 2000. Average household spending on carbonated beverages fell 22 percent during that time, but spending on cheese saw a smaller 5 percent decrease.

Average household spending on groceries is determined by household size, larger households spending more than smaller ones on most items. Average household spending on groceries may decline in the years ahead as boomers become empty-nesters and household size drifts downward. But household demographic characteristics and nutritional claims will continue to affect spending patterns—patterns that will determine the future success of grocery retailers and food manufacturers.

Spending on groceries

(average annual spending of households on groceries, 2000, 2006, and 2010; in 2010 dollars)

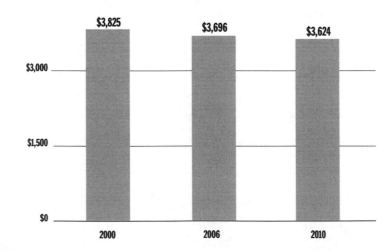

Table 9.1 Spending on groceries, 2000 to 2010

(average annual and percent distribution of household spending on groceries by category, 2000 to 2010; percent change in spending and percentage point change in distribution, 2000–06, 2006–10, and 2000–10; in 2010 dollars; ranked by amount spent)

	2010 average household spending	2006 average household spending (in 2010$)	2000 average household spending (in 2010$)	percent change		
				2006–10	2000–06	2000–10
AVERAGE ANNUAL SPENDING						
Average household spending on groceries	**$3,624.04**	**$3,695.77**	**$3,825.48**	**–1.9%**	**–3.4%**	**–5.3%**
Fruit, fresh (apples, bananas, and citrus also shown separately)	232.24	211.39	206.62	9.9	2.3	12.4
Vegetables, fresh (lettuce, potatoes, and tomatoes also shown separately)	210.47	209.04	200.99	0.7	4.0	4.7
Prepared food (except salads, desserts, and frozen meals)	146.76	143.51	93.59	2.3	53.3	56.8
Carbonated drinks	132.65	145.53	170.16	–8.9	–14.5	–22.1
Milk, fresh	121.03	134.63	151.46	–10.1	–11.1	–20.1
Cheese	115.43	119.79	121.51	–3.6	–1.4	–5.0
Chicken, fresh and frozen	110.25	121.26	144.90	–9.1	–16.3	–23.9
Potato chips and other snacks	99.32	102.99	90.76	–3.6	13.5	9.4
Ground beef	84.67	97.56	111.13	–13.2	–12.2	–23.8
Cereal, ready-to-eat and cooked	82.83	91.65	110.02	–9.6	–16.7	–24.7
Steak	82.27	91.62	119.69	–10.2	–23.4	–31.3
Lunch meats (cold cuts)	81.80	81.79	86.01	0.0	–5.0	–5.0
Candy and chewing gum	77.34	85.59	96.62	–9.6	–11.4	–20.0
Prepared food, frozen (except meals)	71.17	73.05	78.13	–2.6	–6.5	–8.9
Prepared meals, frozen	60.95	74.68	36.09	–18.4	106.9	68.9
Coffee	60.25	53.96	52.99	11.7	1.8	13.7
Bread, other than white	59.72	58.66	60.05	1.8	–2.3	–0.5
Fish and shellfish, fresh	55.25	67.42	84.61	–18.1	–20.3	–34.7
Ice cream and related products	54.26	66.65	71.62	–18.6	–6.9	–24.2
Vegetables, canned	52.51	41.53	47.38	26.4	–12.3	10.8
Sauces and gravies	52.44	52.19	47.14	0.5	10.7	11.2
Water, bottled	52.04	59.74	–	–12.9	–	–
Fruit juice, canned and bottled	51.97	59.80	71.18	–13.1	–16.0	–27.0
Biscuits and rolls	48.84	45.26	48.79	7.9	–7.2	0.1
Dairy products (except butter, cheese, eggs, ice cream, and milk)	46.80	40.63	30.25	15.2	34.3	54.7
Eggs	46.29	39.66	43.64	16.7	–9.1	6.1
Cookies	45.90	48.00	60.41	–4.4	–20.5	–24.0
Soup, canned and packaged	42.30	45.62	45.00	–7.3	1.4	–6.0
Fish and shellfish, frozen	41.67	46.35	35.01	–10.1	32.4	19.0
Bananas	40.88	31.16	40.14	31.2	–22.4	1.8
Bread, white	39.83	34.36	46.37	15.9	–25.9	–14.1
Tomatoes, fresh	39.28	39.65	37.39	–0.9	6.0	5.0
Apples	37.30	36.70	37.34	1.6	–1.7	–0.1
Crackers	36.26	34.43	29.53	5.3	16.6	22.8
Vegetables, frozen	36.16	33.03	33.46	9.5	–1.3	8.1
Potatoes, fresh	36.11	33.81	35.54	6.8	–4.9	1.6
Pork (except bacon, frankfurters, ham, chops, and sausage)	35.60	42.38	49.16	–16.0	–13.8	–27.6
Salads, prepared	35.43	34.95	23.49	1.4	48.8	50.8
Cakes and cupcakes	35.30	37.88	48.65	–6.8	–22.1	–27.4
Pasta, cornmeal, and other cereal products	33.92	26.21	36.27	29.4	–27.7	–6.5

	2010 average household spending	2006 average household spending (in 2010$)	2000 average household spending (in 2010$)	percent change		
				2006–10	2000–06	2000–10
Nuts	$33.65	$35.13	$26.38	–4.2%	33.2%	27.6%
Salt, spices, and other seasonings	32.49	27.41	26.15	18.5	4.8	24.2
Baby food	32.48	36.40	40.85	–10.8	–10.9	–20.5
Ham	31.88	36.80	45.92	–13.4	–19.9	–30.6
Bacon	31.61	29.58	32.99	6.9	–10.3	–4.2
Fats and oils	31.49	30.67	29.57	2.7	3.7	6.5
Citrus fruit, fresh (other than oranges)	31.42	18.24	18.12	72.3	0.6	73.4
Lettuce	30.07	27.41	26.28	9.7	4.3	14.4
Roast beef	29.47	43.30	50.45	–31.9	–14.2	–41.6
Tea	29.20	28.46	19.86	2.6	43.3	47.1
Salad dressings	28.77	28.26	34.42	1.8	–17.9	–16.4
Poultry (except chicken)	27.86	30.72	38.91	–9.3	–21.1	–28.4
Jams, preserves, other sweets	26.49	24.92	25.15	6.3	–0.9	5.3
Baking needs and miscellaneous products	26.18	24.83	21.48	5.4	15.6	21.9
Sausage	26.13	27.90	31.96	–6.3	–12.7	–18.2
Bakery products, frozen and refrigerated	25.19	27.69	31.06	–9.0	–10.9	–18.9
Oranges	24.72	24.06	23.97	2.8	0.4	3.1
Rice	24.72	18.94	24.76	30.5	–23.5	–0.1
Frankfurters	24.51	21.84	26.19	12.2	–16.6	–6.4
Fruit-flavored drinks, noncarbonated	24.25	19.20	24.59	26.3	–21.9	–1.4
Pork chops	23.77	33.41	51.37	–28.9	–35.0	–53.7
Butter	23.03	19.82	21.53	16.2	–8.0	7.0
Sugar	22.76	17.89	21.27	27.2	–15.9	7.0
Sweetrolls, coffee cakes, and doughnuts	22.28	22.51	28.72	–1.0	–21.6	–22.4
Fruit, canned	20.53	19.92	19.60	3.0	1.6	4.7
Beef other than ground, roast, steak	20.28	23.04	20.36	–12.0	13.1	–0.4
Fish and seafood, canned	20.16	17.84	19.84	13.0	–10.1	1.6
Cream	19.88	16.99	14.70	17.0	15.6	35.2
Fruit juice, fresh	19.16	18.85	29.68	1.6	–36.5	–35.4
Sports drinks	19.11	–	–	–	–	–
Vegetables, dried	18.25	12.75	13.30	43.1	–4.1	37.3
Nondairy cream and imitation milk	16.96	13.84	11.59	22.5	19.5	46.4
Desserts, prepared	16.53	13.00	11.79	27.1	10.3	40.2
Pies, tarts, and turnovers	16.30	15.07	16.82	8.2	–10.4	–3.1
Peanut butter	15.46	12.17	14.95	27.1	–18.6	3.4
Flour, prepared mixes	15.25	12.20	16.91	25.0	–27.8	–9.8
Vegetable juice, fresh and canned	15.14	13.13	11.78	15.3	11.5	28.6
Other noncarbonated beverages and ice	15.12	–	–	–	–	–
Olives, pickles, and relishes	14.86	13.82	12.37	7.5	11.7	20.1
Lamb, organ meats, and other meat	10.88	9.82	15.03	10.8	–34.7	–27.6
Margarine	9.92	7.90	14.70	25.6	–46.3	–32.5
Fruit, dried	8.20	9.69	6.96	–15.4	39.2	17.7
Flour	7.89	5.35	10.11	47.4	–47.0	–21.9
Bread and cracker products	7.48	4.71	5.58	59.0	–15.7	33.9
Fruit, frozen	6.78	4.40	4.58	54.0	–4.0	47.9
Fruit juice, frozen	6.11	5.46	13.60	11.9	–59.8	–55.1
Artificial sweeteners	5.40	6.27	5.31	–13.9	18.2	1.8

	2006–10	2000–06	2000–10	percentage point change		
				2006–10	2000–06	2000–10
PERCENT DISTRIBUTION OF SPENDING						
Average household spending on groceries	100.0%	100.0%	100.0%	–	–	–
Fruit, fresh (apples, bananas, and citrus also shown separately)	6.4	5.7	5.4	0.7	0.3	1.0
Vegetables, fresh (potatoes, tomatoes, and lettuce also shown separately)	5.8	5.7	5.3	0.2	0.4	0.6
Prepared food (except salads, desserts, and frozen meals)	4.1	3.9	2.4	0.2	1.4	1.6
Carbonated drinks	3.7	3.9	4.4	–0.3	–0.5	–0.8
Milk, fresh	3.3	3.6	4.0	–0.3	–0.3	–0.6
Cheese	3.2	3.2	3.2	–0.1	0.1	0.0
Chicken, fresh and frozen	3.0	3.3	3.8	–0.2	–0.5	–0.7
Potato chips and other snacks	2.7	2.8	2.4	–0.1	0.4	0.4
Ground beef	2.3	2.6	2.9	–0.3	–0.3	–0.6
Cereal, ready-to-eat and cooked	2.3	2.5	2.9	–0.2	–0.4	–0.6
Steak	2.3	2.5	3.1	–0.2	–0.6	–0.9
Lunch meats (cold cuts)	2.3	2.2	2.3	0.0	–0.0	0.0
Candy and chewing gum	2.1	2.3	2.5	–0.2	–0.2	–0.4
Prepared food, frozen (except meals)	2.0	2.0	2.0	–0.0	–0.1	–0.1
Prepared meals, frozen	1.7	2.0	0.9	–0.3	1.1	0.7
Coffee	1.7	1.5	1.4	0.2	0.1	0.3
Bread, other than white	1.6	1.6	1.6	0.1	0.0	0.1
Fish and shellfish, fresh	1.5	1.8	2.2	–0.3	–0.4	–0.7
Ice cream and related products	1.5	1.8	1.9	–0.3	–0.1	–0.4
Vegetables, canned	1.4	1.1	1.2	0.3	–0.1	0.2
Sauces and gravies	1.4	1.4	1.2	0.0	0.2	0.2
Water, bottled	1.4	1.6	–	–	–	–
Fruit juice, canned and bottled	1.4	1.6	1.9	–0.2	–0.2	–0.4
Biscuits and rolls	1.3	1.2	1.3	0.1	–0.1	0.1
Dairy products (except butter, cheese, eggs, ice cream, and milk)	1.3	1.1	0.8	0.2	0.3	0.5
Eggs	1.3	1.1	1.1	0.2	–0.1	0.1
Cookies	1.3	1.3	1.6	–0.0	–0.3	–0.3
Soup, canned and packaged	1.2	1.2	1.2	–0.1	0.1	–0.0
Fish and shellfish, frozen	1.1	1.3	0.9	–0.1	0.3	0.2
Bananas	1.1	0.8	1.1	0.3	–0.2	0.1
Bread, white	1.1	0.9	1.2	0.2	–0.3	–0.1
Tomatoes, fresh	1.1	1.1	1.0	0.0	0.1	0.1
Apples	1.0	1.0	1.0	0.0	0.0	0.1
Crackers	1.0	0.9	0.8	0.1	0.2	0.2
Vegetables, frozen	1.0	0.9	0.9	0.1	0.0	0.1
Potatoes, fresh	1.0	0.9	0.9	0.1	–0.0	0.1
Pork (except bacon, frankfurters, ham, chops, and sausage)	1.0	1.1	1.3	–0.2	–0.1	–0.3
Salads, prepared	1.0	0.9	0.6	0.0	0.3	0.4
Cakes and cupcakes	1.0	1.0	1.3	–0.1	–0.2	–0.3
Pasta, cornmeal, and other cereal products	0.9	0.7	0.9	0.2	–0.2	–0.0
Nuts	0.9	1.0	0.7	–0.0	0.3	0.2
Salt, spices, and other seasonings	0.9	0.7	0.7	0.2	0.1	0.2

	2006–10	2000–06	2000–10	percentage point change 2006–10	2000–06	2000–10
Baby food	0.9%	1.0%	1.1%	–0.1	–0.1	–0.2
Ham	0.9	1.0	1.2	–0.1	–0.2	–0.3
Bacon	0.9	0.8	0.9	0.1	–0.1	0.0
Fats and oils	0.9	0.8	0.8	0.0	0.1	0.1
Citrus fruit, fresh (other than oranges)	0.9	0.5	0.5	0.4	0.0	0.4
Lettuce	0.8	0.7	0.7	0.1	0.1	0.1
Roast beef	0.8	1.2	1.3	–0.4	–0.1	–0.5
Tea	0.8	0.8	0.5	0.0	0.3	0.3
Salad dressings	0.8	0.8	0.9	0.0	–0.1	–0.1
Poultry (except chicken)	0.8	0.8	1.0	–0.1	–0.2	–0.2
Jams, preserves, other sweets	0.7	0.7	0.7	0.1	0.0	0.1
Baking needs and miscellaneous products	0.7	0.7	0.6	0.1	0.1	0.2
Sausage	0.7	0.8	0.8	–0.0	–0.1	–0.1
Bakery products, frozen and refrigerated	0.7	0.7	0.8	–0.1	–0.1	–0.1
Oranges	0.7	0.7	0.6	0.0	0.0	0.1
Rice	0.7	0.5	0.6	0.2	–0.1	0.0
Frankfurters	0.7	0.6	0.7	0.1	–0.1	–0.0
Fruit-flavored drinks, noncarbonated	0.7	0.5	0.6	0.1	–0.1	0.0
Pork chops	0.7	0.9	1.3	–0.2	–0.4	–0.7
Butter	0.6	0.5	0.6	0.1	–0.0	0.1
Sugar	0.6	0.5	0.6	0.1	–0.1	0.1
Sweetrolls, coffee cakes, and doughnuts	0.6	0.6	0.8	0.0	–0.1	–0.1
Fruit, canned	0.6	0.5	0.5	0.0	0.0	0.1
Beef other than ground, roast, steak	0.6	0.6	0.5	–0.1	0.1	0.0
Fish and seafood, canned	0.6	0.5	0.5	0.1	–0.0	0.0
Cream	0.5	0.5	0.4	0.1	0.1	0.2
Fruit juice, fresh	0.5	0.5	0.8	0.0	–0.3	–0.2
Sports drinks	0.5	–	–	–	–	–
Vegetables, dried	0.5	0.3	0.3	0.2	–0.0	0.2
Nondairy cream and imitation milk	0.5	0.4	0.3	0.1	0.1	0.2
Desserts, prepared	0.5	0.4	0.3	0.1	0.0	0.1
Pies, tarts, and turnovers	0.4	0.4	0.4	0.0	–0.0	0.0
Peanut butter	0.4	0.3	0.4	0.1	–0.1	0.0
Flour, prepared mixes	0.4	0.3	0.4	0.1	–0.1	–0.0
Vegetable juice, fresh and canned	0.4	0.4	0.3	0.1	0.1	0.1
Other noncarbonated beverages and ice	0.4	–	–	–	–	–
Olives, pickles, and relishes	0.4	0.4	0.3	0.0	0.1	0.1
Lamb, organ meats, and other meat	0.3	0.3	0.4	0.0	–0.1	–0.1
Margarine	0.3	0.2	0.4	0.1	–0.2	–0.1
Fruit, dried	0.2	0.3	0.2	–0.0	0.1	0.0
Flour	0.2	0.1	0.3	0.1	–0.1	–0.1
Bread and cracker products	0.2	0.1	0.1	0.1	–0.0	0.1
Fruit, frozen	0.2	0.1	0.1	0.1	–0.0	0.1
Fruit juice, frozen	0.2	0.1	0.4	0.0	–0.2	–0.2
Artificial sweeteners	0.1	0.2	0.1	–0.0	0.0	0.0

Note: Numbers do not add to total because apples, bananas, and citrus fruit are shown separately and are included in the fresh fruit total; lettuce, potatoes, and tomatoes are shown separately and are included in the fresh vegetable total; and not all categories are shown. "–" means not applicable or data are unavailable.

Source: Bureau of Labor Statistics, 2000, 2006, and 2010 Consumer Expenditure Surveys; calculations by New Strategist

Apples

Best customers: **Householders aged 35 to 54**
Married couples with children at home

Customer trends: **Average household spending on apples may fall as more boomers become empty-nesters and household size shrinks.**

The largest households spend the most on apples. Married couples with children at home spend 56 percent more than the average household on apples. Householders aged 35 to 54, most with children at home, spend 17 to 23 percent more than average on apples and control 46 percent of the market.

Average household spending on apples remained steady over the course of the decade, after adjusting for inflation. Behind the stability is the greater availability of conveniently packaged sliced apples, boosting household purchasing despite the baby-boom generation's exit from the best-customer lifestage. Average household spending on apples may fall as more boomers become empty-nesters and household size shrinks.

Table 9.2 Apples

Total household spending $4,517,291,100.00
Average household spends   37.30

	AVERAGE HOUSEHOLD SPENDING	BEST CUSTOMERS (index)	BIGGEST CUSTOMERS (market share)
AGE OF HOUSEHOLDER			
Average household	**$37.30**	**100**	**100.0%**
Under age 25	22.14	59	3.9
Aged 25 to 34	35.88	96	16.0
Aged 35 to 44	45.86	123	22.2
Aged 45 to 54	43.55	117	24.2
Aged 55 to 64	37.72	101	17.8
Aged 65 to 74	32.13	86	9.3
Aged 75 or older	25.54	68	6.5

	AVERAGE HOUSEHOLD SPENDING	BEST CUSTOMERS (index)	BIGGEST CUSTOMERS (market share)
HOUSEHOLD INCOME			
Average household	**$37.30**	**100**	**100.0%**
Under $20,000	21.74	58	12.7
$20,000 to $39,999	28.32	76	17.4
$40,000 to $49,999	28.09	75	7.1
$50,000 to $69,999	36.73	98	14.1
$70,000 to $79,999	39.42	106	6.3
$80,000 to $99,999	49.70	133	11.1
$100,000 or more	69.06	185	31.7
HOUSEHOLD TYPE			
Average household	**37.30**	**100**	**100.0**
Married couples	49.54	133	65.5
Married couples, no children	39.84	107	22.7
Married couples, with children	58.09	156	36.2
Oldest child under age 6	52.31	140	6.0
Oldest child aged 6 to 17	59.82	160	18.9
Oldest child aged 18 or older	58.47	157	11.3
Single parent with child under age 18	31.51	84	5.0
Single person	20.16	54	15.8
RACE AND HISPANIC ORIGIN			
Average household	**37.30**	**100**	**100.0**
Asian	41.24	111	4.7
Black	23.85	64	7.8
Hispanic	42.42	114	13.9
Non-Hispanic white and other	38.60	103	78.5
REGION			
Average household	**37.30**	**100**	**100.0**
Northeast	40.71	109	20.0
Midwest	38.24	103	22.9
South	30.97	83	30.5
West	44.00	118	26.7
EDUCATION			
Average household	**37.30**	**100**	**100.0**
Less than high school graduate	32.41	87	12.4
High school graduate	29.27	78	20.0
Some college	30.75	82	17.3
Associate's degree	39.68	106	10.1
Bachelor's degree or more	50.49	135	40.2
Bachelor's degree	46.67	125	23.6
Master's, professional, doctoral degree	58.01	156	16.8

Note: Market shares may not sum to 100.0 because of rounding and missing categories by household type. "Asian" and "black" include Hispanics and non-Hispanics who identify themselves as being of the respective race alone. "Hispanic" includes people of any race who identify themselves as Hispanic. "Other" includes people who identify themselves as non-Hispanic and as Alaska Native, American Indian, Asian (who are also included in the "Asian" row), or Native Hawaiian or other Pacific Islander as well as non-Hispanics reporting more than one race.

Source: Calculations by New Strategist based on the Bureau of Labor Statistics' 2010 Consumer Expenditure Survey

Artificial Sweeteners

Best customers: Householders aged 65 to 74
Married couples without children at home
Married couples with school-aged children
Households in the South

Customer trends: Average household spending on artificial sweetener may rise as boomers fill the
65-to-74 age group.

Older householders spend the most on artificial sweeteners. Householders aged 65 to 74 spend 87 percent more on artificial sweeteners than the average household. Married couples without children at home (most of them empty-nesters) spend one-half more than the average household on this item, while married couples with school-aged children spend 31 percent more than average on artificial sweeteners.

Average household spending on artificial sweeteners increased 18 percent between 2000 and 2006, after adjusting for inflation, but fell 14 percent over the remainder of the decade. One factor behind the increase was the growing popularity of Splenda as a substitute for sugar. Spending on artificial sweeteners is likely to rise again as boomers fill the 65-to-74 age group and increasingly overweight Americans try to cut calories.

Table 9.3 Artificial sweeteners

Total household spending		$653,977,800.00	
Average household spends		5.40	
	AVERAGE HOUSEHOLD SPENDING	BEST CUSTOMERS (index)	BIGGEST CUSTOMERS (market share)
AGE OF HOUSEHOLDER			
Average household	**$5.40**	**100**	**100.0%**
Under age 25	1.73	32	2.1
Aged 25 to 34	3.41	63	10.5
Aged 35 to 44	4.64	86	15.5
Aged 45 to 54	6.05	112	23.2
Aged 55 to 64	5.78	107	18.9
Aged 65 to 74	10.12	187	20.2
Aged 75 or older	5.31	98	9.4

	AVERAGE HOUSEHOLD SPENDING	BEST CUSTOMERS (index)	BIGGEST CUSTOMERS (market share)
HOUSEHOLD INCOME			
Average household	**$5.40**	**100**	**100.0%**
Under $20,000	4.60	85	18.6
$20,000 to $39,999	5.47	101	23.2
$40,000 to $49,999	5.53	102	9.7
$50,000 to $69,999	5.65	105	15.0
$70,000 to $79,999	3.67	68	4.1
$80,000 to $99,999	6.74	125	10.4
$100,000 or more	5.69	105	18.1
HOUSEHOLD TYPE			
Average household	**5.40**	**100**	**100.0**
Married couples	6.74	125	61.6
Married couples, no children	8.05	149	31.7
Married couples, with children	5.55	103	23.9
Oldest child under age 6	3.73	69	3.0
Oldest child aged 6 to 17	7.08	131	15.4
Oldest child aged 18 or older	4.20	78	5.6
Single parent with child under age 18	3.40	63	3.7
Single person	3.33	62	18.1
RACE AND HISPANIC ORIGIN			
Average household	**5.40**	**100**	**100.0**
Asian	3.14	58	2.5
Black	2.54	47	5.8
Hispanic	4.67	86	10.5
Non-Hispanic white and other	5.96	110	83.7
REGION			
Average household	**5.40**	**100**	**100.0**
Northeast	3.45	64	11.7
Midwest	4.14	77	17.1
South	6.96	129	47.3
West	5.71	106	24.0
EDUCATION			
Average household	**5.40**	**100**	**100.0**
Less than high school graduate	5.76	107	15.2
High school graduate	5.56	103	26.3
Some college	5.79	107	22.5
Associate's degree	6.69	124	11.7
Bachelor's degree or more	4.38	81	24.1
Bachelor's degree	4.07	75	14.2
Master's, professional, doctoral degree	5.00	93	10.0

Note: Market shares may not sum to 100.0 because of rounding and missing categories by household type. "Asian" and "black" include Hispanics and non-Hispanics who identify themselves as being of the respective race alone. "Hispanic" includes people of any race who identify themselves as Hispanic. "Other" includes people who identify themselves as non-Hispanic and as Alaska Native, American Indian, Asian (who are also included in the "Asian" row), or Native Hawaiian or other Pacific Islander as well as non-Hispanics reporting more than one race.

Source: Calculations by New Strategist based on the Bureau of Labor Statistics' 2010 Consumer Expenditure Survey

Baby Food

Best customers: **Householders under age 35**
                                 Married couples with children under age 18
                                 Single parents
                                 Hispanics and Asians

Customer trends: **Average household spending on baby food should stabilize now that the large millennial generation is in the family formation lifestage.**

Not surprisingly, married couples with preschoolers spend much more on baby food than any other household type, more than eight times the average. Householders aged 25 to 34, many with infants, spend almost three times the average on baby food, while those under age 25 spend 60 percent more than average on baby food. Single parents, whose spending on most items is below average, spend 47 percent more than average on this item. Hispanics spend nearly twice the average and Asians spend 41 percent more than the average household on baby food.

Average household spending on baby food is on a decade-long decline. It fell 20 percent between 2000 and 2010, after adjusting for inflation. Behind the decline is price discounting, belt tightening during the economic downturn, and the drop in births. Now that the large millennial generation has filled the family formation lifestage, average household spending on baby food should stabilize, but low incomes may limit the increase.

Table 9.4 **Baby food**

Total household spending $3,933,555,360.00
Average household spends   32.48

	AVERAGE HOUSEHOLD SPENDING	BEST CUSTOMERS (index)	BIGGEST CUSTOMERS (market share)
AGE OF HOUSEHOLDER			
Average household	**$32.48**	**100**	**100.0%**
Under age 25	51.86	160	10.6
Aged 25 to 34	90.83	280	46.6
Aged 35 to 44	39.21	121	21.8
Aged 45 to 54	19.63	60	12.5
Aged 55 to 64	10.16	31	5.5
Aged 65 to 74	7.14	22	2.4
Aged 75 or older	3.29	10	1.0

	AVERAGE HOUSEHOLD SPENDING	BEST CUSTOMERS (index)	BIGGEST CUSTOMERS (market share)
HOUSEHOLD INCOME			
Average household	**$32.48**	**100**	**100.0%**
Under $20,000	22.86	70	15.4
$20,000 to $39,999	25.31	78	17.9
$40,000 to $49,999	42.37	130	12.3
$50,000 to $69,999	43.56	134	19.2
$70,000 to $79,999	15.06	46	2.8
$80,000 to $99,999	37.38	115	9.6
$100,000 or more	41.56	128	21.9
HOUSEHOLD TYPE			
Average household	**32.48**	**100**	**100.0**
Married couples	47.78	147	72.6
Married couples, no children	11.47	35	7.5
Married couples, with children	76.25	235	54.6
Oldest child under age 6	274.08	844	36.1
Oldest child aged 6 to 17	48.97	151	17.7
Oldest child aged 18 or older	15.66	48	3.5
Single parent with child under age 18	47.65	147	8.7
Single person	3.84	12	3.5
RACE AND HISPANIC ORIGIN			
Average household	**32.48**	**100**	**100.0**
Asian	45.92	141	6.0
Black	30.08	93	11.3
Hispanic	63.42	195	23.8
Non-Hispanic white and other	28.23	87	65.9
REGION			
Average household	**32.48**	**100**	**100.0**
Northeast	31.04	96	17.5
Midwest	39.31	121	27.0
South	32.54	100	36.8
West	26.65	82	18.6
EDUCATION			
Average household	**32.48**	**100**	**100.0**
Less than high school graduate	33.99	105	15.0
High school graduate	27.89	86	21.9
Some college	16.38	50	10.6
Associate's degree	53.78	166	15.6
Bachelor's degree or more	40.43	124	37.0
Bachelor's degree	38.93	120	22.6
Master's, professional, doctoral degree	43.38	134	14.5

Note: Market shares may not sum to 100.0 because of rounding and missing categories by household type. "Asian" and "black" include Hispanics and non-Hispanics who identify themselves as being of the respective race alone. "Hispanic" includes people of any race who identify themselves as Hispanic. "Other" includes people who identify themselves as non-Hispanic and as Alaska Native, American Indian, Asian (who are also included in the "Asian" row), or Native Hawaiian or other Pacific Islander as well as non-Hispanics reporting more than one race.

Source: Calculations by New Strategist based on the Bureau of Labor Statistics' 2010 Consumer Expenditure Survey

Bacon

Best customers: **Householders aged 45 to 54**
Married couples with school-aged or older children at home
Hispanics

Customer trends: **Average household spending on bacon may fall as more boomers become empty-nesters and household size shrinks.**

Married couples with children spend the most on bacon. Married couples with school-aged children spend 39 percent more than average on bacon, while those with adult children at home spend 43 percent more. Householders aged 45 to 54, most with children, outspend the average for bacon by 19 percent. Hispanics spend 10 percent more than average on bacon.

Average household spending on bacon has been on a topsy-turvy ride this decade. It declined by 10 percent between 2000 and 2006, after adjusting for inflation, but has rebounded to almost its earlier level since then. One factor behind the earlier spending decline was the growing propensity for households to eat fast-food breakfasts or no breakfast at all. Efforts to reduce fast-food spending may be responsible for the rise since 2006. Average household spending on bacon may fall in the years ahead as more boomers become empty-nesters and household size shrinks.

Table 9.5 Bacon

| Total household spending | $3,828,192,270.00 |
| Average household spends | 31.61 |

	AVERAGE HOUSEHOLD SPENDING	BEST CUSTOMERS (index)	BIGGEST CUSTOMERS (market share)
AGE OF HOUSEHOLDER			
Average household	**$31.61**	**100**	**100.0%**
Under age 25	17.87	57	3.8
Aged 25 to 34	27.49	87	14.5
Aged 35 to 44	32.71	103	18.7
Aged 45 to 54	37.64	119	24.6
Aged 55 to 64	33.76	107	18.8
Aged 65 to 74	35.03	111	11.9
Aged 75 or older	24.95	79	7.5

	AVERAGE HOUSEHOLD SPENDING	BEST CUSTOMERS (index)	BIGGEST CUSTOMERS (market share)
HOUSEHOLD INCOME			
Average household	$31.61	100	100.0%
Under $20,000	23.76	75	16.4
$20,000 to $39,999	27.52	87	20.0
$40,000 to $49,999	31.18	99	9.3
$50,000 to $69,999	34.16	108	15.5
$70,000 to $79,999	35.59	113	6.7
$80,000 to $99,999	34.44	109	9.1
$100,000 or more	42.29	134	22.9
HOUSEHOLD TYPE			
Average household	31.61	100	100.0
Married couples	39.06	124	61.0
Married couples, no children	34.85	110	23.4
Married couples, with children	41.67	132	30.7
Oldest child under age 6	27.78	88	3.8
Oldest child aged 6 to 17	43.97	139	16.4
Oldest child aged 18 or older	45.33	143	10.4
Single parent with child under age 18	28.60	90	5.3
Single person	16.94	54	15.7
RACE AND HISPANIC ORIGIN			
Average household	31.61	100	100.0
Asian	23.58	75	3.2
Black	32.69	103	12.7
Hispanic	34.90	110	13.5
Non-Hispanic white and other	30.85	98	74.0
REGION			
Average household	31.61	100	100.0
Northeast	28.75	91	16.7
Midwest	31.76	100	22.4
South	31.52	100	36.6
West	33.94	107	24.3
EDUCATION			
Average household	31.61	100	100.0
Less than high school graduate	37.99	120	17.2
High school graduate	31.91	101	25.8
Some college	28.28	89	18.8
Associate's degree	34.48	109	10.3
Bachelor's degree or more	29.98	95	28.2
Bachelor's degree	30.65	97	18.3
Master's, professional, doctoral degree	28.66	91	9.8

Note: Market shares may not sum to 100.0 because of rounding and missing categories by household type. "Asian" and "black" include Hispanics and non-Hispanics who identify themselves as being of the respective race alone. "Hispanic" includes people of any race who identify themselves as Hispanic. "Other" includes people who identify themselves as non-Hispanic and as Alaska Native, American Indian, Asian (who are also included in the "Asian" row), or Native Hawaiian or other Pacific Islander as well as non-Hispanics reporting more than one race.

Source: Calculations by New Strategist based on the Bureau of Labor Statistics' 2010 Consumer Expenditure Survey

Bakery Products, Frozen and Refrigerated

Best customers: **Householders aged 35 to 54**
Married couples with school-aged or older children at home
Single parents

Customer trends: **Average household spending on frozen and refrigerated bakery products should
continue to fall as the small generation X fills the best-customer age group.**

Households with children spend the most on frozen and refrigerated bakery products. Married couples with school-aged children spend 78 percent more than the average household on this item, while those with adult children at home spend 44 percent more than average. Many are busy two-earner couples trying to save time by buying heat-and-serve foods. Householders aged 35 to 54, most with children at home, spend 23 to 31 percent more than average on frozen and refrigerated bakery products. Single parents, whose spending on most items is below average, spend 27 percent more than average on this item.

Average household spending on frozen and refrigerated bakery products fell 19 percent between 2000 and 2010, after adjusting for inflation. Behind the decline was the ongoing shift away from meal preparation and toward fast-food meals and snacking. Average household spending on frozen and refrigerated bakery products may continue to decline as the small generation X fills the best-customer age group.

Table 9.6 Bakery products, frozen and refrigerated

| Total household spending | $3,050,685,330.00 |
| Average household spends | 25.19 |

	AVERAGE HOUSEHOLD SPENDING	BEST CUSTOMERS (index)	BIGGEST CUSTOMERS (market share)
AGE OF HOUSEHOLDER			
Average household	**$25.19**	**100**	**100.0%**
Under age 25	13.65	54	3.6
Aged 25 to 34	24.52	97	16.2
Aged 35 to 44	30.90	123	22.2
Aged 45 to 54	32.89	131	27.0
Aged 55 to 64	21.86	87	15.3
Aged 65 to 74	21.63	86	9.2
Aged 75 or older	16.84	67	6.4

	AVERAGE HOUSEHOLD SPENDING	BEST CUSTOMERS (index)	BIGGEST CUSTOMERS (market share)
HOUSEHOLD INCOME			
Average household	$25.19	100	100.0%
Under $20,000	13.53	54	11.7
$20,000 to $39,999	19.61	78	17.8
$40,000 to $49,999	22.87	91	8.6
$50,000 to $69,999	24.25	96	13.8
$70,000 to $79,999	27.15	108	6.5
$80,000 to $99,999	32.29	128	10.7
$100,000 or more	46.16	183	31.4
HOUSEHOLD TYPE			
Average household	25.19	100	100.0
Married couples	32.95	131	64.5
Married couples, no children	26.14	104	22.0
Married couples, with children	38.98	155	36.0
Oldest child under age 6	27.55	109	4.7
Oldest child aged 6 to 17	44.76	178	20.9
Oldest child aged 18 or older	36.20	144	10.4
Single parent with child under age 18	31.91	127	7.5
Single person	11.09	44	12.9
RACE AND HISPANIC ORIGIN			
Average household	25.19	100	100.0
Asian	25.17	100	4.2
Black	27.25	108	13.2
Hispanic	18.93	75	9.2
Non-Hispanic white and other	25.79	102	77.6
REGION			
Average household	25.19	100	100.0
Northeast	25.13	100	18.3
Midwest	29.95	119	26.5
South	23.76	94	34.6
West	22.76	90	20.5
EDUCATION			
Average household	25.19	100	100.0
Less than high school graduate	22.06	88	12.5
High school graduate	21.99	87	22.3
Some college	20.56	82	17.2
Associate's degree	27.62	110	10.4
Bachelor's degree or more	31.93	127	37.7
Bachelor's degree	31.36	124	23.5
Master's, professional, doctoral degree	33.07	131	14.2

Note: Market shares may not sum to 100.0 because of rounding and missing categories by household type. "Asian" and "black" include Hispanics and non-Hispanics who identify themselves as being of the respective race alone. "Hispanic" includes people of any race who identify themselves as Hispanic. "Other" includes people who identify themselves as non-Hispanic and as Alaska Native, American Indian, Asian (who are also included in the "Asian" row), or Native Hawaiian or other Pacific Islander as well as non-Hispanics reporting more than one race.

Source: Calculations by New Strategist based on the Bureau of Labor Statistics' 2010 Consumer Expenditure Survey

Baking Needs and Miscellaneous Products

Best customers: **Householders aged 35 to 54**
Married couples with children at home

Customer trends: **Average household spending on baking needs and miscellaneous products is likely**
to fall as cooking-challenged younger generations marry and have children.

Although cooking from scratch has become a lot less common than it once was, many people enjoy whipping up a home-cooked meal or dessert every now and then. Most are married couples, often with children at home. Married couples with children at home spend 49 percent more than the average household on products for baking. Householders aged 35 to 54 spend 12 to 26 percent more than average on baking needs.

Average household spending on products for baking rose steadily over the entire decade, for a cumulative gain of 22 percent between 2000 and 2010, after adjusting for inflation. The popularity of televised cooking programs may account for some of the increase. In the long-term, however, average household spending on products for baking is likely to decline as cooking-challenged younger generations have children.

Table 9.7 **Baking needs and miscellaneous products**

Total household spending $3,170,581,260.00
Average household spends   26.18

	AVERAGE HOUSEHOLD SPENDING	BEST CUSTOMERS (index)	BIGGEST CUSTOMERS (market share)
AGE OF HOUSEHOLDER			
Average household	**$26.18**	**100**	**100.0%**
Under age 25	13.21	50	3.3
Aged 25 to 34	21.44	82	13.6
Aged 35 to 44	29.37	112	20.3
Aged 45 to 54	33.01	126	26.1
Aged 55 to 64	27.06	103	18.2
Aged 65 to 74	24.98	95	10.3
Aged 75 or older	22.08	84	8.0

	AVERAGE HOUSEHOLD SPENDING	BEST CUSTOMERS (index)	BIGGEST CUSTOMERS (market share)
HOUSEHOLD INCOME			
Average household	**$26.18**	**100**	**100.0%**
Under $20,000	16.06	61	13.4
$20,000 to $39,999	20.46	78	17.9
$40,000 to $49,999	22.51	86	8.1
$50,000 to $69,999	26.79	102	14.7
$70,000 to $79,999	19.79	76	4.5
$80,000 to $99,999	33.73	129	10.7
$100,000 or more	47.22	180	30.9
HOUSEHOLD TYPE			
Average household	**26.18**	**100**	**100.0**
Married couples	34.54	132	65.1
Married couples, no children	30.35	116	24.6
Married couples, with children	38.90	149	34.6
Oldest child under age 6	32.31	123	5.3
Oldest child aged 6 to 17	38.70	148	17.4
Oldest child aged 18 or older	42.58	163	11.7
Single parent with child under age 18	19.24	73	4.3
Single person	13.66	52	15.3
RACE AND HISPANIC ORIGIN			
Average household	**26.18**	**100**	**100.0**
Asian	17.61	67	2.9
Black	18.23	70	8.5
Hispanic	19.88	76	9.3
Non-Hispanic white and other	28.41	109	82.3
REGION			
Average household	**26.18**	**100**	**100.0**
Northeast	27.78	106	19.5
Midwest	30.10	115	25.6
South	23.46	90	32.9
West	25.36	97	21.9
EDUCATION			
Average household	**26.18**	**100**	**100.0**
Less than high school graduate	21.07	80	11.5
High school graduate	22.43	86	21.9
Some college	22.50	86	18.1
Associate's degree	34.05	130	12.3
Bachelor's degree or more	31.76	121	36.0
Bachelor's degree	30.05	115	21.7
Master's, professional, doctoral degree	35.13	134	14.5

Note: Market shares may not sum to 100.0 because of rounding and missing categories by household type. "Asian" and "black" include Hispanics and non-Hispanics who identify themselves as being of the respective race alone. "Hispanic" includes people of any race who identify themselves as Hispanic. "Other" includes people who identify themselves as non-Hispanic and as Alaska Native, American Indian, Asian (who are also included in the "Asian" row), or Native Hawaiian or other Pacific Islander as well as non-Hispanics reporting more than one race.

Source: Calculations by New Strategist based on the Bureau of Labor Statistics' 2010 Consumer Expenditure Survey

Bananas

Best customers:
    Householders aged 35 to 54
    Married couples with children at home
    Hispanics and Asians

Customer trends:
    Average household spending on bananas may decline as more boomers become empty-nesters and household size shrinks.

The largest households spend the most on bananas. Married couples with children at home spend 38 percent more than the average household on bananas. Householders aged 35 to 54, most with children at home, spend 15 to 20 percent more on bananas than the average household. Hispanics, who tend to have large families, spend 40 percent more than average on bananas, while Asians outspend the average by 28 percent.

Average household spending on bananas fell 22 percent between 2000 and 2006, after adjusting for inflation, but has rebounded 31 percent since then, for an overall gain of 2 percent. The greater propensity to eat out and the exit of the baby-boom generation from the best-customer lifestage were factors in the spending decline during the earlier part of the decade. The increased spending since 2006 is due to less eating out as households tightened their belts during the Great Recession. Average household spending on bananas may decline again in the years ahead as more boomers become empty-nesters and household size shrinks.

Table 9.8 Bananas

Total household spending $4,950,854,160.00
Average household spends   40.88

	AVERAGE HOUSEHOLD SPENDING	BEST CUSTOMERS (index)	BIGGEST CUSTOMERS (market share)
AGE OF HOUSEHOLDER			
Average household	**$40.88**	**100**	**100.0%**
Under age 25	18.55	45	3.0
Aged 25 to 34	35.60	87	14.5
Aged 35 to 44	47.14	115	20.9
Aged 45 to 54	49.02	120	24.8
Aged 55 to 64	42.11	103	18.2
Aged 65 to 74	38.43	94	10.1
Aged 75 or older	36.44	89	8.5

	AVERAGE HOUSEHOLD SPENDING	BEST CUSTOMERS (index)	BIGGEST CUSTOMERS (market share)
HOUSEHOLD INCOME			
Average household	**$40.88**	**100**	**100.0%**
Under $20,000	26.27	64	14.0
$20,000 to $39,999	36.48	89	20.4
$40,000 to $49,999	32.07	78	7.4
$50,000 to $69,999	40.80	100	14.3
$70,000 to $79,999	47.48	116	7.0
$80,000 to $99,999	49.81	122	10.2
$100,000 or more	63.95	156	26.8
HOUSEHOLD TYPE			
Average household	**40.88**	**100**	**100.0**
Married couples	52.43	128	63.3
Married couples, no children	43.77	107	22.7
Married couples, with children	56.51	138	32.2
Oldest child under age 6	49.03	120	5.1
Oldest child aged 6 to 17	56.01	137	16.1
Oldest child aged 18 or older	61.09	149	10.8
Single parent with child under age 18	36.28	89	5.2
Single person	21.86	53	15.7
RACE AND HISPANIC ORIGIN			
Average household	**40.88**	**100**	**100.0**
Asian	52.15	128	5.4
Black	36.76	90	11.0
Hispanic	57.40	140	17.1
Non-Hispanic white and other	39.00	95	72.3
REGION			
Average household	**40.88**	**100**	**100.0**
Northeast	44.17	108	19.8
Midwest	39.70	97	21.6
South	36.02	88	32.3
West	47.37	116	26.2
EDUCATION			
Average household	**40.88**	**100**	**100.0**
Less than high school graduate	43.92	107	15.3
High school graduate	37.15	91	23.2
Some college	36.01	88	18.5
Associate's degree	42.33	104	9.8
Bachelor's degree or more	45.84	112	33.3
Bachelor's degree	41.89	102	19.4
Master's, professional, doctoral degree	53.62	131	14.2

Note: Market shares may not sum to 100.0 because of rounding and missing categories by household type. "Asian" and "black" include Hispanics and non-Hispanics who identify themselves as being of the respective race alone. "Hispanic" includes people of any race who identify themselves as Hispanic. "Other" includes people who identify themselves as non-Hispanic and as Alaska Native, American Indian, Asian (who are also included in the "Asian" row), or Native Hawaiian or other Pacific Islander as well as non-Hispanics reporting more than one race.

Source: Calculations by New Strategist based on the Bureau of Labor Statistics' 2010 Consumer Expenditure Survey

Beef, Ground

Best customers:	**Householders aged 35 to 54** **Married couples with school-aged or older children at home** **Single parents** **Hispanics** **Householders without a high school diploma**
Customer trends:	**Average household spending on ground beef may continue to decline as more boomers become empty-nesters and eating out claims more of the food dollar.**

Households with children are the biggest spenders on ground beef. Married couples with school-aged or older children at home spend 47 to 48 percent more than average on this item. Householders aged 35 to 54, most with children, spend 14 to 27 percent more than average on ground beef and control 47 percent of the market. Single parents, whose spending is well below average on most items, spend 2 percent more than average on ground beef. Hispanic householders outspend the average on ground beef by 15 percent. Householders who did not graduate from high school, many of them Hispanic, spend 16 percent more on ground beef than the average household.

Average household spending on ground beef declined 24 percent between 2000 and 2010, after adjusting for inflation. Behind the decline is the growing popularity of fast food as a substitute for home-cooked meals. Average household spending on ground beef may continue to decline as more boomers become empty-nesters and eating out claims more of the food dollar.

Table 9.9 Beef, ground

Total household spending $10,254,129,690.00
Average household spends 84.67

	AVERAGE HOUSEHOLD SPENDING	BEST CUSTOMERS (index)	BIGGEST CUSTOMERS (market share)
AGE OF HOUSEHOLDER			
Average household	**$84.67**	**100**	**100.0%**
Under age 25	61.73	73	4.8
Aged 25 to 34	79.43	94	15.6
Aged 35 to 44	96.60	114	20.6
Aged 45 to 54	107.23	127	26.2
Aged 55 to 64	74.99	89	15.6
Aged 65 to 74	69.39	82	8.8
Aged 75 or older	72.93	86	8.2

	AVERAGE HOUSEHOLD SPENDING	BEST CUSTOMERS (index)	BIGGEST CUSTOMERS (market share)
HOUSEHOLD INCOME			
Average household	**$84.67**	**100**	**100.0%**
Under $20,000	63.20	75	16.3
$20,000 to $39,999	75.13	89	20.3
$40,000 to $49,999	93.53	110	10.4
$50,000 to $69,999	93.04	110	15.8
$70,000 to $79,999	87.95	104	6.2
$80,000 to $99,999	91.57	108	9.0
$100,000 or more	107.23	127	21.7
HOUSEHOLD TYPE			
Average household	**84.67**	**100**	**100.0**
Married couples	108.63	128	63.3
Married couples, no children	93.21	110	23.4
Married couples, with children	117.69	139	32.3
Oldest child under age 6	82.68	98	4.2
Oldest child aged 6 to 17	124.91	148	17.3
Oldest child aged 18 or older	124.84	147	10.6
Single parent with child under age 18	86.35	102	6.0
Single person	36.55	43	12.6
RACE AND HISPANIC ORIGIN			
Average household	**84.67**	**100**	**100.0**
Asian	54.61	64	2.7
Black	83.23	98	12.0
Hispanic	97.65	115	14.1
Non-Hispanic white and other	82.78	98	74.1
REGION			
Average household	**84.67**	**100**	**100.0**
Northeast	81.33	96	17.6
Midwest	87.59	103	23.1
South	84.19	99	36.5
West	85.26	101	22.8
EDUCATION			
Average household	**84.67**	**100**	**100.0**
Less than high school graduate	98.33	116	16.6
High school graduate	86.42	102	26.1
Some college	89.26	105	22.2
Associate's degree	83.56	99	9.3
Bachelor's degree or more	74.13	88	26.0
Bachelor's degree	77.50	92	17.3
Master's, professional, doctoral degree	67.49	80	8.6

Note: Market shares may not sum to 100.0 because of rounding and missing categories by household type. "Asian" and "black" include Hispanics and non-Hispanics who identify themselves as being of the respective race alone. "Hispanic" includes people of any race who identify themselves as Hispanic. "Other" includes people who identify themselves as non-Hispanic and as Alaska Native, American Indian, Asian (who are also included in the "Asian" row), or Native Hawaiian or other Pacific Islander as well as non-Hispanics reporting more than one race.

Source: Calculations by New Strategist based on the Bureau of Labor Statistics' 2010 Consumer Expenditure Survey

Beef, Roast

Best customers:
Householders aged 45 to 54 and aged 75 or older
Married couples without children at home
Married couples with school-aged or older children at home
Hispanics

Customer trends:
Average household spending on roast beef may continue to decline as more boomers become empty-nesters and prepared meals claim more of the food dollar.

Households with children and the oldest householders are the biggest spenders on roast beef. Married couples with school-aged or older children at home spend 53 to 62 percent more than average on this item. Householders aged 45 to 54, many with children at home, spend 27 percent more than average on roast beef. Hispanics, who have the largest families, spend 22 percent more than average on beef roast. Householders aged 75 or older outspend the average household by 18 percent on roast beef, and married couples without children at home (most empty-nesters) do so by 27 percent.

Average household spending on roast beef fell a steep 42 percent between 2000 and 2010, after adjusting for inflation. The decline in spending on this item accelerated between 2006 and 2009. Behind the decline is the growing consumer preference for prepared foods and eating out. Average household spending on roast beef may continue to decline in the years ahead as more boomers become empty-nesters and prepared meals claim more of the food dollar.

Table 9.10 Beef, roast

Total household spending $3,569,023,290.00
Average household spends   29.47

	AVERAGE HOUSEHOLD SPENDING	BEST CUSTOMERS (index)	BIGGEST CUSTOMERS (market share)
AGE OF HOUSEHOLDER			
Average household	**$29.47**	**100**	**100.0%**
Under age 25	10.09	34	2.3
Aged 25 to 34	23.88	81	13.5
Aged 35 to 44	31.21	106	19.2
Aged 45 to 54	37.35	127	26.2
Aged 55 to 64	28.83	98	17.3
Aged 65 to 74	28.19	96	10.3
Aged 75 or older	34.90	118	11.3

	AVERAGE HOUSEHOLD SPENDING	BEST CUSTOMERS (index)	BIGGEST CUSTOMERS (market share)
HOUSEHOLD INCOME			
Average household	**$29.47**	**100**	**100.0%**
Under $20,000	14.89	51	11.0
$20,000 to $39,999	22.71	77	17.7
$40,000 to $49,999	27.24	92	8.7
$50,000 to $69,999	26.09	89	12.7
$70,000 to $79,999	38.68	131	7.9
$80,000 to $99,999	35.20	119	10.0
$100,000 or more	55.56	189	32.3
HOUSEHOLD TYPE			
Average household	**29.47**	**100**	**100.0**
Married couples	41.49	141	69.4
Married couples, no children	37.30	127	26.9
Married couples, with children	43.64	148	34.4
Oldest child under age 6	28.93	98	4.2
Oldest child aged 6 to 17	47.66	162	19.0
Oldest child aged 18 or older	45.15	153	11.1
Single parent with child under age 18	16.62	56	3.3
Single person	13.23	45	13.2
RACE AND HISPANIC ORIGIN			
Average household	**29.47**	**100**	**100.0**
Asian	25.26	86	3.6
Black	15.87	54	6.6
Hispanic	35.87	122	14.8
Non-Hispanic white and other	30.65	104	78.8
REGION			
Average household	**29.47**	**100**	**100.0**
Northeast	31.58	107	19.7
Midwest	30.88	105	23.4
South	25.93	88	32.3
West	32.15	109	24.7
EDUCATION			
Average household	**29.47**	**100**	**100.0**
Less than high school graduate	24.85	84	12.0
High school graduate	32.18	109	27.9
Some college	26.31	89	18.8
Associate's degree	26.17	89	8.4
Bachelor's degree or more	32.55	110	32.8
Bachelor's degree	35.97	122	23.1
Master's, professional, doctoral degree	25.82	88	9.5

Note: Market shares may not sum to 100.0 because of rounding and missing categories by household type. "Asian" and "black" include Hispanics and non-Hispanics who identify themselves as being of the respective race alone. "Hispanic" includes people of any race who identify themselves as Hispanic. "Other" includes people who identify themselves as non-Hispanic and as Alaska Native, American Indian, Asian (who are also included in the "Asian" row), or Native Hawaiian or other Pacific Islander as well as non-Hispanics reporting more than one race.

Source: Calculations by New Strategist based on the Bureau of Labor Statistics' 2010 Consumer Expenditure Survey

Beef, Steak

Best customers: Householders aged 45 to 64 and 75 or older
Married couples without children at home
Married couples with school-aged or older children at home
Hispanics
Households in the West

Customer trends: Average household spending on steak should continue to decline as more boomers become empty-nesters and prepared meals claim more of the food dollar.

The best customers of steak are the largest households as well as older householders. Married couples with school-aged or older children at home spend 36 to 94 percent more than average on steak. Householders ranging in age from 45 to 64 spend 16 to 18 percent more than average on steak, and householders aged 75 or older spend 28 percent more. Married couples without children at home (most empty-nesters) outspend the average by 23 percent. Hispanics, who tend to have large families, spend 29 percent more than average on steak. Households in the West, where many Hispanics reside, spend almost one-third more than average on this item.

Average household spending on steak has been in a decade-long decline. Spending on steak fell 23 percent between 2000 and 2006 and another 10 percent between 2006 and 2010, after adjusting for inflation. Average household spending on steak may continue to decline in the years ahead as more boomers become empty-nesters and prepared meals claim more of the food dollar.

Table 9.11 Beef, steak

Total household spending $9,963,472,890.00
Average household spends 82.27

	AVERAGE HOUSEHOLD SPENDING	BEST CUSTOMERS (index)	BIGGEST CUSTOMERS (market share)
AGE OF HOUSEHOLDER			
Average household	**$82.27**	**100**	**100.0%**
Under age 25	49.40	60	4.0
Aged 25 to 34	63.33	77	12.8
Aged 35 to 44	85.03	103	18.7
Aged 45 to 54	96.94	118	24.4
Aged 55 to 64	95.76	116	20.5
Aged 65 to 74	56.56	69	7.4
Aged 75 or older	105.48	128	12.2

	AVERAGE HOUSEHOLD SPENDING	BEST CUSTOMERS (index)	BIGGEST CUSTOMERS (market share)
HOUSEHOLD INCOME			
Average household	**$82.27**	**100**	**100.0%**
Under $20,000	42.74	52	11.3
$20,000 to $39,999	53.02	64	14.8
$40,000 to $49,999	86.02	105	9.9
$50,000 to $69,999	90.17	110	15.7
$70,000 to $79,999	88.42	107	6.4
$80,000 to $99,999	103.71	126	10.5
$100,000 or more	151.84	185	31.6
HOUSEHOLD TYPE			
Average household	**82.27**	**100**	**100.0**
Married couples	111.70	136	67.0
Married couples, no children	100.90	123	26.0
Married couples, with children	120.00	146	33.9
Oldest child under age 6	66.47	81	3.5
Oldest child aged 6 to 17	111.71	136	16.0
Oldest child aged 18 or older	159.76	194	14.0
Single parent with child under age 18	69.81	85	5.0
Single person	34.49	42	12.3
RACE AND HISPANIC ORIGIN			
Average household	**82.27**	**100**	**100.0**
Asian	65.53	80	3.4
Black	50.47	61	7.5
Hispanic	106.23	129	15.7
Non-Hispanic white and other	83.52	102	77.0
REGION			
Average household	**82.27**	**100**	**100.0**
Northeast	83.31	101	18.6
Midwest	77.22	94	20.9
South	69.61	85	31.1
West	107.38	131	29.6
EDUCATION			
Average household	**82.27**	**100**	**100.0**
Less than high school graduate	72.74	88	12.6
High school graduate	70.89	86	22.0
Some college	94.32	115	24.1
Associate's degree	81.15	99	9.3
Bachelor's degree or more	88.08	107	31.8
Bachelor's degree	88.32	107	20.3
Master's, professional, doctoral degree	87.62	107	11.5

Note: Market shares may not sum to 100.0 because of rounding and missing categories by household type. "Asian" and "black" include Hispanics and non-Hispanics who identify themselves as being of the respective race alone. "Hispanic" includes people of any race who identify themselves as Hispanic. "Other" includes people who identify themselves as non-Hispanic and as Alaska Native, American Indian, Asian (who are also included in the "Asian" row), or Native Hawaiian or other Pacific Islander as well as non-Hispanics reporting more than one race.

Source: Calculations by New Strategist based on the Bureau of Labor Statistics' 2010 Consumer Expenditure Survey

Biscuits and Rolls

Best customers:	Householders aged 35 to 64
	Married couples with school-aged or older children at home
	Households in the Northeast
Customer trends:	Average household spending on biscuits and rolls may resume its decline as more
	boomers become empty-nesters and household size shrinks.

The largest households spend the most on biscuits and rolls. Married couples with school-aged children spend 68 percent more than the average household on this item, and those with adult children at home spend 57 percent more. Householders ranging in age from 35 to 64, many with children at home, spend 14 to 19 percent more than average on biscuits and rolls and control two-thirds of the market. Households in the Northeast spend 24 percent more than average on this item.

Average household spending on biscuits and rolls, in decline before the Great Recession, grew by 8 percent between 2006 and 2010, after adjusting for inflation. Behind the 2006-to-2010 increase was the shift to homemade meals by financially strapped consumers. Average household spending on biscuits and rolls may resume its decline as more boomers become empty-nesters and household size shrinks.

Table 9.12 **Biscuits and rolls**

Total household spending $5,914,865,880.00
Average household spends 48.84

	AVERAGE HOUSEHOLD SPENDING	BEST CUSTOMERS (index)	BIGGEST CUSTOMERS (market share)
AGE OF HOUSEHOLDER			
Average household	**$48.84**	**100**	**100.0%**
Under age 25	25.41	52	3.5
Aged 25 to 34	38.85	80	13.2
Aged 35 to 44	57.62	118	21.3
Aged 45 to 54	58.00	119	24.6
Aged 55 to 64	55.89	114	20.2
Aged 65 to 74	42.36	87	9.3
Aged 75 or older	40.18	82	7.8

	AVERAGE HOUSEHOLD SPENDING	BEST CUSTOMERS (index)	BIGGEST CUSTOMERS (market share)
HOUSEHOLD INCOME			
Average household	**$48.84**	**100**	**100.0%**
Under $20,000	25.69	53	11.5
$20,000 to $39,999	37.53	77	17.6
$40,000 to $49,999	45.71	94	8.8
$50,000 to $69,999	51.42	105	15.1
$70,000 to $79,999	58.66	120	7.2
$80,000 to $99,999	65.38	134	11.2
$100,000 or more	82.14	168	28.8
HOUSEHOLD TYPE			
Average household	**48.84**	**100**	**100.0**
Married couples	65.85	135	66.5
Married couples, no children	55.45	114	24.1
Married couples, with children	73.72	151	35.1
Oldest child under age 6	44.06	90	3.9
Oldest child aged 6 to 17	82.08	168	19.8
Oldest child aged 18 or older	76.44	157	11.3
Single parent with child under age 18	40.45	83	4.9
Single person	23.58	48	14.1
RACE AND HISPANIC ORIGIN			
Average household	**48.84**	**100**	**100.0**
Asian	39.35	81	3.4
Black	34.84	71	8.7
Hispanic	39.80	81	9.9
Non-Hispanic white and other	52.45	107	81.4
REGION			
Average household	**48.84**	**100**	**100.0**
Northeast	60.55	124	22.8
Midwest	46.39	95	21.2
South	42.16	86	31.7
West	52.73	108	24.5
EDUCATION			
Average household	**48.84**	**100**	**100.0**
Less than high school graduate	35.01	72	10.2
High school graduate	43.38	89	22.7
Some college	46.57	95	20.0
Associate's degree	53.22	109	10.3
Bachelor's degree or more	59.95	123	36.5
Bachelor's degree	58.99	121	22.8
Master's, professional, doctoral degree	61.85	127	13.7

Note: Market shares may not sum to 100.0 because of rounding and missing categories by household type. "Asian" and "black" include Hispanics and non-Hispanics who identify themselves as being of the respective race alone. "Hispanic" includes people of any race who identify themselves as Hispanic. "Other" includes people who identify themselves as non-Hispanic and as Alaska Native, American Indian, Asian (who are also included in the "Asian" row), or Native Hawaiian or other Pacific Islander as well as non-Hispanics reporting more than one race.

Source: Calculations by New Strategist based on the Bureau of Labor Statistics' 2010 Consumer Expenditure Survey

Bread and Cracker Products

Best customers: **Householders aged 45 to 54**
                             Married couples with school-aged or older children at home

Customer trends: **Average household spending on bread and cracker products is likely to stabilize**
                             as restaurant and carry-out meals continue to replace home cooking among
                             younger generations.

The biggest spenders on bread and cracker products are married couples with school-aged or older children at home. These households spend 40 to 59 percent more than average on this item. Householders aged 45 to 54, many of them with children at home, outspend the average by 41 percent.

Average household spending on bread and cracker products rose 59 percent between 2006 and 2010, after adjusting for inflation. The robust increase more than reversed the 16 percent decline in spending that had occurred between 2000 and 2006. The increase may be due to belt-tightening in face of the Great Recession, as households opted for more meals at home rather than in restaurants, as well as the introduction of many new products in this category. Average household spending on bread and cracker products is likely to stabilize as restaurant and carry-out meals continue to replace home cooking among younger generations.

Table 9.13 Bread and cracker products

| Total household spending | $905,880,360.00 |
| Average household spends | 7.48 |

	AVERAGE HOUSEHOLD SPENDING	BEST CUSTOMERS (index)	BIGGEST CUSTOMERS (market share)
AGE OF HOUSEHOLDER			
Average household	**$7.48**	**100**	**100.0%**
Under age 25	4.83	65	4.3
Aged 25 to 34	3.91	52	8.7
Aged 35 to 44	8.73	117	21.1
Aged 45 to 54	10.57	141	29.2
Aged 55 to 64	8.05	108	19.0
Aged 65 to 74	6.38	85	9.2
Aged 75 or older	6.56	88	8.4

	AVERAGE HOUSEHOLD SPENDING	BEST CUSTOMERS (index)	BIGGEST CUSTOMERS (market share)
HOUSEHOLD INCOME			
Average household	**$7.48**	**100**	**100.0%**
Under $20,000	4.41	59	12.9
$20,000 to $39,999	6.56	88	20.1
$40,000 to $49,999	6.49	87	8.2
$50,000 to $69,999	7.23	97	13.9
$70,000 to $79,999	11.55	154	9.2
$80,000 to $99,999	8.51	114	9.5
$100,000 or more	11.61	155	26.6
HOUSEHOLD TYPE			
Average household	**7.48**	**100**	**100.0**
Married couples	9.06	121	59.7
Married couples, no children	7.82	105	22.2
Married couples, with children	10.12	135	31.5
Oldest child under age 6	5.78	77	3.3
Oldest child aged 6 to 17	10.45	140	16.4
Oldest child aged 18 or older	11.86	159	11.4
Single parent with child under age 18	6.27	84	4.9
Single person	4.16	56	16.3
RACE AND HISPANIC ORIGIN			
Average household	**7.48**	**100**	**100.0**
Asian	0.87	12	0.5
Black	6.49	87	10.6
Hispanic	6.00	80	9.8
Non-Hispanic white and other	7.86	105	79.7
REGION			
Average household	**7.48**	**100**	**100.0**
Northeast	7.84	105	19.2
Midwest	7.83	105	23.3
South	6.54	87	32.1
West	8.39	112	25.4
EDUCATION			
Average household	**7.48**	**100**	**100.0**
Less than high school graduate	5.87	78	11.2
High school graduate	6.85	92	23.4
Some college	8.57	115	24.1
Associate's degree	7.69	103	9.7
Bachelor's degree or more	7.89	105	31.3
Bachelor's degree	7.54	101	19.0
Master's, professional, doctoral degree	8.58	115	12.4

Note: Market shares may not sum to 100.0 because of rounding and missing categories by household type. "Asian" and "black" include Hispanics and non-Hispanics who identify themselves as being of the respective race alone. "Hispanic" includes people of any race who identify themselves as Hispanic. "Other" includes people who identify themselves as non-Hispanic and as Alaska Native, American Indian, Asian (who are also included in the "Asian" row), or Native Hawaiian or other Pacific Islander as well as non-Hispanics reporting more than one race.

Source: Calculations by New Strategist based on the Bureau of Labor Statistics' 2010 Consumer Expenditure Survey

Bread, Other than White

Best customers:	**Householders aged 35 to 54** **Married couples with school-aged or older children at home**
Customer trends:	**Average household spending on nonwhite bread should remain stable as house-holds switch from white to other types of bread, but shrinking household size may limit gains.**

Bread took a beating a few years back as low-carb diets became popular. Nonwhite bread held its own, however. In 2000, nonwhite bread accounted for 56 percent of total household spending on bread. By 2010, the figure had grown to 60 percent of the total. The best customers of nonwhite bread are the largest households. Married couples with school-aged or older children at home spend 52 to 57 percent more than the average household on nonwhite bread. Householders aged 35 to 54, most with children at home, spend 14 to 15 percent more than average on this item.

Spending on nonwhite bread, in slow decline before the Great Recession, grew by 2 percent between 2006 and 2010, after adjusting for inflation. One factor behind the recent spending increase is the shift to more homemade lunches rather than carry-outs as the Great Recession cut incomes and spending. Average household spending on nonwhite bread should remain stable in the years ahead because of the shift away from white bread, but shrinking household size may take a toll on all bread buying in the years ahead.

Table 9.14 Bread, other than white

Total household spending $7,232,510,040.00
Average household spends   59.72

	AVERAGE HOUSEHOLD SPENDING	BEST CUSTOMERS (index)	BIGGEST CUSTOMERS (market share)
AGE OF HOUSEHOLDER			
Average household	**$59.72**	**100**	**100.0%**
Under age 25	39.28	66	4.4
Aged 25 to 34	48.87	82	13.6
Aged 35 to 44	68.53	115	20.8
Aged 45 to 54	68.22	114	23.6
Aged 55 to 64	64.21	108	19.0
Aged 65 to 74	58.50	98	10.5
Aged 75 or older	50.58	85	8.1

	AVERAGE HOUSEHOLD SPENDING	BEST CUSTOMERS (index)	BIGGEST CUSTOMERS (market share)
HOUSEHOLD INCOME			
Average household	$59.72	100	100.0%
Under $20,000	38.55	65	14.1
$20,000 to $39,999	47.07	79	18.1
$40,000 to $49,999	54.08	91	8.6
$50,000 to $69,999	61.75	103	14.8
$70,000 to $79,999	66.07	111	6.6
$80,000 to $99,999	78.65	132	11.0
$100,000 or more	94.27	158	27.1
HOUSEHOLD TYPE			
Average household	59.72	100	100.0
Married couples	77.72	130	64.2
Married couples, no children	65.84	110	23.4
Married couples, with children	88.61	148	34.5
Oldest child under age 6	68.30	114	4.9
Oldest child aged 6 to 17	93.99	157	18.5
Oldest child aged 18 or older	90.98	152	11.0
Single parent with child under age 18	45.35	76	4.5
Single person	34.13	57	16.7
RACE AND HISPANIC ORIGIN			
Average household	59.72	100	100.0
Asian	54.90	92	3.9
Black	44.57	75	9.1
Hispanic	64.79	108	13.2
Non-Hispanic white and other	61.26	103	77.8
REGION			
Average household	59.72	100	100.0
Northeast	63.98	107	19.7
Midwest	58.46	98	21.8
South	52.94	89	32.5
West	68.68	115	26.1
EDUCATION			
Average household	59.72	100	100.0
Less than high school graduate	51.73	87	12.4
High school graduate	52.46	88	22.4
Some college	56.57	95	19.9
Associate's degree	59.84	100	9.5
Bachelor's degree or more	71.88	120	35.8
Bachelor's degree	68.00	114	21.5
Master's, professional, doctoral degree	79.54	133	14.4

Note: Market shares may not sum to 100.0 because of rounding and missing categories by household type. "Asian" and "black" include Hispanics and non-Hispanics who identify themselves as being of the respective race alone. "Hispanic" includes people of any race who identify themselves as Hispanic. "Other" includes people who identify themselves as non-Hispanic and as Alaska Native, American Indian, Asian (who are also included in the "Asian" row), or Native Hawaiian or other Pacific Islander as well as non-Hispanics reporting more than one race.

Source: Calculations by New Strategist based on the Bureau of Labor Statistics' 2010 Consumer Expenditure Survey

Bread, White

Best customers: **Householders aged 35 to 54**
Married couples with school-aged or older children at home
Hispanics

Customer trends: **Average household spending on white bread is likely to resume its decline in the years ahead as consumers switch to nonwhite bread.**

White bread accounts for 40 percent of the average household's bread spending, down from 44 percent in 2000. The best customers of white bread are the largest households. Married couples with school-aged or older children at home spend 52 to 54 percent more than the average household on this item. Householders aged 35 to 54, many with children at home, spend 18 to 26 percent more than average on white bread. Hispanics, whose households tend to be larger than average, spend 21 percent more than the average household on white bread.

Average household spending on white bread declined by a substantial 26 percent between 2000 and 2006, after adjusting for inflation, but rebounded by 16 percent between 2006 and 2010. Behind the earlier decline was the switch to nonwhite bread, and behind the more recent increase is more brown-bag lunches as the Great Recession cut incomes and spending. Average household spending on white bread is likely to resume its decline in the years ahead as consumers continue to switch to more-nutritious whole-grain bread.

Table 9.15 Bread, white

Total household spending $4,823,691,810.00
Average household spends 39.83

	AVERAGE HOUSEHOLD SPENDING	BEST CUSTOMERS (index)	BIGGEST CUSTOMERS (market share)
AGE OF HOUSEHOLDER			
Average household	**$39.83**	**100**	**100.0%**
Under age 25	27.87	70	4.6
Aged 25 to 34	37.07	93	15.5
Aged 35 to 44	50.14	126	22.8
Aged 45 to 54	46.86	118	24.3
Aged 55 to 64	37.59	94	16.6
Aged 65 to 74	33.78	85	9.1
Aged 75 or older	29.09	73	7.0

	AVERAGE HOUSEHOLD SPENDING	BEST CUSTOMERS (index)	BIGGEST CUSTOMERS (market share)
HOUSEHOLD INCOME			
Average household	**$39.83**	**100**	**100.0%**
Under $20,000	29.81	75	16.3
$20,000 to $39,999	36.66	92	21.1
$40,000 to $49,999	38.92	98	9.2
$50,000 to $69,999	41.91	105	15.1
$70,000 to $79,999	42.05	106	6.3
$80,000 to $99,999	44.75	112	9.4
$100,000 or more	52.41	132	22.6
HOUSEHOLD TYPE			
Average household	**39.83**	**100**	**100.0**
Married couples	49.14	123	60.9
Married couples, no children	37.58	94	20.0
Married couples, with children	57.89	145	33.8
Oldest child under age 6	42.15	106	4.5
Oldest child aged 6 to 17	61.41	154	18.1
Oldest child aged 18 or older	60.69	152	11.0
Single parent with child under age 18	35.84	90	5.3
Single person	21.98	55	16.2
RACE AND HISPANIC ORIGIN			
Average household	**39.83**	**100**	**100.0**
Asian	38.01	95	4.1
Black	37.11	93	11.4
Hispanic	48.31	121	14.8
Non-Hispanic white and other	38.94	98	74.1
REGION			
Average household	**39.83**	**100**	**100.0**
Northeast	44.82	113	20.7
Midwest	40.38	101	22.6
South	36.17	91	33.3
West	41.21	103	23.4
EDUCATION			
Average household	**39.83**	**100**	**100.0**
Less than high school graduate	45.65	115	16.4
High school graduate	40.15	101	25.7
Some college	35.35	89	18.7
Associate's degree	36.35	91	8.6
Bachelor's degree or more	41.39	104	30.9
Bachelor's degree	41.36	104	19.6
Master's, professional, doctoral degree	41.45	104	11.3

Note: Market shares may not sum to 100.0 because of rounding and missing categories by household type. "Asian" and "black" include Hispanics and non-Hispanics who identify themselves as being of the respective race alone. "Hispanic" includes people of any race who identify themselves as Hispanic. "Other" includes people who identify themselves as non-Hispanic and as Alaska Native, American Indian, Asian (who are also included in the "Asian" row), or Native Hawaiian or other Pacific Islander as well as non-Hispanics reporting more than one race.

Source: Calculations by New Strategist based on the Bureau of Labor Statistics' 2010 Consumer Expenditure Survey

Butter

Best customers:	Householders aged 35 to 54 Married couples with school-aged or older children at home
Customer trends:	Average household spending on butter may continue to climb as butter's reputation improves, but shrinking household size due to the aging of the baby-boom generation may limit the increase.

The best customers of butter are the largest households. Married couples with school-aged or older children at home spend 59 to 60 percent more than the average household on butter. Householders aged 35 to 54, most with children, spend 17 to 35 percent more than average on butter.

Average household spending on butter fell in the earlier part of the decade but rebounded with a 16 percent rise between 2006 and 2010, after adjusting for inflation. Spending on butter may continue to climb in the years ahead as butter's reputation improves, but shrinking household size due to the aging of the baby-boom generation may limit the increase.

Table 9.16 **Butter**

Total household spending $2,789,094,210.00
Average household spends   23.03

	AVERAGE HOUSEHOLD SPENDING	BEST CUSTOMERS (index)	BIGGEST CUSTOMERS (market share)
AGE OF HOUSEHOLDER			
Average household	**$23.03**	**100**	**100.0%**
Under age 25	11.22	49	3.2
Aged 25 to 34	16.63	72	12.0
Aged 35 to 44	26.84	117	21.1
Aged 45 to 54	31.19	135	28.0
Aged 55 to 64	23.13	100	17.7
Aged 65 to 74	23.19	101	10.8
Aged 75 or older	16.72	73	6.9

	AVERAGE HOUSEHOLD SPENDING	BEST CUSTOMERS (index)	BIGGEST CUSTOMERS (market share)
HOUSEHOLD INCOME			
Average household	**$23.03**	**100**	**100.0%**
Under $20,000	14.25	62	13.5
$20,000 to $39,999	18.33	80	18.2
$40,000 to $49,999	20.49	89	8.4
$50,000 to $69,999	20.93	91	13.0
$70,000 to $79,999	24.49	106	6.4
$80,000 to $99,999	29.15	127	10.6
$100,000 or more	40.82	177	30.4
HOUSEHOLD TYPE			
Average household	**23.03**	**100**	**100.0**
Married couples	31.21	136	66.8
Married couples, no children	26.83	117	24.7
Married couples, with children	34.35	149	34.7
Oldest child under age 6	22.99	100	4.3
Oldest child aged 6 to 17	36.58	159	18.7
Oldest child aged 18 or older	36.83	160	11.5
Single parent with child under age 18	16.61	72	4.3
Single person	11.19	49	14.2
RACE AND HISPANIC ORIGIN			
Average household	**23.03**	**100**	**100.0**
Asian	13.72	60	2.5
Black	16.69	72	8.9
Hispanic	18.51	80	9.8
Non-Hispanic white and other	24.76	108	81.5
REGION			
Average household	**23.03**	**100**	**100.0**
Northeast	26.86	117	21.4
Midwest	26.91	117	26.0
South	17.81	77	28.4
West	24.55	107	24.1
EDUCATION			
Average household	**23.03**	**100**	**100.0**
Less than high school graduate	16.59	72	10.3
High school graduate	21.62	94	24.0
Some college	23.49	102	21.4
Associate's degree	24.44	106	10.0
Bachelor's degree or more	26.30	114	33.9
Bachelor's degree	26.09	113	21.4
Master's, professional, doctoral degree	26.72	116	12.6

Note: Market shares may not sum to 100.0 because of rounding and missing categories by household type. "Asian" and "black" include Hispanics and non-Hispanics who identify themselves as being of the respective race alone. "Hispanic" includes people of any race who identify themselves as Hispanic. "Other" includes people who identify themselves as non-Hispanic and as Alaska Native, American Indian, Asian (who are also included in the "Asian" row), or Native Hawaiian or other Pacific Islander as well as non-Hispanics reporting more than one race.

Source: Calculations by New Strategist based on the Bureau of Labor Statistics' 2010 Consumer Expenditure Survey

Cakes and Cupcakes

Best customers:	Householders aged 35 to 54
	Married couples with school-aged or older children at home
	Asians and Hispanics

Customer trends:	Average household spending on cakes and cupcakes should continue to decline as
	more boomers become empty-nesters and household size shrinks.

The largest households—those with children—spend the most on cakes and cupcakes. Married couples with school-aged children spend 52 percent more than the average household on this item, and those with adult children at home spend 64 percent above average. Householders aged 35 to 54, most with children, spend 12 to 17 percent more than average on cakes and cupcakes. Asians spend 25 percent more than average on this item and Hispanics, 18 percent.

Average household spending on cakes and cupcakes fell 22 percent between 2000 and 2006, after adjusting for inflation, and another 7 percent between 2006 and 2010. The baby-boom generation's exit from the best-customer lifestage is one factor behind the decline. Average household spending on cakes and cupcakes should continue its decline as more boomers become empty-nesters and household size shrinks.

Table 9.17 Cakes and cupcakes

Total household spending	$4,275,077,100.00
Average household spends	35.30

	AVERAGE HOUSEHOLD SPENDING	BEST CUSTOMERS (index)	BIGGEST CUSTOMERS (market share)
AGE OF HOUSEHOLDER			
Average household	**$35.30**	**100**	**100.0%**
Under age 25	34.97	99	6.6
Aged 25 to 34	35.72	101	16.8
Aged 35 to 44	41.33	117	21.2
Aged 45 to 54	39.46	112	23.1
Aged 55 to 64	32.29	91	16.1
Aged 65 to 74	29.40	83	9.0
Aged 75 or older	26.49	75	7.2

	AVERAGE HOUSEHOLD SPENDING	BEST CUSTOMERS (index)	BIGGEST CUSTOMERS (market share)
HOUSEHOLD INCOME			
Average household	**$35.30**	**100**	**100.0%**
Under $20,000	24.49	69	15.1
$20,000 to $39,999	24.44	69	15.9
$40,000 to $49,999	29.46	83	7.9
$50,000 to $69,999	36.48	103	14.8
$70,000 to $79,999	53.20	151	9.0
$80,000 to $99,999	41.16	117	9.7
$100,000 or more	57.54	163	27.9
HOUSEHOLD TYPE			
Average household	**35.30**	**100**	**100.0**
Married couples	45.31	128	63.3
Married couples, no children	36.11	102	21.7
Married couples, with children	52.35	148	34.5
Oldest child under age 6	38.03	108	4.6
Oldest child aged 6 to 17	53.59	152	17.9
Oldest child aged 18 or older	57.82	164	11.8
Single parent with child under age 18	25.49	72	4.3
Single person	16.72	47	13.9
RACE AND HISPANIC ORIGIN			
Average household	**35.30**	**100**	**100.0**
Asian	43.97	125	5.3
Black	26.35	75	9.1
Hispanic	41.57	118	14.3
Non-Hispanic white and other	35.67	101	76.6
REGION			
Average household	**35.30**	**100**	**100.0**
Northeast	37.63	107	19.6
Midwest	31.08	88	19.6
South	34.77	98	36.2
West	38.52	109	24.7
EDUCATION			
Average household	**35.30**	**100**	**100.0**
Less than high school graduate	33.23	94	13.4
High school graduate	32.30	92	23.4
Some college	36.40	103	21.7
Associate's degree	38.22	108	10.2
Bachelor's degree or more	37.06	105	31.2
Bachelor's degree	36.06	102	19.3
Master's, professional, doctoral degree	39.04	111	12.0

Note: Market shares may not sum to 100.0 because of rounding and missing categories by household type. "Asian" and "black" include Hispanics and non-Hispanics who identify themselves as being of the respective race alone. "Hispanic" includes people of any race who identify themselves as Hispanic. "Other" includes people who identify themselves as non-Hispanic and as Alaska Native, American Indian, Asian (who are also included in the "Asian" row), or Native Hawaiian or other Pacific Islander as well as non-Hispanics reporting more than one race.

Source: Calculations by New Strategist based on the Bureau of Labor Statistics' 2010 Consumer Expenditure Survey

Candy and Chewing Gum

Best customers: **Householders aged 35 to 64**
Married couples with school-aged or older children at home

Customer trends: **Average household spending on candy and chewing gum will fall as more boomers become empty-nesters and household size shrinks.**

Households with children spend the most on candy and chewing gum. Married couples with school-aged children spend 72 percent more than the average household on this item, and those with adult children at home, 49 percent. Householders aged 35 to 64, many with children, spend 15 to 21 percent more than average on candy and chewing gum.

Average household spending on candy and chewing gum fell 20 percent between 2000 and 2010, after adjusting for inflation. Average household spending on candy and chewing gum should continue to fall as the large baby-boom generation exits from the best-customer lifestage, more boomers become empty-nesters, and household size shrinks.

Table 9.18 **Candy and chewing gum**

Total household spending   **$9,366,415,380.00**
Average household spends   **77.34**

	AVERAGE HOUSEHOLD SPENDING	BEST CUSTOMERS (index)	BIGGEST CUSTOMERS (market share)
AGE OF HOUSEHOLDER			
Average household	**$77.34**	**100**	**100.0%**
Under age 25	32.25	42	2.8
Aged 25 to 34	64.13	83	13.8
Aged 35 to 44	89.67	116	21.0
Aged 45 to 54	93.62	121	25.0
Aged 55 to 64	89.14	115	20.3
Aged 65 to 74	70.29	91	9.8
Aged 75 or older	58.69	76	7.2

	AVERAGE HOUSEHOLD SPENDING	BEST CUSTOMERS (index)	BIGGEST CUSTOMERS (market share)
HOUSEHOLD INCOME			
Average household	**$77.34**	**100**	**100.0%**
Under $20,000	43.20	56	12.2
$20,000 to $39,999	56.61	73	16.8
$40,000 to $49,999	74.60	96	9.1
$50,000 to $69,999	83.81	108	15.5
$70,000 to $79,999	84.16	109	6.5
$80,000 to $99,999	107.65	139	11.6
$100,000 or more	128.17	166	28.4
HOUSEHOLD TYPE			
Average household	**77.34**	**100**	**100.0**
Married couples	103.45	134	66.0
Married couples, no children	90.26	117	24.8
Married couples, with children	116.28	150	35.0
Oldest child under age 6	70.48	91	3.9
Oldest child aged 6 to 17	132.95	172	20.2
Oldest child aged 18 or older	114.87	149	10.7
Single parent with child under age 18	64.76	84	4.9
Single person	39.87	52	15.1
RACE AND HISPANIC ORIGIN			
Average household	**77.34**	**100**	**100.0**
Asian	64.93	84	3.6
Black	53.62	69	8.5
Hispanic	53.45	69	8.4
Non-Hispanic white and other	84.77	110	83.1
REGION			
Average household	**77.34**	**100**	**100.0**
Northeast	75.41	98	17.9
Midwest	85.77	111	24.7
South	68.92	89	32.7
West	84.26	109	24.7
EDUCATION			
Average household	**77.34**	**100**	**100.0**
Less than high school graduate	52.31	68	9.7
High school graduate	68.71	89	22.7
Some college	71.71	93	19.5
Associate's degree	87.52	113	10.7
Bachelor's degree or more	96.68	125	37.1
Bachelor's degree	90.49	117	22.1
Master's, professional, doctoral degree	108.87	141	15.2

Note: Market shares may not sum to 100.0 because of rounding and missing categories by household type. "Asian" and "black" include Hispanics and non-Hispanics who identify themselves as being of the respective race alone. "Hispanic" includes people of any race who identify themselves as Hispanic. "Other" includes people who identify themselves as non-Hispanic and as Alaska Native, American Indian, Asian (who are also included in the "Asian" row), or Native Hawaiian or other Pacific Islander as well as non-Hispanics reporting more than one race.

Source: Calculations by New Strategist based on the Bureau of Labor Statistics' 2010 Consumer Expenditure Survey

Carbonated Drinks

Best customers:	**Householders aged 35 to 54**
	Married couples with school-aged or older children at home
	Single parents
	Hispanics
Customer trends:	**Average household spending on carbonated beverages may continue to fall as boomers entirely exit the crowded-nest lifestage, but the substitution of colas for coffee among younger generations may limit the decline.**

The best customers of carbonated drinks are the largest households. Married couples with school-aged or older children at home spend 40 to 52 percent more than average on this item. Householders ranging in age from 35 to 54, many with children at home, spend 18 to 21 percent more than average on sodas and control 46 percent of the market. Single parents, whose spending is below average on most items, spend slightly more than average on carbonated beverages. Hispanics, who have the largest households, outspend the average by 14 percent.

Average household spending on carbonated beverages purchased at grocery or convenience stores fell 22 percent between 2000 and 2010, after adjusting for inflation. Lower-priced private brands and discounts are one factor behind the decline. Average household spending on sodas may continue to fall as more boomers become empty-nesters and household size shrinks. But younger generations, drinking cola rather than coffee, may limit the decline.

Table 9.19 Carbonated drinks

Total household spending	$16,064,843,550.00
Average household spends	132.65

	AVERAGE HOUSEHOLD SPENDING	BEST CUSTOMERS (index)	BIGGEST CUSTOMERS (market share)
AGE OF HOUSEHOLDER			
Average household	**$132.65**	**100**	**100.0%**
Under age 25	105.78	80	5.3
Aged 25 to 34	129.32	97	16.2
Aged 35 to 44	156.39	118	21.3
Aged 45 to 54	160.26	121	25.0
Aged 55 to 64	141.34	107	18.8
Aged 65 to 74	112.20	85	9.1
Aged 75 or older	57.60	43	4.1

	AVERAGE HOUSEHOLD SPENDING	BEST CUSTOMERS (index)	BIGGEST CUSTOMERS (market share)
HOUSEHOLD INCOME			
Average household	**$132.65**	**100**	**100.0%**
Under $20,000	97.30	73	16.0
$20,000 to $39,999	121.65	92	21.0
$40,000 to $49,999	146.69	111	10.5
$50,000 to $69,999	141.32	107	15.3
$70,000 to $79,999	117.98	89	5.3
$80,000 to $99,999	152.19	115	9.6
$100,000 or more	170.70	129	22.1
HOUSEHOLD TYPE			
Average household	**132.65**	**100**	**100.0**
Married couples	161.67	122	60.1
Married couples, no children	131.93	99	21.1
Married couples, with children	181.18	137	31.8
Oldest child under age 6	129.38	98	4.2
Oldest child aged 6 to 17	185.60	140	16.5
Oldest child aged 18 or older	201.08	152	10.9
Single parent with child under age 18	135.50	102	6.0
Single person	69.93	53	15.4
RACE AND HISPANIC ORIGIN			
Average household	**132.65**	**100**	**100.0**
Asian	93.29	70	3.0
Black	107.52	81	9.9
Hispanic	151.18	114	13.9
Non-Hispanic white and other	133.62	101	76.4
REGION			
Average household	**132.65**	**100**	**100.0**
Northeast	123.45	93	17.1
Midwest	137.65	104	23.1
South	141.15	106	39.1
West	121.14	91	20.7
EDUCATION			
Average household	**132.65**	**100**	**100.0**
Less than high school graduate	144.05	109	15.5
High school graduate	140.98	106	27.1
Some college	126.82	96	20.1
Associate's degree	134.71	102	9.6
Bachelor's degree or more	123.85	93	27.7
Bachelor's degree	121.45	92	17.3
Master's, professional, doctoral degree	128.58	97	10.5

Note: Market shares may not sum to 100.0 because of rounding and missing categories by household type. "Asian" and "black" include Hispanics and non-Hispanics who identify themselves as being of the respective race alone. "Hispanic" includes people of any race who identify themselves as Hispanic. "Other" includes people who identify themselves as non-Hispanic and as Alaska Native, American Indian, Asian (who are also included in the "Asian" row), or Native Hawaiian or other Pacific Islander as well as non-Hispanics reporting more than one race.

Source: Calculations by New Strategist based on the Bureau of Labor Statistics' 2010 Consumer Expenditure Survey

Cereal, Ready-to-Eat and Cooked

Best customers:
Householders aged 35 to 44
Married couples with children at home
Single parents
Hispanics

Customer trends:
Average household spending on cereal should stabilize and possibly grow as the large millennial generation enters the best-customer lifestage.

The biggest spenders on cereal are households with children. Married couples with children at home spend 59 percent more than the average household on cereal, the figure peaking at 78 percent among those with school-aged children. Householders aged 35 to 44, most of them parents, spend 30 percent more than average on cereal. Single parents, whose spending approaches the average on only a few items, spend just about an average amount on cereal. Hispanics, who tend to have the largest families, outspend the average on cereal by 11 percent.

Average household spending on cereal fell 25 percent between 2000 and 2010, after adjusting for inflation. Behind the decline was the entry of the small generation X into the best-customer age group. Average household spending on cereal should stabilize and possibly grow as the large millennial generation enters the best-customer lifestage.

Table 9.20 Cereal, ready-to-eat and cooked

Total household spending $10,031,292,810.00
Average household spends   82.83

	AVERAGE HOUSEHOLD SPENDING	BEST CUSTOMERS (index)	BIGGEST CUSTOMERS (market share)
AGE OF HOUSEHOLDER			
Average household	**$82.83**	**100**	**100.0%**
Under age 25	55.07	66	4.4
Aged 25 to 34	76.37	92	15.4
Aged 35 to 44	107.80	130	23.5
Aged 45 to 54	97.87	118	24.4
Aged 55 to 64	75.62	91	16.1
Aged 65 to 74	69.32	84	9.0
Aged 75 or older	62.18	75	7.2

	AVERAGE HOUSEHOLD SPENDING	BEST CUSTOMERS (index)	BIGGEST CUSTOMERS (market share)
HOUSEHOLD INCOME			
Average household	**$82.83**	**100**	**100.0%**
Under $20,000	50.34	61	13.3
$20,000 to $39,999	73.61	89	20.4
$40,000 to $49,999	73.05	88	8.3
$50,000 to $69,999	79.45	96	13.8
$70,000 to $79,999	93.73	113	6.8
$80,000 to $99,999	112.26	136	11.3
$100,000 or more	127.28	154	26.3
HOUSEHOLD TYPE			
Average household	**82.83**	**100**	**100.0**
Married couples	107.41	130	64.0
Married couples, no children	77.02	93	19.8
Married couples, with children	131.55	159	36.9
Oldest child under age 6	112.12	135	5.8
Oldest child aged 6 to 17	147.07	178	20.9
Oldest child aged 18 or older	118.36	143	10.3
Single parent with child under age 18	82.25	99	5.9
Single person	43.21	52	15.3
RACE AND HISPANIC ORIGIN			
Average household	**82.83**	**100**	**100.0**
Asian	60.31	73	3.1
Black	74.49	90	11.0
Hispanic	91.96	111	13.5
Non-Hispanic white and other	82.88	100	75.9
REGION			
Average household	**82.83**	**100**	**100.0**
Northeast	86.73	105	19.2
Midwest	81.47	98	21.9
South	78.46	95	34.8
West	88.23	107	24.1
EDUCATION			
Average household	**82.83**	**100**	**100.0**
Less than high school graduate	78.43	95	13.5
High school graduate	71.79	87	22.1
Some college	74.90	90	19.0
Associate's degree	88.24	107	10.1
Bachelor's degree or more	98.42	119	35.3
Bachelor's degree	95.46	115	21.8
Master's, professional, doctoral degree	104.25	126	13.6

Note: Market shares may not sum to 100.0 because of rounding and missing categories by household type. "Asian" and "black" include Hispanics and non-Hispanics who identify themselves as being of the respective race alone. "Hispanic" includes people of any race who identify themselves as Hispanic. "Other" includes people who identify themselves as non-Hispanic and as Alaska Native, American Indian, Asian (who are also included in the "Asian" row), or Native Hawaiian or other Pacific Islander as well as non-Hispanics reporting more than one race.

Source: Calculations by New Strategist based on the Bureau of Labor Statistics' 2010 Consumer Expenditure Survey

Cheese

Best customers: **Householders aged 35 to 54**
                          Married couples with children at home

Customer trends: **Average household spending on cheese may continue to decline in the years ahead as more boomers become empty-nesters and household size shrinks.**

The largest households spend the most on cheese. Married couples with children at home spend 50 percent more than the average household on this item, the figure peaking at 59 percent more among couples with school-aged children. Householders aged 35 to 54, most with children at home, spend 18 to 20 percent more than average on cheese.

Average household spending on cheese declined 5 percent between 2000 and 2010, after adjusting for inflation. Spending on cheese may continue to decline in the years ahead as more boomers become empty-nesters and household size shrinks.

Table 9.21 Cheese

Total household spending $13,979,381,010.00
Average household spends 115.43

	AVERAGE HOUSEHOLD SPENDING	BEST CUSTOMERS (index)	BIGGEST CUSTOMERS (market share)
AGE OF HOUSEHOLDER			
Average household	**$115.43**	**100**	**100.0%**
Under age 25	68.30	59	3.9
Aged 25 to 34	110.84	96	16.0
Aged 35 to 44	138.23	120	21.7
Aged 45 to 54	136.29	118	24.4
Aged 55 to 64	113.27	98	17.3
Aged 65 to 74	108.76	94	10.1
Aged 75 or older	78.74	68	6.5

	AVERAGE HOUSEHOLD SPENDING	BEST CUSTOMERS (index)	BIGGEST CUSTOMERS (market share)
HOUSEHOLD INCOME			
Average household	**$115.43**	**100**	**100.0%**
Under $20,000	66.58	58	12.6
$20,000 to $39,999	83.39	72	16.6
$40,000 to $49,999	110.41	96	9.0
$50,000 to $69,999	115.23	100	14.3
$70,000 to $79,999	137.66	119	7.1
$80,000 to $99,999	148.72	129	10.7
$100,000 or more	202.22	175	30.0
HOUSEHOLD TYPE			
Average household	**115.43**	**100**	**100.0**
Married couples	151.17	131	64.6
Married couples, no children	122.84	106	22.6
Married couples, with children	173.68	150	35.0
Oldest child under age 6	141.37	122	5.2
Oldest child aged 6 to 17	183.99	159	18.7
Oldest child aged 18 or older	174.85	151	10.9
Single parent with child under age 18	90.30	78	4.6
Single person	59.45	52	15.1
RACE AND HISPANIC ORIGIN			
Average household	**115.43**	**100**	**100.0**
Asian	49.96	43	1.8
Black	64.42	56	6.8
Hispanic	128.65	111	13.6
Non-Hispanic white and other	121.54	105	79.8
REGION			
Average household	**115.43**	**100**	**100.0**
Northeast	131.41	114	20.9
Midwest	122.69	106	23.7
South	99.36	86	31.6
West	121.47	105	23.8
EDUCATION			
Average household	**115.43**	**100**	**100.0**
Less than high school graduate	96.22	83	11.9
High school graduate	96.62	84	21.4
Some college	111.79	97	20.4
Associate's degree	114.82	99	9.4
Bachelor's degree or more	143.31	124	36.9
Bachelor's degree	137.51	119	22.5
Master's, professional, doctoral degree	154.73	134	14.5

Note: Market shares may not sum to 100.0 because of rounding and missing categories by household type. "Asian" and "black" include Hispanics and non-Hispanics who identify themselves as being of the respective race alone. "Hispanic" includes people of any race who identify themselves as Hispanic. "Other" includes people who identify themselves as non-Hispanic and as Alaska Native, American Indian, Asian (who are also included in the "Asian" row), or Native Hawaiian or other Pacific Islander as well as non-Hispanics reporting more than one race.

Source: Calculations by New Strategist based on the Bureau of Labor Statistics' 2010 Consumer Expenditure Survey

Chicken, Fresh and Frozen

Best customers:	**Householders aged 35 to 54** **Married couples with children at home** **Single parents** **Hispanics, blacks, and Asians**
Customer trends:	**Average household spending on chicken may rise as minority populations grow** **and the large millennial generation begins to fill the best-customer lifestage.**

Families with children are the best customers of chicken. Married couples with children at home spend 51 percent more than the average household on this item. Single parents, whose spending approaches average on only a few items, spend 18 percent more than average on chicken. Householders aged 35 to 54, most with children at home, spend 24 to 28 percent more than average on chicken. Asians spend 19 percent more, blacks spend 33 percent more, and Hispanics 49 percent more than average on chicken. Together, the three minority groups account for 40 percent of household spending on this item.

Average household spending on chicken fell 24 percent between 2000 and 2010, after adjusting for inflation. One factor behind the decline was the baby-boom generation's exit from the best-customer lifestage, as well as competition from fast-food restaurants. Spending on chicken may rise in the years ahead as minority populations grow and the large millennial generation fills the best-customer lifestage.

Table 9.22 Chicken, fresh and frozen

Total household spending $13,352,046,750.00
Average household spends   110.25

	AVERAGE HOUSEHOLD SPENDING	BEST CUSTOMERS (index)	BIGGEST CUSTOMERS (market share)
AGE OF HOUSEHOLDER			
Average household	**$110.25**	**100**	**100.0%**
Under age 25	70.19	64	4.2
Aged 25 to 34	122.67	111	18.5
Aged 35 to 44	136.46	124	22.4
Aged 45 to 54	141.15	128	26.5
Aged 55 to 64	96.94	88	15.5
Aged 65 to 74	76.85	70	7.5
Aged 75 or older	61.50	56	5.3

	AVERAGE HOUSEHOLD SPENDING	BEST CUSTOMERS (index)	BIGGEST CUSTOMERS (market share)
HOUSEHOLD INCOME			
Average household	**$110.25**	**100**	**100.0%**
Under $20,000	85.79	78	17.0
$20,000 to $39,999	92.15	84	19.2
$40,000 to $49,999	107.20	97	9.2
$50,000 to $69,999	109.67	99	14.3
$70,000 to $79,999	104.22	95	5.7
$80,000 to $99,999	135.12	123	10.2
$100,000 or more	158.17	143	24.6
HOUSEHOLD TYPE			
Average household	**110.25**	**100**	**100.0**
Married couples	134.89	122	60.4
Married couples, no children	90.40	82	17.4
Married couples, with children	166.88	151	35.2
Oldest child under age 6	129.08	117	5.0
Oldest child aged 6 to 17	174.86	159	18.7
Oldest child aged 18 or older	174.32	158	11.4
Single parent with child under age 18	130.56	118	7.0
Single person	53.29	48	14.2
RACE AND HISPANIC ORIGIN			
Average household	**110.25**	**100**	**100.0**
Asian	131.43	119	5.1
Black	147.05	133	16.3
Hispanic	164.49	149	18.2
Non-Hispanic white and other	96.37	87	66.3
REGION			
Average household	**110.25**	**100**	**100.0**
Northeast	128.47	117	21.4
Midwest	87.51	79	17.7
South	115.58	105	38.5
West	109.55	99	22.5
EDUCATION			
Average household	**110.25**	**100**	**100.0**
Less than high school graduate	121.22	110	15.7
High school graduate	109.91	100	25.5
Some college	95.05	86	18.1
Associate's degree	115.76	105	9.9
Bachelor's degree or more	114.91	104	31.0
Bachelor's degree	115.71	105	19.8
Master's, professional, doctoral degree	113.34	103	11.1

Note: Market shares may not sum to 100.0 because of rounding and missing categories by household type. "Asian" and "black" include Hispanics and non-Hispanics who identify themselves as being of the respective race alone. "Hispanic" includes people of any race who identify themselves as Hispanic. "Other" includes people who identify themselves as non-Hispanic and as Alaska Native, American Indian, Asian (who are also included in the "Asian" row), or Native Hawaiian or other Pacific Islander as well as non-Hispanics reporting more than one race.

Source: Calculations by New Strategist based on the Bureau of Labor Statistics' 2010 Consumer Expenditure Survey

Citrus Fruit Other than Oranges

Best customers:	Householders aged 35 to 54
	Married couples with children at home
	Asians and Hispanics
	Households in the West
Customer trends:	Average household spending on fresh citrus fruit other than oranges should rise as the Asian and Hispanic populations grow.

The largest households are the best customers of fresh citrus fruit other than oranges. Married couples with children at home spend 50 percent more than average on fresh citrus fruit excluding oranges. Householders aged 35 to 54 spend 17 to 19 percent more than average on this item. Hispanics, whose families tend to be relatively large, spend 56 percent more than average on fresh citrus fruit, and Asians spend 63 percent more. Together the two minority groups account for a sizeable 26 percent of the market. Households in the West, where many Asians and Hispanics reside and where fresh citrus fruit is widely available, spend 29 percent more than average on this item.

Average household spending on fresh citrus fruit other than oranges, which had stagnated in the earlier part of the decade, increased by a substantial 72 percent between 2006 and 2010, after adjusting for inflation. One factor behind the increase is the greater availability of a variety of citrus fruit in grocery stores. Average household spending on fresh citrus may continue to rise as the Asian and Hispanic populations grow.

Table 9.23 Citrus fruit other than oranges

Total household spending $3,805,181,940.00
Average household spends 31.42

	AVERAGE HOUSEHOLD SPENDING	BEST CUSTOMERS (index)	BIGGEST CUSTOMERS (market share)
AGE OF HOUSEHOLDER			
Average household	**$31.42**	**100**	**100.0%**
Under age 25	17.92	57	3.8
Aged 25 to 34	32.49	103	17.2
Aged 35 to 44	37.42	119	21.5
Aged 45 to 54	36.91	117	24.3
Aged 55 to 64	31.06	99	17.4
Aged 65 to 74	25.18	80	8.6
Aged 75 or older	23.30	74	7.1

	AVERAGE HOUSEHOLD SPENDING	BEST CUSTOMERS (index)	BIGGEST CUSTOMERS (market share)
HOUSEHOLD INCOME			
Average household	**$31.42**	**100**	**100.0%**
Under $20,000	18.62	59	12.9
$20,000 to $39,999	26.74	85	19.5
$40,000 to $49,999	26.00	83	7.8
$50,000 to $69,999	28.88	92	13.2
$70,000 to $79,999	30.20	96	5.8
$80,000 to $99,999	33.74	107	9.0
$100,000 or more	59.35	189	32.4
HOUSEHOLD TYPE			
Average household	**31.42**	**100**	**100.0**
Married couples	40.58	129	63.7
Married couples, no children	32.17	102	21.7
Married couples, with children	47.05	150	34.8
Oldest child under age 6	44.52	142	6.1
Oldest child aged 6 to 17	47.79	152	17.9
Oldest child aged 18 or older	47.23	150	10.9
Single parent with child under age 18	25.43	81	4.8
Single person	18.60	59	17.3
RACE AND HISPANIC ORIGIN			
Average household	**31.42**	**100**	**100.0**
Asian	51.37	163	7.0
Black	23.30	74	9.1
Hispanic	49.10	156	19.0
Non-Hispanic white and other	29.91	95	72.2
REGION			
Average household	**31.42**	**100**	**100.0**
Northeast	32.18	102	18.8
Midwest	31.16	99	22.1
South	25.71	82	30.0
West	40.45	129	29.2
EDUCATION			
Average household	**31.42**	**100**	**100.0**
Less than high school graduate	29.85	95	13.6
High school graduate	23.40	74	19.0
Some college	26.06	83	17.4
Associate's degree	29.17	93	8.8
Bachelor's degree or more	43.79	139	41.4
Bachelor's degree	38.55	123	23.2
Master's, professional, doctoral degree	54.11	172	18.6

Note: Market shares may not sum to 100.0 because of rounding and missing categories by household type. "Asian" and "black" include Hispanics and non-Hispanics who identify themselves as being of the respective race alone. "Hispanic" includes people of any race who identify themselves as Hispanic. "Other" includes people who identify themselves as non-Hispanic and as Alaska Native, American Indian, Asian (who are also included in the "Asian" row), or Native Hawaiian or other Pacific Islander as well as non-Hispanics reporting more than one race.

Source: Calculations by New Strategist based on the Bureau of Labor Statistics' 2010 Consumer Expenditure Survey

Coffee

Best customers:	**Householders aged 45 to 74** **Married couples without children at home** **Married couples with adult children at home**
Customer trends:	**Average household spending on coffee may decline in the years ahead as the millennial generation—which prefers cola to coffee—enters middle age.**

Starbucks has been successful in promoting coffee to the masses, and it may be the reason for the greater spending on coffee purchased at grocery and convenience stores. The best customers are householders ranging in age from 45 to 74, who spend 15 to 32 percent more than average on coffee. Married couples without children at home (most of them middle-aged and older) spend 33 percent more than average on this item, while those with adult children at home spend 41 percent more.

Average household spending on coffee purchased at grocery or convenience stores climbed slightly between 2000 and 2006 (up 2 percent after adjusting for inflation), then rose more strongly between 2006 and 2010 (up 12 percent). The surprising growth in spending on coffee purchased at groceries and convenience stores may be due to fewer trips to Starbucks and other restaurants as the Great Recession sapped incomes and reduced restaurant spending. Average household spending on coffee may decline in the years ahead, however, as the millennial generation—which prefers cola to coffee—enters middle age.

Table 9.24 Coffee

Total household spending	$7,296,696,750.00
Average household spends	60.25

	AVERAGE HOUSEHOLD SPENDING	BEST CUSTOMERS (index)	BIGGEST CUSTOMERS (market share)
AGE OF HOUSEHOLDER			
Average household	**$60.25**	**100**	**100.0%**
Under age 25	25.54	42	2.8
Aged 25 to 34	35.90	60	9.9
Aged 35 to 44	58.04	96	17.4
Aged 45 to 54	79.33	132	27.2
Aged 55 to 64	76.78	127	22.5
Aged 65 to 74	69.25	115	12.4
Aged 75 or older	47.53	79	7.5

	AVERAGE HOUSEHOLD SPENDING	BEST CUSTOMERS (index)	BIGGEST CUSTOMERS (market share)
HOUSEHOLD INCOME			
Average household	**$60.25**	**100**	**100.0%**
Under $20,000	37.01	61	13.4
$20,000 to $39,999	48.42	80	18.4
$40,000 to $49,999	57.28	95	9.0
$50,000 to $69,999	61.26	102	14.6
$70,000 to $79,999	68.21	113	6.8
$80,000 to $99,999	71.00	118	9.8
$100,000 or more	99.17	165	28.2
HOUSEHOLD TYPE			
Average household	**60.25**	**100**	**100.0**
Married couples	75.89	126	62.1
Married couples, no children	80.04	133	28.2
Married couples, with children	71.45	119	27.6
Oldest child under age 6	50.46	84	3.6
Oldest child aged 6 to 17	69.67	116	13.6
Oldest child aged 18 or older	84.83	141	10.2
Single parent with child under age 18	33.42	55	3.3
Single person	40.15	67	19.5
RACE AND HISPANIC ORIGIN			
Average household	**60.25**	**100**	**100.0**
Asian	43.86	73	3.1
Black	33.05	55	6.7
Hispanic	53.29	88	10.8
Non-Hispanic white and other	65.65	109	82.6
REGION			
Average household	**60.25**	**100**	**100.0**
Northeast	67.94	113	20.7
Midwest	51.56	86	19.1
South	57.48	95	35.0
West	67.30	112	25.3
EDUCATION			
Average household	**60.25**	**100**	**100.0**
Less than high school graduate	50.56	84	12.0
High school graduate	51.09	85	21.7
Some college	51.25	85	17.9
Associate's degree	61.77	103	9.7
Bachelor's degree or more	78.61	130	38.8
Bachelor's degree	72.75	121	22.8
Master's, professional, doctoral degree	90.17	150	16.2

Note: Market shares may not sum to 100.0 because of rounding and missing categories by household type. "Asian" and "black" include Hispanics and non-Hispanics who identify themselves as being of the respective race alone. "Hispanic" includes people of any race who identify themselves as Hispanic. "Other" includes people who identify themselves as non-Hispanic and as Alaska Native, American Indian, Asian (who are also included in the "Asian" row), or Native Hawaiian or other Pacific Islander as well as non-Hispanics reporting more than one race.

Source: Calculations by New Strategist based on the Bureau of Labor Statistics' 2010 Consumer Expenditure Survey

Cookies

Best customers: Householders aged 35 to 64
Married couples with school-aged or older children at home
Single parents

Customer trends: Average household spending on cookies may continue to decline until the large
millennial generation fills the best-customer lifestage.

The biggest spenders on cookies are households with children. Married couples with school-aged or older children at home spend 53 to 60 percent more than the average household on this item. Householders aged 35 to 64, many with children at home, spend 11 to 23 percent more than average on cookies. Single parents, whose spending approaches average on only a few items, outspend the average on cookies by 13 percent.

Average household spending on cookies fell 24 percent between 2000 and 2010, after adjusting for inflation. Behind the decline was increased competition with other snack foods for the dollars of shoppers as well as the baby-boom generation's exit from the best-customer lifestage. Average household spending on cookies may continue to decline until the large millennial generation fills the best-customer lifestage.

Table 9.25 Cookies

Total household spending $5,558,811,300.00
Average household spends 45.90

	AVERAGE HOUSEHOLD SPENDING	BEST CUSTOMERS (index)	BIGGEST CUSTOMERS (market share)
AGE OF HOUSEHOLDER			
Average household	**$45.90**	**100**	**100.0%**
Under age 25	21.63	47	3.1
Aged 25 to 34	37.49	82	13.6
Aged 35 to 44	52.01	113	20.5
Aged 45 to 54	56.43	123	25.4
Aged 55 to 64	50.99	111	19.6
Aged 65 to 74	41.97	91	9.8
Aged 75 or older	37.71	82	7.8

	AVERAGE HOUSEHOLD SPENDING	BEST CUSTOMERS (index)	BIGGEST CUSTOMERS (market share)
HOUSEHOLD INCOME			
Average household	**$45.90**	**100**	**100.0%**
Under $20,000	26.49	58	12.6
$20,000 to $39,999	39.15	85	19.5
$40,000 to $49,999	36.17	79	7.4
$50,000 to $69,999	43.09	94	13.5
$70,000 to $79,999	55.19	120	7.2
$80,000 to $99,999	62.10	135	11.3
$100,000 or more	76.86	167	28.7
HOUSEHOLD TYPE			
Average household	**45.90**	**100**	**100.0**
Married couples	58.62	128	63.0
Married couples, no children	47.38	103	21.9
Married couples, with children	66.96	146	33.9
Oldest child under age 6	44.48	97	4.1
Oldest child aged 6 to 17	70.18	153	18.0
Oldest child aged 18 or older	73.65	160	11.6
Single parent with child under age 18	51.99	113	6.7
Single person	21.25	46	13.6
RACE AND HISPANIC ORIGIN			
Average household	**45.90**	**100**	**100.0**
Asian	40.05	87	3.7
Black	39.29	86	10.5
Hispanic	43.51	95	11.5
Non-Hispanic white and other	47.40	103	78.3
REGION			
Average household	**45.90**	**100**	**100.0**
Northeast	51.39	112	20.5
Midwest	46.60	102	22.6
South	42.29	92	33.8
West	46.63	102	23.0
EDUCATION			
Average household	**45.90**	**100**	**100.0**
Less than high school graduate	41.03	89	12.8
High school graduate	39.66	86	22.1
Some college	37.49	82	17.2
Associate's degree	54.58	119	11.2
Bachelor's degree or more	56.74	124	36.7
Bachelor's degree	56.01	122	23.1
Master's, professional, doctoral degree	58.17	127	13.7

Note: Market shares may not sum to 100.0 because of rounding and missing categories by household type. "Asian" and "black" include Hispanics and non-Hispanics who identify themselves as being of the respective race alone. "Hispanic" includes people of any race who identify themselves as Hispanic. "Other" includes people who identify themselves as non-Hispanic and as Alaska Native, American Indian, Asian (who are also included in the "Asian" row), or Native Hawaiian or other Pacific Islander as well as non-Hispanics reporting more than one race.

Source: Calculations by New Strategist based on the Bureau of Labor Statistics' 2010 Consumer Expenditure Survey

Crackers

Best customers: **Householders aged 35 to 54**
                         Married couples with children at home

Customer trends: **Average household spending on crackers is likely to stabilize now that boomers**
                         are exiting the best-customer lifestage.

Married couples with children at home are the biggest spenders on crackers. This household type spends 56 percent more than the average household on crackers. The figure peaks at 64 percent more than average among households with school-aged children. Householders aged 35 to 54, most with children, spend 23 to 25 percent more than average on this item and account for almost half the market (48 percent).

Average household spending on crackers grew 23 percent between 2000 and 2010, after adjusting for inflation. Several factors account for this increase, such as the greater variety of crackers available and consumers' substitution of crackers for cookies in an attempt to cut calories. Average household spending on crackers is likely to stabilize now that boomers have are exiting the best-customer lifestage.

Table 9.26 Crackers

| Total household spending | $4,391,339,820.00 |
| Average household spends | 36.26 |

	AVERAGE HOUSEHOLD SPENDING	BEST CUSTOMERS (index)	BIGGEST CUSTOMERS (market share)
AGE OF HOUSEHOLDER			
Average household	$36.26	100	100.0%
Under age 25	17.54	48	3.2
Aged 25 to 34	29.62	82	13.6
Aged 35 to 44	45.21	125	22.6
Aged 45 to 54	44.56	123	25.4
Aged 55 to 64	34.77	96	16.9
Aged 65 to 74	34.86	96	10.3
Aged 75 or older	30.17	83	7.9

	AVERAGE HOUSEHOLD SPENDING	BEST CUSTOMERS (index)	BIGGEST CUSTOMERS (market share)
HOUSEHOLD INCOME			
Average household	$36.26	100	100.0%
Under $20,000	23.79	66	14.3
$20,000 to $39,999	28.87	80	18.2
$40,000 to $49,999	30.28	84	7.9
$50,000 to $69,999	32.95	91	13.0
$70,000 to $79,999	41.64	115	6.9
$80,000 to $99,999	44.21	122	10.2
$100,000 or more	63.50	175	30.0
HOUSEHOLD TYPE			
Average household	36.26	100	100.0
Married couples	46.97	130	63.9
Married couples, no children	36.02	99	21.1
Married couples, with children	56.46	156	36.2
Oldest child under age 6	46.48	128	5.5
Oldest child aged 6 to 17	59.51	164	19.3
Oldest child aged 18 or older	57.02	157	11.4
Single parent with child under age 18	30.84	85	5.0
Single person	19.07	53	15.4
RACE AND HISPANIC ORIGIN			
Average household	36.26	100	100.0
Asian	19.01	52	2.2
Black	25.84	71	8.7
Hispanic	28.30	78	9.5
Non-Hispanic white and other	39.15	108	81.9
REGION			
Average household	36.26	100	100.0
Northeast	38.60	106	19.5
Midwest	39.24	108	24.1
South	34.37	95	34.8
West	34.45	95	21.5
EDUCATION			
Average household	36.26	100	100.0
Less than high school graduate	29.27	81	11.5
High school graduate	32.48	90	22.9
Some college	31.75	88	18.4
Associate's degree	35.51	98	9.3
Bachelor's degree or more	46.22	127	37.9
Bachelor's degree	42.35	117	22.1
Master's, professional, doctoral degree	53.85	149	16.1

Note: Market shares may not sum to 100.0 because of rounding and missing categories by household type. "Asian" and "black" include Hispanics and non-Hispanics who identify themselves as being of the respective race alone. "Hispanic" includes people of any race who identify themselves as Hispanic. "Other" includes people who identify themselves as non-Hispanic and as Alaska Native, American Indian, Asian (who are also included in the "Asian" row), or Native Hawaiian or other Pacific Islander as well as non-Hispanics reporting more than one race.

Source: Calculations by New Strategist based on the Bureau of Labor Statistics' 2010 Consumer Expenditure Survey

Cream

Best customers: **Householders aged 35 to 54**
Married couples without children at home
Married couples with school-aged or older children at home
Households in the Northeast

Customer trends: **Average household spending on cream should stabilize now that boomers are**
exiting the best-customer lifestage.

Like butter, cream made a comeback when lower-carb diets became popular, especially among baby boomers. The biggest spenders on cream are the largest households—middle-aged married couples with children. Householders aged 35 to 54 spend 22 to 23 percent more than the average household on cream. Married couples with school-aged or older children at home spend 45 to 66 percent more than average on this item. Married couples without children at home, most empty-nesters, spend 27 percent more than average on cream. The spending on cream by households in the Northeast is 22 percent above average.

Average household spending on cream rose 35 percent between 2000 and 2010, after adjusting for inflation. Behind the increase is the improved reputation of cream because of the popularity of low-carb diets. Spending on cream should stabilize now that boomers are exiting the best-customer lifestage.

Table 9.27 Cream

| Total household spending | $2,407,607,160.00 |
| Average household spends | 19.88 |

	AVERAGE HOUSEHOLD SPENDING	BEST CUSTOMERS (index)	BIGGEST CUSTOMERS (market share)
AGE OF HOUSEHOLDER			
Average household	**$19.88**	**100**	**100.0%**
Under age 25	9.20	46	3.1
Aged 25 to 34	16.43	83	13.8
Aged 35 to 44	24.21	122	22.0
Aged 45 to 54	24.39	123	25.4
Aged 55 to 64	21.33	107	18.9
Aged 65 to 74	17.64	89	9.5
Aged 75 or older	15.12	76	7.3

	AVERAGE HOUSEHOLD SPENDING	BEST CUSTOMERS (index)	BIGGEST CUSTOMERS (market share)
HOUSEHOLD INCOME			
Average household	**$19.88**	**100**	**100.0%**
Under $20,000	11.30	57	12.4
$20,000 to $39,999	15.98	80	18.4
$40,000 to $49,999	16.82	85	8.0
$50,000 to $69,999	19.45	98	14.0
$70,000 to $79,999	18.45	93	5.6
$80,000 to $99,999	25.66	129	10.8
$100,000 or more	36.15	182	31.2
HOUSEHOLD TYPE			
Average household	**19.88**	**100**	**100.0**
Married couples	27.50	138	68.2
Married couples, no children	25.22	127	26.9
Married couples, with children	28.90	145	33.8
Oldest child under age 6	20.96	105	4.5
Oldest child aged 6 to 17	28.90	145	17.1
Oldest child aged 18 or older	32.97	166	12.0
Single parent with child under age 18	14.89	75	4.4
Single person	9.32	47	13.7
RACE AND HISPANIC ORIGIN			
Average household	**19.88**	**100**	**100.0**
Asian	11.02	55	2.4
Black	11.65	59	7.2
Hispanic	18.41	93	11.3
Non-Hispanic white and other	21.42	108	81.7
REGION			
Average household	**19.88**	**100**	**100.0**
Northeast	24.29	122	22.4
Midwest	20.67	104	23.2
South	16.32	82	30.1
West	21.33	107	24.3
EDUCATION			
Average household	**19.88**	**100**	**100.0**
Less than high school graduate	17.15	86	12.3
High school graduate	17.08	86	21.9
Some college	19.14	96	20.2
Associate's degree	19.42	98	9.2
Bachelor's degree or more	24.25	122	36.2
Bachelor's degree	22.24	112	21.1
Master's, professional, doctoral degree	28.22	142	15.4

Note: Market shares may not sum to 100.0 because of rounding and missing categories by household type. "Asian" and "black" include Hispanics and non-Hispanics who identify themselves as being of the respective race alone. "Hispanic" includes people of any race who identify themselves as Hispanic. "Other" includes people who identify themselves as non-Hispanic and as Alaska Native, American Indian, Asian (who are also included in the "Asian" row), or Native Hawaiian or other Pacific Islander as well as non-Hispanics reporting more than one race.

Source: Calculations by New Strategist based on the Bureau of Labor Statistics' 2010 Consumer Expenditure Survey

Dairy Products Other than Butter, Cheese, Cream, Ice Cream, and Milk

Best customers: **Householders aged 35 to 54**
          Married couples with children at home
          Households in the Northeast

Customer trends: **Average household spending on dairy products other than butter, cheese, cream,**
          ice cream, and milk should continue to grow as more consumers seek the health
          benefits of yogurt.

Some dairy products, such as yogurt, are growing in popularity. The biggest spenders on dairy products other than butter, cheese, cream, ice cream, and milk—a category that includes yogurt—are the largest households. Married couples with children at home spend 58 percent more than the average household on such dairy products. Householders aged 35 to 54, many with children, spend 22 to 23 percent more than average on this item and account for 47 percent of the market. Households in the Northeast spend 23 percent more than average on dairy products other than butter, cheese, cream, ice cream, and milk.

Average household spending on other dairy products rose by a substantial 55 percent between 2000 and 2010, after adjusting for inflation. Behind the increase is the growing popularity of yogurt and yogurt-based drinks. Average household spending on such dairy products may continue to rise as more consumers seek the health benefits of yogurt.

Table 9.28 Dairy products other than butter, cheese, cream, ice cream, and milk

Total household spending	$5,667,807,600.00
Average household spends	46.80

	AVERAGE HOUSEHOLD SPENDING	BEST CUSTOMERS (index)	BIGGEST CUSTOMERS (market share)
AGE OF HOUSEHOLDER			
Average household	**$46.80**	**100**	**100.0%**
Under age 25	26.39	56	3.7
Aged 25 to 34	46.15	99	16.4
Aged 35 to 44	57.52	123	22.2
Aged 45 to 54	57.05	122	25.2
Aged 55 to 64	42.96	92	16.2
Aged 65 to 74	41.75	89	9.6
Aged 75 or older	32.25	69	6.6

	AVERAGE HOUSEHOLD SPENDING	BEST CUSTOMERS (index)	BIGGEST CUSTOMERS (market share)
HOUSEHOLD INCOME			
Average household	**$46.80**	**100**	**100.0%**
Under $20,000	24.63	53	11.5
$20,000 to $39,999	35.42	76	17.3
$40,000 to $49,999	36.15	77	7.3
$50,000 to $69,999	48.38	103	14.8
$70,000 to $79,999	52.36	112	6.7
$80,000 to $99,999	54.94	117	9.8
$100,000 or more	90.67	194	33.2
HOUSEHOLD TYPE			
Average household	**46.80**	**100**	**100.0**
Married couples	62.55	134	65.9
Married couples, no children	48.82	104	22.2
Married couples, with children	74.13	158	36.8
Oldest child under age 6	73.13	156	6.7
Oldest child aged 6 to 17	75.95	162	19.1
Oldest child aged 18 or older	71.93	154	11.1
Single parent with child under age 18	33.67	72	4.2
Single person	23.82	51	14.9
RACE AND HISPANIC ORIGIN			
Average household	**46.80**	**100**	**100.0**
Asian	59.38	127	5.4
Black	31.31	67	8.2
Hispanic	53.29	114	13.9
Non-Hispanic white and other	48.26	103	78.2
REGION			
Average household	**46.80**	**100**	**100.0**
Northeast	57.64	123	22.6
Midwest	47.06	101	22.4
South	40.42	86	31.7
West	48.17	103	23.3
EDUCATION			
Average household	**46.80**	**100**	**100.0**
Less than high school graduate	35.88	77	11.0
High school graduate	36.08	77	19.7
Some college	40.19	86	18.1
Associate's degree	46.54	99	9.4
Bachelor's degree or more	65.95	141	41.9
Bachelor's degree	57.86	124	23.4
Master's, professional, doctoral degree	81.88	175	18.9

Note: Market shares may not sum to 100.0 because of rounding and missing categories by household type. "Asian" and "black" include Hispanics and non-Hispanics who identify themselves as being of the respective race alone. "Hispanic" includes people of any race who identify themselves as Hispanic. "Other" includes people who identify themselves as non-Hispanic and as Alaska Native, American Indian, Asian (who are also included in the "Asian" row), or Native Hawaiian or other Pacific Islander as well as non-Hispanics reporting more than one race.

Source: Calculations by New Strategist based on the Bureau of Labor Statistics' 2010 Consumer Expenditure Survey

Desserts, Prepared

Best customers:	**Householders aged 35 to 64** **Married couples with school-aged or older children at home**
Customer trends:	**Average household spending on prepared desserts may decline in the years ahead as boomers exit the best-customer lifestage and household size shrinks.**

The best customers of prepared desserts are the largest households. For convenience, they are buying prepared desserts rather than cooking from scratch. Couples with school-aged children spend 36 percent more than the average household on this item, and those with adult children at home spend 67 percent more than the average. Householders ranging in age from 35 to 64 outspend the average by 6 to 24 percent.

Average household spending on prepared desserts climbed 40 percent between 2000 and 2010, after adjusting for inflation. Behind the increase is the consumer preference for the convenience of prepared food. Average household spending on prepared desserts may decline in the years ahead as boomers exit the best-customer lifestage and household size shrinks.

Table 9.29 Desserts, prepared

Total household spending $2,001,898,710.00
Average household spends   16.53

	AVERAGE HOUSEHOLD SPENDING	BEST CUSTOMERS (index)	BIGGEST CUSTOMERS (market share)
AGE OF HOUSEHOLDER			
Average household	**$16.53**	**100**	**100.0%**
Under age 25	6.90	42	2.8
Aged 25 to 34	12.48	75	12.6
Aged 35 to 44	17.47	106	19.1
Aged 45 to 54	19.53	118	24.4
Aged 55 to 64	20.45	124	21.8
Aged 65 to 74	14.49	88	9.4
Aged 75 or older	17.02	103	9.8

	AVERAGE HOUSEHOLD SPENDING	BEST CUSTOMERS (index)	BIGGEST CUSTOMERS (market share)
HOUSEHOLD INCOME			
Average household	**$16.53**	**100**	**100.0%**
Under $20,000	13.14	80	17.4
$20,000 to $39,999	13.08	79	18.1
$40,000 to $49,999	13.48	82	7.7
$50,000 to $69,999	14.87	90	12.9
$70,000 to $79,999	16.30	99	5.9
$80,000 to $99,999	22.61	137	11.4
$100,000 or more	26.11	158	27.1
HOUSEHOLD TYPE			
Average household	**16.53**	**100**	**100.0**
Married couples	20.45	124	61.0
Married couples, no children	18.78	114	24.1
Married couples, with children	22.42	136	31.6
Oldest child under age 6	12.00	73	3.1
Oldest child aged 6 to 17	22.54	136	16.0
Oldest child aged 18 or older	27.57	167	12.0
Single parent with child under age 18	15.58	94	5.6
Single person	9.93	60	17.6
RACE AND HISPANIC ORIGIN			
Average household	**16.53**	**100**	**100.0**
Asian	10.97	66	2.8
Black	10.54	64	7.8
Hispanic	15.70	95	11.6
Non-Hispanic white and other	17.59	106	80.7
REGION			
Average household	**16.53**	**100**	**100.0**
Northeast	18.07	109	20.1
Midwest	18.01	109	24.3
South	14.83	90	32.9
West	16.58	100	22.7
EDUCATION			
Average household	**16.53**	**100**	**100.0**
Less than high school graduate	15.77	95	13.6
High school graduate	16.28	98	25.1
Some college	15.11	91	19.2
Associate's degree	16.09	97	9.2
Bachelor's degree or more	18.28	111	32.9
Bachelor's degree	18.09	109	20.7
Master's, professional, doctoral degree	18.66	113	12.2

Note: Market shares may not sum to 100.0 because of rounding and missing categories by household type. "Asian" and "black" include Hispanics and non-Hispanics who identify themselves as being of the respective race alone. "Hispanic" includes people of any race who identify themselves as Hispanic. "Other" includes people who identify themselves as non-Hispanic and as Alaska Native, American Indian, Asian (who are also included in the "Asian" row), or Native Hawaiian or other Pacific Islander as well as non-Hispanics reporting more than one race.

Source: Calculations by New Strategist based on the Bureau of Labor Statistics' 2010 Consumer Expenditure Survey

Eggs

Best customers:	Householders aged 35 to 54
	Married couples with school-aged or older children at home
	Hispanics and Asians
	Households in the West
Customer trends:	Average household spending on eggs may decline as more boomers become empty-nesters and household size shrinks.

Household size is the most-important factor in determining spending on eggs, the largest households spending the most. Married couples with school-aged children spend 48 percent more than the average household on eggs, and those with adult children at home, 42 percent. Householders aged 35 to 54, most with children, outspend the average for eggs by 17 to 20 percent. Hispanics, whose families are larger than average, spend 56 percent more than average on eggs. Asians spend 27 percent more. Households in the West, where many Asians and Hispanics reside, spend 20 percent more than average on this item.

Average household spending on eggs declined 9 percent between 2000 and 2006, after adjusting for inflation, but rebounded by 17 percent between 2006 and 2010. Behind the rise was the improving reputation of eggs thanks to the popularity of low-carb diets, as well as consumers' increased propensity to eat at home as the Great Recession reduced incomes. Spending on eggs is likely to stabilize or even decline as more boomers become empty-nesters and household size shrinks.

Table 9.30 **Eggs**

Total household spending	$5,606,043,030.00
Average household spends	46.29

	AVERAGE HOUSEHOLD SPENDING	BEST CUSTOMERS (index)	BIGGEST CUSTOMERS (market share)
AGE OF HOUSEHOLDER			
Average household	**$46.29**	**100**	**100.0%**
Under age 25	30.68	66	4.4
Aged 25 to 34	45.81	99	16.5
Aged 35 to 44	54.32	117	21.2
Aged 45 to 54	55.40	120	24.8
Aged 55 to 64	43.74	94	16.7
Aged 65 to 74	42.22	91	9.8
Aged 75 or older	32.09	69	6.6

	AVERAGE HOUSEHOLD SPENDING	BEST CUSTOMERS (index)	BIGGEST CUSTOMERS (market share)
HOUSEHOLD INCOME			
Average household	$46.29	100	100.0%
Under $20,000	35.42	77	16.7
$20,000 to $39,999	41.97	91	20.8
$40,000 to $49,999	41.69	90	8.5
$50,000 to $69,999	46.93	101	14.5
$70,000 to $79,999	44.86	97	5.8
$80,000 to $99,999	53.73	116	9.7
$100,000 or more	65.31	141	24.2
HOUSEHOLD TYPE			
Average household	46.29	100	100.0
Married couples	56.79	123	60.5
Married couples, no children	43.60	94	20.0
Married couples, with children	64.14	139	32.2
Oldest child under age 6	47.76	103	4.4
Oldest child aged 6 to 17	68.65	148	17.4
Oldest child aged 18 or older	65.79	142	10.3
Single parent with child under age 18	42.67	92	5.4
Single person	25.06	54	15.9
RACE AND HISPANIC ORIGIN			
Average household	46.29	100	100.0
Asian	58.60	127	5.4
Black	46.83	101	12.4
Hispanic	72.21	156	19.0
Non-Hispanic white and other	42.15	91	69.0
REGION			
Average household	46.29	100	100.0
Northeast	50.66	109	20.1
Midwest	39.85	86	19.2
South	42.37	92	33.6
West	55.70	120	27.3
EDUCATION			
Average household	46.29	100	100.0
Less than high school graduate	53.30	115	16.5
High school graduate	44.61	96	24.6
Some college	43.01	93	19.5
Associate's degree	45.09	97	9.2
Bachelor's degree or more	47.45	103	30.5
Bachelor's degree	46.66	101	19.0
Master's, professional, doctoral degree	49.01	106	11.5

Note: Market shares may not sum to 100.0 because of rounding and missing categories by household type. "Asian" and "black" include Hispanics and non-Hispanics who identify themselves as being of the respective race alone. "Hispanic" includes people of any race who identify themselves as Hispanic. "Other" includes people who identify themselves as non-Hispanic and as Alaska Native, American Indian, Asian (who are also included in the "Asian" row), or Native Hawaiian or other Pacific Islander as well as non-Hispanics reporting more than one race.

Source: Calculations by New Strategist based on the Bureau of Labor Statistics' 2010 Consumer Expenditure Survey

Fats and Oils

Best customers:

Householders aged 35 to 54
Married couples with school-aged or older children at home
Single parents
Hispanics, Asians, and blacks
Households in the Northeast
Householders without a high school diploma

Customer trends:

Average household spending on fats and oils may level out in the years ahead if eating out regains its pre–Great Recession popularity.

The biggest spenders on fats and oils are Hispanics, Asians, and blacks. Hispanics spend 70 percent more, Asians 61 percent more, and blacks 20 percent more than average on fats and oils. Together the three minorities, which represent 29 percent of the population, account for 42 percent of the market for fats and oils. Married couples with school-aged or older children at home spend 41 to 53 percent more than average on fats and oils. Single parents, whose spending approaches average on only a few items, spend 5 percent more than average on this item. Households in the Northeast outspend the average by 24 percent. The spending on fats and oils of householders who did not complete high school is one-third above average.

Average household spending on fats and oils rose 7 percent between 2000 and 2010, after adjusting for inflation. Behind the increase was the popularity of high-priced specialty oils, as well as the growth of the Asian, black, and Hispanic populations. Average household spending on fats and oils may level out in the years ahead if eating out regains its pre–Great Recession popularity.

Table 9.31 Fats and oils

Total household spending $3,813,659,430.00
Average household spends   31.49

	AVERAGE HOUSEHOLD SPENDING	BEST CUSTOMERS (index)	BIGGEST CUSTOMERS (market share)
AGE OF HOUSEHOLDER			
Average household	**$31.49**	**100**	**100.0%**
Under age 25	23.67	75	5.0
Aged 25 to 34	27.23	86	14.4
Aged 35 to 44	36.58	116	21.0
Aged 45 to 54	35.58	113	23.4
Aged 55 to 64	32.45	103	18.2
Aged 65 to 74	31.88	101	10.9
Aged 75 or older	23.44	74	7.1

	AVERAGE HOUSEHOLD SPENDING	BEST CUSTOMERS (index)	BIGGEST CUSTOMERS (market share)
HOUSEHOLD INCOME			
Average household	$31.49	100	100.0%
Under $20,000	24.74	79	17.1
$20,000 to $39,999	27.17	86	19.8
$40,000 to $49,999	32.14	102	9.6
$50,000 to $69,999	29.44	93	13.4
$70,000 to $79,999	24.23	77	4.6
$80,000 to $99,999	36.18	115	9.6
$100,000 or more	47.76	152	26.0
HOUSEHOLD TYPE			
Average household	31.49	100	100.0
Married couples	38.33	122	60.0
Married couples, no children	29.92	95	20.2
Married couples, with children	42.58	135	31.5
Oldest child under age 6	26.22	83	3.6
Oldest child aged 6 to 17	44.39	141	16.6
Oldest child aged 18 or older	48.25	153	11.1
Single parent with child under age 18	33.00	105	6.2
Single person	15.89	50	14.8
RACE AND HISPANIC ORIGIN			
Average household	31.49	100	100.0
Asian	50.83	161	6.9
Black	37.69	120	14.6
Hispanic	53.53	170	20.7
Non-Hispanic white and other	27.00	86	65.0
REGION			
Average household	31.49	100	100.0
Northeast	39.02	124	22.7
Midwest	26.23	83	18.6
South	32.41	103	37.8
West	29.11	92	20.9
EDUCATION			
Average household	31.49	100	100.0
Less than high school graduate	41.94	133	19.0
High school graduate	27.62	88	22.4
Some college	28.43	90	19.0
Associate's degree	30.12	96	9.0
Bachelor's degree or more	32.94	105	31.1
Bachelor's degree	31.05	99	18.6
Master's, professional, doctoral degree	36.67	116	12.6

Note: Market shares may not sum to 100.0 because of rounding and missing categories by household type. "Asian" and "black" include Hispanics and non-Hispanics who identify themselves as being of the respective race alone. "Hispanic" includes people of any race who identify themselves as Hispanic. "Other" includes people who identify themselves as non-Hispanic and as Alaska Native, American Indian, Asian (who are also included in the "Asian" row), or Native Hawaiian or other Pacific Islander as well as non-Hispanics reporting more than one race.

Source: Calculations by New Strategist based on the Bureau of Labor Statistics' 2010 Consumer Expenditure Survey

Fish and Seafood, Canned

Best customers: **Householders aged 45 to 64**
Married couples with children at home
Asians
Households in the Northeast

Customer trends: **Average household spending on canned fish and seafood may resume its slow
decline as consumer preferences shift from canned to frozen fish.**

The biggest spenders on canned fish and seafood are older householders. Householders ranging in age from 45 to 64 spend 19 to 24 percent more than the average household on this item and account for 46 percent of the market. Couples with adult children at home spend 43 percent more than average on canned fish and seafood, and those with younger children, 23 to 27 percent more. Asians outspend the average by 12 percent. Households in the Northeast spend one-third more than average on canned fish.

Average household spending on canned fish and seafood fell 10 percent between 2000 and 2006, after adjusting for inflation, but spending rebounded between 2006 and 2010 for a 2 percent increase over the decade. Behind the earlier decline was the shift from canned to frozen fish and the then-growing preference for eating out rather than preparing meals from scratch. Average household spending on canned fish and seafood may resume its slow decline as consumer preferences shift from canned to frozen fish.

Table 9.32 Fish and seafood, canned

| Total household spending | $2,441,517,120.00 |
| Average household spends | 20.16 |

	AVERAGE HOUSEHOLD SPENDING	BEST CUSTOMERS (index)	BIGGEST CUSTOMERS (market share)
AGE OF HOUSEHOLDER			
Average household	**$20.16**	**100**	**100.0%**
Under age 25	6.40	32	2.1
Aged 25 to 34	15.41	76	12.7
Aged 35 to 44	20.14	100	18.1
Aged 45 to 54	23.91	119	24.5
Aged 55 to 64	24.98	124	21.9
Aged 65 to 74	21.44	106	11.4
Aged 75 or older	19.43	96	9.2

	AVERAGE HOUSEHOLD SPENDING	BEST CUSTOMERS (index)	BIGGEST CUSTOMERS (market share)
HOUSEHOLD INCOME			
Average household	**$20.16**	**100**	**100.0%**
Under $20,000	14.18	70	15.4
$20,000 to $39,999	16.79	83	19.1
$40,000 to $49,999	17.58	87	8.2
$50,000 to $69,999	20.11	100	14.3
$70,000 to $79,999	18.93	94	5.6
$80,000 to $99,999	21.50	107	8.9
$100,000 or more	34.11	169	29.0
HOUSEHOLD TYPE			
Average household	**20.16**	**100**	**100.0**
Married couples	24.73	123	60.5
Married couples, no children	22.22	110	23.4
Married couples, with children	26.29	130	30.3
Oldest child under age 6	25.53	127	5.4
Oldest child aged 6 to 17	24.88	123	14.5
Oldest child aged 18 or older	28.77	143	10.3
Single parent with child under age 18	17.14	85	5.0
Single person	13.32	66	19.4
RACE AND HISPANIC ORIGIN			
Average household	**20.16**	**100**	**100.0**
Asian	22.55	112	4.8
Black	21.50	107	13.1
Hispanic	18.77	93	11.3
Non-Hispanic white and other	20.16	100	75.8
REGION			
Average household	**20.16**	**100**	**100.0**
Northeast	26.61	132	24.2
Midwest	18.42	91	20.4
South	17.01	84	31.0
West	21.83	108	24.5
EDUCATION			
Average household	**20.16**	**100**	**100.0**
Less than high school graduate	16.47	82	11.7
High school graduate	19.11	95	24.2
Some college	18.35	91	19.1
Associate's degree	17.57	87	8.2
Bachelor's degree or more	24.91	124	36.7
Bachelor's degree	22.96	114	21.5
Master's, professional, doctoral degree	28.76	143	15.4

Note: Market shares may not sum to 100.0 because of rounding and missing categories by household type. "Asian" and "black" include Hispanics and non-Hispanics who identify themselves as being of the respective race alone. "Hispanic" includes people of any race who identify themselves as Hispanic. "Other" includes people who identify themselves as non-Hispanic and as Alaska Native, American Indian, Asian (who are also included in the "Asian" row), or Native Hawaiian or other Pacific Islander as well as non-Hispanics reporting more than one race.

Source: Calculations by New Strategist based on the Bureau of Labor Statistics' 2010 Consumer Expenditure Survey

Fish and Shellfish, Fresh

Best customers:	**Householders aged 35 to 64**
	Married couples with school-aged or older children at home
	Asians, Hispanics, and blacks
	Households in the Northeast
Customer trends:	**Average household spending on fresh fish may continue its decline if consumers opt for prepared meals rather than home cooking.**

The best customers of fresh fish and shellfish are minorities and the largest households. Asians spend two-and-one-half times the average on fresh fish, while Hispanics and blacks spend, respectively, 32 and 24 percent above average on fresh fish. Together the three minority groups, which represent 29 percent of the population, account for 42 percent of the market for fresh fish. Householders ranging in age from 35 to 64 spend 16 to 30 percent more than average on fresh fish. Married couples with school-aged or older children at home spend 47 to 62 percent more than average on this item. Households in the Northeast spend 39 percent more than average on fresh fish.

Average household spending on fresh fish fell 20 percent between 2000 and 2006, after adjusting for inflation, and another 18 percent between 2006 and 2010. Behind the earlier decline was the shift from fresh to frozen fish, as well as the then-growing propensity of Americans to eat out rather than prepare a meal from scratch. Average household spending on fresh fish may continue its decline if consumers opt for prepared meals rather than home cooking.

Table 9.33 Fish and shellfish, fresh

Total household spending	$6,691,161,750.00
Average household spends	55.25

	AVERAGE HOUSEHOLD SPENDING	BEST CUSTOMERS (index)	BIGGEST CUSTOMERS (market share)
AGE OF HOUSEHOLDER			
Average household	**$55.25**	**100**	**100.0%**
Under age 25	19.98	36	2.4
Aged 25 to 34	45.38	82	13.7
Aged 35 to 44	64.20	116	21.0
Aged 45 to 54	71.57	130	26.8
Aged 55 to 64	64.40	117	20.6
Aged 65 to 74	52.77	96	10.3
Aged 75 or older	29.69	54	5.1

	AVERAGE HOUSEHOLD SPENDING	BEST CUSTOMERS (index)	BIGGEST CUSTOMERS (market share)
HOUSEHOLD INCOME			
Average household	**$55.25**	**100**	**100.0%**
Under $20,000	30.61	55	12.1
$20,000 to $39,999	38.72	70	16.1
$40,000 to $49,999	42.88	78	7.3
$50,000 to $69,999	51.94	94	13.5
$70,000 to $79,999	43.49	79	4.7
$80,000 to $99,999	68.48	124	10.3
$100,000 or more	118.40	214	36.7
HOUSEHOLD TYPE			
Average household	**55.25**	**100**	**100.0**
Married couples	70.78	128	63.2
Married couples, no children	60.65	110	23.3
Married couples, with children	79.20	143	33.3
Oldest child under age 6	52.92	96	4.1
Oldest child aged 6 to 17	81.17	147	17.3
Oldest child aged 18 or older	89.72	162	11.7
Single parent with child under age 18	49.44	89	5.3
Single person	30.28	55	16.1
RACE AND HISPANIC ORIGIN			
Average household	**55.25**	**100**	**100.0**
Asian	137.53	249	10.6
Black	68.37	124	15.1
Hispanic	73.07	132	16.1
Non-Hispanic white and other	50.53	91	69.3
REGION			
Average household	**55.25**	**100**	**100.0**
Northeast	76.73	139	25.5
Midwest	33.75	61	13.6
South	53.85	97	35.8
West	61.71	112	25.3
EDUCATION			
Average household	**55.25**	**100**	**100.0**
Less than high school graduate	51.69	94	13.4
High school graduate	44.04	80	20.4
Some college	48.00	87	18.3
Associate's degree	46.90	85	8.0
Bachelor's degree or more	74.75	135	40.2
Bachelor's degree	63.02	114	21.5
Master's, professional, doctoral degree	97.84	177	19.2

Note: Market shares may not sum to 100.0 because of rounding and missing categories by household type. "Asian" and "black" include Hispanics and non-Hispanics who identify themselves as being of the respective race alone. "Hispanic" includes people of any race who identify themselves as Hispanic. "Other" includes people who identify themselves as non-Hispanic and as Alaska Native, American Indian, Asian (who are also included in the "Asian" row), or Native Hawaiian or other Pacific Islander as well as non-Hispanics reporting more than one race.

Source: Calculations by New Strategist based on the Bureau of Labor Statistics' 2010 Consumer Expenditure Survey

Fish and Shellfish, Frozen

Best customers: **Householders aged 35 to 54**
Married couples with school-aged or older children at home
Asians, Hispanics, and blacks

Customer trends: **Average household spending on frozen fish could continue to decline for the next few years because the small generation X is in the best-customer lifestage.**

The largest households are the best customers of frozen fish. Married couples with school-aged or older children at home spend 39 to 58 percent more than average on this item. Householders aged 35 to 54, most with children, spend 14 to 17 percent more than average on frozen fish. Asian households spend more than twice the average on this item. Hispanics and blacks spend, respectively, 20 and 17 percent above average on frozen fish. Together the three minority groups, which represent 29 percent of the population, account for 38 percent of the market for frozen fish.

Average household spending on frozen fish rose by a healthy 32 percent between 2000 and 2006, after adjusting for inflation, but spending declined by 10 percent since then. Behind the earlier increase were nutritional claims regarding the benefits of fish consumption and the shift away from canned and fresh fish to the greater convenience of frozen fish. Average household spending on frozen fish could continue to decline for the next few years because the small generation X is in the best-customer lifestage.

Table 9.34 Fish and shellfish, frozen

Total household spending $5,046,528,690.00
Average household spends   41.67

	AVERAGE HOUSEHOLD SPENDING	BEST CUSTOMERS (index)	BIGGEST CUSTOMERS (market share)
AGE OF HOUSEHOLDER			
Average household	**$41.67**	**100**	**100.0%**
Under age 25	18.16	44	2.9
Aged 25 to 34	43.60	105	17.4
Aged 35 to 44	47.58	114	20.7
Aged 45 to 54	48.68	117	24.2
Aged 55 to 64	42.76	103	18.1
Aged 65 to 74	35.95	86	9.3
Aged 75 or older	32.58	78	7.5

	AVERAGE HOUSEHOLD SPENDING	BEST CUSTOMERS (index)	BIGGEST CUSTOMERS (market share)
HOUSEHOLD INCOME			
Average household	**$41.67**	**100**	**100.0%**
Under $20,000	29.51	71	15.5
$20,000 to $39,999	35.27	85	19.4
$40,000 to $49,999	40.47	97	9.2
$50,000 to $69,999	35.71	86	12.3
$70,000 to $79,999	33.59	81	4.8
$80,000 to $99,999	49.32	118	9.9
$100,000 or more	70.77	170	29.1
HOUSEHOLD TYPE			
Average household	**41.67**	**100**	**100.0**
Married couples	52.66	126	62.3
Married couples, no children	45.37	109	23.1
Married couples, with children	57.16	137	31.9
Oldest child under age 6	37.66	90	3.9
Oldest child aged 6 to 17	58.00	139	16.4
Oldest child aged 18 or older	65.87	158	11.4
Single parent with child under age 18	34.06	82	4.8
Single person	22.95	55	16.1
RACE AND HISPANIC ORIGIN			
Average household	**41.67**	**100**	**100.0**
Asian	91.20	219	9.3
Black	48.93	117	14.4
Hispanic	49.89	120	14.6
Non-Hispanic white and other	39.19	94	71.3
REGION			
Average household	**41.67**	**100**	**100.0**
Northeast	45.43	109	20.0
Midwest	33.51	80	17.9
South	42.36	102	37.3
West	45.69	110	24.8
EDUCATION			
Average household	**41.67**	**100**	**100.0**
Less than high school graduate	43.84	105	15.0
High school graduate	40.92	98	25.1
Some college	31.28	75	15.8
Associate's degree	37.78	91	8.6
Bachelor's degree or more	50.22	121	35.8
Bachelor's degree	46.79	112	21.2
Master's, professional, doctoral degree	56.97	137	14.8

Note: Market shares may not sum to 100.0 because of rounding and missing categories by household type. "Asian" and "black" include Hispanics and non-Hispanics who identify themselves as being of the respective race alone. "Hispanic" includes people of any race who identify themselves as Hispanic. "Other" includes people who identify themselves as non-Hispanic and as Alaska Native, American Indian, Asian (who are also included in the "Asian" row), or Native Hawaiian or other Pacific Islander as well as non-Hispanics reporting more than one race.

Source: Calculations by New Strategist based on the Bureau of Labor Statistics' 2010 Consumer Expenditure Survey

Flour

Best customers: **Householders aged 35 to 44**
                                    Married couples with children at home
                                    Asians and Hispanics
                                    Householders without a high school diploma

Customer trends: **Average household spending on flour should resume its decline if discretionary income begins to grow again and eating out regains its popularity.**

The biggest spenders on flour are the households most likely to cook from scratch—typically married couples with children at home. This household type spends 58 percent more than average on flour, the figure peaking at 76 percent above average among couples with preschoolers. Householders aged 35 to 44, many with young children, spend 34 percent more than average on this item. Asians spend twice the average amount on flour, and Hispanics spend 42 percent more. Households headed by people without a high school diploma spend 71 percent more than average on flour.

Average household spending on flour fell 47 percent between 2000 and 2006, after adjusting for inflation, then rebounded with a 47 percent increase between 2006 and 2010 for an overall minus of 22 percent. Behind the earlier decline was the rise of eating out as busy families found less time to cook from scratch. The Great Recession then shifted restaurant dollars back to the grocery store as families endeavored to cut spending. Average household spending on flour should resume its decline if discretionary income begins to grow again and eating out regains its popularity.

Table 9.35　Flour

Total household spending $955,534,230.00
Average household spends   7.89

	AVERAGE HOUSEHOLD SPENDING	BEST CUSTOMERS (index)	BIGGEST CUSTOMERS (market share)
AGE OF HOUSEHOLDER			
Average household	**$7.89**	**100**	**100.0%**
Under age 25	3.88	49	3.3
Aged 25 to 34	7.19	91	15.2
Aged 35 to 44	10.57	134	24.2
Aged 45 to 54	8.55	108	22.4
Aged 55 to 64	7.60	96	17.0
Aged 65 to 74	8.77	111	12.0
Aged 75 or older	4.92	62	5.9

	AVERAGE HOUSEHOLD SPENDING	BEST CUSTOMERS (index)	BIGGEST CUSTOMERS (market share)
HOUSEHOLD INCOME			
Average household	**$7.89**	**100**	**100.0%**
Under $20,000	5.59	71	15.5
$20,000 to $39,999	6.17	78	17.9
$40,000 to $49,999	8.45	107	10.1
$50,000 to $69,999	7.58	96	13.8
$70,000 to $79,999	12.81	162	9.7
$80,000 to $99,999	8.89	113	9.4
$100,000 or more	10.93	139	23.8
HOUSEHOLD TYPE			
Average household	**7.89**	**100**	**100.0**
Married couples	10.81	137	67.6
Married couples, no children	8.36	106	22.5
Married couples, with children	12.50	158	36.9
Oldest child under age 6	13.90	176	7.5
Oldest child aged 6 to 17	12.96	164	19.3
Oldest child aged 18 or older	11.09	141	10.1
Single parent with child under age 18	5.53	70	4.1
Single person	3.30	42	12.3
RACE AND HISPANIC ORIGIN			
Average household	**7.89**	**100**	**100.0**
Asian	16.09	204	8.7
Black	7.25	92	11.2
Hispanic	11.20	142	17.3
Non-Hispanic white and other	7.46	95	71.7
REGION			
Average household	**7.89**	**100**	**100.0**
Northeast	9.64	122	22.4
Midwest	8.20	104	23.2
South	6.22	79	28.9
West	8.88	113	25.5
EDUCATION			
Average household	**7.89**	**100**	**100.0**
Less than high school graduate	13.49	171	24.4
High school graduate	7.05	89	22.8
Some college	6.04	77	16.1
Associate's degree	4.70	60	5.6
Bachelor's degree or more	8.55	108	32.2
Bachelor's degree	7.58	96	18.1
Master's, professional, doctoral degree	10.47	133	14.4

Note: Market shares may not sum to 100.0 because of rounding and missing categories by household type. "Asian" and "black" include Hispanics and non-Hispanics who identify themselves as being of the respective race alone. "Hispanic" includes people of any race who identify themselves as Hispanic. "Other" includes people who identify themselves as non-Hispanic and as Alaska Native, American Indian, Asian (who are also included in the "Asian" row), or Native Hawaiian or other Pacific Islander as well as non-Hispanics reporting more than one race.

Source: Calculations by New Strategist based on the Bureau of Labor Statistics' 2010 Consumer Expenditure Survey

Flour, Prepared Mixes

Best customers: Householders aged 35 to 54
                         Married couples with school-aged or older children at home
                         Households in the Midwest

Customer trends: Average household spending on flour mixes should resume its decline if discretionary income begins to grow again and eating out regains its popularity.

The biggest spenders on prepared flour mixes—such as cake and biscuit mixes—are married couples with children. Couples with school-aged or older children at home spend 57 to 67 percent more than average on flour mixes. Householders aged 35 to 54, most with children, spend 25 to 40 percent more than average on prepared flour mixes. Households in the Midwest outspend the average by 19 percent.

Average household spending on prepared flour mixes fell 28 percent between 2000 and 2006, after adjusting for inflation, then rebounded by growing 25 percent between 2006 and 2010. Behind the earlier spending cut was the decline in home cooking. Behind the rebound is the Great Recession, with more consumers baking at home to save money. Average household spending on flour mixes should resume its decline if discretionary income begins to grow again and eating out regains its popularity.

Table 9.36 Flour, prepared mixes

Total household spending $1,846,881,750.00
Average household spends   15.25

	AVERAGE HOUSEHOLD SPENDING	BEST CUSTOMERS (index)	BIGGEST CUSTOMERS (market share)
AGE OF HOUSEHOLDER			
Average household	**$15.25**	**100**	**100.0%**
Under age 25	7.49	49	3.3
Aged 25 to 34	12.36	81	13.5
Aged 35 to 44	19.11	125	22.7
Aged 45 to 54	21.42	140	29.1
Aged 55 to 64	15.56	102	18.0
Aged 65 to 74	10.50	69	7.4
Aged 75 or older	9.65	63	6.0

	AVERAGE HOUSEHOLD SPENDING	BEST CUSTOMERS (index)	BIGGEST CUSTOMERS (market share)
HOUSEHOLD INCOME			
Average household	**$15.25**	**100**	**100.0%**
Under $20,000	9.20	60	13.2
$20,000 to $39,999	9.78	64	14.7
$40,000 to $49,999	13.31	87	8.2
$50,000 to $69,999	16.79	110	15.8
$70,000 to $79,999	15.57	102	6.1
$80,000 to $99,999	20.05	131	11.0
$100,000 or more	28.00	184	31.5
HOUSEHOLD TYPE			
Average household	**15.25**	**100**	**100.0**
Married couples	20.38	134	65.9
Married couples, no children	16.17	106	22.5
Married couples, with children	23.23	152	35.4
Oldest child under age 6	15.18	100	4.3
Oldest child aged 6 to 17	25.46	167	19.6
Oldest child aged 18 or older	24.01	157	11.4
Single parent with child under age 18	12.19	80	4.7
Single person	7.23	47	13.9
RACE AND HISPANIC ORIGIN			
Average household	**15.25**	**100**	**100.0**
Asian	7.62	50	2.1
Black	12.73	83	10.2
Hispanic	12.49	82	10.0
Non-Hispanic white and other	16.06	105	79.8
REGION			
Average household	**15.25**	**100**	**100.0**
Northeast	16.08	105	19.4
Midwest	18.20	119	26.6
South	12.59	83	30.3
West	15.98	105	23.7
EDUCATION			
Average household	**15.25**	**100**	**100.0**
Less than high school graduate	12.93	85	12.1
High school graduate	14.86	97	24.9
Some college	13.16	86	18.1
Associate's degree	16.89	111	10.5
Bachelor's degree or more	17.60	115	34.3
Bachelor's degree	17.44	114	21.6
Master's, professional, doctoral degree	17.92	118	12.7

Note: Market shares may not sum to 100.0 because of rounding and missing categories by household type. "Asian" and "black" include Hispanics and non-Hispanics who identify themselves as being of the respective race alone. "Hispanic" includes people of any race who identify themselves as Hispanic. "Other" includes people who identify themselves as non-Hispanic and as Alaska Native, American Indian, Asian (who are also included in the "Asian" row), or Native Hawaiian or other Pacific Islander as well as non-Hispanics reporting more than one race.

Source: Calculations by New Strategist based on the Bureau of Labor Statistics' 2010 Consumer Expenditure Survey

Frankfurters

Best customers: Householders aged 35 to 54
Married couples with children at home
Single parents

Customer trends: Average household spending on frankfurters may resume its decline because the small generation X is in the best-customer lifestage.

Households with children are the biggest spenders on frankfurters. Married couples with children at home spend 43 percent more than average on this item; the figure peaks at 58 percent above average among couples with school-aged children. Householders aged 35 to 54, most with children, spend 13 to 20 percent more than average on hot dogs. Single parents, whose spending approaches the average on only a few items, spend an average amount on frankfurters.

Average household spending on frankfurters fell 17 percent between 2000 and 2006, after adjusting for inflation, but spending has rebounded by 12 percent since then. Average household spending on hot dogs may resume its decline because the small generation X is in the best-customer lifestage.

Table 9.37 Frankfurters

Total household spending $2,968,332,570.00
Average household spends 24.51

	AVERAGE HOUSEHOLD SPENDING	BEST CUSTOMERS (index)	BIGGEST CUSTOMERS (market share)
AGE OF HOUSEHOLDER			
Average household	**$24.51**	**100**	**100.0%**
Under age 25	19.43	79	5.3
Aged 25 to 34	24.17	99	16.4
Aged 35 to 44	29.52	120	21.8
Aged 45 to 54	27.62	113	23.3
Aged 55 to 64	23.40	95	16.8
Aged 65 to 74	22.34	91	9.8
Aged 75 or older	16.82	69	6.5

	AVERAGE HOUSEHOLD SPENDING	BEST CUSTOMERS (index)	BIGGEST CUSTOMERS (market share)
HOUSEHOLD INCOME			
Average household	$24.51	100	100.0%
Under $20,000	17.50	71	15.6
$20,000 to $39,999	21.54	88	20.1
$40,000 to $49,999	25.11	102	9.7
$50,000 to $69,999	22.93	94	13.4
$70,000 to $79,999	27.48	112	6.7
$80,000 to $99,999	27.22	111	9.3
$100,000 or more	36.12	147	25.3
HOUSEHOLD TYPE			
Average household	24.51	100	100.0
Married couples	30.30	124	61.0
Married couples, no children	24.39	100	21.1
Married couples, with children	35.07	143	33.3
Oldest child under age 6	33.80	138	5.9
Oldest child aged 6 to 17	38.79	158	18.6
Oldest child aged 18 or older	30.16	123	8.9
Single parent with child under age 18	24.55	100	5.9
Single person	11.18	46	13.4
RACE AND HISPANIC ORIGIN			
Average household	24.51	100	100.0
Asian	20.29	83	3.5
Black	26.72	109	13.3
Hispanic	27.38	112	13.6
Non-Hispanic white and other	23.69	97	73.3
REGION			
Average household	24.51	100	100.0
Northeast	26.69	109	20.0
Midwest	23.75	97	21.6
South	23.91	98	35.8
West	24.48	100	22.6
EDUCATION			
Average household	24.51	100	100.0
Less than high school graduate	25.14	103	14.7
High school graduate	26.98	110	28.1
Some college	23.72	97	20.3
Associate's degree	23.40	95	9.0
Bachelor's degree or more	23.01	94	27.9
Bachelor's degree	23.28	95	17.9
Master's, professional, doctoral degree	22.49	92	9.9

Note: Market shares may not sum to 100.0 because of rounding and missing categories by household type. "Asian" and "black" include Hispanics and non-Hispanics who identify themselves as being of the respective race alone. "Hispanic" includes people of any race who identify themselves as Hispanic. "Other" includes people who identify themselves as non-Hispanic and as Alaska Native, American Indian, Asian (who are also included in the "Asian" row), or Native Hawaiian or other Pacific Islander as well as non-Hispanics reporting more than one race.

Source: Calculations by New Strategist based on the Bureau of Labor Statistics' 2010 Consumer Expenditure Survey

Fruit, Canned

Best customers: **Married couples**

Customer trends: **Average household spending on canned fruit may decline as sliced and conveniently packaged fresh fruit becomes more widely available.**

The biggest spenders on canned fruit are older householders and the largest households. Householders aged 75 or older spend 11 percent more than average on canned fruit as do those aged 55 to 64. Married couples spend 30 percent more than average on this item, the figure peaking at 54 percent among those with school-aged children.

Average household spending on canned fruit rose 5 percent between 2000 and 2010, after adjusting for inflation. Behind the small but steady increase was the aging of the population and the attempt by consumers to add more fruit to their diet. Average household spending on canned fruit may decline as sliced and conveniently packaged fresh fruit becomes more widely available.

Table 9.38 Fruit, canned

Total household spending $2,486,326,710.00
Average household spends   20.53

	AVERAGE HOUSEHOLD SPENDING	BEST CUSTOMERS (index)	BIGGEST CUSTOMERS (market share)
AGE OF HOUSEHOLDER			
Average household	**$20.53**	**100**	**100.0%**
Under age 25	10.07	49	3.3
Aged 25 to 34	16.75	82	13.6
Aged 35 to 44	21.63	105	19.1
Aged 45 to 54	22.49	110	22.7
Aged 55 to 64	22.69	111	19.5
Aged 65 to 74	21.60	105	11.3
Aged 75 or older	22.84	111	10.6

	AVERAGE HOUSEHOLD SPENDING	BEST CUSTOMERS (index)	BIGGEST CUSTOMERS (market share)
HOUSEHOLD INCOME			
Average household	$20.53	100	100.0%
Under $20,000	12.97	63	13.8
$20,000 to $39,999	16.01	78	17.9
$40,000 to $49,999	19.45	95	9.0
$50,000 to $69,999	20.24	99	14.1
$70,000 to $79,999	23.90	116	7.0
$80,000 to $99,999	25.20	123	10.2
$100,000 or more	34.04	166	28.4
HOUSEHOLD TYPE			
Average household	20.53	100	100.0
Married couples	26.71	130	64.2
Married couples, no children	25.30	123	26.2
Married couples, with children	27.25	133	30.9
Oldest child under age 6	31.58	154	6.6
Oldest child aged 6 to 17	26.72	130	15.3
Oldest child aged 18 or older	25.82	126	9.1
Single parent with child under age 18	17.94	87	5.2
Single person	10.08	49	14.4
RACE AND HISPANIC ORIGIN			
Average household	20.53	100	100.0
Asian	16.55	81	3.4
Black	18.61	91	11.1
Hispanic	16.14	79	9.6
Non-Hispanic white and other	21.48	105	79.3
REGION			
Average household	20.53	100	100.0
Northeast	21.46	105	19.2
Midwest	22.42	109	24.3
South	18.23	89	32.6
West	21.63	105	23.9
EDUCATION			
Average household	20.53	100	100.0
Less than high school graduate	17.62	86	12.3
High school graduate	19.22	94	23.9
Some college	18.64	91	19.1
Associate's degree	20.74	101	9.5
Bachelor's degree or more	24.27	118	35.1
Bachelor's degree	20.37	99	18.7
Master's, professional, doctoral degree	31.95	156	16.8

Note: Market shares may not sum to 100.0 because of rounding and missing categories by household type. "Asian" and "black" include Hispanics and non-Hispanics who identify themselves as being of the respective race alone. "Hispanic" includes people of any race who identify themselves as Hispanic. "Other" includes people who identify themselves as non-Hispanic and as Alaska Native, American Indian, Asian (who are also included in the "Asian" row), or Native Hawaiian or other Pacific Islander as well as non-Hispanics reporting more than one race.

Source: Calculations by New Strategist based on the Bureau of Labor Statistics' 2010 Consumer Expenditure Survey

Fruit, Dried

Best customers: **Householders aged 45 to 64**
                                           Married couples

Customer trends: **Average household spending on dried fruit should increase again as the population ages.**

The biggest spenders on dried fruit are older householders and the largest households. Married couples with children at home spend 43 percent more than average on dried fruit, and couples without children at home (most of them older empty-nesters) spend 24 percent more than average on this item. Householders aged 45 to 64 outspend the average by 18 to 20 percent.

Average household spending on dried fruit, which had risen strongly between 2000 and 2006, declined 15 percent between 2006 and 2010, after adjusting for inflation. Behind the earlier increase was the greater availability of dried fruit and its growing popularity as a snack food. Spending on dried fruit should increase again as the population ages.

Table 9.39 Fruit, dried

Total household spending $993,077,400.00
Average household spends   8.20

	AVERAGE HOUSEHOLD SPENDING	BEST CUSTOMERS (index)	BIGGEST CUSTOMERS (market share)
AGE OF HOUSEHOLDER			
Average household	**$8.20**	**100**	**100.0%**
Under age 25	4.58	56	3.7
Aged 25 to 34	5.86	71	11.9
Aged 35 to 44	8.13	99	17.9
Aged 45 to 54	9.80	120	24.7
Aged 55 to 64	9.64	118	20.7
Aged 65 to 74	8.29	101	10.9
Aged 75 or older	8.65	105	10.1

	AVERAGE HOUSEHOLD SPENDING	BEST CUSTOMERS (index)	BIGGEST CUSTOMERS (market share)
HOUSEHOLD INCOME			
Average household	**$8.20**	**100**	**100.0%**
Under $20,000	4.14	50	11.0
$20,000 to $39,999	5.48	67	15.3
$40,000 to $49,999	6.87	84	7.9
$50,000 to $69,999	8.05	98	14.1
$70,000 to $79,999	9.80	120	7.2
$80,000 to $99,999	14.57	178	14.8
$100,000 or more	14.30	174	29.9
HOUSEHOLD TYPE			
Average household	**8.20**	**100**	**100.0**
Married couples	10.93	133	65.7
Married couples, no children	10.18	124	26.4
Married couples, with children	11.69	143	33.2
Oldest child under age 6	9.81	120	5.1
Oldest child aged 6 to 17	9.30	113	13.3
Oldest child aged 18 or older	16.22	198	14.3
Single parent with child under age 18	5.34	65	3.8
Single person	3.91	48	14.0
RACE AND HISPANIC ORIGIN			
Average household	**8.20**	**100**	**100.0**
Asian	7.91	96	4.1
Black	8.03	98	12.0
Hispanic	8.65	105	12.9
Non-Hispanic white and other	8.14	99	75.3
REGION			
Average household	**8.20**	**100**	**100.0**
Northeast	9.38	114	21.0
Midwest	9.43	115	25.6
South	6.31	77	28.2
West	9.11	111	25.2
EDUCATION			
Average household	**8.20**	**100**	**100.0**
Less than high school graduate	4.63	56	8.1
High school graduate	5.83	71	18.2
Some college	6.82	83	17.5
Associate's degree	9.93	121	11.4
Bachelor's degree or more	12.29	150	44.5
Bachelor's degree	11.96	146	27.6
Master's, professional, doctoral degree	12.92	158	17.0

Note: Market shares may not sum to 100.0 because of rounding and missing categories by household type. "Asian" and "black" include Hispanics and non-Hispanics who identify themselves as being of the respective race alone. "Hispanic" includes people of any race who identify themselves as Hispanic. "Other" includes people who identify themselves as non-Hispanic and as Alaska Native, American Indian, Asian (who are also included in the "Asian" row), or Native Hawaiian or other Pacific Islander as well as non-Hispanics reporting more than one race.

Source: Calculations by New Strategist based on the Bureau of Labor Statistics' 2010 Consumer Expenditure Survey

Fruit-Flavored Drinks, Noncarbonated

Best customers:	Householders aged 35 to 54
	Married couples with children at home
	Single parents
	Asians, blacks, and Hispanics
	Households in the Northeast
Customer trends:	Average household spending on noncarbonated fruit-flavored drinks should continue to grow in the years ahead as the millennial generation enters the best-customer age group.

The best customers of noncarbonated fruit-flavored drinks are parents with children. Married couples with children at home spend 54 percent more than the average household on this item, the number peaking at 78 percent among those with school-aged children. Single parents, whose spending approaches average on only a few items, spend a whopping 67 percent more than average on fruit-flavored drinks. Householders aged 35 to 54, most with children at home, spend 20 to 36 percent more than average on this item. Hispanics, blacks, and Asians spend 32 to 40 percent more than average on fruit-flavored drinks and account for 38 percent of the market. Households in the Northeast spend 27 percent more than average on this item.

Average household spending on noncarbonated fruit-flavored drinks purchased at grocery or convenience stores declined rapidly before the Great Recession, then rebounded strongly. Behind the spending increase are growing minority populations, as well as the switch from fruit juice to less-expensive fruit-flavored drinks by some households. Average household spending on noncarbonated fruit-flavored drinks should continue to grow in the years ahead as the millennial generation enters the best-customer age group.

Table 9.40 Fruit-flavored drinks, noncarbonated

Total household spending $2,936,844,750.00
Average household spends   24.25

	AVERAGE HOUSEHOLD SPENDING	BEST CUSTOMERS (index)	BIGGEST CUSTOMERS (market share)
AGE OF HOUSEHOLDER			
Average household	**$24.25**	**100**	**100.0%**
Under age 25	15.09	62	4.1
Aged 25 to 34	27.73	114	19.0
Aged 35 to 44	32.92	136	24.6
Aged 45 to 54	29.09	120	24.8
Aged 55 to 64	21.02	87	15.3
Aged 65 to 74	14.36	59	6.4
Aged 75 or older	14.86	61	5.8

	AVERAGE HOUSEHOLD SPENDING	BEST CUSTOMERS (index)	BIGGEST CUSTOMERS (market share)
HOUSEHOLD INCOME			
Average household	**$24.25**	**100**	**100.0%**
Under $20,000	16.81	69	15.1
$20,000 to $39,999	19.85	82	18.8
$40,000 to $49,999	24.95	103	9.7
$50,000 to $69,999	23.95	99	14.2
$70,000 to $79,999	24.35	100	6.0
$80,000 to $99,999	30.71	127	10.6
$100,000 or more	36.91	152	26.1
HOUSEHOLD TYPE			
Average household	**24.25**	**100**	**100.0**
Married couples	30.74	127	62.5
Married couples, no children	19.38	80	17.0
Married couples, with children	37.44	154	35.9
Oldest child under age 6	29.13	120	5.1
Oldest child aged 6 to 17	43.19	178	20.9
Oldest child aged 18 or older	33.13	137	9.9
Single parent with child under age 18	40.51	167	9.9
Single person	9.35	39	11.3
RACE AND HISPANIC ORIGIN			
Average household	**24.25**	**100**	**100.0**
Asian	33.91	140	5.9
Black	32.35	133	16.3
Hispanic	32.08	132	16.1
Non-Hispanic white and other	21.78	90	68.1
REGION			
Average household	**24.25**	**100**	**100.0**
Northeast	30.89	127	23.4
Midwest	21.92	90	20.2
South	22.58	93	34.2
West	23.91	99	22.3
EDUCATION			
Average household	**24.25**	**100**	**100.0**
Less than high school graduate	24.44	101	14.4
High school graduate	21.92	90	23.1
Some college	22.17	91	19.2
Associate's degree	26.22	108	10.2
Bachelor's degree or more	27.06	112	33.2
Bachelor's degree	24.07	99	18.7
Master's, professional, doctoral degree	32.96	136	14.7

Note: Market shares may not sum to 100.0 because of rounding and missing categories by household type. "Asian" and "black" include Hispanics and non-Hispanics who identify themselves as being of the respective race alone. "Hispanic" includes people of any race who identify themselves as Hispanic. "Other" includes people who identify themselves as non-Hispanic and as Alaska Native, American Indian, Asian (who are also included in the "Asian" row), or Native Hawaiian or other Pacific Islander as well as non-Hispanics reporting more than one race.

Source: Calculations by New Strategist based on the Bureau of Labor Statistics' 2010 Consumer Expenditure Survey

Fruit, Fresh, Total

Best customers:	Householders aged 35 to 54
	Married couples with children at home
	Asians and Hispanics
	Households in the West
Customer trends:	Average household spending on fresh fruit should continue to rise because of growing minority populations and the interest in healthy eating.

The biggest spenders on fresh fruit are the largest households. Married couples with children at home spend 48 percent more than average on fresh fruit, the figure peaking at 54 percent among couples with school-aged children. Householders aged 35 to 54, most with children, spend 18 percent more than average on fresh fruit. Asians spend 42 percent more than average on this item, and Hispanics, 23 percent. Households in the West, where many Asians and Hispanics live, spend 21 percent above average on fresh fruit.

Fresh fruit is the grocery category on which the average household spends the most. Average household spending on fresh fruit climbed 12 percent between 2000 and 2010, after adjusting for inflation. Behind the increase was the growing variety of sliced and packaged fresh fruit available in grocery stores, boosting sales. Average household spending on fresh fruit should continue to rise because of growing minority populations and the interest in healthy eating.

Table 9.41 **Fruit, fresh, total**

Total household spending	$28,125,889,680.00
Average household spends	232.24

	AVERAGE HOUSEHOLD SPENDING	BEST CUSTOMERS (index)	BIGGEST CUSTOMERS (market share)
AGE OF HOUSEHOLDER			
Average household	**$232.24**	**100**	**100.0%**
Under age 25	119.10	51	3.4
Aged 25 to 34	209.63	90	15.0
Aged 35 to 44	273.39	118	21.3
Aged 45 to 54	274.04	118	24.4
Aged 55 to 64	242.75	105	18.4
Aged 65 to 74	213.98	92	9.9
Aged 75 or older	182.06	78	7.5

	AVERAGE HOUSEHOLD SPENDING	BEST CUSTOMERS (index)	BIGGEST CUSTOMERS (market share)
HOUSEHOLD INCOME			
Average household	$232.24	100	100.0%
Under $20,000	133.97	58	12.6
$20,000 to $39,999	186.56	80	18.4
$40,000 to $49,999	180.00	78	7.3
$50,000 to $69,999	214.73	92	13.3
$70,000 to $79,999	256.35	110	6.6
$80,000 to $99,999	294.81	127	10.6
$100,000 or more	430.26	185	31.8
HOUSEHOLD TYPE			
Average household	232.24	100	100.0
Married couples	304.32	131	64.6
Married couples, no children	251.71	108	23.0
Married couples, with children	343.56	148	34.4
Oldest child under age 6	308.12	133	5.7
Oldest child aged 6 to 17	357.00	154	18.1
Oldest child aged 18 or older	341.65	147	10.6
Single parent with child under age 18	195.19	84	5.0
Single person	127.59	55	16.1
RACE AND HISPANIC ORIGIN			
Average household	232.24	100	100.0
Asian	330.47	142	6.1
Black	181.82	78	9.6
Hispanic	286.51	123	15.0
Non-Hispanic white and other	231.87	100	75.7
REGION			
Average household	232.24	100	100.0
Northeast	255.49	110	20.2
Midwest	231.50	100	22.2
South	192.00	83	30.3
West	280.22	121	27.3
EDUCATION			
Average household	232.24	100	100.0
Less than high school graduate	210.97	91	13.0
High school graduate	180.45	78	19.8
Some college	193.53	83	17.5
Associate's degree	222.21	96	9.0
Bachelor's degree or more	318.62	137	40.8
Bachelor's degree	291.17	125	23.7
Master's, professional, doctoral degree	372.66	160	17.4

Note: Market shares may not sum to 100.0 because of rounding and missing categories by household type. "Asian" and "black" include Hispanics and non-Hispanics who identify themselves as being of the respective race alone. "Hispanic" includes people of any race who identify themselves as Hispanic. "Other" includes people who identify themselves as non-Hispanic and as Alaska Native, American Indian, Asian (who are also included in the "Asian" row), or Native Hawaiian or other Pacific Islander as well as non-Hispanics reporting more than one race.

Source: Calculations by New Strategist based on the Bureau of Labor Statistics' 2010 Consumer Expenditure Survey

Fruit, Frozen

Best customers:	Householders aged 35 to 74
	Married couples without children at home
	Married couples with school-aged children
Customer trends:	Average household spending on frozen fruit may continue to rise as aging boomers attempt to improve their diet.

The largest households and older householders are the best customers of frozen fruit. Householders aged 35 to 44, many with children at home, spend 53 percent more than the average household on this item. Householders ranging in age from 45 to 74 spend 8 to 21 percent more than average on this item. Married couples with school-aged children spend 57 percent more than average on frozen fruit. Those without children at home, most of them empty-nesters, outspend the average by 48 percent. Households in the Midwest spend one-third more than average on frozen fruit.

Average household spending on frozen fruit grew by a substantial 48 percent between 2000 and 2010, after adjusting for inflation. One factor behind the rise was growing health consciousness among consumers, who were adding more fruit to their diet. Average household spending on frozen fruit may continue to rise as aging boomers attempt to improve their diet.

Table 9.42 Fruit, frozen

Total household spending $821,105,460.00
Average household spends   6.78

	AVERAGE HOUSEHOLD SPENDING	BEST CUSTOMERS (index)	BIGGEST CUSTOMERS (market share)
AGE OF HOUSEHOLDER			
Average household	**$6.78**	**100**	**100.0%**
Under age 25	3.06	45	3.0
Aged 25 to 34	3.33	49	8.2
Aged 35 to 44	10.39	153	27.7
Aged 45 to 54	7.94	117	24.2
Aged 55 to 64	7.32	108	19.0
Aged 65 to 74	8.18	121	13.0
Aged 75 or older	3.43	51	4.8

	AVERAGE HOUSEHOLD SPENDING	BEST CUSTOMERS (index)	BIGGEST CUSTOMERS (market share)
HOUSEHOLD INCOME			
Average household	**$6.78**	**100**	**100.0%**
Under $20,000	3.96	58	12.7
$20,000 to $39,999	5.08	75	17.2
$40,000 to $49,999	3.89	57	5.4
$50,000 to $69,999	7.44	110	15.7
$70,000 to $79,999	7.89	116	7.0
$80,000 to $99,999	7.26	107	8.9
$100,000 or more	13.29	196	33.6
HOUSEHOLD TYPE			
Average household	**6.78**	**100**	**100.0**
Married couples	9.43	139	68.6
Married couples, no children	10.06	148	31.5
Married couples, with children	8.18	121	28.1
Oldest child under age 6	2.93	43	1.9
Oldest child aged 6 to 17	10.64	157	18.5
Oldest child aged 18 or older	7.19	106	7.7
Single parent with child under age 18	6.53	96	5.7
Single person	3.40	50	14.7
RACE AND HISPANIC ORIGIN			
Average household	**6.78**	**100**	**100.0**
Asian	5.83	86	3.7
Black	2.19	32	4.0
Hispanic	5.04	74	9.1
Non-Hispanic white and other	7.78	115	87.0
REGION			
Average household	**6.78**	**100**	**100.0**
Northeast	7.04	104	19.1
Midwest	9.07	134	29.8
South	4.63	68	25.1
West	7.80	115	26.1
EDUCATION			
Average household	**6.78**	**100**	**100.0**
Less than high school graduate	4.72	70	9.9
High school graduate	4.83	71	18.2
Some college	6.01	89	18.6
Associate's degree	6.64	98	9.3
Bachelor's degree or more	10.01	148	43.9
Bachelor's degree	9.85	145	27.4
Master's, professional, doctoral degree	10.35	153	16.5

Note: Market shares may not sum to 100.0 because of rounding and missing categories by household type. "Asian" and "black" include Hispanics and non-Hispanics who identify themselves as being of the respective race alone. "Hispanic" includes people of any race who identify themselves as Hispanic. "Other" includes people who identify themselves as non-Hispanic and as Alaska Native, American Indian, Asian (who are also included in the "Asian" row), or Native Hawaiian or other Pacific Islander as well as non-Hispanics reporting more than one race.

Source: Calculations by New Strategist based on the Bureau of Labor Statistics' 2010 Consumer Expenditure Survey

Fruit Juice, Canned and Bottled

Best customers:	Householders aged 35 to 54
	Married couples with children at home
	Single parents
	Hispanics, Asians, and blacks
	Households in the Northeast and West
Customer trends:	Average household spending on canned and bottled fruit juice may continue to decline now that the small generation X is in the best-customer lifestage.

Households with children are the biggest spenders on canned and bottled fruit juice, which dominates fruit juice sales. Married couples with children at home spend 52 percent more than average on canned and bottled fruit juice. Despite their low incomes single parents spend 10 percent more than the average household on this item. Householders aged 35 to 54, most with children at home, spend 17 to 22 percent more than average on canned and bottled fruit juice. Blacks, Asians, and Hispanics outspend the average by 16 to 45 percent and account for 37 percent of the market. Households in the Northeast and West outspend the average household on this item by 14 and 13 percent, respectively.

Average household spending on canned and bottled fruit juice purchased at grocery or convenience stores fell 27 percent between 2000 and 2010. Behind the decline is the growing propensity of consumers to eat fast-food breakfasts or no breakfast at all, and the rise of fruit-flavored drinks as a substitute for juice. Spending on canned and bottled fruit juice may continue to decline now that the small generation X is in the best-customer lifestage.

Table 9.43 **Fruit juice, canned and bottled**

Total household spending $6,293,930,790.00
Average household spends 51.97

	AVERAGE HOUSEHOLD SPENDING	BEST CUSTOMERS (index)	BIGGEST CUSTOMERS (market share)
AGE OF HOUSEHOLDER			
Average household	**$51.97**	**100**	**100.0%**
Under age 25	36.13	70	4.6
Aged 25 to 34	54.82	105	17.6
Aged 35 to 44	61.04	117	21.3
Aged 45 to 54	63.38	122	25.2
Aged 55 to 64	48.30	93	16.4
Aged 65 to 74	37.29	72	7.7
Aged 75 or older	39.38	76	7.2

	AVERAGE HOUSEHOLD SPENDING	BEST CUSTOMERS (index)	BIGGEST CUSTOMERS (market share)
HOUSEHOLD INCOME			
Average household	**$51.97**	**100**	**100.0%**
Under $20,000	33.54	65	14.1
$20,000 to $39,999	42.54	82	18.8
$40,000 to $49,999	49.62	95	9.0
$50,000 to $69,999	54.39	105	15.0
$70,000 to $79,999	49.84	96	5.7
$80,000 to $99,999	58.59	113	9.4
$100,000 or more	85.60	165	28.2
HOUSEHOLD TYPE			
Average household	**51.97**	**100**	**100.0**
Married couples	63.03	121	59.8
Married couples, no children	43.19	83	17.7
Married couples, with children	78.74	152	35.2
Oldest child under age 6	71.49	138	5.9
Oldest child aged 6 to 17	78.41	151	17.7
Oldest child aged 18 or older	82.94	160	11.5
Single parent with child under age 18	57.28	110	6.5
Single person	28.64	55	16.1
RACE AND HISPANIC ORIGIN			
Average household	**51.97**	**100**	**100.0**
Asian	67.77	130	5.5
Black	60.27	116	14.2
Hispanic	75.58	145	17.7
Non-Hispanic white and other	47.01	90	68.6
REGION			
Average household	**51.97**	**100**	**100.0**
Northeast	59.24	114	20.9
Midwest	45.00	87	19.3
South	48.58	93	34.3
West	58.67	113	25.6
EDUCATION			
Average household	**51.97**	**100**	**100.0**
Less than high school graduate	43.01	83	11.8
High school graduate	47.36	91	23.3
Some college	49.93	96	20.2
Associate's degree	52.46	101	9.5
Bachelor's degree or more	61.33	118	35.1
Bachelor's degree	60.63	117	22.0
Master's, professional, doctoral degree	62.70	121	13.1

Note: Market shares may not sum to 100.0 because of rounding and missing categories by household type. "Asian" and "black" include Hispanics and non-Hispanics who identify themselves as being of the respective race alone. "Hispanic" includes people of any race who identify themselves as Hispanic. "Other" includes people who identify themselves as non-Hispanic and as Alaska Native, American Indian, Asian (who are also included in the "Asian" row), or Native Hawaiian or other Pacific Islander as well as non-Hispanics reporting more than one race.

Source: Calculations by New Strategist based on the Bureau of Labor Statistics' 2010 Consumer Expenditure Survey

Fruit Juice, Fresh

Best customers: **Householders aged 35 to 54**
Married couples with children at home
Blacks and Hispanics
Households in the Northeast

Customer trends: **Average household spending on fresh fruit juice may resume its decline in the years ahead because the small generation X has entered the best-customer lifestage.**

Middle-aged married couples are the biggest spenders on fresh fruit juice. Householders aged 35 to 54 spend 18 to 32 percent more than average on this item. Married couples with children at home spend 46 percent more than average on fresh fruit juice, the figure peaking among those with adult children at home at 59 percent above average. Blacks and Hispanics spend, respectively, 19 and 12 percent more than average on this item. Households in the Northeast outspend the average by 43 percent.

Average household spending on fresh fruit juice purchased at grocery or convenience stores fell by a substantial 36 percent between 2000 and 2006, after adjusting for inflation, but has stabilized since. Behind the decline in the earlier part of the decade (before the Great Recession) was the baby-boom generation's exit from the best-customer lifestage and the growing propensity of consumers to eat fast-food breakfasts or no breakfast at all. As the Great Recession shifted household spending toward groceries and away from restaurants, spending on fresh fruit juice began to grow. Average household spending on fresh fruit juice may resume its decline in the years ahead because the small generation X has entered the best-customer lifestage.

Table 9.44 Fruit juice, fresh

Total household spending $2,320,410,120.00
Average household spends   19.16

	AVERAGE HOUSEHOLD SPENDING	BEST CUSTOMERS (index)	BIGGEST CUSTOMERS (market share)
AGE OF HOUSEHOLDER			
Average household	**$19.16**	**100**	**100.0%**
Under age 25	10.01	52	3.5
Aged 25 to 34	16.03	84	13.9
Aged 35 to 44	25.36	132	23.9
Aged 45 to 54	22.59	118	24.4
Aged 55 to 64	18.97	99	17.5
Aged 65 to 74	17.27	90	9.7
Aged 75 or older	14.22	74	7.1

	AVERAGE HOUSEHOLD SPENDING	BEST CUSTOMERS (index)	BIGGEST CUSTOMERS (market share)
HOUSEHOLD INCOME			
Average household	**$19.16**	**100**	**100.0%**
Under $20,000	11.88	62	13.5
$20,000 to $39,999	15.70	82	18.8
$40,000 to $49,999	15.49	81	7.6
$50,000 to $69,999	19.04	99	14.3
$70,000 to $79,999	20.74	108	6.5
$80,000 to $99,999	17.68	92	7.7
$100,000 or more	35.89	187	32.1
HOUSEHOLD TYPE			
Average household	**19.16**	**100**	**100.0**
Married couples	24.49	128	63.0
Married couples, no children	20.17	105	22.4
Married couples, with children	28.06	146	34.1
Oldest child under age 6	25.86	135	5.8
Oldest child aged 6 to 17	27.26	142	16.7
Oldest child aged 18 or older	30.38	159	11.4
Single parent with child under age 18	19.37	101	6.0
Single person	9.27	48	14.2
RACE AND HISPANIC ORIGIN			
Average household	**19.16**	**100**	**100.0**
Asian	18.85	98	4.2
Black	22.72	119	14.5
Hispanic	21.37	112	13.6
Non-Hispanic white and other	18.35	96	72.6
REGION			
Average household	**19.16**	**100**	**100.0**
Northeast	27.34	143	26.2
Midwest	18.86	98	21.9
South	15.65	82	30.0
West	18.53	97	21.9
EDUCATION			
Average household	**19.16**	**100**	**100.0**
Less than high school graduate	19.22	100	14.3
High school graduate	15.89	83	21.2
Some college	16.00	84	17.6
Associate's degree	17.90	93	8.8
Bachelor's degree or more	24.71	129	38.3
Bachelor's degree	24.99	130	24.6
Master's, professional, doctoral degree	24.15	126	13.6

Note: Market shares may not sum to 100.0 because of rounding and missing categories by household type. "Asian" and "black" include Hispanics and non-Hispanics who identify themselves as being of the respective race alone. "Hispanic" includes people of any race who identify themselves as Hispanic. "Other" includes people who identify themselves as non-Hispanic and as Alaska Native, American Indian, Asian (who are also included in the "Asian" row), or Native Hawaiian or other Pacific Islander as well as non-Hispanics reporting more than one race.

Source: Calculations by New Strategist based on the Bureau of Labor Statistics' 2010 Consumer Expenditure Survey

Fruit Juice, Frozen

Best customers:	**Householders aged 35 to 54** **Married couples with school-aged or older children at home** **Single parents** **Hispanics** **Households in the Midwest and West**
Customer trends:	**Average household spending on frozen fruit juice may resume its decline as the small generation X moves into the best-customer lifestage.**

Households with children are the best customers of frozen fruit juice. Married couples with school-aged children spend 70 percent more than average on frozen fruit juice, and those with adult children at home spend 55 percent more. Single parents, whose spending approaches average on only a few items, spend 18 percent more than average on frozen fruit juice. Householders aged 35 to 54, most with children, outspend the average by 19 to 28 percent. Households in the Midwest and West spend, respectively, 39 and 24 percent more than average on frozen fruit juice.

Average household spending on frozen fruit juice fell steeply between 2000 and 2006 (down 60 percent), after adjusting for inflation, but rebounded 12 percent from 2006 to 2010. The decline occurred because consumers were looking for more convenience from fruit juice, and they were increasingly eating breakfast away from home—a trend slowed by household belt tightening in face of the Great Recession. Although average household spending on frozen fruit juice recovered between 2006 and 2010, it is likely that spending will resume its decline as the small generation X moves into the best-customer lifestage.

Table 9.45 Fruit juice, frozen

Total household spending	$739,963,770.00
Average household spends	6.11

	AVERAGE HOUSEHOLD SPENDING	BEST CUSTOMERS (index)	BIGGEST CUSTOMERS (market share)
AGE OF HOUSEHOLDER			
Average household	**$6.11**	**100**	**100.0%**
Under age 25	4.16	68	4.5
Aged 25 to 34	5.20	85	14.2
Aged 35 to 44	7.28	119	21.6
Aged 45 to 54	7.84	128	26.5
Aged 55 to 64	5.29	87	15.3
Aged 65 to 74	6.15	101	10.8
Aged 75 or older	4.48	73	7.0

	AVERAGE HOUSEHOLD SPENDING	BEST CUSTOMERS (index)	BIGGEST CUSTOMERS (market share)
HOUSEHOLD INCOME			
Average household	**$6.11**	**100**	**100.0%**
Under $20,000	3.61	59	12.9
$20,000 to $39,999	4.52	74	17.0
$40,000 to $49,999	6.68	109	10.3
$50,000 to $69,999	5.36	88	12.6
$70,000 to $79,999	6.33	104	6.2
$80,000 to $99,999	8.10	133	11.1
$100,000 or more	10.74	176	30.1
HOUSEHOLD TYPE			
Average household	**6.11**	**100**	**100.0**
Married couples	7.86	129	63.5
Married couples, no children	6.57	108	22.8
Married couples, with children	9.07	148	34.5
Oldest child under age 6	4.58	75	3.2
Oldest child aged 6 to 17	10.36	170	19.9
Oldest child aged 18 or older	9.44	155	11.2
Single parent with child under age 18	7.19	118	6.9
Single person	3.06	50	14.7
RACE AND HISPANIC ORIGIN			
Average household	**6.11**	**100**	**100.0**
Asian	3.21	53	2.2
Black	5.69	93	11.4
Hispanic	7.53	123	15.0
Non-Hispanic white and other	5.97	98	74.1
REGION			
Average household	**6.11**	**100**	**100.0**
Northeast	5.75	94	17.3
Midwest	8.49	139	31.0
South	3.96	65	23.8
West	7.55	124	28.0
EDUCATION			
Average household	**6.11**	**100**	**100.0**
Less than high school graduate	4.93	81	11.5
High school graduate	5.55	91	23.2
Some college	4.67	76	16.1
Associate's degree	8.57	140	13.3
Bachelor's degree or more	7.35	120	35.7
Bachelor's degree	7.51	123	23.2
Master's, professional, doctoral degree	7.02	115	12.4

Note: Market shares may not sum to 100.0 because of rounding and missing categories by household type. "Asian" and "black" include Hispanics and non-Hispanics who identify themselves as being of the respective race alone. "Hispanic" includes people of any race who identify themselves as Hispanic. "Other" includes people who identify themselves as non-Hispanic and as Alaska Native, American Indian, Asian (who are also included in the "Asian" row), or Native Hawaiian or other Pacific Islander as well as non-Hispanics reporting more than one race.

Source: Calculations by New Strategist based on the Bureau of Labor Statistics' 2010 Consumer Expenditure Survey

Ham

Best customers: **Married couples with school-aged or older children at home**
Hispanics

Customer trends: **Average household spending on ham may continue its decline as more boomers**
become empty-nesters.

Households with children are the biggest spenders on ham. Married couples with school-aged or older children at home spend 46 to 60 percent more than average on this item. Hispanics, who tend to have larger-than-average families, outspend the average by 29 percent.

Average household spending on ham declined 20 percent between 2000 and 2006, after adjusting for inflation, and another 13 percent since then. Average household spending on ham may continue its decline as more boomers become empty-nesters.

Table 9.46 Ham

Total household spending	$3,860,891,160.00
Average household spends	31.88

	AVERAGE HOUSEHOLD SPENDING	BEST CUSTOMERS (index)	BIGGEST CUSTOMERS (market share)
AGE OF HOUSEHOLDER			
Average household	**$31.88**	**100**	**100.0%**
Under age 25	15.81	50	3.3
Aged 25 to 34	29.05	91	15.2
Aged 35 to 44	37.45	117	21.3
Aged 45 to 54	34.92	110	22.7
Aged 55 to 64	32.68	103	18.1
Aged 65 to 74	35.58	112	12.0
Aged 75 or older	25.14	79	7.5

	AVERAGE HOUSEHOLD SPENDING	BEST CUSTOMERS (index)	BIGGEST CUSTOMERS (market share)
HOUSEHOLD INCOME			
Average household	**$31.88**	**100**	**100.0%**
Under $20,000	19.14	60	13.1
$20,000 to $39,999	26.98	85	19.4
$40,000 to $49,999	41.47	130	12.3
$50,000 to $69,999	32.47	102	14.6
$70,000 to $79,999	37.40	117	7.0
$80,000 to $99,999	35.84	112	9.4
$100,000 or more	44.20	139	23.8
HOUSEHOLD TYPE			
Average household	**31.88**	**100**	**100.0**
Married couples	41.30	130	63.9
Married couples, no children	35.43	111	23.6
Married couples, with children	45.40	142	33.1
Oldest child under age 6	26.93	84	3.6
Oldest child aged 6 to 17	50.98	160	18.8
Oldest child aged 18 or older	46.54	146	10.5
Single parent with child under age 18	29.53	93	5.5
Single person	14.26	45	13.1
RACE AND HISPANIC ORIGIN			
Average household	**31.88**	**100**	**100.0**
Asian	27.70	87	3.7
Black	30.75	96	11.8
Hispanic	41.11	129	15.7
Non-Hispanic white and other	30.55	96	72.7
REGION			
Average household	**31.88**	**100**	**100.0**
Northeast	33.82	106	19.5
Midwest	35.20	110	24.6
South	31.21	98	35.9
West	28.03	88	19.9
EDUCATION			
Average household	**31.88**	**100**	**100.0**
Less than high school graduate	31.76	100	14.2
High school graduate	32.86	103	26.3
Some college	30.87	97	20.4
Associate's degree	33.00	104	9.8
Bachelor's degree or more	31.43	99	29.3
Bachelor's degree	29.00	91	17.2
Master's, professional, doctoral degree	36.22	114	12.3

Note: Market shares may not sum to 100.0 because of rounding and missing categories by household type. "Asian" and "black" include Hispanics and non-Hispanics who identify themselves as being of the respective race alone. "Hispanic" includes people of any race who identify themselves as Hispanic. "Other" includes people who identify themselves as non-Hispanic and as Alaska Native, American Indian, Asian (who are also included in the "Asian" row), or Native Hawaiian or other Pacific Islander as well as non-Hispanics reporting more than one race.

Source: Calculations by New Strategist based on the Bureau of Labor Statistics' 2010 Consumer Expenditure Survey

Ice Cream and Related Products

Best customers:	Married couples without children at home
	Married couples with school-aged or older children at home
	Single parents

| Customer trends: | Average household spending on ice cream will continue to fall as household size shrinks. |

Households with children spend the most on ice cream and related products. Married couples with school-aged or older children at home spend 41 to 61 percent more than the average household on this item. Single parents, whose spending approaches average on only a few items, spend 7 percent more than average on ice cream. Married couples without children at home, most older empty-nesters, outspend the average by one-fifth.

Average household spending on ice cream and related products fell 24 percent between 2000 and 2010, after adjusting for inflation. Behind the decline was price discounting as private-label brands competed with premium brands in the grocery store. Average household spending on ice cream will continue to fall as household size shrinks.

Table 9.47 Ice cream and related products

| Total household spending | $6,571,265,820.00 |
| Average household spends | 54.26 |

	AVERAGE HOUSEHOLD SPENDING	BEST CUSTOMERS (index)	BIGGEST CUSTOMERS (market share)
AGE OF HOUSEHOLDER			
Average household	**$54.26**	**100**	**100.0%**
Under age 25	24.12	44	2.9
Aged 25 to 34	44.21	81	13.6
Aged 35 to 44	57.99	107	19.3
Aged 45 to 54	64.12	118	24.4
Aged 55 to 64	60.45	111	19.6
Aged 65 to 74	58.06	107	11.5
Aged 75 or older	48.15	89	8.5

	AVERAGE HOUSEHOLD SPENDING	BEST CUSTOMERS (index)	BIGGEST CUSTOMERS (market share)
HOUSEHOLD INCOME			
Average household	**$54.26**	**100**	**100.0%**
Under $20,000	30.83	57	12.4
$20,000 to $39,999	43.72	81	18.5
$40,000 to $49,999	51.50	95	9.0
$50,000 to $69,999	58.88	109	15.6
$70,000 to $79,999	49.89	92	5.5
$80,000 to $99,999	72.20	133	11.1
$100,000 or more	88.83	164	28.1
HOUSEHOLD TYPE			
Average household	**54.26**	**100**	**100.0**
Married couples	69.65	128	63.3
Married couples, no children	65.02	120	25.5
Married couples, with children	75.11	138	32.2
Oldest child under age 6	47.61	88	3.8
Oldest child aged 6 to 17	76.45	141	16.6
Oldest child aged 18 or older	87.21	161	11.6
Single parent with child under age 18	58.31	107	6.3
Single person	27.39	50	14.8
RACE AND HISPANIC ORIGIN			
Average household	**54.26**	**100**	**100.0**
Asian	55.54	102	4.4
Black	40.47	75	9.1
Hispanic	50.73	93	11.4
Non-Hispanic white and other	56.98	105	79.6
REGION			
Average household	**54.26**	**100**	**100.0**
Northeast	59.01	109	20.0
Midwest	53.91	99	22.1
South	51.49	95	34.8
West	55.29	102	23.1
EDUCATION			
Average household	**54.26**	**100**	**100.0**
Less than high school graduate	48.54	89	12.8
High school graduate	50.29	93	23.7
Some college	49.56	91	19.2
Associate's degree	58.62	108	10.2
Bachelor's degree or more	62.24	115	34.1
Bachelor's degree	57.54	106	20.0
Master's, professional, doctoral degree	71.50	132	14.3

Note: Market shares may not sum to 100.0 because of rounding and missing categories by household type. "Asian" and "black" include Hispanics and non-Hispanics who identify themselves as being of the respective race alone. "Hispanic" includes people of any race who identify themselves as Hispanic. "Other" includes people who identify themselves as non-Hispanic and as Alaska Native, American Indian, Asian (who are also included in the "Asian" row), or Native Hawaiian or other Pacific Islander as well as non-Hispanics reporting more than one race.

Source: Calculations by New Strategist based on the Bureau of Labor Statistics' 2010 Consumer Expenditure Survey

Jams, Preserves, and Other Sweets

Best customers: **Householders aged 35 to 54**
                          Married couples with school-aged or older children at home

Customer trends: **Average household spending on jams, preserves, and other sweets is likely to
                          decline as more boomers become empty-nesters and household size shrinks.**

Married couples with school-aged or older children at home spend the most on jams, preserves, and other sweets—61 to 68 percent more than the average household. Householders aged 35 to 54, most with children at home, spend 20 to 22 percent more than average on jams.

Average household spending on jams, preserves, and other sweets held steady between 2000 and 2006, but increased 6 percent between 2006 and 2010, after adjusting for inflation. One factor behind the increase is more brown-bag lunches as the Great Recession reduced eating out. Average household spending on jams is likely to fall in the years ahead as more boomers become empty-nesters and household size shrinks.

Table 9.48 Jams, preserves, and other sweets

Total household spending $3,208,124,430.00
Average household spends   26.49

	AVERAGE HOUSEHOLD SPENDING	BEST CUSTOMERS (index)	BIGGEST CUSTOMERS (market share)
AGE OF HOUSEHOLDER			
Average household	**$26.49**	**100**	**100.0%**
Under age 25	14.23	54	3.6
Aged 25 to 34	22.52	85	14.2
Aged 35 to 44	31.89	120	21.8
Aged 45 to 54	32.33	122	25.2
Aged 55 to 64	25.54	96	17.0
Aged 65 to 74	26.61	100	10.8
Aged 75 or older	20.56	78	7.4